# THE DISCIPLINE

## of

# THE WESLEYAN CHURCH

## 2000

WESLEYAN PUBLISHING HOUSE
INDIANAPOLIS, INDIANA

**Published by authority of the Ninth General Conference held in Greensboro, North Carolina July 15-19, 2000**

**Editing Committee**

**Ronald D. Kelly, chair**
**Wayne E. Caldwell**
**Craig A. Dunn**
**Lee M. Haines**
**Jerry G. Pence**
**Wayne A. Richards**


**Printed in the United States of America**
**International Standard Book Number 0-89827-224-6**

# CONTENTS

**Note:** The basic unit in *The Discipline* is the paragraph, rather than page, chapter, or section. The paragraphs are numbered in order through the entire volume, but with many numbers skipped, in order to allow for future additions or amendments, and to fit into the following plan:



If a paragraph is divided into numbered parts, each is called a subparagraph. When a paragraph number is followed by a subparagraph number, the two numbers are joined by a colon. For example, 725:1 means paragraph 725, subparagraph 1. If a subparagraph is further divided into parts, they are identified by letter. For example, 1233:9b means paragraph 1233, subparagraph 9, division b. A comparative or "cf." reference, when found within a sentence applies only to that sentence. When the "Cf." appears parenthetically outside the sentence the comparative reference(s) apply to the whole of the preceding paragraph.

## PART I

## Basic Principles



## PART II

## Local Church Government



## PART III

## District Church Government

## PART IV

### General Church Government



## PART V

### World Organization



## PART VI

### Ministry



## PART VII

### Corporations

## PART VIII

## Property



## PART IX

## Judiciary



## PART X

## The Ritual

## PART XI

### Forms



## APPENDICES



## INDEX

# PART I

# BASIC PRINCIPLES

## Chapter I

## HISTORY

### A. The Origin of the Wesleyan Movement

**1.** The Wesleyan movement centers around the scriptural truth concerning the doctrine and experience of holiness, which declares that the atonement in Christ provides not only for the regeneration of sinners but for the entire sanctification of believers. A revival of these scriptural truths concerning Christian perfection and scriptural holiness took place under the leadership of John Wesley in the eighteenth century, and continues in various ways until the present.

**2.** Nurtured in a devout home, John Wesley committed himself to a search after God from earliest childhood. While at Oxford, together with his brother Charles and a few other serious-minded collegians, he methodically pursued holiness through systematic Bible study, prayer, good works, intensive examination, and reproof. The group earned the nicknames of the "Holy Club" and of "Methodists," but Wesley did not earn the assurance of salvation. Having graduated from Oxford, and having been ordained as a clergyman in the state church, he intensified his search for peace through legalism and self-discipline. The turning point came at a prayer meeting in Aldersgate Street, London, May 24, 1738, when he perceived the way of faith and found his heart "strangely warmed" in the new birth. As he went on to the experience of entire sanctification, he shared his testimony and teaching with others, and a spiritual awakening spread across the British Isles and to America.

**3.** It was not Wesley's purpose to found a church, but the awakening brought about the spontaneous origin of the "societies" which grew into the Methodist movement. Near the end of 1739, there came to Wesley, in London, eight or ten persons who appeared to be deeply convinced of sin and earnestly groaning for redemption. They desired, as did two or three more the next day, that he would spend some time with them in prayer, and advise them how to flee from the wrath to come, which they saw continually hanging over their heads. A day was appointed when they might all come together, which from thence forward they did every week; namely, on Thursday in the evening. To these, and as many more as desired to join with them (for their number increased daily), he gave those advices which he judged most needful for them and they always concluded their meeting with prayer. The Covenant Membership Commitments found in this *Discipline* (260-268) represent in revised form the General Rules which Wesley gave to the members of the societies to enable them to test the sincerity of their purpose and to guide them in holy living.

**4.** The movement spread to America by the emigration of Methodists, who, beginning in 1766, began to organize the Methodist "classes" and "societies" in the colonies. In December 1784, the Methodist Episcopal Church was organized at the Christmas Conference in Baltimore, Maryland. The new church experienced a miraculous growth, especially on the frontier, and quickly became one of the major religious forces in the new nation.

## B. The Organization of The Wesleyan Methodist Connection

**6.** John Wesley and the early Methodist leaders in America had been uncompromising in their denunciation of human slavery. But with the invention of the cotton gin, the economic advantages of slavery involved many ministers and members of the Methodist Episcopal Church in slaveholding. When a group of ministers in the New England Conference, led by Orange Scott, began to agitate anew for the abolition of slavery, the bishops and others in the church sought to silence them lest the peace of the church be disturbed.

**7.** The inward compulsion of truth met by the outward compulsion of ecclesiastical authority led to a series of withdrawals of churches and ministers from the Methodist Episcopal Church. The earliest extensive withdrawal was in Michigan, and led on May 13, 1841, to the formation of the annual conference using the name, "The Wesleyan Methodist Church." The withdrawal which had the most far-reaching consequences occurred in New England and New York late in 1842. In November 1842, Orange Scott, Jotham Horton, and LaRoy Sunderland withdrew, publishing their reasons in the first issue of *The True Wesleyan*, and they were joined in the following month by Luther Lee and Lucius C. Matlack. A call was issued to those interested in the ultimate formation of a new church, free from episcopacy and slavery, to meet at Andover, Massachusetts, February 1, 1843. At Andover a call was issued for an organizing convention.

**8.** The organizing convention for the Wesleyan Methodist Connection of America was held at Utica, New York, May 31 to June 8, 1843. The new organization was a "Connection" of local churches organized in annual conferences. It avoided the episcopacy, and provided for equal ministerial a. lay representation in all of its governing bodies. Moral and social reform wer strongly emphasized, with slaveholding and all involvements with intoxicating liquors being prohibited.

## C. The Revival of the Wesleyan Experience

**11.** The Wesleyan Methodist Connection saw the crusade against slavery carried to a conclusion in the Civil War. Afterwards, many felt there was no reason for the Connection as such to continue, and returned to the larger Methodist bodies. Others felt, as was expressed by the 1867 General Conference, that the effects of slavery were not yet eradicated, and that the historic stand against intoxicating liquors, and the increasingly firm stand against lodges and secret societies, could only be maintained by the continued existence and activity of the Connection.

**12.** At its first General Conference in 1844, the Connection had adopted an article of religion on "Sanctification," becoming the first denomination to do so. But the doctrine and experience suffered neglect and decline among all branches of Methodism in the mid-nineteenth century. To renew them, God raised up a revival of holiness promoted through literature, evangelistic meetings, and camp meetings that swept throughout Methodism and across denominational lines. The first national camp meeting, which developed into the National Holiness Association, was held in 1867. The revival led to the establishment of several new holiness denominations and to the renewing and redirecting of others.

**13.** This spiritual revival, promoted vigorously by a corps of itinerant evangelists, soon established holiness as the major tenet of the Wesleyan Methodist Connection, which had formerly majored on social and political reform. In 1883, the General Conference adopted a resolution requiring the preaching of entire sanctification, and by 1893 new articles of religion on regeneration and entire sanctification had been adopted by the General Conference, the annual conferences, and local churches.

## D. The Development of The Wesleyan Methodist Church

**16.** The revival of holiness which swept the Wesleyan Methodist Connection introduced a new emphasis on evangelism. The need for organized efforts of church extension and the need to conserve converts led to the gradual development of a more formal organization as a
than a connection. In 1891, the name was changed to the *Wesle*
*Connection (or Church) of America*, and the denomination mc

.ership largely confined to publications (editor and publisher) to elect a neral missionary superintendent. Gradually other departmental executives vere added. In 1947, the name was changed to *The Wesleyan Methodist Church of America,* and a central supervisory authority was established with the general conference president as the full-time leader of the denomination, and the Board of Administration as the central and coordinating board of control. In 1957, the denominational headquarters was moved from Syracuse, New York, where it had been for over a century, to Marion, Indiana. In 1959, the plan for a general conference president was superseded by one calling for three general superintendents.

**17.** Various ministers and local churches affiliated themselves with The Wesleyan Methodist Church at different times throughout its history. But its home base and missionary work were appreciably augmented by the affiliation of three organizations.

(1) *The Hephzibah Faith Missionary Society* was organized in 1893 and eventually established headquarters at Tabor, Iowa. Some of its ministers and churches in Nebraska, its Brainerd Indian School near Hot Springs, South Dakota, and its mission field in Haiti became part of The Wesleyan Methodist Church in 1948.

(2) *The Missionary Bands of the World*, organized in 1885 as the Pentecost Bands, an auxiliary of the Free Methodist Church, became a separate organization in 1895, changed names in 1925, and in 1958 merged its churches in Indiana and its mission fields in central India and Jamaica with The Wesleyan Methodist Church.

(3) *The Alliance of the Reformed Baptist Church of Canada* was organized in 1888 as the result of the sanctification of several Baptist ministers. In 1966 it merged its churches in New Brunswick, Nova Scotia, and Maine, and its mission fields in Africa with The Wesleyan Methodist Church.

**18.** The Wesleyan Methodist Church became international with its spread to Canada, and the establishment, development, and acquisition through merger of mission fields in Sierra Leone, India, Colombia, Japan, Haiti, Jamaica, Puerto Rico, Honduras, Mexico, Taiwan, Australia, Papua New Guinea, Nepal, Rhodesia, and South Africa.

### E. The Formation and Development of The Pilgrim Holiness Church

**23.** The Pilgrim Holiness Church came into being as a result of the revival of scriptural holiness that swept across the various denominations in America in the last half of the nineteenth century, the same awakening that had channeled the energies of the Wesleyan Methodist Connection from social political reform to holiness evangelism (12-13). The awakening crystallized in the establishment of many nondenominational a interdenominational holiness unions and associations and independen churches. Toward the close of the nineteenth century many of like precious faith began to draw together in the unity of the Spirit.

**24.** A focal point for the beginning of The Pilgrim Holiness Church as an organization was the formation of the *International Holiness Union and Prayer League* in September 1897, at Cincinnati, Ohio, in the home of Martin Wells Knapp. Rev. Seth C. Rees was chosen President, and Rev. Martin Wells Knapp, Vice-President. The Union was not thought of as a church, nor intended as such, but was an interdenominational fellowship, marked by simplicity and the absence of restrictions. The primary purpose of the Union was to unite holiness people in promoting worldwide holiness evangelism. A fourfold emphasis was declared concerning the regeneration of sinners, the entire sanctification of believers, the premillennial and imminent return of the Lord Jesus Christ, and the evangelization of the world. The Union met the need of many people for fellowship and cooperation in the spread of scriptural holiness and grew rapidly. Extensive revival work was carried on by members of the Union, resulting in the formation of the many city missions, churches, rescue homes, and camp meetings.

**25.** In the annual meeting of the Union held in July 1900, the name was changed to *International Apostolic Holiness Union* in order to express more fully the aim of promoting a return to apostolic principles and practices. Also in 1900 the foreign missionary work began as members of the Union went out as faith missionaries to South Africa, India, Japan, the West Indies, and South America.

**26.** The Union gradually developed into a church organization in order to provide church homes for the converts and the conservation of the work. In 1905 the name was changed to *International Apostolic Holiness Union and Churches*. The interdenominational features also faded out, and in 1913 the name was altered to *International Apostolic Holiness Church*.

**27.** In 1919, the Indiana, Illinois-Missouri, and Kansas-Oklahoma Conferences of the *Holiness Christian Church* were received by the *General Assembly of the International Apostolic Holiness Church*. The Holiness Christian Church had its beginning in a revival movement around Philadelphia, Pennsylvania, in 1882, and was organized at Linwood, Pennsylvania, in 1889 as the *Holiness Christian Association*. By 1919 it was known as the Holiness Christian Church and was composed of four conferences; it also sponsored a missionary work in Central America.

**28.** The *Pentecostal Rescue Mission* joined the International Holiness Church in March 1922, and became the New York District. It had [illegible] at Binghamton, New York, in 1897, and had spread until it inclu[illegible] cue work, camp meetings, orphanage activities, churches, and a missionary ork in Alaska.

**29.** In October 1922, the General Assembly, in special session, received *The Pilgrim Church* of California and adopted the name, *The Pilgrim Holiness Church*. The Pilgrim Church was first organized on May 27, 1917, as the *Pentecost-Pilgrim Church* in Pasadena, California. By 1922, a school known as Pilgrim Bible School had been established and a periodical was being published at Pasadena, California, and missionaries had been sent out to Mexico.

**30.** In 1924, a group of several churches known as the *Pentecostal Brethren in Christ* united with and became a part of the Ohio District of The Pilgrim Holiness Church.

**31.** In 1925, *The People's Mission Church*, with headquarters at Colorado Springs, Colorado, became a part of The Pilgrim Holiness Church. It was the outgrowth of revival work that began in 1898 in Colorado Springs and spread through several surrounding states. A Bible school was operated, a periodical published, and a camp meeting maintained at Colorado Springs.

**32.** In 1946, *The Holiness Church* of California was received by the General Conference into The Pilgrim Holiness Church. This Church, which began in a revival movement in 1880 and was first known as *The Holiness Bands*, maintained a Bible school at El Monte, California, and a growing missionary work in Peru and Palestine.

**33.** *The Africa Evangelistic Mission*, with headquarters at Boksburg, Transvaal, South Africa, was received by The Pilgrim Holiness Church in 1962. The Mission carried on work organized into three districts, two of which were located in the Orange Free State and Transvaal in the Republic of South Africa, and a third district comprising extensive work in Mozambique.

**34.** The growth of The Pilgrim Holiness Church continued through revival work and evangelism in greater measure than by the uniting of other bodies. An important turning point in the organizational structure was reached in 1930 when the General Assembly unified the administration of the denomination by providing for one general superintendent, one general board, and a general headquarters at Indianapolis, Indiana. In 1958 a plan for three general superintendents was inaugurated. In 1962 the general conference, known until 1942 as the General Assembly, was designated as the International Conference in recognition of the growth and development of the overseas work.

**35.** The original purpose of the founders of The Pilgrim Holiness Church to promote worldwide holiness evangelism remained an indelible characteristic. Missionary work was carried on in many lands, and The Pilgrim Holiness Church extended beyond the United States and Canada to the llowing places: South Africa, including Natal, Transvaal, Cape Province, and

Orange Free State; Swaziland; Mozambique; Zambia; the Caribbean area, including Grand Cayman, Jamaica, St. Croix, St. Thomas, Saba, St. Kitts, Nevis, Antigua, Barbuda, Barbados, St. Vincent, Trinidad and Tobago, and Curacao; Guyana; Suriname; Brazil; Peru; Mexico; Philippine Islands; and England.

### F. The Formation of The Wesleyan Church

**50.** Merger between The Pilgrim Holiness Church and The Wesleyan Methodist Church of America was proposed at various times, and was voted upon by the General Conferences of the two bodies in 1958 and 1959, failing to pass in the Wesleyan Methodist General Conference by a margin of a single vote. In 1962, the General Conference of The Pilgrim Holiness Church took action expressing renewed interest in union with The Wesleyan Methodist Church. In 1963, the General Conference of The Wesleyan Methodist Church took like action, instructing its Committee on Church Union to pursue its work with all due diligence. On June 15, 1966, the Thirty-Second General Conference of The Wesleyan Methodist Church adopted The Basis for Merger and Constitution, and subsequently the annual conferences and local churches ratified the action. On June 16, 1966, the Twenty-Fifth International Conference of The Pilgrim Holiness Church also adopted The Basis for Merger and Constitution. Thus the formation of *The Wesleyan Church* was authorized. The General Board of The Pilgrim Holiness Church and the General Board of Administration of The Wesleyan Methodist Church cooperated in planning the uniting General Conference, and in preparing the new book of *Discipline* for its consideration. On June 26, 1968, The Pilgrim Holiness Church and The Wesleyan Methodist Church of America were united to form The Wesleyan Church.

### G. The Development of the World Organization

**60.** The merging General Conference provided tentatively for the development of the overseas churches into national or regional general conferences, as they matured and qualified for such status. As a result, the General Board of Administration appointed a World Organization Planning Committee. Its work led to a meeting of miss... coordinators and national representatives from around the world in... World Organization Planning Conference, June 6-9, 1972, prior to the ...econd General Conference. The Planning Conference recommended ...ting apart those portions of the Constitution which contained the ...cles, doctrines, and standards of conduct, as the Essentials of The Wesleyan ... plus some new organization... ...ng upon all General Conferen... Church, which would be ... ...ended the formation of a Wes... Wesleyan Church. It r...

fellowship governed by a Charter, functioning through a General Council, with eventually an International Board of Review assisting in maintaining faithfulness to the Essentials. The entire plan was approved by the 1972 General Conference, and subsequently the members of the World Organization Planning Conference effected the organization of the General Council. During the following quadrennium two provisional general conferences, one step short of full status, were formed. The Caribbean Provisional General Conference was organized April 3, 1974, and the Provisional General Conference of the Philippines was organized April 22-23, 1975. The 1984 General Conference incorporated the Essentials in the Charter as an historic statement of faith with which all disciplines must agree. On June 20, 1988, the General Conference approved the elevation of The Wesleyan Church of the Philippines to full standing equivalent to that of the North American General Conference, providing for the formation of the International Board of Review.

### H. Official Church Names

**80.** In keeping with the provisions of paragraphs 205 and 340:2, the following adaptations of the Church name have been approved for the various units of The Wesleyan Church as listed. These are printed for information only. Changes may be authorized when necessary by the General Board (340:2; 1655:31).

Australia: *The Wesleyan Methodist Church*
Brazil: *Igreja Evangelica Wesleyana*
British Isles: *The Wesleyan Holiness Church*
Caribbean: *The Wesleyan Holiness Church*
Colombia: *La Iglesia Wesleyana de Colombia*
Guyana: *The Wesleyan Church*
Haiti: *L'Eglise Wesleyenne d'Haiti*
Honduras: *Mision Methodista Zion*
India: *The Wes[illegible]eyan Methodist Church*
Indonesia: *Yaya[illegible]n Gereja Wesleyan Indonesia*
Liberia: *The Wesley[illegible] Church of Liberia*
Mexico: *Iglesia Evang[illegible]a de los Peregrinos*
Mozambique: *Igreja Em[illegible]uel Evangelica Wesleyana*
Myanmar: *The Wesleyan M[illegible]dist Church*
Peru: *Iglesia Wesleyana*
Philippines (cf. 2560): *The Wesle[illegible]hurch of the Philippines*
Sierra Leone: *The Wesleyan Church[illegible]rra Leone*
South Korea: *Jesus Korea Wesleyan C[illegible]*
South Africa: *The Wesleyan Church of So[illegible] Africa*

Suriname: *De Wesleyaanse Gemeente*
United States and Canada: *The Wesleyan Church*
Zambia: *The Pilgrim Wesleyan Church*
Zimbabwe: *The Wesleyan Church*

## Chapter II

# MISSION OF THE WESLEYAN CHURCH

**100.** The Wesleyan Church has grown out of a revival movement which has historically given itself to one mission — the spreading of scriptural holiness throughout every land. The message which ignited the Wesleyan revival was the announcement that God through Christ can forgive men and women of their sins, transform them, free them from inbred sin, enable them to live a holy life, and bear witness to their hearts that they are indeed children of God. The message was based on the Scriptures, was verified in personal experience, and came not only in word but in the power of the Spirit. It was dynamic and contagious, and was communicated from heart to heart and from land to land. It adapted itself and gave new vitality and purpose to various kinds of church organizations.

**105.** The Wesleyan Church believes that to spread scriptural holiness throughout every land involves joining the entire church of Christ in a full-orbed mission to the world, including the following:

(1) Sharing the divine revelation of full salvation through Christ as recorded in the Holy Scriptures so as to evangelize the lost and to minister redemptively to human society and its institutions.

(2) Relating new converts to local churches and providing Spirit-filled and well-trained pastors and leaders for the same.

(3) Developing in the converts patterns of worship to God and of fellowship with other believers.

(4) Discipling new believers in turn to be witnesses for their Lord.

(5) Guiding believers to experience entire sanctification so they are enabled to live whole and holy lives.

(6) [illegible]iding for developing Christians lifelong nurture and instruction, encouraging [illegible] grow toward spiritual maturity in Christ Jesus.

(7) Helping [illegible]ing Christians to develop a Christian interpretation of life and the univers[illegible] them to be good stewards of the talents, time, opportunities, and reso[illegible] which Christ has entrusted them.

(8) Equipping belie[illegible] of dynamic service toward God and humanity, so that the full pot[illegible] designed for each of them may be realized.

# Chapter III

# CLASSIFICATION OF CHURCH LAW

## A. Constitutional Law

**125. Relationship to Essentials.** The Essentials of The Wesleyan Church consist of an historic statement of faith and practice and are set forth in the Charter of the Wesleyan World Fellowship (see Appendix A). Each general conference of the Wesleyan World Fellowship must subscribe to the Essentials' pronouncements and must not contravene any of its provisions in its constitutions, articles of religion, or discipline. The North American General Conference does so subscribe. The Articles of Religion and other statements of faith and practice which are a part of the Constitution of the North American General Conference are in accord with the Essentials of The Wesleyan Church and are not intended to contravene or contradict them at any point.

**135. Identification.** The Constitution of the North American General Conference of The Wesleyan Church consists of Articles I through XI, paragraph 200 through 385, including the Preamble, Name, Articles of Religion, Covenant Membership Commitments, Elementary Principles, Observance of Sacraments, Membership, The Ministry, Organization and Government, Powers and Restrictions of the General Conference, The Supreme Judiciary, and Amendments to the Constitution. The Constitution may be amended as set forth in paragraph 385.

**145. Function.** The Constitution is that body of laws (cf. 135) that sets forth fundamental doctrines and practices, the basic laws, principles, and restrictions by which the Church is governed, and guarantees certain rights to its members and ministers. The Constitution takes precedence over statutory law, ritual, and all other laws and official actions of the governing bodies and officers within its jurisdiction (cf. 185). It is the law to which all statutory law, ritual, and any other legislative or official actions must conform.

## B. Statutory Law

**155.** Statutory law consists of legislation passed by the General Conference by a majority vote in fulfillment of its duties as set forth in the Constitution and in keeping with its provisions and restrictions and printed by order of the General Conference in *The Discipline of The Wesleyan Church*. Such statutory law is the authority for all of the North American General Conference of The Wesleyan Church, including its members, mi churches, districts, institutions, auxiliary organizations, corporations, general departments and offices, agencies, and any other official bodies (cf. 185). Statutory law remains in effect until amended, rescinded, or declared unconstitutional.

**165.** All changes in or additions to the statutory laws take effect when *The Discipline* is published following the adjournment of the General Conference unless an earlier time is ordered by a two-thirds vote of the General Conference.

### C. Ritual

**175.** The ritual of The Wesleyan Church consists of those rites and ceremonies contained in *The Discipline of The Wesleyan Church* (cf. 5500-5999), officially approved by the General Conference by a majority of those present and voting. The "Reception of Covenant Members," "Covenant Questions," and "Declaration of Purpose," in the ritual for the "Reception of Covenant Members" (5565-5567); the "Examination of Candidates" in the rituals for the "Ordination of Ministers" (5772); and the "Commissioning of Ministers" (5825) have the authority of statutory law and must be followed as prescribed. In the remainder of the Ritual, a measure of flexibility is permitted as long as nothing contradicts the Articles of Religion or any other part of the Constitution.

### D. Current Authority

**185.** The current issue of *The Discipline of The Wesleyan Church* is the only valid authority for the North American General Conference and its subordinate units, with the exception of those units under the General Department of World Missions which have been authorized to have their own disciplines by the General Board (cf. 340:2; 2500:4-5; 2610:6).

### E. Scripture References and Explanatory Notes

**190.** Listings of Scripture references and explanatory notes have been appended in support of the Articles of Religion and Covenant Membership Commitments. These have the status of statutory law (155).

# Chapter IV

# THE CONSTITUTION OF THE NORTH AMERICAN GENERAL CONFERENCE

## Preamble

**200.** In order that we may wisely preserve and pass on to posterity the heritage of doctrine and principles of Christian living transmitted to us as evangelicals in the Arminian-Wesleyan tradition, and to insure church order by sound principles of ecclesiastical polity, and to prepare the way for more effective cooperation with other branches of the church of Christ in all that makes for the advancement of God's kingdom among all people, we, the ministers and lay members of The Wesleyan Church meeting in official assemblies, do hereby ordain, establish, and set forth as the fundamental law, or constitution of The Wesleyan Church, the articles of religion, rules of Christian living, privileges and conditions of church membership, and articles of organization and government, here following:

## Article I. Name

**205.** The name of this communion is *The Wesleyan Church*. Wherever the use of this name is impossible or impractical, adaptation may be made by the authorized body (340:2).

## Article II. Articles of Religion

### *I. Faith in the Holy Trinity*

**210.** We believe in the one living and true God, both holy and loving, eternal, unlimited in power, wisdom, goodness, the Creator and Preserver of all things. Within this unity there are three persons of one essential nature, power and eternity — the Father, the Son and the Holy Spirit.

**Gen. 1:1; 17:1; Ex. 3:13-15; 33:20; Deut. 6:4; Ps. 90:2; Isa. 40:28-29; Matt. 3:16-17; 28:19; John 1:1-2; 4:24; 16:13; 17:3; Acts 5:3-4; 17:24-25; 1 Cor. 8:4, 6; Eph. 2:18; Phil. 2:6; Col. 1:16-17; 1 Tim. 2 1:17; Heb. 1:8; 1 John 5:20.**

### *II. The Father*

**212.** We believe the Father is the Source of all that exists, whether of matter or spirit. With the Son and the Holy Spirit, He made man in His image. By intention He relates to people as Father, thereby forever declaring His goodwill toward them. In love, He both seeks and receives penitent sinners.

**Ps. 68:5; Isa. 64:8; Matt. 7:11; John 3:17; Rom. 8:15; 1 Peter 1:17.**

### *III. The Son of God*

**214.** We believe in Jesus Christ, the only begotten Son of God. He was conceived by the Holy Spirit and born of the Virgin Mary, truly God and truly man. He died on the cross and was buried, to be a sacrifice both for original sin and for all human transgressions, and to reconcile us to God. Christ rose bodily from the dead, and ascended into heaven, and there intercedes for us at the Father's right hand until He returns to judge all humanity at the last day.

**Ps. 16:8-10; Matt. 1:21, 23; 11:27; 16:28; 27:62-66; 28:5-9, 16-17; Mark 10:45; 15; 16:6-7; Luke 1:27, 31, 35; 24:4-8, 23; John 1:1, 14, 18; 3:16-17; 20:26-29; 21; Acts 1:2-3; 2:24-31; 4:12; 10:40; Rom. 5:10, 18; 8:34; 14:9; 1 Cor. 15:3-8, 14; 2 Cor. 5:18-19; Gal. 1:4; 2:20; 4:4-5; Eph. 5:2; 1 Tim. 1:15; Heb 2:17; 7:27; 9:14, 28; 10:12; 13:20; 1 Peter 2:24; 1 John 2:2; 4:14.**

### *IV. The Holy Spirit*

**216.** We believe in the Holy Spirit who proceeds from the Father and the Son, and is of the same essential nature, majesty, and glory, as the Father and the Son, truly and eternally God. He is the Administrator of grace to all mankind, and is particularly the effective Agent in conviction for sin, in regeneration, in sanctification, and in glorification. He is ever present, assuring, preserving, guiding, and enabling the believer.

**Job 33:4; Matt. 28:19; John 4:24; 14:16-17; 15:26; 16:13-15; Acts 5:3-4; Rom. 8:9; 2 Cor. 3:17; Gal. 4:6.**

### *V. The Sufficiency and Full Authority of the Holy Scriptures for Salvation*

**218.** We believe that the books of the Old and New Testaments constitute the Holy Scriptures. They are the inspired and infallibly written Word of God, fully inerrant in their original manuscripts and superior to all human authority, and have been transmitted to the present without corruption of any essential doctrine. We believe that they contain all things necessary to salvation; so that whatever is not read therein, nor may be proved thereby, is not to be required of any man or woman that it should be believed as an article of faith, or be thought requisite or necessary to salvation. Both in the Old and New Testaments life is offered ultimately through Christ, who is the only Mediator between God and humanity. The New Testament teaches Christians how to fulfill the moral principles of the Old Testament, calling for loving obedience to God made possible by the indwelling presence of His Holy Spirit.

The canonical books of the Old Testament are:

Genesis, Exodus, Leviticus, Numbers, Deuteronomy, Joshua, Judges, Ruth, 1 Samuel, 2 Samuel, 1 Kings, 2 Kings, 1 Chronicles, 2 Chronicles, Ezra, Nehemiah, Esther, Job, Psalms, Proverbs, Ecclesiastes, The Song of Solomon, Isaiah, Jeremiah, Lamentations, Ezekiel, Daniel, Hosea, Joel, Amos, Obadiah, Jonah, Micah, Nahum, Habakkuk, Zephaniah, Haggai, Zechariah and Malachi.

The canonical books of the New Testament are:

Matthew, Mark, Luke, John, Acts, Romans, 1 Corinthians, 2 Corinthians, Galatians, Ephesians, Philippians, Colossians, 1 Thessalonians, 2 Thessalonians, 1 Timothy, 2 Timothy, Titus, Philemon, Hebrews, James, 1 Peter, 2 Peter, 1 John, 2 John, 3 John, Jude and Revelation.

**Ps. 19:7; Matt. 5:17-19; 22:37-40; Luke 24:27, 44; John 1:45; 5:46; 17:17; Acts 17:2, 11; Rom. 1:2; 15:4, 8; 16:26; 2 Cor. 1:20; Gal. 1:8; Eph. 2:15-16; 1 Tim. 2:5; 2 Tim. 3:15-17; Heb. 4:12; 10:1; 11:39; James 1:21; 1 Peter 1:23; 2 Peter 1:19-21; 1 John 2:3-7; Rev. 22:18-19.**

### *VI. God's Purpose for Humanity*

**220.** We believe that the two great commandments which require us to love the Lord our God with all the heart, and our neighbors as ourselves, summarize the divine law as it is revealed in the Scriptures. They are the perfect measure and norm of human duty, both for the ordering and directing of families and nations, and all other social bodies, and for individual acts, by which we are required to acknowledge God as our only Supreme Ruler, and all persons as created by Him, equal in all natural rights. Therefore all persons should so order all their individual, social and political acts as to give to God entire and absolute obedience, and to assure to all the enjoyment of every natural right, as well as to promote the fulfillment of each in the possession and exercise of such rights.

**Lev. 19:18, 34; Deut. 1:16-17; Job 31:13-14; Jer. 21:12; 22:3; Micah 6:8; Matt. 5:44-48; 7:12; Mark 12:28-31; Luke 6:27-29, 35; John 13:34-35;**

**Acts 10:34-35; 17:26; Rom. 12:9; 13:1, 7-8, 10; Gal. 5:14; 6:10; Titus 3:1; James 2:8; 1 Peter 2:17; 1 John 2:5; 4:12-13; 2 John 6.**

### *VII. Marriage and the Family*

**222.** We believe that every person is created in the image of God, that human sexuality reflects that image in terms of intimate love, communication, fellowship, subordination of the self to the larger whole, and fulfillment. God's Word makes use of the marriage relationship as the supreme metaphor for His relationship with His covenant people and for revealing the truth that that relationship is of one God with one people. Therefore God's plan for human sexuality is that it is to be expressed only in a monogamous lifelong relationship between one man and one woman within the framework of marriage. This is the only relationship which is divinely designed for the birth and rearing of children and is a covenant union made in the sight of God, taking priority over every other human relationship.

**Gen. 1:27-28; 2:18, 20, 23-24; Isa. 54:4-8; 62:5b; Jer. 3:14; Ezek. 16:3ff.; Hosea 2; Mal. 2:14; Matt. 19:4-6; Mark 10:9; John 2:1-2, 11; 1 Cor. 9:5; Eph. 5:23-32; 1 Tim. 5:14; Heb. 13:4; Rev. 19:7-8.**

### *VIII. Personal Choice*

**224.** We believe that humanity's creation in the image of God included ability to choose between right and wrong. Thus individuals were made morally responsible for their choices. But since the fall of Adam, people are unable in their own strength to do the right. This is due to original sin, which is not simply the following of Adam's example, but rather the corruption of the nature of each mortal, and is reproduced naturally in Adam's descendants. Because of it, humans are very far gone from original righteousness, and by nature are continually inclined to evil. They cannot of themselves even call upon God or exercise faith for salvation. But through Jesus Christ the prevenient grace of God makes possible what humans in self effort cannot do. It is bestowed freely upon all, enabling all who will to turn and be saved.

**Gen. 6:5; 8:21; Deut. 30:19; Josh. 24:15; 1 Kings 20:40; Ps. 51:5; Isa. 64:6; Jer. 17:9; Mark 7:21-23; Luke 16:15; John 7:17; Rom. 3:10-12; 5:12-21; 1 Cor. 15:22; Eph. 2:1-3; 1 Tim. 2:5; Titus 3:5; Heb. 11:6; Rev. 22:17.**

### *IX. The Atonement*

**226.** We believe that Christ's offering of himself, once and for all, through His sufferings and meritorious death on the cross, provides the perfect redemption and atonement for the sins of the whole world, both original and actual. There is no other ground of salvation from sin but that alone. This atonement is sufficient for every individual of Adam's race. It is unconditionally effective in the salvation of those mentally incompetent from birth, of those converted persons who have become mentally incompetent, and of children under the age of accountability. But it is effective for the salvation of those who reach the age of accountability only when they repent and exercise faith in Christ.

**Isa. 52:13-53:12; Luke 24:46-47; John 3:16; Acts 3:18; 4:12; Rom. 3:20, 24-26; 5:8-11, 13, 18-20; 7:7; 8:34; 1 Cor. 6:11; 15:22; Gal. 2:16; 3:2-3; Eph. 1:7; 2:13, 16; 1 Tim. 2:5-6; Heb. 7:23-27; 9:11-15, 24-28; 10:14; 1 John 2:2; 4:10.**

### *X. Repentance and Faith*

**228.** We believe that for men and women to appropriate what God's prevenient grace has made possible, they must voluntarily respond in repentance and faith. The ability comes from God, but the act is the individual's.

Repentance is prompted by the convicting ministry of the Holy Spirit. It involves a willful change of mind that renounces sin and longs for righteousness, a godly sorrow for and a confession of past sins, proper restitution for wrongdoings, and a resolution to reform the life. Repentance is the precondition for saving faith, and without it saving faith is impossible. Faith, in turn, is the only condition of salvation. It begins in the agreement of the mind and the consent of the will to the truth of the gospel, but issues in a complete reliance by the whole person in the saving ability of Jesus Christ and a complete trusting of oneself to Him as Savior and Lord. Saving faith is expressed in a public acknowledgment of His Lordship and an identification with His church.

**Mark 1:15; Luke 5:32; 13:3; 24:47; John 3:16; 17:20; 20:31; Acts 5:31; 10:43; 11:18; 16:31; 20:21; 26:20; Rom. 1:16; 2:4; 10:8-10, 17; Gal. 3:26; Eph. 2:8; 4:4-6; Phil. 3:9; 2 Thess. 2:13; 2 Tim. 2:25; Heb. 11:6; 12:2; 1 Peter 1:9; 2 Peter 3:9.**

### *XI. Justification, Regeneration and Adoption*

**230.** We believe that when one repents of personal sin and believes on the Lord Jesus Christ, that at the same moment that person is justified, regenerated, adopted into the family of God, and assured of personal salvation through the witness of the Holy Spirit.

We believe that justification is the judicial act of God whereby a person is accounted righteous, granted full pardon of all sin, delivered from guilt, completely released from the penalty of sins committed, by the merit of our Lord and Savior Jesus Christ, by faith alone, not on the basis of works.

We believe that regeneration, or the new birth, is that work of the Holy Spirit whereby, when one truly repents and believes, one's moral nature is given a distinctively spiritual life with the capacity for love and obedience. This new life is received by faith in Jesus Christ, it enables the pardoned sinner to serve God with the will and affections of the heart, and by it the regenerate are delivered from the power of sin which reigns over all the unregenerate.

We believe that adoption is the act of God by which the justified and regenerated believer becomes a partaker of all the rights, privileges and responsibilities of a child of God.

**Justification: Hab. 2:4; Acts 13:38-39; 15:11; 16:31; Rom. 1:17; 3:28; 4:2-5; 5:1-2; Gal. 3:6-14; Eph. 2:8-9; Phil 3:9; Heb. 10:38.**
**Regeneration: John 1:12-13; 3:3, 5-8; 2 Cor. 5:17; Gal. 3:26; Eph. 2:5, 10, 19; 4:24; Col. 3:10; Titus 3:5; James 1:18; 1 Peter 1:3-4; 2 Peter 1:4; 1 John 3:1.**
**Adoption: Rom. 8:15; Gal. 4:5, 7; Eph. 1:5.**
**Witness of the Spirit: Rom. 8:16-17; Gal. 4:6; 1 John 2:3; 3:14, 18-19.**

### *XII. Good Works*

**232.** We believe that although good works cannot save us from our sins or from God's judgment, they are the fruit of faith and follow after regeneration. Therefore they are pleasing and acceptable to God in Christ, and by them a living faith may be as evidently known as a tree is discerned by its fruit.

**Matt. 5:16; 7:16-20; John 15:8; Rom 3:20; 4:2, 4, 6; Gal. 2:16; 5:6; Eph. 2:10; Phil. 1:11; Col. 1:10; 1 Thess. 1:3; Titus 2:14; 3:5; James 2:18, 22; 1 Peter 2:9, 12.**

### *XIII. Sin After Regeneration*

**234.** We believe that after we have experienced regeneration, it is possible to fall into sin, for in this life there is no such height or strength of holiness from which it is impossible to fall. But by the grace of God one who has fallen into sin may by true repentance and faith find forgiveness and restoration.

**Mal. 3:7; Matt. 18:21-22; John 15:4-6; 1 Tim. 4:1, 16; Heb. 10:35-39; 1 John 1:9; 2:1, 24-25.**

### *XIV. Sanctification: Initial, Progressive, Entire*

**236.** We believe that sanctification is that work of the Holy Spirit by which the child of God is separated from sin unto God and is enabled to love God with all the heart and to walk in all His holy commandments blameless. Sanctification is initiated at the moment of justification and regeneration. From that moment there is a gradual or progressive sanctification as the believer walks with God and daily grows in grace and in a more perfect obedience to God. This prepares for the crisis of entire sanctification which is wrought instantaneously when believers present themselves as living sacrifices, holy and acceptable to God, through faith in Jesus Christ, being effected by the baptism with the Holy Spirit who cleanses the heart from all inbred sin. The crisis of entire sanctification perfects the believer in love and empowers that person for effective service. It is followed by lifelong growth in grace and the knowledge of our Lord and Savior Jesus Christ. The life of holiness continues through faith in the sanctifying blood of Christ and evidences itself by loving obedience to God's revealed will.

**Gen. 17:1; Deut. 30:6; Ps. 130:8; Isa. 6:1-6; Ezek. 36:25-29; Matt. 5:8, 48; Luke 1:74-75; 3:16-17; 24:49; John 17:1-26; Acts 1:4-5, 8; 2:1-4; 15:8-9; 26:18; Rom. 8:3-4; 1 Cor. 1:2; 6:11; 2 Cor. 7:1; Eph. 4:13, 24; 5:25-27; 1 Thess. 3:10, 12-13; 4:3, 7-8; 5:23-24; 2 Thess. 2:13; Titus 2:11-14; Heb. 10:14; 12:14; 13:12; James 3:17-18; 4:8; 1 Peter 1:2; 2 Peter 1:4; 1 John 1:7, 9; 3:8-9; 4:17-18; Jude 24.**

### *XV. The Gifts of the Spirit*

**238.** We believe that the Gift of the Spirit is the Holy Spirit himself, and He is to be desired more than the gifts of the Spirit which He in His wise counsel bestows upon individual members of the Church to enable them properly to fulfill their function as members of the body of Christ. The gifts of the Spirit, although not always identifiable with natural abilities, function through them for the edification of the whole church. These gifts are to be exercised in love under the administration of the Lord of the church, not through human volition. The relative value of the gifts of the Spirit is to be tested by their usefulness in the church and not by the ecstasy produced in the ones receiving them.

**Luke 11:13; 24:49; Acts 1:4; 2:38-39; 8:19-20; 10:45; 11:17; Rom. 12:4-8; 1 Cor. 12:1-14:40; Eph. 4:7-8, 11-16; Heb. 2:4; 13:20-21; 1 Peter 4:8-11.**

*XVI. The Church*

**240.** We believe that the Christian church is the entire body of believers in Jesus Christ, who is the founder and only Head of the church. The church includes both those believers who have gone to be with the Lord and those who remain on the earth, having renounced the world, the flesh and the devil, and having dedicated themselves to the work which Christ committed unto His church until He comes. The church on earth is to preach the pure Word of God, properly administer the sacraments according to Christ's instructions, and live in obedience to all that Christ commands. A local church is a body of believers formally organized on gospel principles, meeting regularly for the purposes of evangelism, nurture, fellowship and worship. The Wesleyan Church is a denomination consisting of those members within district conferences and local churches who, as members of the body of Christ, hold the faith set forth in these Articles of Religion and acknowledge the ecclesiastical authority of its governing bodies.

**Matt. 16:18; 18:17; Acts 2:41-47; 9:31; 11:22; 12:5; 14:23; 15:22; 20:28; 1 Cor. 1:2; 12:28; 16:1; 2 Cor. 1:1; Gal. 1:2; Eph. 1:22-23; 2:19-22; 3:9-10, 21; 5:22-33; Col. 1:18, 24; 1 Thess. 1:1; 2 Thess. 1:1; 1 Tim. 3:15; Heb. 12:23; James 5:14.**

*XVII. The Sacraments: Baptism and the Lord's Supper*

**242.** We believe that water baptism and the Lord's Supper are the sacraments of the church commanded by Christ and ordained as a means of grace when received through faith. They are tokens of our profession of Christian faith and signs of God's gracious ministry toward us. By them, He works within us to quicken, strengthen and confirm our faith.

We believe that water baptism is a sacrament of the church, commanded by our Lord and administered to believers. It is a symbol of the new covenant of grace and signifies acceptance of the benefits of the atonement of Jesus Christ. By means of this sacrament, believers declare their faith in Jesus Christ as Savior.

**Matt. 3:13-17; 28:19; Mark 1:9-11; John 3:5, 22, 26; 4:1-2; Acts 2:38-39, 41; 8:12-17, 36-38; 9:18; 16:15, 33; 18:8; 19:5; 22:16; Rom 2:28-29; 4:11; 6:3-4; 1 Cor. 12:13; Gal. 3:27-29; Col. 2:11-12; Titus 3:5.**

We believe that the Lord's Supper is a sacrament of our redemption by Christ's death and of our hope in His victorious return, as well as a sign of the love that Christians have for each other. To such as receive it humbly, with a proper spirit and by faith, the Lord's Supper is made a means through which God communicates grace to the heart.

Matt. 26:26-28; Mark 14:22-24; Luke 22:19-20; John 6:48-58; 1 Cor. 5:7-8; 10:3-4, 16-17; 11:23-29.

### *XVIII. The Second Coming of Christ*

**244.** We believe that the certainty of the personal and imminent return of Christ inspires holy living and zeal for the evangelization of the world. At His return He will fulfill all prophecies made concerning His final and complete triumph over evil.

**Job 19:25-27; Isa. 11:1-12; Zech. 14:1-11; Matt. 24:1-51; 25; 26:64; Mark 13:1-37; Luke 17:22-37; 21:5-36; John 14:1-3; Acts 1:6-11; 1 Cor. 1:7-8; 1 Thess. 1:10; 2:19; 3:13; 4:13-18; 5:1-11, 23; 2 Thess. 1:6-10; 2:1-12; Titus 2:11-14; Heb. 9:27-28; James 5:7-8; 2 Peter 3:1-14; 1 John 3:2-3; Rev. 1:7; 19:11-16; 22:6-7, 12, 20.**

### *XIX. The Resurrection of the Dead*

**246.** We believe in the bodily resurrection from the dead of all mankind--of the just unto the resurrection of life, and of the unjust unto the resurrection of damnation. The resurrection of the righteous dead will occur at Christ's Second Coming, and the resurrection of the wicked will occur at a later time. The resurrection of Christ is the guarantee of the resurrection of those who are in Christ. The raised body will be a spiritual body, but the person will be whole and identifiable.

**Job 19:25-27; Dan. 12:2; Matt. 22:30-32; 28:1-20; Mark 16:1-8; Luke 14:14; 24:1-53; John 5:28-29; 11:21-27; 20:1--21:25; Acts 1:3; Rom. 8:11; 1 Cor. 6:14; 15:1-58; 2 Cor. 4:14; 5:1-11; 1 Thess. 4:13-17; Rev. 20:4-6, 11-13.**

### *XX. The Judgment of All Persons*

**248.** We believe that the Scriptures reveal God as the Judge of all and the acts of His judgment are based on His omniscience and eternal justice. His administration of judgment will culminate in the final meeting of all persons before His throne of great majesty and power, where records will be examined and final rewards and punishments will be administered.

**Eccl. 12:14; Matt. 10:15; 25:31-46; Luke 11:31-32; Acts 10:42; 17:31; Rom. 2:16; 14:10-12; 2 Cor. 5:10; 2 Tim. 4:1; Heb. 9:27; 2 Peter 3:7; Rev. 20:11-13.**

### *XXI. Destiny*

**250.** We believe that the Scriptures clearly teach that there is a conscious personal existence after death. The final destiny of each person is determined by God's grace and that person's response, evidenced inevitably by a moral character which results from that individual's personal and volitional choices and not from any arbitrary decree of God. Heaven with its eternal glory and the blessedness of Christ's presence is the final abode of those who choose the salvation which God provides through Jesus Christ, but hell with its everlasting misery and separation from God is the final abode of those who neglect this great salvation.

**Dan. 12:2; Matt. 25:34-46; Mark 9:43-48; Luke 13:3; John 8:21-23; 14:2-3; 2 Cor. 5:6, 8, 10; Heb. 2:1-3; 9:27-28; 10:26-31; Rev. 20:14-15; 21:1-22:5, 14-15.**

## Article III. Covenant Membership Commitments

**260.** To be identified with an organized church is the blessed privilege and sacred duty of all who are saved from their sins and are seeking completeness in Christ Jesus. From the church's beginnings in the New Testament age, it has been understood that such identification involves putting off the old patterns of conduct and putting on the mind of Christ. In maintaining this Christian concept of a transformed life, The Wesleyan Church intends to relate timeless biblical principles to the conditions of contemporary society in such a way as to respect the integrity of the individual believer, yet maintain the purity of the Church and the effectiveness of its witness. This is done in the conviction that there is validity in the concept of the collective Christian conscience as illuminated and guided by the Holy Spirit. The following items (265) represent historic, ethical and practical standards of The Wesleyan Church. While it is hoped that our people will earnestly seek the aid of the Spirit in cultivating a sensitivity to evil which transcends the mere letter of the law, it is expected that those entering into Covenant Membership shall follow carefully and conscientiously these guides and helps to holy living. Disregard of the principles embraced in these Covenant Membership Commitments subjects a member to Church discipline (268).

**265.** Those admitted to Covenant Membership in our churches commit themselves to demonstrate their life in Christ in such ways as:

### *Toward God*

(1) To reverence the name of God and to honor the Lord's Day by divine worship and spiritual edification, participating in those activities which contribute to the moral and spiritual purposes of this day.

**Gen. 2:3; Ex. 20:3, 7-11; Deut. 5:11-15; Isa. 58:13-14; Mark 2:27; Acts 20:7; Heb. 4:9.**

(2) To seek only the leading of the Holy Spirit and to abstain from all forms of spiritism, such as the occult, witchcraft, astrology and other similar practices.

**Lev. 19:31; 20:6; Deut. 18:10-14; Acts 19:18-19; Gal. 5:19-20.**

### *Toward Self*

(3) To exercise faithful stewardship through the wise use of their time and material resources, practicing careful self-discipline in order to further the mission of Christ's church (remembering the principle of tithing which is basic to the New Testament standard of stewardship) and to demonstrate compassion to those in need.

**Prov. 3:9; Mal. 3:10; Matt. 25:34-40; Acts 20:35; 1 Cor. 16:2; 2 Cor. 9:7; Eph. 5:16; Col. 3:17; James 2:15-16; 1 John 3:17.**

(4) To demonstrate a positive social witness by abstaining from all forms of gambling and by abstaining from using or trafficking (production, sale or purchase)* in any substances destructive to their physical, mental and spiritual health, such as alcoholic beverages, tobacco and drugs (other than proper medical purposes of drugs); and by refraining from membership in secret societies and lodges which are oath bound, believing that the quasi-religious nature of such organizations divides the Christian's loyalty, their secret nature contravenes the Christian's open witness and the secret nature of their oaths is repugnant to the Christian conscience.

**Ex. 20:17; Rom. 14:21; 1 Cor. 6:12.** Gambling violates the principle of Christian stewardship and the tenth commandment, is harmful to the individual in that it is emotionally addictive, is a poor example to others, and pollutes the moral climate of society.

**Prov. 20:1; Rom. 6:12; 14:21; 1 Cor. 6:12-20; 10:23; 2 Cor. 7:1 Eph. 5:18; 1 Thess. 5:22.** Christians are to regard their bodies as temples of the Holy Spirit. While no "thing" of itself is sinful, the Christian should avoid the use of

*See 6805 in Appendix B

anything which would not help build the fellowship of the church, would not help the believers to realize their full potential in Christ, or which would enslave them. In the light of the scientific knowledge of our day concerning the actual and potential harm of these substances, total abstinence is more in keeping with these biblical principles than is moderation.

**Ex. 20:3; Matt. 5:34-36; John 18:20; Acts 4:12; James 5:12.** These prohibitions do not restrict membership in labor, civic or other organizations which do not contradict loyalty to Christ and the Church. When in these relationships Christian principles are violated, members shall be dealt with because of such violations and not because of the membership itself.

*Toward Family*

(5) To follow the teachings of the Scriptures regarding marriage and divorce. We affirm that sexual relationships outside of marriage and sexual relationships between persons of the same sex are immoral and sinful. We further affirm that heterosexual monogamy is God's plan for marriage, and we regard sexual sin of the spouse, such as adultery, homosexual behavior, bestiality or incest, as the only biblical grounds for considering divorce, and then only when appropriate counseling has failed to restore the relationship.

**Ex. 20:14, 17; 22:19; Lev. 20:10-16; Matt. 5:32; 19:19; Mark 10:11-12; Luke 16:18.**

(6) To preserve the sanctity of the home by honoring Christ in every phase of family life and by demonstrating Christ-like love (always avoiding spousal or child abuse), and by living peacefully with one another, thereby encouraging the nurture and education of the children in the Christian faith so as to bring them early to the saving knowledge of Christ.

**Prov. 22:6; Mark 10:9; Eph. 5:28; 6:4.**

*Toward The Church*

(7) To work together for the advancement of God's kingdom and for the mutual edification of fellow believers in holiness, knowledge and love; to walk together in Christian fellowship by giving and receiving counsel with gentleness and affection; by praying for each other; by helping each other in sickness and distress; and by demonstrating love, purity and courtesy to all.

**Rom. 15:1-2; Eph. 4; 1 Thess. 5.**

(8) To grow in the knowledge, love and grace of God by participating in public worship, the ministry of the Word of God, the Lord's Supper, family and personal devotions and fasting.

**Mark 2:18-20; Acts 13:2-3; 14:23; Rom. 12:12; 1 Cor. 11:23-28; Eph. 6:18; Phil. 4:6; 1 Tim. 2:1-2; 2 Tim. 3:16-17; Heb. 10:25; 1 Peter 2:2; 2 Peter 3:18.**

(9) To preserve the fellowship and witness of the Church with reference to the use of languages. The Wesleyan Church believes in the miraculous use of languages and the interpretation of languages in its biblical and historical setting. But it is contrary to the Word of God to teach that speaking in an unknown tongue or the gift of tongues is the evidence of the baptism of the Holy Spirit or of that entire sanctification which the baptism accomplishes; therefore, only a language readily understood by the congregation is to be used in public worship. The Wesleyan Church believes that the use of an ecstatic prayer language has no clear scriptural sanction, or any pattern of established historical usage in the Church; therefore, the use of such a prayer language shall not be promoted among us.

**Acts 8:14-17; 1 Cor. 12:1-14:40; Gal. 5:22-24.**

### *Toward Others*

(10) To do good as much as is possible to all people as God gives opportunity, especially to those in the body of Christ; by giving food to the hungry, by clothing the destitute, by visiting or helping those who are sick or in prison; by instructing, correcting or encouraging them in love.

**Matt. 25:31-46; Eph. 5:11; 1 Thess. 5:14; Heb. 3:13; 10:23-25.**

(11) To respect the inherent individual rights of all persons, regardless of race, color or sex.

**1 Cor. 8:13; 12:13; Gal. 3:28; 1 Tim. 5:21.**

(12) To live honestly, be just in all dealings and faithful in all commitments.

**Eccl. 5:4-5; Rom. 12:17; Phil. 4:8-9; 1 Peter 2:12.**

**268.** These are the Covenant Membership Commitments of our Church. We believe all these to be consistent with the principles of Christ as taught in the Word of God, which is the only and sufficient rule both of our faith and practice. If any among us do not observe them, and/or habitually break any of them, we will admonish such persons in love with the hope of restoring them to lives of harmony with the above Membership Commitments. If such efforts of restoration continue to prove fruitless, official action should be taken toward termination of said persons' church membership. However, the church members are encouraged to continue efforts toward the spiritual restoration of these persons.

**Matt. 18:15-17; 1 Cor. 5:6-7, 9-13; 2 Cor. 2:5-7; 5:18-20; 6:14-18; Gal. 6:1-10; Eph. 4:25-32; Titus 3:10-11.**

### Article IV. Elementary Principles

**270.** Christ is the only Head of the church, and the Word of God the only rule of faith and conduct.

**272.** No person who loves the Lord Jesus Christ, and obeys the gospel of God our Savior, ought to be deprived of church membership.

**274.** Every person has an inalienable right to private judgment in matters of religion, and an equal right to express personal opinions in any way which will not violate the laws of God or the rights of others.

**276.** All church trials should be conducted on gospel principles only; and no minister or member should be excommunicated except for immorality, the propagation of unchristian doctrines, or for neglect of duties enjoined by the Word of God.

**278.** The pastoral or ministerial office and duties are of divine appointment, and all ordained ministers in the church of God are equal; but ministers are forbidden to be lords over God's heritage, or to have dominion over the faith of the saints.

**280.** The Church has a right to form and enforce such rules and regulations only as are in accordance with the Holy Scriptures, and may be necessary or have a tendency to carry into effect the great system of practical Christianity.

**282.** Whatever power may be necessary to the formation of rules and regulations is inherent in the ministers and members of the Church; but so much of that power may be delegated from time to time, upon a plan of representation, as they may judge necessary and proper.

**284.** It is the duty of all ministers and members of the Church to maintain godliness and oppose all moral evil.

**286.** It is obligatory upon ministers of the gospel to be faithful in the discharge of their pastoral and ministerial duties, and it is also obligatory upon the members to esteem ministers highly for the works' sake, and to render them a righteous compensation for their labors.

## Article V. Observance of Sacraments

**290.** All persons to be baptized shall have the choice of baptism by immersion, pouring or sprinkling. Since children are born into this world with natures inclined to sin, and yet the prevenient grace of God provides for their redemption during the period before reaching the age of accountability, those parents who so choose may testify to their faith in God's provision by presenting their small children for baptism, while those who prefer to emphasize baptism as a testimony by the individual believer to his own act of faith may present their children for dedication.

**Mark 10:13-16; Acts 2:38-39; 16:15; 18:8.**

**293.** The Lord's Supper shall be observed in each local Wesleyan church at least once each three months.

## Article VI. Membership

**295.** The privileges and conditions of covenant membership in the Church are constitutional, and changes therein may be made only by constitutional enactment. The General Conference may at its own discretion establish categories of membership other than covenant membership. Nothing shall be included in the membership ritual that is contrary to the following definitions, conditions and privileges of membership.

**297.** The conditions of covenant membership are:

(1) Confession of a personal experience in regeneration, and a pledge to seek diligently until sanctified wholly if that grace has not been obtained.

(2) Christian baptism.

(3) Acceptance of the Articles of Religion which are summarized in 299, the Covenant Membership Commitments, the Elementary Principles, and the authority of *The Discipline* in matters of church government.

(4) A covenant to support the Church, to live in fellowship with the members thereof, and to seek God's glory in all things.

(5) The approving vote of the members of the receiving church who are present and voting, unless the church by vote shall delegate this right to the church board. In both cases, it shall be by majority vote, provided that when objections are urged against the reception of a member, it shall require a vote of two-thirds of those present and voting to receive.

**299.** Candidates for covenant membership shall declare their agreement with the following summary of the Articles of Religion:

We believe in God the Father, the Son and the Holy Spirit.

We believe that Jesus Christ the Son suffered in our place on the cross, that He died but rose again, that He now sits at the Father's right hand until He returns to judge every person at the last day.

We believe in the Holy Scriptures as the inspired and inerrant Word of God.

We believe that by the grace of God every person has the ability and responsibility to choose between right and wrong, and that those who repent of their sin and believe in the Lord Jesus Christ are justified by faith.

We believe that God not only counts the believer as righteous, but that He makes such persons righteous, freeing them from sin's dominion at conversion, purifying their hearts by faith, perfecting them in love at entire sanctification, and providing for their growth in grace at every stage of spiritual life, enabling them through the presence and power of the Holy Spirit to live victorious lives.

**302.** The rights of covenant membership are:

(1) The fellowship of the saints and the encouragement, admonition and spiritual guidance of the ministry.

(2) The access to the sacraments and ordinances of the Church.

(3) The right to vote and the eligibility to hold any office for which a person in covenant membership is eligible, if not under discipline.

(4) The right to trial and appeal if charged with failure to maintain the conditions of membership, with the specific provision that joining another religious body shall of itself sever membership in the Church.

(5) A covenant member in good standing in any Wesleyan church is entitled to membership privileges in any Wesleyan church to which a transfer of membership may be desired, subject to 297:5.

**305.** Church membership may be terminated only by one or more of the following:

(1) Voluntary withdrawal.

(2) Joining another religious body or a secret order.

(3) Expulsion after proper trial and conviction.

(4) Persistent neglect of church relationship as defined by *The Discipline*.

## Article VII. The Ministry

**310.** The General Conference shall from time to time enact provisions for the training, qualification and ordination of the ministry. Every Wesleyan minister must be a member of some Wesleyan church, and each ordained minister must be a member of a district. An ordained minister is a minister of the gospel fully invested with all the functions of the Christian ministry.

**313.** The constitutional rights of ministers in The Wesleyan Church if not under discipline shall include the following:

(1) To preach the gospel and in the case of ordained ministers to administer baptism and the Lord's Supper, to perform all parts of divine worship, and to solemnize the rite of matrimony.

(2) To be eligible, in the case of ordained ministers, for election to any office in the Church for which ordained ministers are eligible.

(3) To contract the pastoral relationship with local Wesleyan churches subject to the other provisions of this Constitution (313:6; 323:1-2).

(4) To enjoy the use for religious meetings of the church building or buildings of the pastoral charge to which appointment has been made by the district conference.

(5) To serve the assigned pastoral charge without interference by unauthorized activities of another minister of The Wesleyan Church.

(6) To transfer in the manner prescribed by *The Discipline* from one district to another, subject to the approval of the district superintendent and the general superintendent supervising the area which includes the district into which the transfer is sought.

(7) To have recourse, even if under discipline, to a proper court of jurisdiction in any matters involving complaint against the minister's character or ministerial conduct and to appeal the decision of such court.

## Article VIII. Organization and Government

### Local

**315. Pastoral Charges.** The members of the denomination shall be grouped into local churches, one or more of which shall constitute a pastoral charge. The following are the constitutional rights of each pastoral charge:

(1) To receive and expel or discontinue members subject to the provisions of *The Discipline*. This right vests severally in each local church.

(2) To call its own pastor, subject to confirmation by the district conference.

(3) To grant or revoke local licenses for various ministries as provided in *The Discipline*. This right may be delegated to the church board.

(4) To recommend persons for various ministries to the district conference. This right may be delegated to the church board.

(5) To elect its own officers and to remove the same for cause. No pastor or other official has any right to appoint an officer or declare an office vacant. This right belongs to the church alone, and vests severally in each local church.

(6) To elect trustees and through such trustees to supervise, control and maintain its property for the use and benefit of the ministry and members of The Wesleyan Church and subject to its regulations and appointments as from time to time legislated and declared. This right vests severally in each local church.

(7) To be represented in the voting membership of its district conference, if not under discipline.

(8) To have recourse to a proper court of jurisdiction in any matters of controversy between itself and other local, or district, or general units or agencies of the denomination. This right vests severally in each local church.

### District

**317.** The General Conference shall organize the work at large into districts, which shall operate under its jurisdiction and promote the interests of the denomination, and whose voting membership shall include the following: All ordained ministers on the appointed, retired, reserve and educational leave lists; licensed ministers elected to ordained minister's status; all commissioned and licensed ministers serving as pastors of Wesleyan churches; all commissioned and licensed ministers serving as full-time associate or assistant pastors of Wesleyan churches; members of the district board of administration who are not members by some other right; and lay delegates elected as provided in *The Discipline*. In addition the district conference shall include such nonvoting members as *The Discipline* shall provide. The principle of equal representation of the ministry and the laity in the district conference shall be maintained.

**320.** In transacting the business of the district conference the ministers and lay members shall deliberate as one body; but on the final vote on any question, at the call of one-fourth of the members, the house shall divide, and the ministers and lay members shall vote separately; and it shall require a majority vote of each branch to pass any question upon which the division has been called.

**323.** The constitutional rights of each district shall include the following:

(1) The right to take charge of all the ministers and churches within its bounds, as modified by 360:3e (except those serving the general church as the

General Conference shall define who shall be amenable to the General Board of Administration for their official conduct and to their districts for their moral character, and except the district superintendent who shall be amenable both to the district and to the General Board of Administration), and subject to the right of the ministers and churches to enter into pastoral engagements.

(2) To alter the agreement entered into by any pastor and charge, or veto the action of the church and appoint another pastor on said charge when it deems this to be for the best interest of the charge or pastor involved or when the general interest of the work of the district would be better served by such change; and the said church or charge shall receive the pastor appointed by the district conference, provided that any such alteration of a previous arrangement between a pastor and church shall be separately reported and passed by vote of the district conference to be effective.

(3) To elect and ordain ministers, and to receive ordained ministers from other denominations subject to the restrictions of *The Discipline*.

(4) To receive or decline persons recommended to it for various ministries by the pastoral charges within its bounds.

(5) To organize and receive local churches within the boundaries of the territory assigned to it by the General Conference, and to fix the boundaries of its circuits and stations.

(6) To take such actions and adopt such rules as it shall judge necessary to promote the interest and prosperity of the church and to amend or rescind the same, provided it shall not add to or take from any provision of the Constitution or of *The Discipline*, and provided further that if three members of a district shall take exception to its action on the ground that it violates this restriction, they may make an appeal therefrom through the channels prescribed by *The Discipline*.

(7) To elect its own officers as outlined in *The Discipline* and to dismiss them for cause.

(8) To elect in the manner prescribed by *The Discipline* its own board of trustees and through them to receive, hold, encumber and dispose of all district property within the bounds of the district, including local property held by the district, according to the provisions of *The Discipline* and the laws of the state. All properties held by the district shall be held in trust for the use and benefit of the ministry and members of The Wesleyan Church and subject to its regulations and appointments as from time to time legislated and declared.

(9) To be represented in the lay and ministerial voting membership of the General Conference, if not under discipline.

(10) To have recourse to a proper court of jurisdiction in any matters of controversy between itself and other district, local or general units or agencies of the denomination.

## General

**325. General Conference Membership.** The General Conference shall be composed of an equal number of ordained ministers and lay members elected by the several districts, and each district superintendent and a lay delegate elected on the district superintendent's behalf; the presidents of the general educational institutions; such officers serving the general church as the General Conference may establish by legislation, provided that it shall at the same time enact provisions to secure such further representation as shall be necessary to continue the principle of equal lay and ministerial membership; and of voting and/or nonvoting delegates from units under the General Department of World Missions according to a plan approved by the General Board of Administration.

**327. General Conference Delegates.**

(1) Each district, if not under discipline, shall be entitled to send one ordained minister and one lay member as delegates to the General Conference and additional ministerial and lay delegates according to membership on a basis of representation to be fixed by the General Conference.

(2) The delegates shall be elected by ballot. The ministerial delegates must be ordained, and at the time of their election, as also at the time of General Conference, must be members of the district which elected them.

(3) The lay delegates shall be chosen from the members of the Church in full relation within the bounds of the district they represent, and at the time of the General Conference they must be members of a church within the bounds of the district which elected them.

**330. General Conference Sessions.**

(1) The General Conference shall meet quadrennially, except that in cases of emergency or other unusual circumstances the General Board of Administration shall have the power to shorten or lengthen the interval. Each session shall be held at a time of the year specified in *The Discipline* at a place determined by the General Board of Administration; in case of emergency the General Board of Administration shall have power to change the time.

(2) The president or other elected officer of the General Conference whenever two-thirds of the districts shall request it, or the General Board of Administration, by such vote as the General Conference shall determine, shall call an extra session of the General Conference, fixing the place thereof and the time of assembling later than the next session of each district conference.

**332. General Conference Presidency.** The various sittings of the General Conference shall be presided over by the general superintendents in such order as these may determine; but in case no general superintendent be present, the General Conference shall elect by ballot an ordained minister as president pro tem.

**334. Other Officers.** The General Conference shall elect by ballot a secretary and such other officers as it shall decide upon.

**336. General Conference Quorum.** At all times when the General Conference is in session, it shall require a majority of all the delegates elected by the districts to form a quorum to do business, but a smaller number may adjourn from time to time, until a quorum is obtained.

**338. General Conference Voting.** The ministers and lay members shall deliberate in the sessions of the General Conference as one body, but upon the final vote on any question except proposed amendments to the Constitution, on a call of one-fourth of the members, the house shall divide and ministers and lay members shall vote separately; and it shall require a majority vote of each branch to pass any question upon which the division has been called.

**340. General Board of Administration.**

(1) There shall be a General Board of Administration to carry out the will of the General Conference during the quadrennium. Such Board shall be composed of the general superintendent(s) and such other general officers as shall be designated by the General Conference together with an equal number of ordained ministers and lay members chosen by the General Conference to represent equitably the several administrative areas of the Church. The number of such representative members shall be determined by the action of the General Conference.

(2) The General Board of Administration is the chief governing body of the Church in the interim of the General Conferences, and as such is empowered to perfect all plans necessary to the performance of its duties; it shall constitute or create the basic board of control of each and all of the Wesleyan societies and institutions now incorporated or hereafter incorporated under the laws of any state of the United States or of any province of Canada or under any other jurisdiction where such is permitted by the laws of said jurisdiction. The General Board of Administration shall have jurisdiction over mission units under the General Department of World Missions. It shall have the authority to approve a discipline for each unit achieving recognition as a fully established general conference and for each mission unit. In so doing, it shall have the power to adapt the name of the Church within the restrictions of paragraph 205, and to adapt the provisions of *The Discipline* of the North American General Conference, including both constitutional and statutory law, provided that it does not contravene the Essentials of The Wesleyan Church. In authorizing the adaptation of the name for a unit achieving recognition as an established general conference, it shall first consult with the highest interim administrative bodies of the

other established general conferences which are members of the Wesleyan World Fellowship.

**350. The General Superintendency.**

(1) The General Conference shall elect by ballot from among the ordained ministers one or more general superintendents, who shall be considered as the general spiritual and administrative leader(s) of the Church.

(2) They shall be elected for a four-year term of office to begin on the date determined by the General Conference.

(3) The general superintendents shall preside over the sittings of the General Conference and over the district conferences assigned to their supervision. At the district conference over which a general superintendent is presiding, the district superintendent shall serve by being seated at the presiding officer's table to advise and assist the chair. In the event a general superintendent is unable to be present at a district conference, a representative appointed by the General Superintendent shall serve as chair, and if neither the General Superintendent nor an appointed representative is present, it is the duty of the district superintendent to preside or to take responsibility for the same.

(4) Further duties of the general superintendent(s) shall be defined by the General Conference.

## Article IX. Powers and Restrictions of the General Conference

**360.** The General Conference shall have full power:

(1) To designate a criterion for parliamentary procedure for itself and for the other bodies of The Wesleyan Church.

(2) To elect such officers as it shall choose and to define their duties and responsibilities.

(3) To make and administer rules and regulations for The Wesleyan Church subject to the Constitution and the following restrictions:

(a) It shall not have power to revoke, alter or change our Articles of Religion, Elementary Principles or any Covenant Membership Commitment, or the conditions of membership, or to establish any standards of doctrine contrary to our present existing and established standards of doctrine.

(b) It shall not change or alter any part or rule of our government, so as to destroy the principle of equal representation of ministers and lay members in the representative bodies of the Church; or to do away with the right of each General Conference to elect its own officers, or the maintenance of an itinerant ministry.

(c) It shall make no rule that shall deny any church the right to receive, discontinue or expel its own members subject to their right of appeal; or to elect and remove its own officers; or that shall deny to the district conference the final disposition of all pastoral arrangements, except those districts in which the General Conference or the General Board has transferred the supervision to a general superintendent or other related general official, or that shall deny to preachers and churches initial negotiations concerning the same.

(d) It shall make no rule that will discriminate against any member or minister on account of ancestry, color or sex.

(e) It shall make no rule that will interfere with the supervision of established districts (in distinction from mission districts) over the ministers and churches within their bounds, unless said district (or districts) is under discipline.

(f) It shall not have the power to deprive any member or minister of the right of trial by an impartial committee, or of the right of appeal.

### Article X. The Supreme Judiciary

**370.** There shall be a judicial council to be known as the Board of Review whose number of members, qualifications, terms of office, and method of election shall be determined by the General Conference.

**375.** The Board of Review shall have authority:

(1) To determine the constitutionality of any act of the General Conference upon appeal of the general superintendents, or one-fifth of the members of the General Conference.

(2) To hear and determine any appeal from the decisions of the general superintendents as to the constitutionality of an action by a district or upon a point of Church law.

(3) To hear and determine the legality of any action by any general church board upon appeal of one-third the members thereof, or by request of the general superintendents.

(4) To settle questions in dispute between districts upon appeal by a two-thirds vote of a district that claims it has a grievance against another district.

(5) To determine the validity of any complaints against books used in the course of study or in our schools.

(6) To settle and determine the legality of issues arising between a district and the General Conference.

**380.** A decision of the Board of Review shall be final unless the General Conference votes to overrule the same by a two-thirds vote of those present and voting.

### Article XI. Amendments to the Constitution

**385.** Upon the recommendation of a two-thirds vote of all members of the several district conferences who are present and vote on a proposed change of any matter involving the Constitution, the next ensuing General Conference may by a two-thirds vote ratify the same and it shall become constitutional law. Also, when the General Conference shall originate and recommend by a two-thirds vote any such change, as soon as all members of the several district conferences present and voting shall have concurred by a two-thirds aggregate vote, the same shall be declared constitutional law.

# Chapter V

# SPECIAL DIRECTIONS

**400.** The special directions are expressions by which The Wesleyan Church seeks to bear witness to contemporary society concerning the Christian life and character required by its Articles of Religion and Covenant Membership Commitments. While they are not covenant membership commitments, they are official admonitions to the members, ministers and officials of The Wesleyan Church, and provide guidelines for bearing public testimony on the issues discussed.

## A. Christian Social Concern

**410.** The Wesleyan Church seeks recognition by the society which surrounds it of the authority of Almighty God, and the authority of the Lord Jesus Christ, in civil, political and temporal as well as spiritual matters, and the transformation of that society into the image of Christ insofar as is possible in this present age. It believes that such a transformation of society shall primarily be accomplished by the divine transformation through faith in Christ of the individuals who compose society, but that Christians ought also to manifest social concern in every manner that is in keeping with their Christian testimony. To this end:

(1) **Equal Rights.** The Wesleyan Church upholds the right of all individuals to equal opportunity politically, economically and religiously, and pledges itself to an active effort to bring about the possession of dignity and happiness by all people everywhere (cf. 220; 265:10, 11; 360:3d).

(2) **Peace.** The Wesleyan Church, knowing that war results in great suffering for the bodies, minds and souls of men and women, staggering economic loss with its legacy of debt for future generations, and the unleashing of the baser passions of life, urges that persons and nations seek by every legitimate means to avoid armed conflict among the peoples and nations of the world. The Wesleyan Church also urges that holy people everywhere pray earnestly for those in authority, so that peace may prevail (1 Tim. 2:2), and for the quick return of the Prince of Peace.

(3) **Military Service.** The Wesleyan Church teaches respect for properly constituted civil authority and the proper loyalty to one's country. It recognizes the responsibility of the individual to answer the call of government and to enter into military service. However, there are those within the fellowship of The Wesleyan Church who believe that military service is contrary to the teaching of the New Testament and that their consciences are violated by being compelled to take part in such. The

Wesleyan Church will therefore lend moral support to any member who asks and claims exemption by legal processes from military service as a sincere conscientious objector and who asks to serve one's country as a noncombatant.

(4) **Substance Abuse.** The Wesleyan Church is opposed to the production, sale, purchase and use of alcoholic beverages, tobacco, narcotics and other harmful drugs, unless for mechanical, chemical or medicinal purposes (cf. 265:4). The unprescribed use of hallucinogens, stimulants and depressants, and the misuse and abuse of regularly prescribed medicines should be prohibited; only on competent medical advice and under medical supervision should such drugs be used.

(5) **Human Sexuality.** The Wesleyan Church abhors the trend to ignore God's laws of chastity and purity, and vigorously opposes public acceptance of sexual promiscuity and all factors and practices which promote it. The Wesleyan Church maintains a biblical view of human sexuality which makes the sexual experience, within the framework of marriage, a gift of God to be enjoyed as communion of a man and woman, as well as for the purpose of procreation. Sexual relationships outside of marriage and sexual relationships between persons of the same sex are immoral and sinful. The depth of the sinfulness of homosexual practice is recognized, and yet we believe the grace of God sufficient to overcome both the practice of such activity and the perversion leading to its practice.

(6) **Divorce and Remarriage.** On the basis of a careful study of the Scriptures, and in keeping with its Covenant Membership Commitments (265:5), The Wesleyan Church teaches the following with reference to divorce and remarriage after divorce:

(a) To obtain a divorce on other than scriptural grounds is a sin against God and humanity. Such putting asunder of what God has joined is a direct and deliberate act of disobedience against both the Law and the Gospel. It separates one from God and subjects a member to Church discipline (5350; 5370).

(b) However, recognizing the fallen state of humanity, divorce has been recognized in the Scriptures as a valid and permanent dissolution of marriage with all its rights and responsibilities. Divorce is not reversible. There is no way to "restore" a dissolved marriage. The divorced (unmarried) status can be changed only by a new marriage to the same person or another person. No divorced and remarried person has two spouses, only a former spouse and a present spouse, as in Deuteronomy 24:1-4 and 1 Corinthians 7.

(c) Divorce, however sinful the act and however serious the consequences, is not "unpardonable." A redeemed sinner or reclaimed backslider is "free" to marry "in the Lord" or to remain unmarried, a eunuch for the kingdom of God's sake. The one exception to this freedom of choice is mentioned by the Apostle Paul. It is a believer who disobeys the commandment of God and puts away a believing spouse. That person must remain unmarried to leave room for reconciliation to the spouse (1 Cor. 7).

(d) The right to remarry in no way excuses the sin of divorce. It only implies that the Church must forgive and restore those whom the Lord forgives and restores. Neither penance nor penalty remain to the truly penitent and restored sinner, or backslider, whatever the traumatic consequences of the sin may be.

(7) **Merchandising on the Lord's Day.** The Wesleyan Church opposes the legalization of merchandising on the Lord's Day (cf. 265:1).

(8) **Religion in Public Life.** The Wesleyan Church, believing that it is possible to allow recognition of God and the invoking of His aid in public functions without violating the Constitution of the United States, advocates the enactment of suitable legislation by the Congress which will strengthen the present provision for the free exercise of religion in national life and allow reference to, or the invoking of the aid of God, in any governmental or public document, proceeding, activity, ceremony or institution. The Wesleyan Church further affirms its belief in the public school's duty to do full justice to the large place of the Judeo-Christian tradition in our American heritage, and its conviction that the Bible is an appropriate book for reading in the public schools and that the right of students to pray should not be abridged.

(9) **Public School Activities.** The Wesleyan Church protests the inclusion of such questionable items as social dancing in the public school curriculum and maintains the right of its members to seek exemption from participation by their children in all matters that are contrary to scriptural doctrines and principles as expressed in the Articles of Religion, Covenant Membership Commitments or Elementary Principles of The Wesleyan Church, without prejudice to academic standing.

(10) **Judicial Oaths**. The Wesleyan Church reserves for its members the right to affirm the truth in testimony before the civil and criminal courts rather than to engage in a judicial oath.

(11) **Abortion.** The Wesleyan Church seeks to recognize and preserve the sanctity of human life from conception to natural death and, thus, is opposed to the use of induced abortion. However, it recognizes that there may be rare pregnancies where there are grave medical conditions threatening the life of the mother, which could raise a serious question about taking the life of the unborn child. In such a case, a decision should be made only after very prayerful consideration following medical and spiritual counseling. The Wesleyan Church encourages its members to become informed about the abortion issue and to become actively involved locally and nationally in the

preparation and passage of appropriate legislation guaranteeing protection of life under law to unborn children.

(12) **Use of Leisure Time.** The Wesleyan Church believes that its members should exercise responsible stewardship of their leisure time. This will include careful regulation of the use in the home of mass media, such as current literature, radio and television, guarding the home against the encroachment of evil (cf. 265:6). It will also involve witnessing against social evils by appropriate forms of influence, the refusal to participate in social dancing, the refusal to patronize the motion picture theater (cinema), together with other commercial ventures as they feature the cheap, the violent or the sensual and pornographic, and the refusal to engage in playing games which tend to be addictive or conducive to gambling (cf. 265:4).

(13) **Modesty in Attire.** The Wesleyan Church believes that our people should provide clear testimony to Christian purity and modesty by properly clothing the body and by dressing with Christian simplicity.

### B. Christian Worship and Fellowship

**420. Rites and Ceremonies of Churches.** True religion does not consist in any ritual observances such as forms or ceremonies, even of the most excellent kind, be they ever so decent and significant, ever so expressive of inward things. The religion of Christ rises infinitely higher and lies infinitely deeper than all these. Let no one conceive that rites and ceremonies have any intrinsic worth, or that true worship cannot subsist without them. Therefore, it is not necessary that rites and ceremonies should in all places be the same or exactly alike, for they have always been different and may be changed according to the diversities of countries, times and customs, provided that nothing be ordained against God's Word.

**Acts 15:10, 28-29; Rom. 14:2-6, 15, 17, 21; 1 Cor. 1:10; 12:25; 14:26; 2 Cor. 13:11; Gal. 5:1, 13; Col. 2:16-17; 2 Thess. 3:6, 14; 1 Tim. 1:4, 6; 1 Peter 2:16.**

**430. Healing.** The truth that Jesus is both able and willing to heal the body as well as the human soul, whenever such healing is for His glory, is clearly set forth in God's Word and attested by the experience of many of His people at the present day. Prayer for healing according to the pattern set forth in the Scriptures shall be encouraged.

**Matt. 10:8; Luke 9:2; 10:9; Acts 4:10, 14; 1 Cor. 12:9, 28, James 5:14-16.**

**440. Christian Liberty.** Christ, through His death on the cross, has freed His followers from sin and from bondage to the law. Christians are "called unto liberty" (Gal. 5:13), and are not under the law as a means of salvation. They are rather exhorted, "Stand fast therefore in the liberty wherewith Christ hath made us free, and be not entangled again with the yoke of bondage" (Gal. 5:1).

This liberty, however, is not to be construed as license (Gal. 5:13). Rather, love for Christ constrains the Christian to live righteously and holily as God demands. By the Spirit of God, His laws are written on the heart (Heb. 8:10). So Christians resist evil and cleave to the good, not in order to be saved, but because they have been saved.

Within the bounds of Christian liberty, there will be differences of opinion. In such cases, the believer seeks to avoid offending other believers. The stronger one is mindful of the opinions of the one with the weaker conscience (1 Cor. 8 and 10), and is careful not to put a stumbling block in another's way (1 Cor. 10:24; Gal 5:13). On the other hand, the weak does not criticize the strong (1 Cor. 10:29-30), for the conscience of the weak may need instruction.

The recognition and exercise of that liberty which Christ affords will glorify God and promote the unity of the Church.

**450. Christian Unity.** The Wesleyan Church, having originated through merger between those of like precious faith, is fully committed to that true Christian unity which is based on scriptural truth and the fellowship of the Spirit, and deplores the separation or division of Christians over peripheral and nonessential matters. While The Wesleyan Church opposes the building of one all-inclusive ecclesiastical organization which regards neither scriptural doctrine nor practice, it welcomes fellowship with those who are committed to the same doctrines and standards of holy living, and cooperation across denominational lines with those who hold the cardinal doctrines of the Christian religion revealed in the Bible.

### C. Christian Stewardship

**460. Meaning of Stewardship.** The Scriptures teach that God is the owner of all persons and all things, that people are His stewards of both life and possessions, that God's ownership and one's stewardship ought to be acknowledged, and that every person shall be held personally accountable to God for the exercise of their stewardship (cf. 265:3). God, as a God of system and order in all of His ways, has established a system of giving which acknowledges His ownership and humankind's stewardship. To this end all His children should faithfully tithe and present offerings for the support of the gospel.

**465. Storehouse Tithing.** Storehouse tithing is a scriptural and practical performance of faithfully and regularly placing the tithe into that church to which the member belongs. Therefore, the financing of the church shall be based on the plan of storehouse tithing, and The Wesleyan Church shall be regarded by all its people as the storehouse. All who are a part of The Wesleyan Church are urged to contribute faithfully one-tenth of all their increase as a minimum financial obligation to the Lord and freewill offerings in addition as God has prospered them.

**Gen. 14:20; 28:22; Lev. 27:30-32; Deut. 14:22; Prov. 3:9-10; 11:24-25; Mal. 3:10-11; Matt. 23:23; Acts 4:34-35; 6:1-3; 1 Cor. 16:2; 2 Cor. 8:13-14; Heb. 7:1-2, 6, 9.**

**470. Methods of Fund Raising.** In the light of the scriptural teaching concerning the giving of tithes and offerings (cf. 465) for the support of the gospel, and for the erection of church buildings, no Wesleyan church should engage in any method of fund raising which would detract from these principles, hinder the gospel message, sully the name of the Church, discriminate against the poor, or misdirect the people's energies from promoting the gospel.

**475. Wills, Bequests and Annuities.** It is essential in the exercise of Christian stewardship that careful thought be given as to what shall be done with one's estate after death. Civil laws often do not provide for the distribution of an estate in such a way as to glorify God. Each Christian should give careful attention to the preparation of a last will and testament in a careful and legal manner, and The Wesleyan Church and its various ministries through the local church, the district, world missions, extension and evangelism, education and benevolences are recommended for consideration. The General Director of Estate and Gift Planning is prepared to assist in these matters (2070-2075; 4240; 4940).

# PART II

# LOCAL CHURCH GOVERNMENT

## Chapter I

## LOCAL CHURCH ORGANIZATION

### A. Function of Local Churches

**500.** The local Wesleyan church is a body of Christian believers who hold the faith set forth in the Articles of Religion of The Wesleyan Church, who have been duly received as members of The Wesleyan Church and formally organized according to its *Discipline*, who acknowledge the ecclesiastical authority of The Wesleyan Church, who support its worldwide mission, and who meet together regularly for the purposes of evangelism, nurture, fellowship and worship (240).

### B. Types of Organization

**503.** A pastoral charge may consist of a single church, or of two or more churches designated by the district conference as a circuit; is supplied as a regular pastoral appointment by the district conference; and transacts business through a local conference of the covenant members. The constitutional rights of a pastoral charge are given in 315. If the district conference desires to appoint a minister to serve two or more churches that shall continue as separate pastoral charges, it may appoint the minister as pastor of one church and supply pastor of the other (3255-3260).

#### 1. Developing Church

**510.** A new work, or a work which does not meet the requirements for an established church (518), shall be organized as a developing church (cf. 807). It shall be authorized by the district conference (1180:24) or the district board of administration (1233:29), and shall be governed as follows:

(1) The pastor shall be selected by the district board of administration and appointed by the district conference, except in the interim of district

conference sessions when the district board of administration shall have full power of appointment.

(2) A membership roll shall be maintained, ordinarily for one to eleven members. Candidates for membership shall be examined and recommended by the pastor until such a time as a local advisory council is formed and assumes this duty; and their reception shall be authorized by the district superintendent (1310:15).

(3) As soon as qualified members are available, the district superintendent, in cooperation with the pastor, may appoint a local advisory council of three to five members. The pastor shall serve as chair of this council (cf. 807; 1310:15). They shall exercise the duties and powers of a local board of administration (782), making all recommendations to the district superintendent or the district board of administration instead of the local church conference (1310:15). All investments in land, buildings and equipment (1233:32; 4650-4660), matters involving employed staff, and other major decisions must be authorized by the district board of administration; and all actions of the local advisory council shall be subject to the review and approval of the district superintendent. The local advisory council shall be responsible to assist the district superintendent in qualifying the church as quickly as possible for organization as an established church.

(4) All property of a developing church shall be held by the district, with titles secured as given in 4660.

(5) A developing church may have one lay delegate to the district conference when so assigned by the district board of administration (1086; 1100:2; 1103).

### 2. Established Church

**518. Authorization for Organization.** The organization of a developing church as a fully established church, or of a group of believers who have applied to a district superintendent for organization as a Wesleyan church, empowering it to assemble for business as a local church conference and to elect a local board of administration, and investing it with all the rights, powers and duties of a local church as given in the Constitution (315) and as set forth elsewhere in *The Discipline*, may be authorized by the district board of administration and effected by the district superintendent when it meets these requirements:

(1) Twelve or more persons who are covenant members or are approved and ready to be received as covenant members when the organization shall be effected.

(2) A reasonable degree of financial stability, including the meeting of such obligations as it may have to the general church and the district.

(3) A reasonable degree of leadership and organizational maturity, with sufficient qualified persons to staff the minimum organization provided for in 810.

(4) The holding of all property in trust for The Wesleyan Church as required in 4610 (4680) or steps taken to accomplish the same.

(5) An established church may be reclassified by the district board of administration as a developing church if such is recommended by the district superintendent and:

(a) if its covenant membership drops to ten or fewer (cf. 1180:24; 1233:29; 5190); or

(b) if it ceases to meet one or more of the other conditions set forth in 510:2-4 (cf. 4670).

**520. Organizational Meeting.** When the organization of an established church has been authorized by the district board of administration, the district superintendent shall consult with the pastor and the local advisory council, or if there are none, with those interested in forming the church, and appoint a time for an organizational meeting. The organizational meeting shall be conducted by the district superintendent or a representative appointed by the district superintendent as follows:

(1) The reading of the Summary of the Articles of Religion (299) and the Covenant Membership Commitments by the presiding officer.

(2) An examination of each of the candidates for membership, conducted by the presiding officer, using the questions commonly addressed to such candidates (cf. 5560-5575), and the baptism of such as have not previously been baptized. When the organization involves a church previously organized as a developing church, those who have been accepted as members of the developing church need not be reexamined.

(3) A mutual pledge of purpose and fellowship on the part of all covenant members, including those being received. The presiding officer shall ask each one:

**Question 1:** "Are you in Christian fellowship with all those who present themselves for membership in this church organization?"

**Answer:** "I am."

**Question 2:** "In that Christian fellowship will you promise to walk with each other in love, giving and receiving counsel, sympathy and instruction in the Spirit of Christ?"

**Answer:** "I will."

(4) A declaration made by the presiding officer:

"On the basis of these mutual pledges in the presence of God, I proceed to give you each the right hand of fellowship, and declare by this act that you are a Christian church organized on the basis of *The Discipline of The Wesleyan Church*, and are invested with all the rights, powers and duties assigned to an established church by *The Discipline*."

(5) The first session of the local church conference, with the election of officers who shall serve for the remainder of the year, or until specified, and the installation of the officers (5915) by the person presiding over the organizational service.

(6) The report of the organization by the district superintendent to the next regular session of the district board of administration, and to the next regular session of the district conference (1180:24; 1310:14).

(7) The taking of steps to provide for the pastoral oversight and care of the new church, if such has not already been done.

### 3. Circuit

**525. Relationship of Circuit and Church.** A circuit is a pastoral charge in which a district conference has grouped two or more local churches under one pastor, and designated them as a circuit, with business to be transacted by a circuit conference. Each church on the circuit shall be organized and shall conduct its business according to the regulations for an established church, and shall exercise its constitutional rights to receive, expel and discontinue its members, to elect its own officers and trustees, and to have recourse to a proper court of jurisdiction in matters of controversy between itself and other units or agencies of The Wesleyan Church (315:1, 5, 6, 8). The circuit shall exercise all of the constitutional rights of a pastoral charge which are not reserved to the local church (315:2-4, 7), and take charge of all matters of circuit business as given in 525-535.

**526. Developing Circuit Conference.** When the churches on the circuit are all developing churches, the regulations governing a developing church will be applied to the developing circuit (510).

**528. Circuit Conference.** The covenant members of the several churches on a circuit, duly called and assembled together to do business, shall constitute a circuit conference. It shall follow the same organizational and procedural pattern as a local church conference (cf. 630-650). Its duties and powers shall be:

(1) To call the pastor and set the terms of pastoral service (315:2; 690-722).

(2) To license lay ministers (3410-3420) and to recommend suitable members to the district conference for district licenses as ministerial students and special workers (3015:3-4; 3033:1-2; 3460).

(3) To elect lay delegates to the district conference (315:7; 1100-1109).

(4) To elect a circuit secretary, such members of the circuit advisory council (530) in addition to the *ex officio* members as the circuit conference shall determine are needed to assure proper representation, and a circuit board of trustees (if such is needed, cf. 532).

(5) To determine all matters involving two or more of the churches on the circuit, including the authorization of transactions involved in the purchase, erection, encumbrance, sale or other disposition of a circuit parsonage or other property (4740-4750).

**530. Circuit Advisory Council.** The circuit advisory council shall direct circuit affairs between sessions of the circuit conference, bearing the same relationship to the circuit conference that the local board of administration bears to the local church conference (750; 782). It shall consist of the pastor as chair, the circuit secretary as secretary, the chair of the circuit board of trustees, the treasurer of each local church, and such other representatives as the circuit conference shall determine are needed to assure proper representation. It shall elect one of its members as vice-chair, and shall meet at least quarterly at such time and place as it shall determine. It shall nominate the pastor, make recommendations on all matters over which the circuit conference has authority, and carry out and administer the decisions of the circuit conference (690).

**532. Circuit Trustees.** The circuit board of trustees shall consist of three to five members elected by the circuit conference. They shall organize themselves and carry on their work under the direction of the circuit advisory council in the same manner as the board of trustees for a local church (850-859), except that they shall have jurisdiction only over that property owned by the circuit, such as the circuit parsonage (cf. 4740-4750).

**535. Circuit Committees.** The circuit advisory council may appoint such committees as are necessary to the proper conduct of circuit affairs, including a nominating committee to nominate the circuit officers (cf. 820-823).

### 4. Mission

**537.** A special evangelistic, rescue or missionary work which cannot appropriately be organized as a developing church or church shall be carried on as a mission. A mission may be conducted by an established church subject to the approval of the district board of administration (655:15), by a district (1180:24; 1233:29) or by the General Department of Evangelism and Church Growth. It shall not maintain a membership roll nor receive members. A mission shall have no local boards, officers or committees except such as are appointed by the mission director, are amenable to the mission director, and can be replaced at the discretion of the mission director.

### 5. Local Churches in a Developing District

**542.** Missions, developing churches, churches and circuits located in developing district shall be authorized, organized, and governed according to the *GB Policy for Evangelism and Church Growth*, which shall be in harmony with *The Discipline* (cf. 4800).

### 6. Affiliate Church

**548.** An independent congregation of the Wesleyan tradition which seeks a less than full relationship with The Wesleyan Church may be recognized and listed as an Affiliate Church. This relationship shall exist to encourage fellowship, to include and involve the affiliated body in ministries and opportunities available to Wesleyan churches, and to eventually lead the affiliated unit into full relationship with The Wesleyan Church. Provisions and procedures to establish and govern an Affiliate Church relationship are located in Appendix H, paragraph 7900 et seq.

# Chapter II

# MEMBERSHIP

### A. Essence and Necessity of Membership

**550.** Membership in The Wesleyan Church is conditioned upon an experience of conversion whereby a person becomes a member of the body of Jesus Christ, followed by discipleship within a family of believers for spiritual life and growth. Therefore it is of high importance that immediate steps be taken to shepherd, disciple and train believers through the process of membership for mutual accountability and ministry to the church, community, and the world (cf. 568-570; 725:11; 782:7, 880:11; 2300:5).

**551.** The overall mission objective of membership in The Wesleyan Church is: To acknowledge believers as belonging to the body of Christ; to disciple them into covenant relationship with The Wesleyan Church; and to equip them to minister to the church, community, and the world.

(1) **The Vision of Membership**. It is our belief and practice that The Wesleyan Church is not a collection of independent churches unrelated to each other nor just merely an association of churches, but rather we constitute a "family" of believers connected by our identity in Christ and our identity with one another. Membership serves as the common thread that unifies us within our diversity as a community with the passion for developing fully committed disciples of Christ. Membership is a ministry tool to use in the process of spiritual development, subsequent to conversion and leading to maturity in Christ. To enhance the discipleship process of maturing people toward Christlikeness, membership is used as a means of accountability. The accountability used within the community of faith is based on the primary authority of the Scriptures. We also acknowledge the role of tradition, experience, and reason to shape the collective conscience reflected in the membership accountability commitments. Membership becomes the channel whereby people are discipled and equipped to do ministry within the church and as a witness to the world at large.

(2) **The Value of Membership**. Membership in The Wesleyan Church is built on the premise that it is a discipleship tool within the life of the church. Each local fellowship adapts its ministry scope and sequence but a common path would involve the following steps:

**Relationship** – The personal conversion experience with Christ. This relationship with Christ incorporates the person in the universal church and identifies one with the fellowship of believers.

**Discipleship** – The process of becoming more and more like Christ with the goal to proceed further in spiritual pilgrimage and spiritual leadership.

**Ministry** – The potential for believers to use their gifts and abilities to serve Christ and others, and demonstrate their allegiance and accountability to the doctrine, polity, and ministry of The Wesleyan Church.

Membership provides the personal and corporate benefits of:

**Believing** – Membership helps people identify the essential beliefs taught in the Bible, and how these beliefs impact our lifestyle, relationships, and our witness for Christ within the church and beyond.

**Belonging** – Every person being served by our churches needs a sense of belonging, which in turn gives the Church a wonderful opportunity to enhance the discipling process.

**Building** – The task of building or discipling our believers is the paramount task of the Church, and is best accomplished through the membership process.

**Blessing** – A member is expected to do what makes life worthwhile – contributing and serving with the ultimate goal of reaching the world for Christ.

**552. Membership Structure**. Membership in The Wesleyan Church shall be covenant membership. A local church that has a discipleship program may choose to implement the community membership category as part of that discipleship process. Community membership shall not be transferable. After consultation with the district superintendent, a local church may institute the community membership option upon two-thirds vote of the covenant members present and voting at a duly called local church conference. The community membership option may be discontinued upon the recommendation of the local board of administration, and approval of the district board of administration.

## B. Categories of Membership

### 1. Covenant Membership

**553.** Those persons shall be admitted to covenant membership in The Wesleyan Church who meet the conditions set forth in the Constitution (297:1-5).

(1) Candidates for covenant membership shall be examined as provided for by the local board of administration (782:7; 835-837), to determine

whether they meet the requirements of the Constitution concerning their experience of regeneration, Christian baptism, their acceptance of the Articles of Religion, Covenant Membership Commitments, Elementary Principles and the authority of *The Discipline* in matters of church government, and their willingness to enter into covenant with The Church.

(2) Covenant members will further demonstrate their life in Christ and commitment to the local church upon becoming a covenant member, by signing a covenant affirming their personal experience in regeneration and commitment to an experience of heart holiness and a life of practical holiness; their acceptance of the Articles of Religion, the Covenant Membership Commitments, the Elementary Principles and the authority of *The Discipline* in matters of church government; their support of the church; their commitment to live in fellowship with the members thereof and to seek God's glory in all things.

(3) Candidates for covenant membership who have satisfactorily passed the examination by the local board of administration, shall be voted upon by the local church conference unless the local church conference has delegated this right to the local board of administration (297:5; 655:1). In either case, it shall require a majority vote of those present and voting to receive; and if objections are urged against the reception of a member, it shall require a two-thirds vote of those present and voting.

(4) Persons who have been duly accepted for covenant membership as explained in 553:3, should be formally received into covenant membership in a public service, in which they shall make their confession and vows public, according to the manner given in 5565, and be given the right hand of fellowship by the pastor or the representative of the pastor.

**555.** The rights of covenant membership are set forth in the Constitution (302). Any covenant member charged with failure to uphold the Articles of Religion or to observe the Covenant Membership Commitments must be dealt with by judicial process as given in *The Discipline* (5000-5140).

### 2. Community Membership

**558.** A local church may choose to implement the community membership category. Those who are converted to Christ but who are not yet able to assume the responsibility of covenant membership, either because they are young in Christ, young in years or come from a religious background different from The Wesleyan Church in areas of doctrine or discipline, yet demonstrate willingness to be discipled in the Wesleyan convictions, may be received as community members.

(1) The local board of administration, having provided for their examination concerning their Christian experience and their intention to

prepare for covenant membership may, if satisfied, receive them by majority vote.

(2) Community members will further demonstrate their life in Christ and commitment to growth and development in the body by signing, upon becoming a community member, a Community Member Agreement affirming their personal experience in regeneration and commitment to seek after an experience of heart holiness and a life of practical holiness; their participation in a discipleship program including further instruction in the Articles of Religion, Covenant Membership Commitments and the Elementary Principles; and by their support of the church and purpose to live in fellowship with the members thereof.

(3) Community members shall be formally received according to the manner given in 5575.

**560.** The rights of community membership are:

(1) The fellowship of the saints and the encouragement, admonition and spiritual guidance of the ministry.

(2) Access to the sacraments and ordinances of the Church. (This does not mean that The Wesleyan Church practices closed communion—cf. 5605; 5615.)

(3) Eligibility to fill any office or position in the local church other than those for which covenant membership is required by *The Discipline*, provided that the local board of administration considers the community member sufficiently mature in years and spiritual development, exemplary in conduct and gifted for such service.

(4) Community members have the right to vote on all issues presented to the local church conference except votes on the calling or renewal of the call of pastors or associate pastors, election of members to the local board of administration, reception of covenant members, election of nominating committee members and the delegates to district conference.

(5) The right of a hearing before the local board of administration in the event of dismissal from community membership, but if after such hearing the board reaffirms the vote of dismissal there shall be no further right of appeal; joining another religious body shall of itself sever membership in the church.

**563.** A community member may become a covenant member at any time the community member is qualified and received as given in 553. It shall be the duty of the pastor and the local board of administration to assist a community member in qualifying for covenant membership. If upon reception into community status, the member is sufficiently mature in years, every effort shall be put forth to prepare the community member for reception into community membership. As a part of its annual review of the church membership roll (cf. 782:10), the local board of administration shall review the status of each community member and assess progress toward covenant membership.

### C. Reception of Members

**565.** Covenant members in The Wesleyan Church may be received by confession of faith or by letter. Community members shall be received by confession of faith.

**568**. Those who are received as covenant members after having been community members, shall be considered as having joined on confession of faith. The pastor and the local board of administration shall be responsible to provide membership training classes for all community members, training them in the biblical doctrines and standards of the Church, acquainting them with the history and organization of The Wesleyan Church, and explaining to them the meaning of the vows and covenant of covenant membership (297; cf. 5565).

**570.** Those who present letters of recommendation from other denominations shall be examined by the pastor and the local board of administration. If it is discovered that the persons involved have indeed been previously converted and are fully committed to the doctrines and standards of The Wesleyan Church, they may be received as by letter (cf. 5570). But if it is discovered that these persons have only now given their hearts to Christ and are seeking after a full knowledge of the truth, they shall be encouraged to prepare for covenant membership.

### D. Transfer of Membership

**575.** When any covenant member shall request a letter of transfer to another Wesleyan church, the pastor and local church secretary shall grant it on the proper form as given in 6000-6020 providing the member is neither under discipline nor under charges. Both pastor and secretary shall sign the letter, and shall forward it to the pastor and local church secretary of the church to which the member is transferring. The letter shall be presented to the local board of administration of the receiving church at its next session, but not later than thirty days from the date of issuance, and acted upon in the manner indicated in 578. When the member has been duly received, the second part of the form shall be completed by the receiving church and forwarded to the church granting the transfer. The date the return letter is received shall mark the expiration of membership in the church granting the letter, and in the official membership record the local church secretary shall enter opposite the member's name, the date and "Withdrawn by letter of transfer."

**578.** The receiving church shall handle transfers as follows:

(1) Covenant members shall be received, subject to the approving vote of the local church conference, unless the local church conference shall have delegated this right to the local board of administration (297:5). The transfer of covenant membership may be questioned by the receiving church if it is evident that the person involved is not in a state of grace or is living in open violation of the Articles of Religion or the Covenant Membership Commitments.

(2) The membership of a pastor, senior pastor, associate pastor, or assistant pastor and of such members of the pastor's family as so desire and have the proper credentials, shall be automatically transferred to the church to which appointed, or if the pastoral charge consists of more than one church, to the church of choice. The secretary of the church from which the pastor is moving shall forward the proper forms for the pastor's membership and that of family members who so desire to the secretary of the receiving church who shall record them without any further action by the local church conference or local board of administration.

**580.** A covenant member of The Wesleyan Church transferring from one local church to another shall not be required to be involved in a public service of reception.

**581.** Community membership is not transferable.

### E. Termination of Membership

**585.** Covenant membership in The Wesleyan Church may be terminated only by one or more of the following (305):

(1) Voluntary withdrawal.
(2) Joining another religious body or joining a secret order.
(3) Expulsion after proper trial and conviction (5350:5).
(4) Persistent neglect of church relationship as defined in 600-605.
(5) Death.

**588.** Community membership in a local church may be terminated by one or more the following:

(1) Voluntary withdrawal.
(2) Joining another religious body.
(3) Removal by the local board of administration.
(4) Persistent neglect of church relationship.
(5) Death.
(6) The discontinuance of the community membership category in the local church.

**590.** When any covenant member requests a letter of recommendation to some other denomination, the pastor and local church secretary shall grant it on the proper form provided in 6030, if the member is neither under discipline nor under charges. Such a person's membership in the local church granting the letter shall cease immediately, and the secretary shall enter opposite the member's name, the date and "Withdrawn by letter of recommendation."

**592.** When any covenant member requests a letter of withdrawal, the pastor and local church secretary shall grant it on the proper form provided in 6040. The secretary shall enter on the record book (610), opposite the member's name, the date the letter was granted and "Withdrawn by letter of withdrawal." If the member's withdrawal occurs during the course of a judicial investigation, the secretary shall note on the membership record, "Withdrawn under accusation," and if withdrawal occurs during the course of a trial, "Withdrawn under charges " (cf. 5302).

**595.** When any covenant member joins another denomination, or other religious body exercising the functions of a church, or a secret society, no trial is necessary to remove such a member. The pastor, having investigated and ascertained the facts, shall report the same to the next session of the local board of administration, and upon the board's order the local church secretary shall enter opposite the member's name the date of the session and "Withdrawn through having joined another body."

**598.** When any covenant member moves away from the church in which membership is held, and it is evident that distance will not permit full and regular participation in the life of the church, the pastor shall encourage the member to transfer membership to the Wesleyan church nearest the new residence. To that end, the pastor shall notify the General Secretary of The Wesleyan Church of the name and address of the member.

**600.** When any covenant member moves away from the church in which membership is held, and does not leave a forwarding address, or fails to report spiritual standing or to send financial support, or to transfer membership to the nearest Wesleyan church, after one year the member may be dropped from the roll provided that every effort has been made to contact the member and notify the member of such an intention. The member's name shall be dropped upon the recommendation of the local board of administration and the majority vote of the local church conference, unless the local church conference shall have delegated full responsibility in such matters to the local board of administration. The secretary shall enter opposite the member's name the date of the vote, and *Discontinued by vote.*

**605.** When any covenant member fails to attend the services of the church where membership is held for one year without a reason deemed justifiable by the local board of administration, or to support the church financially, as able, the pastor and local board of administration shall seek to restore the member to active fellowship, but if unable to do so, the member's name may be dropped upon the recommendation of the local board of administration and the majority vote of the local church conference, unless the local church conference shall have delegated full responsibility in such matters to the local board of administration. The secretary shall enter opposite the member's name the date of the vote, and *Discontinued by vote for persistent neglect.*

### F. Record of Membership

**610.** Each local church shall have a permanent record maintained by the local church secretary, in which shall be recorded all the names of the members, category of membership, the time when received and whether by profession of faith or by letter, the time and manner of termination of membership, whether by some manner of withdrawal, or by discontinuance for neglect, dismissal or death; and all dedications, baptisms, marriages, pastoral terms and other information essential to a permanent written record of the life and ministry of the local church.

# Chapter III

# LOCAL CHURCH CONFERENCE

### A. Composition and Function

**625.** The covenant members of a local church, duly called and assembled together to do business, constitute the local church conference. It is the highest governing body of a local Wesleyan church, and exercises those powers granted to the local church by the Constitution (315), and other powers specifically granted to the local church conference by the General Conference as set forth in *The Discipline* (cf. 302; 555; 560:4). In churches which choose to implement the community membership category, community members will attend the local church conference and participate in keeping with the limits set forth in 560:3-4.

### B. Sessions

**630. Regular Sessions.**

(1) **Annual Sessions.** The local church conference shall meet annually, near the close of the fiscal year, as established by the district conference (1180:18), at a time approved by the district superintendent in consultation with the pastor and announced from the pulpit, and in the weekly bulletin when such is available, at least two weeks in advance (cf. 625). Reports shall be made; the officers, local board of administration and trustees shall be elected (cf. 823; 965; 1103); and such other business shall be transacted as necessary (cf. 650).

(2) **Quarterly Sessions.** The local church conference may choose to meet quarterly at such times as the district superintendent and pastor shall arrange, unless the district superintendent shall in writing delegate to the pastor full authority for setting such dates. Such quarterly sessions shall be announced from the pulpit, and in the weekly bulletin when such is available, at least two weeks in advance of the appointed time. At each session, reports shall be given and other business transacted as necessary (cf. 650).

**633. Special Session.**

(1) **General Business.** The local church conference may be called into special session by the pastor, or in times of emergency by the district superintendent, for the transaction of any business other than the election of officers, with announcement from the pulpit in two regular services, the first of which shall be given not less than one week before the appointed time. Notice shall also be given one week in advance in the church bulletin, when

such is available. The requirements for special sessions dealing with legal or property matters are set forth in 4040 and 4700.

(2) **Reception of Members.** In those churches in which the local church conference must vote on the reception of covenant members (297:5), the pastor may call a special session for such a vote, with announcement from the pulpit in one regular service in advance of the appointed time.

(3) **Pastoral Vote.** The vice-chair of the local board of administration (773), when authorized to do so by the local board of administration, and having notified the district superintendent, may call a special session of the local church conference to conduct a pastoral vote, with announcement from the pulpit, and in the weekly bulletin when such is available, at least two weeks in advance of the appointed time, except that during negotiations for calling a new pastor the announcement need be made only from the pulpit and in only one regular service in advance of the appointed time.

## C. Organization and Procedure

### 1. Officers

**635. Chair.** The district superintendent, or a representative appointed by the district superintendent, shall preside over the local church conference whenever present. In their absence, the pastor shall preside, except over sessions dealing with the securing or retaining of a pastor. The vice-chair of the local board of administration (773) shall preside over sessions dealing with the securing or retaining of a pastor, if the district superintendent, or a representative appointed by the district superintendent, is not present. The district superintendent may also preside, at the request of the pastor, over other sessions of the local church conference. In emergencies, when the pastor is absent or incapacitated, the vice-chair may preside over other sessions with the permission of the district superintendent.

**638. Secretary.** The local church secretary, elected annually by the local church conference, shall serve as secretary of the local church conference by virtue of this office (830:1).

### 2. Procedure

**640. Quorum.** Those covenant members who assemble for a meeting of the local church conference when such has been duly called shall constitute a quorum.

**643. Voting.** A majority vote of those present and voting in the local church conference shall be sufficient in all items of business unless otherwise required by *The Discipline* or by local laws when dealing with legal matters.

**645. Rules of Order.** The business of the local church conference shall be conducted according to the current edition of ***Robert's Rules of Order, Newly Revised,*** except when formally suspended or otherwise ordered by ***The Discipline***.

**650. Order of Business.** The local church conference, in all regular sessions, whether annually or quarterly, shall give special attention to the spiritual, numerical and financial progress of the church, including the following items:

(1) Reading of minutes of last session, unless authority to approve the minutes has been delegated by the local church conference to the local board of administration.

(2) Receiving the reports of the pastor(s), Sunday school superintendent, president of Wesleyan Men, director of Wesleyan Women International, coordinator of Wesleyan Kids for Missions, director of Christian Youth Clubs International, president of Wesleyan Youth, chair of Young Adults International and any others the local church conference shall order.

(3) Receiving the reports of the various treasurers (cf. 863).

(4) Receiving and acting upon the reports of boards and committees.

(5) Receiving the reports of the lay ministers.

(6) Granting or renewing of local licenses for lay ministers.

(7) Recommending suitable members to the district conference for district licenses as ministerial students and special workers (315:3-4).

(8) Electing of officers, trustees and delegates.

(9) Miscellaneous business.

### D. Duties and Powers

**655.** The local church conference has duties and powers:

(1) To approve by vote the reception of covenant members and to expel or discontinue covenant members unless it delegates full authority concerning membership to the local board of administration (297:5; 315:1). Such authority may be withdrawn from the local board of administration at any annual session of the local church conference.

(2) To call a pastor or renew the call (315:2; 692; 705; 718; 720; 735), or to vote on the termination of a renewed call as set forth in 722:2.

(3) To authorize a nominating committee, which shall be chaired by the pastor, to which the local board of administration shall elect two covenant members from its membership, and to which the local church conference may, at its option, elect four additional covenant members who are not members of the local board of administration (820-823).

(4) To elect the church officers, which shall consist of the lay leader (if any; cf. 833), the local church secretary, the local church treasurer (if any, cf.

842), the Sunday school superintendent (if any; cf. 889), the trustees (designating annually at least one trustee to serve as a member of the local board of administration), members-at-large of the local board of administration (cf. 752), and lay delegates to the district conference (315:5, 7).

(5) To receive reports from the pastor(s), church officers, lay ministers and other persons, boards and committees as desired, and as listed in 650:2-5.

(6) To remove, when such is in the best interests of the church, by a majority vote of those present and voting, any church officer, trustee, or delegate mentioned in 655:4 (cf. 782:25).

(7) To license lay ministers (315:3), and to renew or revoke such license (cf. 782:19; 3410; 3420; 3440:2). This power may be delegated to the local board of administration.

(8) To recommend suitable members to the district conference for district licenses as ministerial students, licensed ministers, or special workers (315:3). This power may be delegated to the local board of administration.

(9) To adopt petitions or resolutions to the district conference, including memorials proposed for recommendation to the General Conference (1150-1156).

(10) To adopt financial policies, which policies shall be administered by the local board of administration (cf. 782:29).

(11) To authorize the enlargement or decrease of the employed staff (cf. 782:16).

(12) To adopt an annual budget (cf. 782:30), and to authorize all expenditures not provided for in the annual budget; or to delegate to the local board of administration (782:30) full authority over the annual budget.

(13) To authorize the purchase or sale of property, the erection or major remodeling of buildings (1345:2), and all mortgages or other indebtedness which encumbers the property, subject to the prior approval of the district board of administration, according to the procedure set forth in 4700-4720.

(14) To petition the district board of administration for the incorporation of the local church when it is deemed necessary as set forth in 4000, and to authorize the local board of administration to incorporate the church when such incorporation has been approved by the district board of administration (1233:32).

(15) To authorize, subject to the approval of the district board of administration, the establishment and operation of a mission (cf. 537; 782:5; 1233:29), a branch Sunday school, or a developing church, in order to share the benefits of the gospel with others.

(16) To delegate such responsibilities as it shall choose to the local board of administration.

(17) To have recourse to a proper court of jurisdiction in any matters of controversy between itself and other local, or district, or general units or agencies of the denomination (315:8; 5162:4; 5185:1; 5218).

(18) To authorize the establishment of a day care and/or a day school of preschool, elementary and secondary levels only, when such is desired, subject to approval by the district board of administration; and to delegate governance of the day care and/or day school to the local board of administration (cf. 782:35; 1233:34; 2305). A local church conference shall not formalize post-secondary education in terms of an institute or of junior college or college-level programs, without prior approval of the district conference and the General Board. (Cf. 1180:24; 1655:35.)

(19) To authorize significant changes in mission, facilities, or finances of an established day care and/or day school, subject to approval by the district board of administration (cf. 1233:34).

# Chapter IV

# PASTORS

## A. Function

**675.** A pastor is an ordained, commissioned or licensed minister, who is called of God and appointed by the Church to serve as the spiritual shepherd, teacher and administrative overseer of the local church, preaching the Word, directing the worship, administering the sacraments and ordinances of the Church, taking the comforts of the gospel to the sin-burdened, the sick and the distressed, discipling converts, nurturing and instructing believers, equipping and enabling them for their part in ministry, and serving as chief executive officer in the government of the local church.

**678.** A minister who serves as the sole pastor of a church shall be referred to simply as "the pastor." The term "senior pastor" shall be applied to the presiding minister of a multiple pastoral staff. The pastor shall be expected to carry out the full pastoral function as set forth in 675, and ultimate responsibility for the same shall rest upon the senior pastor. An associate pastor is a helping member of a multiple staff who normally shares a broad range of the shepherding and teaching responsibilities and such administrative responsibilities as are delegated (cf. 738). An assistant pastor is a helping member of a multiple staff who normally is assigned more limited and specific aspects of the pastoral function (cf. 741).

## B. Manner of Pastoral Voting

### 1. Jurisdiction in Pastoral Voting

**690.** All matters related to voting on securing or retaining a pastor are the concern of a pastoral charge (503), whether it consists of a single church or a circuit. In most instances, a pastoral charge will consist of one local church, and the following paragraphs are so written. If a circuit is involved, the vice-chair of the circuit advisory council (530) assumes leadership in all negotiations, the circuit advisory council fills the role of the local board of administration, and the circuit conference rather than the local church conference is the voting body.

## 2. Regulations for All Pastoral Voting

**691. Procedures of Candidating.** In all matters related to pastoral candidating the following regulations shall be observed:

(1) Only one pastoral candidate at a time shall be presented to the congregation for a message. A decision by the local board of administration to recommend a pastor for a congregational vote, and the vote, if recommended, must take place before another candidate is considered.

(2) The support including salary, expense allowances, housing, fringe benefits, moving expenses and related matters which the church proposes to maintain must be provided for the candidate prior to a pastoral vote.

(3) A minister who has agreed to give a candidating message and to submit to a pastoral vote at one church, cannot do the same with another church until the first candidating situation is resolved. If the local board of administration does not recommend the candidating pastor for a congregational vote within seven days the waiting restriction no longer applies.

**692. Procedure of Pastoral Voting.** In all matters related to voting on securing or retaining a pastor, the following regulations shall be observed:

(1) All pastoral votes shall be taken at a duly announced session of the local church conference (630-633).

(2) The district superintendent, or a representative appointed by the district superintendent, shall preside over the local church conference for the taking of the pastoral vote. If neither can be present, the vice-chair of the local board of administration shall preside.

(3) All pastoral votes shall be taken by secret ballot by covenant members with special provision for absentee ballots (695).

(4) A favorable vote by a majority of covenant members voting shall be required (705; 718; 720; 722).

(5) The minister shall be notified by the local board of administration of the results of the vote,

(6) If the vote is favorable, the minister shall notify the local board of administration and the district superintendent by phone and in writing of a decision within seven days following the official notification of such call by the local church.

**695. Absentee Ballots**. A covenant member who cannot attend a pastoral vote session of the local church conference because of confining illness, required employment or necessary out-of-town travel or seasonal residency, may cast an absentee ballot subject to the following conditions:

(1) The member shall secure a standard ballot from the local church secretary, identical to the ballots to be used at the session, and

submit the marked ballot prior to the session in a sealed envelope identified with the name of the absent member.

(2) The local church secretary must certify the envelope as being submitted by a member to whom the secretary has supplied a ballot, and who is eligible to cast an absentee ballot. In the event that the local church secretary is unable to certify the eligibility of the person casting an absentee ballot, the secretary may consult the vice-chair of the local board of administration to determine eligibility.

(3) Envelopes containing such absentee ballots shall be opened at the session in which the vote is taken, by the secretary in the presence of the chair, prior to the tallying of the vote, and these ballots placed without inspection with the others for counting by the tellers.

**697. District Approval of Pastoral Agreement.** A pastoral agreement, whether for an initial call or a renewal of call, must be reviewed and recommended by the district board of administration, and becomes final upon the approval of the district conference. Each year the district board of administration shall review those pastoral agreements which are continuing before making its report to the district conference (1180:26; 1233:9).

**700. Time of Pastoral Changes.** Except for such emergencies as resignations, removals or deaths, pastoral changes shall take place on the Monday following the second Sunday of July.

**702. Annual Review of Pastoral Support.** The pastor's cash salary and other benefits, including health insurance and employer contributions for the Wesleyan Pension Fund (WPF) shall be reviewed annually by the local board of administration prior to the annual session of the local church conference, whether or not a vote is being taken on the securing or retaining of a pastor. Proper health insurance coverage should be provided by the local church for pastor and family except in cases in which they have adequate coverage through other employment of pastor and/or spouse, or in the case of pastors serving in Canada, through the national health program. Full participation in the Wesleyan Pension Fund by the local church on behalf of all pastors is expected in the plan of support of all pastors. The obligation, responsibility and liability for both health insurance premiums and employer contributions to WPF belong solely to the local church. The district and general Church have no obligation, responsibility, nor liability for these matters, either expressed or implied. A report of the final action on the pastor's support, whether by the local board of administration or by the local church conference, shall be sent by the local board of administration in writing to both the pastor (or pastor-elect, cf. 692:5) and the district superintendent.

### 3. Regulations for Initial Call of Pastor

**705. Procedure of Initial Call of Pastor.** Whenever it is necessary for a pastoral charge to secure a new pastor, the following regulations shall be observed:

(1) The vote shall be for a two-year call, subject to such adjustment as the district superintendent shall approve, so that the term shall expire at the uniform time set by the general conference (700).

(2) The initial call may be for four years or an extended call if such is recommended by the local board of administration and approved by the district superintendent. In case of an extended call the rules governing an extended call shall apply (720).

(3) The local board of administration, under the leadership of its vice-chair, shall counsel with the district superintendent concerning possible candidates. If the church desires to call a minister from another district or from outside the denomination, the local board of administration shall first secure from its own district superintendent assurance that the transfer of the minister would be approved (cf. 313:6).

(4) When a candidate has been approved by a majority vote of the local board of administration (cf. 782:13), the candidate's name shall be presented as a nomination to the local church conference, and the vote shall be taken in keeping with the regulations governing all pastoral voting (692).

**708. Waiver of Local Church Rights.** If a pastoral charge has been unable to secure a pastor prior to thirty days before the annual session of the district conference, the local church conference may, at any time thereafter, by majority vote delegate full authority for the employment of a pastor to the local board of administration, or it may waive its rights and leave the selection of a pastor to the nomination of the district board of administration and appointment by the district conference. If a pastoral charge waives its rights, or if neither local church conference nor local board of administration shall have secured a pastor by the time the annual session of the district conference convenes, the district board of administration shall nominate a pastor for appointment by the district conference. A pastor so appointed shall be received and supported by the pastoral charge the same as if the pastor had been employed in the usual manner.

**710. Initial Call Resignation**. If a pastor resigns during the initial call term of service to a church, the pastor must notify the local board of administration and the district superintendent sixty days in advance. If the district superintendent and the local board of administration deem it wise, the pastor may be released sooner.

**712. Initial Call Removal.** During the initial call term of a pastor's service, the district board of administration may remove the pastor by a two-thirds majority vote of all members, provided such has been requested by the local board of administration by a two-thirds majority vote in a meeting presided over by the district superintendent, or such has been recommended by the district superintendent (cf. 1233:38).

**715. Ad Interim Procedures.** If a pastoral charge is left without a pastor between sessions of the district conference due to death, resignation or removal, the local board of administration and the local church conference shall follow the regular procedures for securing a new pastor with all arrangements subject to the approval of the district board of administration (cf. 1233:38).

### 4. Regulations for Renewal of Call

**718. Procedure for Renewal of Call.** Whenever a pastor's term of service is expiring, unless the pastor shall give notice otherwise to the vice-chair of the local board of administration (773) and the district superintendent, in writing and at least sixty days prior to the convening of the district conference, the pastor shall be considered as available, and a vote on the renewal of the pastoral call shall be taken in keeping with the regulations governing all pastoral voting (692).

(1) One of the following alternative procedures shall be followed:

(a) A vote for a four-year renewal of the call shall be taken. If the vote on a four-year renewal of the call is favorable, the local board of administration, after consulting with the pastor, may then recommend that a ballot vote be taken to renew the call for an extended period (720).

(b) Or, prior to the vote on renewing the call, the local board of administration, after consultation with the pastor, shall recommend to the local church conference a specific call for four years, or an extended call.

(2) A vote for a one or two-year renewal of the call may be authorized by the district superintendent upon the joint request of the pastor and the local board of administration when such is due to extenuating circumstances.

**720. Special Regulations for Extended Call.**

(1) When a pastor is serving for an extended period, the pastor may, when deemed advisable and when approval has been granted by the district superintendent, ask the local board of administration to conduct a vote by the local church conference on renewing the extended call. Such a vote shall be conducted in keeping with 692.

(2) When a pastor is serving for an extended period, the district superintendent shall review the pastoral agreement with the local board of administration at least quadrennially. The local board of administration by a majority vote shall either reaffirm the call or ask the local church conference

to vote on renewing the call. Such a vote shall be conducted in keeping with 692.

**722. Termination of Renewed Call.** The service of a pastor whose call has been renewed may be terminated prior to the expiration of the term or in the interim of quadrennial reviews of an extended call (720:2) in one of three ways:

(1) The pastor may resign, provided that the termination of service is first approved by the district superintendent. Except as otherwise mutually agreed upon by the local board of administration and the district board of administration, notification of the pastor's resignation shall be given at least sixty days in advance and the resignation shall become effective in sixty days or at the time set by the district for pastoral changes (700).

(2) If one-third of the members of the local board of administration so request the district superintendent in writing, the district superintendent or a representative appointed by the district superintendent shall call and preside over a special session of the local board of administration for the purpose of deciding on whether to call for a pastoral vote by the local church conference. If the local board of administration by majority vote calls for the taking of such a vote, and the district superintendent approves the taking of the same, it shall be taken in keeping with 692. If there is a majority vote of the local church conference in favor of retaining the pastor, and the pastor agrees to remain, the pastor shall be free to continue as if the vote had not been taken. If less than a majority are favorable to retaining the pastor, pastoral service shall terminate at the time set by the district for pastoral changes (700), or at a time mutually agreed upon by the pastor, the local board of administration and the district superintendent.

(3) The district board of administration may, by a majority vote, order the district superintendent to conduct a pastoral vote in keeping with 692. Or the district board of administration, upon the recommendation of the district superintendent (1310:19), and for the sake of the pastoral charge involved, may remove the pastor by a two-thirds majority vote of all members (1233:38), with the services of the pastor terminating in sixty days unless ordered otherwise by the district board of administration. If at any time the district board of administration shall deem it in the interests of the district as a whole that the pastor be free to serve elsewhere, it may by majority vote request the pastor to resign.

### C. Duties and Powers

**725.** The pastor shall administer the spiritual and temporal affairs of the work in keeping with *The Discipline* and other general and district regulations and shall be responsible:

**General**

(1) To diligently study the Scriptures, pray and do the work assigned.

(2) To seek, by all means, the conversion of sinners, the sanctification of believers, and the upbuilding of God's people in the most holy faith.

(3) To pray to God for and with the flock.

(4) To feed the flock by reading, expounding, teaching and preaching the Word.

(5) To have the general guidance, under the Holy Spirit, of the religious services, including the midweek service, appointing musicians (cf. 870) and cultivating the practice of corporate worship.

(6) To administer, if an ordained (313:1), commissioned (3059:2a) or licensed minister (3044:1), the sacraments of baptism and the Lord's Supper. Each pastor shall provide for the observance of the Lord's Supper at least once every three months. A supply pastor shall secure the services of an ordained (313:1), commissioned (3059:2) or licensed minister (3044:1) who is a pastor, for such observance (3260:2), except when authorization has been granted by a district superintendent as provided in 3260:2.

(7) To solemnize, if an ordained (313:1), commissioned (3059:2a) or licensed minister (3044:1), the rite of matrimony, in keeping with the Scriptures and *The Discipline* (265:5; 3111); to counsel with those being married and those already married, emphasizing the spiritual values in all phases of marital and parental life, seeking to develop the spiritual ideals and resources necessary to build permanent unions and godly homes (cf. 410:6).

(8) To comfort the bereaved and to bury the dead.

(9) To provide pastoral guidance and oversight through visitation and counsel to the members of the church and to others in need of a pastor's help. The minister, as counselor, has the right to protect the conversation with a counselee as privileged communication.

(10) To keep all members fully conversant with the Christian life-style set forth in the Covenant Membership Commitments and the biblical basis for the same, and to maintain with diligence and love adherence to these membership requirements (cf. 260-268).

(11) To be responsible for the instruction of all prospective members in the Articles of Religion, Covenant Membership Commitments and polity of The Wesleyan Church, and in the meaning and purpose of church membership, holding or arranging for membership classes for community members that they might be adequately prepared for covenant membership (cf. 568-570; 782:7; 880:11).

(12) To administer the ritual of membership and to give the right hand of fellowship on behalf of the church to new members (553:4; 5550-5595).

(13) To report the names and addresses of members who have moved away to the General Secretary of The Wesleyan Church (598).

(14) To grant, in conjunction with the local church secretary, letters of transfer, recommendation or withdrawal (575; 590; 592; 6000-6040).

(15) To receive any complaint or accusation against any member of a church under personal care, and to give such prompt and careful attention as required under the Judiciary (5100:1, 4; 5254), and to refer any matter requiring official investigation or judicial proceedings to the local board of administration for disposition (782:11).

### Administrative

(16) To preside as chair of the local church conference and the local board of administration except as otherwise provided (635; 770-773), and to oversee and direct all departments and local church organizations as the chief executive officer.

(17) To serve as a voting member of boards and committees established by the local board of administration, and to meet with boards and committees as time will permit.

(18) To meet with Wesleyan Men, Wesleyan Women, Wesleyan Youth and Young Adults International and any of their committees as deemed best and to call a special meeting of an auxiliary or any of its committees; to serve as an *ex officio* member of the executive committees of the auxiliaries (7125:1; 7325:1; 7530:3f; 7730:1), and as chair, or to appoint a representative as chair, of the nominating committees of the auxiliaries (7125:5; 7325:5; 7730:5).

(19) To give leadership to the missionary, evangelistic, educational and devotional programs of the local church in harmony with objectives and programs of the district and the general church; to request the approval of the district superintendent for the use of an evangelist or worker who is not a member of The Wesleyan Church for a revival or any other event (cf. 1310:21).

(20) To promote all the interests of the general church and the district in the local church, in the manner and to the extent authorized by the General Conference, the General Board and the district conference.

(21) To instruct the people concerning the financial plans of the general church and of the district, and to see, together with the local board of administration, that the United Stewardship Fund and all other obligations are met in full; and to protect the church from solicitations not authorized by the general church or the district.

(22) To promote stewardship, emphasizing tithing and the storehouse plan as a part of the Christian's total stewardship (cf. 460-475), and to see that tithes and freewill offerings are collected regularly.

(23) To see that trustees are elected and all church property properly secured according to *The Discipline* and the local laws, with all legal papers submitted to the district superintendent for approval.

(24) To see that no steps are taken involving the church in financial liability without proper authorization from the local board of administration and local church conference, or without the approval of the district board of administration when such financial liability involves the mortgaging or other encumbering of the church property (655:12-13; 782:30-31; 1233:32).

(25) To see that all property and building transactions are carried out as set forth in 4700-4720.

(26) To circulate holiness literature, promoting all subscription campaigns for the official church publication and other official general church or district periodicals, setting a proper example with personal subscriptions; and to use in all educational departments and agencies curriculum materials provided by The Wesleyan Church.

(27) To have general supervision of the educational program of the local church, organizing classes for the instruction of adults, youth and children in the Word of God and for Christian living, attending all sessions possible, promoting the faithful attendance of members, and providing for the instruction and inspiration of the leaders in educational work.

(28) To enlist youth for the gospel ministry, and for missionary and other special work, encouraging and helping them to prepare for their God-appointed task at educational institutions provided by The Wesleyan Church; to sign, in conjunction with the local church secretary (830:3), licenses for lay ministers granted by the local church conference (655:7; 782:19); and to have the oversight over all lay ministers employing their services as constantly and effectively as possible.

(29) To recommend to the local board of administration a potential associate pastor (738); to nominate to the local board of administration an assistant pastor (741) or a lay assistant to the pastor (744); to nominate to the local board of administration all members of the employed staff; and to supervise, with the assistance of the local board of administration, the services of all employed staff members, including the custodians (cf. 782:16).

(30) To see that up-to-date files are kept on church constituency, membership, Sunday school enrollment, the membership of subsidiary organizations, and subscriptions to the various general church and district publications, and to be ready to turn over such lists to the successor in office (cf. 610; 830:2, 5; 895; 928; 7130:4; 7330:5; 7530:3c; 7740:3).

(31) To see that adequate historical records and financial records are maintained for the church (cf. 610; 842:2, 6; 898; 7130:5; 7330:6; 7530:3c; 7740:3).

(32) To see that all necessary data are collected for the various statistical and financial reports, and to present reports to the local board of administration monthly, to the local church conference at its regular sessions, to the district superintendent as requested, to the district conference annually on forms approved by the Board of General Superintendents, and to various general church or district departmental officers as required.

(33) To attend district conference sessions, institutes and conventions planned for edification by the general church or the district, and to participate in the life and work of the district and the general church as opportunity affords.

### D. Pastoral Staff

**735. Pastor/Senior Pastor.** An ordained, commissioned or licensed minister who is called of God and appointed by the Church to serve as sole pastor of a church shall be referred to simply as "the pastor." The term "senior pastor" is applied to the presiding minister in a multiple pastoral staff who bears ultimate responsibility for carrying out the function set forth in 675.

**738. Associate Pastor.** An associate pastor is an ordained minister or a commissioned or licensed minister, who is called of God and appointed by the church to serve along with the senior pastor and under the direction of the senior pastor as assigned by the senior pastor and approved by the local board of administration; this assignment normally includes a broad range of the shepherding and teaching responsibilities and such administrative responsibilities as are delegated, but may be concentrated on one or more specific aspects of ministry (cf. 675). The calling and assignment of the associate pastor shall be subject to the following guidelines:

(1) The associate pastor shall have training, experience and ministerial standing compatible with those of the senior pastor.

(2) The associate pastor is recommended to the local board of administration by the senior pastor. The associate pastor cannot be employed initially without the express recommendation of the senior pastor and the written approval of the district superintendent. The call cannot be renewed without the express recommendation of the senior pastor. Otherwise, the call is made and renewed by the local church conference in the same manner as that of the senior pastor, except that the termination point for the call can never be later than that of the senior pastor.

(3) The associate pastor's appointment may be terminated in the same manner as that for a pastor, with the additional provision that the term of

service will end whenever there is a change in senior pastor in the local church where service is rendered. Whenever a senior pastor terminates service at a time other than the uniform time of pastoral change (700), the associate pastor's term shall expire at the succeeding uniform time for such change. The newly called senior pastor may recommend renewal of the call for the associate pastor to the local board of administration.

(4) If a clergy couple is appointed to the pastoral staff, only one shall be designated as senior pastor, unless the local church conference should vote to call the persons as co-pastors. In such case, the district shall appoint them as co-pastors and they shall be listed as such in the district journal (1332:8). (Cf. 752.)

**741. Assistant Pastor.** An assistant pastor is an ordained minister or a commissioned or licensed minister, who is called of God and appointed by the Church to serve under the direction of the senior pastor as assigned by the senior pastor and approved by the local board of administration; this assignment normally includes more limited and specific aspects of the pastoral ministry (cf. 678). The calling and assignment of the assistant pastor shall be subject to the following guidelines:

(1) The assistant pastor shall have the training, experience, and ministerial standing which are suitable for this assignment.

(2) The assistant pastor is recommended to the local board of administration by the senior pastor. The assistant pastor cannot be employed initially without the express recommendation of the senior pastor and the written approval of the district superintendent. The call cannot be renewed without the express recommendation of the senior pastor. While the local church conference creates the position, the local board of administration employs the person subject to the recommendation of the pastor and approval of the district conference. Employment shall be for one year at a time except that its termination point can never be later than that of the senior pastor.

(3) The assistant pastor's appointment may be terminated at any time at the pastor's recommendation and the vote of the local board of administration. The term of service will end whenever there is a change in senior pastor in the local church where service is rendered. Whenever a senior pastor terminates service at a time other than the uniform time of pastoral change (700), the assistant pastor's term shall expire at the succeeding uniform time for such change. The newly called senior pastor may recommend the reemployment of the assistant pastor to the local board of administration.

(4) The office of assistant pastor is an employed position, subject to final approval by the district conference. It is to be assigned to no one as an honor or to provide special status.

**744. Lay Assistant to the Pastor.** Lay members may also serve as paid assistants. While the local church conference creates the position, the local board of administration employs the person subject to the recommendation of the pastor.

(1) The lay assistant must be a member of the local church where employed.

(2) Employment shall be for one year at a time.

(3) Employment of a licensed or commissioned special worker shall be subject to review by the district board of administration and appointment by the district conference.

**746. Annual Review of Staff Support**. The salaries and benefits of the pastoral staff and other employees of the church, including health insurance and employee contributions for the Wesleyan Pension Fund, shall be reviewed annually by the local board of administration in a manner parallel to that provided for the pastor in 702. Reports on the provisions for staff and employees shall be sent to the district superintendent only for those under district appointment.

# Chapter V
# LOCAL BOARD OF ADMINISTRATION

## A. Function

**750.** The local board of administration carries out the will of the local church conference, serving as the chief governing and coordinating body of the local church in the interim of local church conference sessions.

## B. Membership

**752.** The local board of administration shall consist of one of the following:

(1) The pastor as chair, the associate pastor (except when the pastor's spouse), the church secretary, the church treasurer, the Sunday school superintendent and at least one member of the board of trustees designated by the local church conference. In addition, the local church conference may designate the assistant pastor(s), lay assistant(s) to the pastor, lay leader and other trustees as *ex officio* members of the local board of administration. In case the local church conference chooses not to elect a local church treasurer and/or a Sunday school superintendent but to assign their duties to employed or appointed staff, and such are covenant members of the local church, it may designate such persons as *ex officio* members of the local board of administration.

(2) Or, the pastor as chair, and ministry leaders of the church as recommended by the local board of administration and approved by the local church conference. They shall be qualified and elected as set forth in 815.

(3) In either of the above, the local church conference may also elect members-at-large to provide for proper representation within larger congregations. If there is a co-pastor arrangement (738:4), only one of the pastors shall be designated to serve as chair of the local board of administration, while the other may attend its meetings as a non-voting member.

**755.** It is recommended that no two persons of the same household be elected to serve on the same local board of administration, that no person shall be elected to more than one office carrying *ex officio* membership on the board, and it is recommended that a former pastor should not serve on the local board of administration. (3097).

**757.** A local church conference may, by a two-thirds majority vote, recommend the limitation to three of the number of successive terms of the members of the local board of administration.

### C. Sessions

**760. Regular Sessions.** It is recommended that the local board of administration meet monthly.

**763. Special Sessions.** The local board of administration may authorize special sessions as it deems necessary, or it may be called into special session by the pastor, the vice-chair (for sessions dealing with a pastoral vote or with the pastor's financial support and related matters), or in times of emergency by the district superintendent or a representative appointed by the district superintendent. A special session may be held at any time if all members of the local board of administration are present. Otherwise, each shall have been notified either personally or by a notice mailed to the residence of the board member at least forty-eight hours prior to the convening of the session. A special session may not be conducted in the absence of the pastor except as provided for in 773.

**767. Evaluation Session.** Periodically, either during regular sessions or in a session called specifically for self-evaluation, the local board of administration shall consider its priorities, review the distribution of its time and evaluate the effectiveness of its efforts, using the duties and powers listed in *The Discipline* as a guide. The method and extent of each evaluation shall be determined by the board, but special attention should be focused on those responsibilities that are most likely to contribute to future outreach and growth to the glory of God.

### D. Organization and Procedure

#### 1. Officers

**770. Chair.** The pastor shall be chair of the local board of administration, *ex officio*, presiding over all sessions except as noted in 773.

**773. Vice-chair.** The local board of administration shall elect one of its members as vice-chair. The vice-chair may preside over meetings of the local board of administration when a pastoral vote or the pastor's support is under discussion (for exceptions, cf. 712; 722:2). The vice-chair may also preside over sessions or portions of sessions of the local church conference dealing with a pastoral vote or the pastor's support when neither the district superintendent nor a representative of the district superintendent are present

(635; 692:2). The vice-chair may preside, at the request of the pastor, over other sessions of the local board of administration or of the local church conference. In emergencies, when the pastor is absent or incapacitated, the vice-chair may also preside over other sessions of the local board of administration and local church conference with the permission of the district superintendent. The district superintendent or a representative of the district superintendent shall preside over all sessions of the local board of administration considering the termination of a pastoral agreement (712; 722:2), and in times of emergency.

**775. Secretary.** The local church secretary shall be secretary of the local board of administration *ex officio* (830). If the secretary is absent, the local board of administration may elect a secretary pro tem.

### 2. Procedure

**778. Quorum.** A majority of the members of the local board of administration shall constitute a quorum.

**780. Voting.** A majority vote of those present and voting shall be sufficient in all items of business except when voting on the reception of a covenant member against whom an objection has been made, which shall require a two-thirds majority vote of those present and voting (297:5; 782:8); and when petitioning the district board of administration to remove a pastor during the initial call, which shall require a two-thirds majority vote of those present and voting (712; 782:13).

## E. Duties and Powers

**782.** The local board of administration shall administer the affairs of the church in keeping with *The Discipline*, other general and district regulations, and the directions of the local church conference, and shall be responsible:

### General

(1) To direct all activities of the church toward the spiritual, moral and social maturity of its people.

(2) To provide a place of worship.

(3) To counsel with the pastor, as the pastor may request, concerning all phases of the pastor's work, and to coordinate the work of all the officers, boards, committees and auxiliaries of the church (cf. 920:3; 7110; 7310; 7515; 7715).

(4) To receive monthly reports from the pastor (725:32), associate and assistant pastor(s), church treasurer (842:3), Sunday school treasurer (898);

quarterly reports from the Sunday school superintendent (889:7); and reports as the local board of administration shall require from all officers, boards, committees, auxiliaries and auxiliary officers (7130:5b; 7330:6b).

(5) To direct the church in its evangelistic outreach, seeking to win its community to Christ; to establish an extension department of the Sunday school (880:15; 913); to recommend to the local church conference the establishment and operation of a mission, a branch Sunday school or a developing church, as it deems necessary and proper (cf. 537; 655:15).

(6) To adopt an annual calendar of events (cf. 655:16).

## Membership

(7) To provide for the examination of all candidates for church membership, which may be done by delegating the actual examination to a committee on witness and membership (835-837); and to assist the pastor in providing church membership classes (568-570; 725:11; 880:11).

(8) To make recommendations concerning the reception of covenant members to the local church conference, unless full authority concerning such reception has been delegated by the local church conference to the local board of administration (297:5; 655:1); and when such authority has been delegated, to authorize the reception of covenant members by a majority vote, except that when an objection is raised against the reception of a member it shall require a two-thirds majority of those present and voting to receive (297:5; 553:3; 780).

(9) To approve, when the local church conference has authorized the implementation of the community membership category (558), the reception of community members (558); or to drop community members from the roll (563; 588-605).

(10) To examine the church membership roll annually, and to provide for its revision according to the provisions of *The Discipline* (553-610; cf. 655:1).

(11) To consider all accusations and charges against members of the local church (cf. 5100), and to appoint a committee of investigation and a local judicial committee as provided for in the Judiciary (5100:1, 4; 5115; 5278; cf. 5130; 5162:1).

(12) To instruct the local church secretary concerning the removal of the name of a member who has joined another religious body or secret society (595); to recommend to the local church conference that it remove from the roll by majority vote the name of a member who has moved away and neither transferred membership to the nearest Wesleyan church nor maintained contact with and support of the former church (600), and that it remove by a majority vote the name of a member who has failed to attend or support the

church where membership is held for one year without proper reason (605), unless the local church conference shall have delegated full responsibilities in such matters to the local board of administration (655:1).

**Pastors, Staff and Licensed Workers**

(13) To nominate pastor and associate pastor to the local church conference (705:3-4; 738:2); to assume full responsibility for securing a pastor when such is delegated by the local church conference (708); and to recommend to the district board of administration by a two-thirds majority vote the termination of a pastoral agreement if such becomes necessary during the initial call (712).

(14) To recommend to the local church conference after a favorable vote has been received for a four-year renewal of the call, the renewal of the pastor's call for an extended period (718:1a); or to recommend prior to the vote on the renewal of call, and after consultation with the pastor, a specific call for four years or, an extended call (718:1b); to review at least quadrennially with the district superintendent an extended call and by majority vote to reaffirm the call or recommend for the local church conference to vote on renewing the call (720:2); to meet, at the request of one-third of its members and under the district superintendent as chair or a representative appointed by the district superintendent, to consider the possibility of ordering a pastoral vote before the expiration of a renewed call, and to call for such a vote by majority vote (722:2).

(15) To review annually the pastor's support and related matters (702).

(16) To recommend to the local church conference the number of employed staff positions, including office secretary, custodian and assistant pastor(s) (655:11); to employ persons for all such staff positions as have been authorized by the local church conference, subject to the pastor's nominations for office employees and assistant pastors and the board of trustees' nominations for custodians; to define the duties and working conditions of all such employees; and to assist the pastor in the supervision of all employed staff members.

(17) To employ evangelists, evangelistic singers and other special workers as needed (cf. 1310:21).

(18) To provide, in cooperation with the pastor, for the supply of the pulpit during the pastor's absence; and to provide, in cooperation with the district superintendent, for the supply of the pulpit during temporary vacancies.

(19) To recommend to the local church conference the licensing and the renewing or revoking of licenses of lay ministers (cf. 655:7).

(20) To recommend ministerial students and special workers to the local church conference for their approval and recommendation to the district conference for district licenses (cf. 315:4; 655:8).

### Officers, Boards, Committees and Auxiliaries

(21) To elect, when so authorized by the local church conference (655:3), two members of a nominating committee from among the members of the local board of administration to serve as set forth in 820-823.

(22) To elect annually at such time as it shall determine, an auditing committee (863); all Sunday school officers except the superintendent, and all departmental supervisors and teachers (880:7; 895-900; 906); one or more offering tellers (845:3); a local director for Church periodicals (840); and such of the following as are needed and can be supplied: financial or tithing secretary (845:2), CYCI director (920:1), children's church director (cf. 880:7), vacation Bible school superintendent (cf. 880:7), local educational director (926), literature secretary (928), local missions director (930), local evangelism director (935), adult youth leader (7530:2a) and other special assignments (cf. 7325:1a).

(23) To approve two or more nominees submitted by the nominating committees, or to present other nominations as desired, for the president of Wesleyan Men (7125:5), the director of Wesleyan Women (7325:5) and the chair of Young Adults International (7730:5), and to ratify the election of officers by these auxiliaries; to ratify the election of Wesleyan Youth officers (7530:2b), and to review and approve the actions of all the auxiliaries (7125:5; 7130:2, 6; 7135; 7325:5, 8; 7330:7; 7530:2b, 3a, f; 7545; 7730:5, 7; 7740:4; 7745).

(24) To organize and elect such boards and committees as it deems necessary to the proper organization of the church, such as the committee on witness and membership (835-837), committee on finance and stewardship (865-868), music committee (870-873), ushering committee (873), communion committee (873), committee on missions (955) and committee on evangelism (960); and to receive and evaluate their recommendations, including their appointment of subcommittees; to serve as or to establish a local board of Christian education, to determine its membership and to elect such members and to delegate full authority of the duties listed in 880:1-21 as it deems wise (cf. 875; 880:1-22).

(25) To recommend to the local church conference the removal from office of any church officer, trustee or delegate (315:5; 655:4, 6) and to remove by majority vote of the local board of administration all who fill other positions (825:4) and officers of auxiliaries (7125:7; 7325:8; 7530:5; 7730:7).

(26) To fill all vacancies occurring in those offices elected by the local church conference, in the interim of its annual sessions, and all vacancies occurring in offices elected by the local board of administration; and to provide for the filling of vacancies in the auxiliaries in keeping with their respective constitutions (7125:7; 7325:8; 7530:5; 7730:7).

### Property and Finance

(27) To direct the local board of trustees in the maintenance of church property, the signing of notes and mortgages and the attending to all legal matters connected with the church, in keeping with the requirements of local laws (4510), and *The Discipline* (850-859; 4500-4720; 4760); or if trustee responsibility is delegated to the local board of administration by the local church conference, to care for such matters.

(28) To direct the local board of trustees to secure sufficient property and liability insurance to cover all buildings and vehicles owned and operated by the local church (856:8); or if trustee responsibility is delegated to the local board of administration by the local church conference, to care for such matters.

(29) To recommend to the local church conference financial policies, and to administer such as are adopted (cf. 655:10). The local board of administration shall review all plans of support annually, adjusting salaries as advisable, recommending changes in the financial policies as necessary (cf. 702; 746).

(30) To recommend an annual budget to the local church conference, to assist the pastor in securing the money necessary to fund the adopted budget and to authorize expenditures within the limits of the adopted budget (655:12; cf. 865-868); or to assume, if such authority is delegated by the local church conference (655:12), authority to adopt the annual budget and authorize all expenditures within the limits of the budget and any expenditures not provided for in the annual budget; to provide for annual audits of all funds (cf. 863).

(31) To recommend to the local church conference: all major expenditures or investments; the purchase or sale of property, the erection or remodeling of buildings, all mortgages or other indebtedness which encumbers the property and major items of equipment (655:13; 4700-4720); and other expenditures not provided for in the annual budget (cf. 655:12).

(32) To implement all general church and district plans which apply to the local church, and to see that the local church raises its assigned portion of the United Stewardship Fund, supports all other general church financial campaigns and offerings and raises the amount assigned to it by the district conference for the support of the district work.

(33) To open the doors of the local church to properly authorized representatives of the general church, the general educational institutions of the area and the district for the presentation of their interests and for the receiving of offerings in keeping with the approved financial plan.

(34) To seek advice from the district board of administration or from an investment committee authorized by the district board of administration when making investment or distribution of funds received as an undesignated estate gift, property for sale or other out-of-pattern contribution with value equal to or exceeding the total contributions for all purposes of the preceding year (cf. 1233:32)..

**Day Care and/or Day School**

(35) To present to the district board of administration for approval a plan for a day care and/or day school following authorization by the local church conference (655:18; 19) or any plans for a significant change in mission, facilities or finances of an established day care and/or day school (1233:34); to govern and direct a day care and/or day school when such has been properly approved (1233:34), or to govern while delegating the operation to a separate school committee; to elect the separate school committee and name its chair when thus delegating said operation; to submit an annual report to the district board of administration including organization, administration and fiscal operations (655:18), for its approval.

(36) To establish treasuries, distinct and separate from that of a local church, to provide for the financial administration of day care centers, day schools, retirement homes, nursing homes and such enterprises (cf. 655:18, 19; 1233:34) and to adopt financial policies to assure adequate supervision and accountability.

### F. Pastor's Advisory Committee

**795.** The local board of administration may establish a pastor's advisory committee when recommended by the pastor. This committee shall have no authority for final action in any matter except that for which the local board of administration grants such authority.

# Chapter VI

# LOCAL CHURCH OFFICERS AND COMMITTEES

### A. List of Local Church Officers, Boards and Committees

**800.** The following summarizes for quick reference the various officers, boards and committees of the local church:

(1) The church *shall* have:
auditor or auditing committee (863)
board of administration, local (750-782)
church secretary (830)
church treasurer or business manager (842)
delegate to district conference (965; 1086; 1100-1109)
offering teller (845:3)
pastor (675-725)
trustees (850-859)
vice-chair of local board of administration (773)

(2) The church *may* have:
advisory committee (795)
assistant treasurer (845:1)
associate or assistant pastor (735-744)
building committee (856:6)
children's church director, staff and committee (880:2, 7-8)
Christian education board (875-880)
Christian education director (880:5)
Christian Youth Clubs International director, staff and committee (915; 920:1-2)
communion committee (873)
Church periodicals director (840)
custodial staff (782:16; 856:5)
day care and/or day school committee (655:18; 19; 782:35-36; 1233:34)
director of discipleship (890)
educational director (926)
evangelism director and committee (935; 960)
fellowship committee (880:19)

finance and stewardship committee (865-868)
financial or tithing secretary (845:2)
judicial committee (970; 5115)
lay leader (833)
literature secretary (928)
missions director and committee (930; 955)
musicians and music committee (870-873)
nominating committee (820-823)
office staff (725:29; 782:16)
Sunday school superintendent, staff and committee (885-913)
ushering committee (873)
vacation Bible school superintendent, staff and committee (880:2, 7-8)
witness and membership committee (835-837)

(3) The church *may* have the following auxiliary officers and committees:

Wesleyan Men officers and committees (7125-7130)
Wesleyan Women officers and committees (7325-7330)
Wesleyan Youth officers and committees (7530)
Young Adults International officers and committees (7730-7740)
Wesleyan Kids for Missions coordinator (7330:7)

## B. General Regulations

### 1. Minimum Organization

**807. Developing church.** A developing church may operate without any regularly constituted officers other than the pastor, but will ordinarily have a local advisory council of three to five members appointed by the district superintendent in cooperation with the pastor. The pastor and these members will form the local advisory council. This council may then appoint such other officers and committees as are needed and for which qualified personnel are available. (Cf. 510:3; 7125:4; 7325:4; 7530; 7730:4.)

**810. Church.** An established church, in addition to the local church conference and the local board of administration, shall have a minimum organization consisting of a local church secretary (830), a local church treasurer (842), an offering teller (845:3), an auditing committee (863) and a board of trustees consisting of at least three members (850-859). Normally it would have a Sunday school superintendent and staff (889-910). Additional offices, positions and committees may be added as provided herewith by the local church conference and the local board of administration as need requires and as qualified personnel are available.

### 2. Church Officers

**815.** The church officers shall include all members of the local board of administration, local church trustees, lay leader, delegates to district conference and assistant treasurer, who shall serve subject to the following regulations:

(1) They must be covenant members of the local Wesleyan church electing them (302:3).

(2) They shall be elected by the local church conference at its annual session (315:5-7; cf. 820-823), except assistant treasurers (see 845) and persons filling offices designated by the local church conference as *ex officio* members of the local board of administration but chosen by the local board of administration (cf. 752). Vacancies occurring between annual sessions of the local church conference shall be filled for the unexpired term by the local board of administration. Vacancies may occur by death, by cessation of membership in The Wesleyan Church, by resignation from office or by removal (815:4).

(3) They shall carry out their duties as given in *The Discipline* and as further defined by the local church conference and the local board of administration.

(4) They shall be under the general supervision of the pastor, shall be amenable to the local church conference, and may be removed for cause or when the best interests of the church so require, upon recommendation of the local board of administration and by a majority vote of the local church conference, or as otherwise provided for.

### 3. Nominating Committee

**820.** Each established church may have a nominating committee consisting of the pastor as chair and two covenant members elected by the local board of administration from its membership (655:3; 782:21). The local church conference may, at its option, elect up to four additional covenant members who are not members of the local board of administration. If the local church conference does not exercise its option to elect at least one additional covenant member, then the local board of administration shall elect one additional covenant member who may or may not be a member of the local board of administration.

**823.** When a nominating committee has been established, it shall present to the local church conference, at its annual session, nominations for each of the following officers: lay leader (if any), local church secretary, local church treasurer (if any), the Sunday school superintendent (if any), and one or more trustees (850). One or more names shall be presented for each office (cf. 755). The nominating committee shall present, at the properly announced session of the local church conference (cf. 965; 1103), nominations for as many delegates to the district conference as the district board of administration shall determine (1100). The nominating committee may be used for other nominations as ordered by the local church conference, or as ordered by the local board of administration for positions elected by the board (cf. 825).

### 4. Other Positions

**825.** Persons holding positions of service within the local church, other than those specifically designated as church officers in 815, and including membership on committees, shall be governed by the following regulations:

(1) They shall be covenant members of the local Wesleyan church electing them in those instances in which *The Discipline* requires it.

(2) They shall be elected annually by the local board of administration (782:22, 24), or as otherwise provided (cf. 880:7).

(3) They shall carry out their duties as given in *The Discipline* and as further defined by the local church conference and local board of administration.

(4) They shall be under the general supervision of the pastor, shall be amenable to the local board of administration, and may be removed for cause or when the best interests of the church so require, by a majority vote of the local board of administration.

(5) Vacancies may occur by death, by cessation of membership in The Wesleyan Church, by resignation from office or by removal (825:4) and shall be filled for the unexpired term by the local board of administration.

### 5. Installation Service

**828.** Those elected to church offices and to other positions of service within the local church may be installed in office at an annual installation service following the ritual given in 5915-5925.

## C. Witness and Membership

### 1. Church Secretary

**830.** The local church conference, at its annual session, shall elect by ballot, from among its covenant members, a church secretary (cf. 820-823), to serve for one year or until a successor is elected. The church secretary shall be an *ex officio* member of the local board of administration (775). General regulations covering this office are given in 815. The duties and powers of the local church secretary shall be:

(1) To record correctly and to preserve faithfully the minutes of all sessions of the local church conference and the local board of administration.

(2) To maintain the local church's record of membership, record of baptisms, marriages and pastoral terms, and other information essential to a permanent written record of the life and ministry of the church (610).

(3) To issue, in conjunction with the pastor, all letters of transfer, recommendation and withdrawal (575; 590-592; 6000-6040); and to sign, in conjunction with the pastor (725:28), licenses for lay ministers granted by the local church conference (655:7; 782:19).

(4) To send to the district secretary a certified list of lay delegates to the district conference duly elected by the local church conference, immediately upon their election, and subsequently to certify an alternate delegate (cf. 965; 1100-1109).

(5) To have custody of all record books of all departments of the church, including auxiliary organizations, after such books are full or in disuse, and to take whatever steps are necessary to preserve them and other historical records and materials, as directed by the pastor and the local board of administration.

### 2. Lay Leader

**833.** The local church conference, at its annual session, may elect by ballot, from among its covenant members a lay leader (cf. 820-823), who shall serve for one year or until a successor is elected, and whose function shall be to assist the pastor in such manner as the pastor shall recommend and the local church conference shall approve. General regulations concerning this office are given in 815. The duties of the lay leader may include any or all of the following: member *ex officio* of the local board of administration (752), leader under the pastor's direction of church prayer meetings or of small groups, classes or neighborhood prayer cells for the deepening of spiritual life and home evangelism.

### 3. Committee on Witness and Membership

**835.** The local board of administration may establish a committee on witness and membership, composed of the pastor, the vice-chair of the local board of administration, the local church secretary, the lay leader (if any) and such other members as the local board of administration shall elect. The local board of administration shall name a board member as chair of the committee, and the committee shall choose its own vice-chair and secretary. General regulations governing membership on this committee are given in 825.

**837.** The local board of administration shall assign such duties to the committee on witness and membership as it deems best, including any or all of the following:

(1) To conduct the examination of candidates for membership; to counsel with members concerning any failure to observe the Covenant Membership Commitments (265); to have initial responsibility in the annual revision of the membership roll; to assist the pastor in any attempts to restore members who have ceased to attend or support the church; and to make recommendations concerning all these matters to the local board of administration in accordance with the principles of Christian discipline (268; 782:7-12).

(2) To make recommendations to the local board of administration concerning revivals and other evangelistic efforts.

(3) To alert the local church to its responsibilities in the area of community social and political reform, recommending courses of action it deems necessary to the local board of administration (cf. 410).

(4) To nominate, for election by the local board of administration, such standing or special subcommittees as the local board of administration shall approve, with a member of the committee as chair of each.

#### 4. Local Director for Church Periodicals

**840.** The local board of administration, at the time of its annual election, may elect a director for church periodicals to serve for one year or until a successor is elected. General regulations concerning this office are given in 825. The director for church periodicals shall be responsible to organize and manage the subscription campaign for the district and Church periodicals in cooperation with the pastor (725:26) and auxiliary solicitors.

### D. Finance and Stewardship

#### 1. Church Treasurer

**842.** The local church shall have either a local church treasurer or a business manager. If there is a church treasurer, that officer shall be elected by the local church conference, at its annual election, by ballot, from among the covenant members, to serve for one year or until a successor is elected. Or the local church conference may authorize the local board of administration to appoint a treasurer or to appoint or employ a business manager who will assume the duties of the treasurer. The financial concerns may be represented on the local board of administration by the church treasurer or the business manager or the chair of the finance and stewardship committee as provided in 865. The duties and powers of the person charged with the local church treasury are:

(1) To receive, hold and disburse, as ordered by the local church conference or the local board of administration, and in harmony with the financial plans of the general church and of the district, all moneys of the local church, including such of the departments and auxiliary organizations as the local board of administration shall order. All funds raised by the local departments, other than the auxiliaries, for general church or district work or for purposes other than local church work, and all money or pledges raised by representatives of the general church or district in deputation work, shall be transferred to or placed in the local church treasury and shall be disbursed for their designated purpose by the local church treasurer.

(2) To keep complete and accurate records of all moneys raised and of the manner in which they are disbursed, and to provide the pastor with information concerning the same as the pastor shall require.

(3) To make monthly reports to the local board of administration, which should be duplicated and distributed to the members of the church, and to make reports to all regular sessions of the local church conference.

(4) To make monthly remittances of all USF and district funds to the district treasurer and remittances of all other general church funds to the General Treasurer or directly to the general department for which the funds are intended.

(5) To issue receipts annually to all regular contributors showing their total tithes and offerings and the various items of giving, and to issue other receipts as requested or by order of the local board of administration.

(6) To submit all books for audit by the auditing committee annually (863), or more frequently if so ordered by the local board of administration, and to submit to the local board of administration the complete treasurer's records at such time as the person shall cease to hold the office of treasurer.

**845.** Assistants for the local church treasurer are provided for as follows:

(1) An assistant treasurer may be elected by the local board of administration, with authority to sign checks when the treasurer is unable to do so.

(2) A financial secretary or tithing secretary may be elected by the local board of administration to assist the treasurer in keeping the record of individual tithes and offerings (842:5).

(3) One or more tellers shall be elected by the local board of administration to assist the treasurer in the counting of all tithes and offerings,

all moneys being counted by two or more persons and recorded as to date of reception, purpose of the offering, and amount. These records shall be preserved and made available to the auditor or auditing committee.

### 2. Board of Trustees

**850. Election.** The local church conference, unless the duties and powers of the board of trustees have been delegated to the local board of administration, shall elect by ballot from among its covenant members a board of trustees (cf. 315:6; 820-823), three to seven in number, one or more being elected at a given annual session for a term of three years, so that the terms of all shall not expire at the same time, or they may be elected to serve until their successors are elected; provided that the manner and conditions of election may be altered to conform to the local laws. At least one of the trustees shall be designated annually by the local church conference as a member of the local board of administration (752). If the local church conference delegates the duties and powers of the trustees to the local board of administration, that board may from its membership elect from three to seven to serve as the board of trustees. General regulations covering this office are given in 815.

**853. Organization and Procedure.** The board of trustees shall meet following the annual session of the local church conference to elect a chair, vice-chair and secretary, and shall meet at such other times as ordered by the local board of administration or as made necessary by their duties.

**856. Duties and Powers.** The local board of trustees shall carry out their duties as required by *The Discipline* (cf. 4500-4780) and shall be responsible:

(1) To carry out the instructions of the local church conference and the local board of administration in supervising, controlling, maintaining and improving all church property (315:6; 655:13; 782:27).

(2) To supervise such expenditures as have been approved by the local church conference or the local board of administration for repairs, improvements and alterations.

(3) To attend to all legal matters regarding the acquisition, purchase, sale, mortgage, transfer or other disposition of property as properly authorized (4700-4720); to see that titles are correct, contain the proper trust clause (4610), are approved by the district superintendent (1310:11; 4700:5), and are recorded (4540); and to see that property and legal records are properly stored (4760).

(4) To attend to all other legal matters pertaining to the local church, as authorized and directed by the local church conference or the local board of administration, including renting property, borrowing money and receiving and administering bequests and trusts.

(5) To nominate to the local board of administration all custodians.

(6) To serve, unless the local church conference shall order a larger or separate committee, as a building committee for the planning and erection of a new sanctuary, educational unit or parsonage or a major remodeling program and to assist the pastor in preparing and submitting all building plans to the district building committee for their approval (1345).

(7) To carry out the directions of the local church conference or local board of administration concerning the purchase, sale, mortgage, transfer or other disposition of property, provided that such transactions have been approved by the district building committee and district board of administration as set forth in 4700-4780.

(8) To make recommendations to the local board of administration concerning sufficient property and liability insurance on the property and for any vehicles owned and operated by the local church, and to carry out the instructions of the local board of administration in securing such insurance (782:28).

(9) To make such reports as are requested by the local church conference or the local board of administration.

**859. Restrictions.** The local board of trustees shall be subject to the following restrictions:

(1) The local board of trustees must carry out the instructions of the local board of administration, the local church conference and the district board of administration. If a local trustee refuses to carry out such instructions when the instructions meet all the requirements of local laws and of *The Discipline*, the trustee may be removed from office as given in 815:4 (cf. 4530).

(2) The local board of trustees cannot mortgage or otherwise encumber local church property without the express authorization of the local church conference and the approval of the district board of administration as set forth in 4700-4720.

(3) The local board of trustees cannot deny the use of the parsonage, church building or other local church buildings, to the pastor who has been duly appointed by the district conference or district board of administration, nor the use of the church building to the membership of the local church and duly elected officials of The Wesleyan Church (cf. 4770).

(4) The local board of trustees cannot divert church property from The Wesleyan Church (4550; 4780).

(5) When a church is reclassified as a developing church (cf. 518:5; 1233:29), the office and power of the local board of trustees shall cease, and all property shall pass directly under the control of the district board of administration (cf. 4670).

### 3. Auditing Committee

**863.** The local board of administration shall be responsible to provide for the annual auditing of the books of the local church treasurer and of all departmental and auxiliary treasurers, either through the election of an auditing committee or the employment of an auditor. If an auditing committee is used for some or all of the treasuries, it shall consist of one to three persons. A report to certify the results of the annual audit shall be presented to the local board of administration. General regulations concerning committee members are given in 825.

### 4. Committee on Finance and Stewardship

**865.** The local board of administration may establish a committee on finance and stewardship. The local board of administration shall name a board member as chair of the committee, and the committee shall choose its own vice-chair and secretary. General regulations governing membership on this committee are given in 825.

**868.** The local board of administration shall assign such duties to the committee on finance and stewardship as it deems best.

## E. Worship

**870.** Musicians, including song leaders, choir directors organists and pianists shall be appointed by the pastor (cf. 725:5). The local board of administration may appoint or, if authorized by the local church conference, may employ a minister or director of music nominated by the pastor (738-744). The duties of the minister or director of music shall be defined by the pastor and the local board of administration. General regulations covering these offices are given in 825.

**873.** The local board of administration may establish committees on music, ushering and communion services, electing their members and defining their duties. General regulations governing membership on such committees are given in 825.

## F. Christian Education

### 1. Local Board of Christian Education

**875. Membership.** The local board of administration shall serve as or shall establish a local board of Christian education (782:24). The pastor shall serve as chair unless the pastor shall recommend and the local board of administration shall assign this duty to another member of the local board of administration, such as the associate or assistant pastor or other qualified person. If a separate board is established, the local board of administration shall determine its membership, electing qualified members in keeping with the provisions of 825 and/or designating *ex officio* members from among the heads of the various educational agencies and auxiliaries (870; 889; 920-928; 7130:2; 7330:7), assigning such duties to it as the local board of administration deems fit (cf. 880). The local board of Christian education shall elect its own secretary.

**878. Age-level Divisions.** Whenever the local board of Christian education shall so recommend, and the local board of administration shall so authorize, the local board of Christian education may organize its members and such other educational leaders and workers as it shall choose into three age-level committees: the children's committee, the youth committee and the adult committee. Each committee shall be organized with a chair and a secretary, and shall serve to coordinate all educational and fellowship activities conducted by the local church or any of its branches for the age level assigned.

**880. Duties and Powers.** The duties and powers of the local board of Christian education shall be:

(1) To study, organize, promote and conduct, under the leadership of the pastor, and subject to the direction of the local board of administration, the total program of Christian education for the local church, in keeping with the denominational objectives for Christian education (2300), and the standards established by the General Board and promoted through the General Departments of Sunday School and Discipleship Ministries, Youth, and Education and the Ministry.

(2) To establish, structure and supervise, in keeping with *The Discipline*, and the standards adopted by the General Board, such educational agencies as are authorized by the local board of administration, including the Sunday school, Christian Youth Clubs International, Wesleyan Youth, Young Adults International, Wesleyan Kids for Missions, children's church, weekday church school, released time classes and vacation Bible school.

(3) To coordinate all educational agencies (cf. 880:2), activities and functions of the local church, setting goals, evaluating procedures, exploring new areas of need and assigning responsibilities to the various departments and auxiliaries.

(4) To determine, in keeping with *The Discipline* and the standards adopted by the General Board, the curricula of the various agencies, always using curriculum materials approved by the General Board and secured from the Wesleyan Publishing House.

(5) To recommend to the local board of administration for the consideration of the local church conference the appointment and/or the

employment of a minister or director of Christian education, and to advise the pastor and the local board of administration in defining all duties. Such a person must be a covenant member of the local church appointing and/or employing the person (cf. 738-744).

(6) To enlist and train administrators and teachers for all phases of the local church's educational task, in keeping with the leadership training program adopted by the General Board.

(7) To submit nominations, or to appoint a committee of its membership to submit nominations, to the local board of administration for all Sunday school officers other than the superintendent, all Sunday school departmental supervisors and teachers, CYCI director, children's church director and vacation Bible school superintendent, and to elect all other officers and teachers except the officers of Wesleyan Youth and WKFM unless the local board of administration instructs the church nominating committee to fulfill these duties (820-823).

(8) To appoint administrative committees for each educational agency other than WY (7530:3f) or Young Adults International (7740:4) or WKFM (7330:7), including in each such committee the executive officer involved and other workers or advisors as shall be deemed best (cf. 903; 920:2).

(9) To remove from office by majority vote any worker elected by the local board of Christian education when such is in the best interest of the work, and to recommend to the local board of administration the removal of any officer or teacher in local Christian education (875-928) elected by the local board of administration.

(10) To organize a training hour, providing for all age levels, selecting the necessary leaders and instructors and assigning responsibilities to the appropriate agencies (cf. 880:2-3).

(11) To assist the pastor and the local board of administration in conducting classes in membership preparation (cf. 725:11; 782:7; 2300:5).

(12) To conduct or assign responsibility for conducting workers' conferences.

(13) To recommend to the local board of administration modifications or enlargement of educational facilities, and the purchase of educational equipment including audiovisuals; to allocate space for various schools and agencies, both for assemblies and classes; and to supervise the storage and use of all equipment.

(14) To promote the interests of The Wesleyan Church educational institutions in cooperation with the General Director of Education and the Ministry, the officials of the general educational institutions within the area and the district educational director.

(15) To conduct extension classes and branch Sunday schools when such are properly authorized (cf. 655:15; 782:5).

(16) To minister to persons on nearby college campuses and military bases in keeping with the programs promoted by the General Department of Youth.

(17) To observe such special days as shall be designated by the General Board and promoted by the General Departments of Sunday School and Discipleship Ministries, Youth, and Education and the Ministry, and as shall be designated by district agencies.

(18) To be responsible for special programs, such as Christmas and vacation Bible school, assigning responsibilities as it deems best, with all plans subject to the approval of the pastor and the local board of administration.

(19) To serve as a committee on fellowship, or to nominate a subcommittee on fellowship for election by the local board of administration.

(20) To encourage and direct ministries of Christian family life in order to enrich the quality of homes and families within the local church constituency.

(21) To nominate, for election by the local board of administration, such standing or special subcommittees as the local board of administration shall approve, with a member of the local board of Christian education as chair of each.

(22) To exercise full authority in such of the duties covered under 880:1-21 as shall be delegated by the local board of administration.

## 2. Sunday School

### a. Function

**885.** Each local church shall provide for systematic Bible study. The Sunday school normally serves as the basic agency for such study.

### b. Administration

**887. General.** The Sunday school shall be governed by the local church conference and the local board of administration through the local board of Christian education, under the general supervision of the pastor. Immediate administration shall be the responsibility of either a Sunday school superintendent and a Sunday school committee or a minister or director of Christian education. If administration is through a superintendent and a committee, the structure outlined in paragraphs 889-910 shall be followed. If administration is through a minister or director of Christian education, the local board of administration may determine the structure and assign responsibilities as it sees fit. In all cases, administrators shall carry out their assignment in keeping with *The Discipline*, the *General Board Policy for Sunday School and Discipleship Ministries*, the standard adopted by the General Board and promoted through the General Department of Sunday School and Discipleship Ministries, and the programs of the general department and of the district Sunday school committee.

**889. Sunday School Superintendent.** The local church conference, at its annual session, may elect by ballot, from among its covenant members, a Sunday school superintendent (cf. 820-823), to serve for one year or until a successor is elected. The superintendent shall be an *ex officio* member of the local board of administration (752), unless the local church conference by prior action has voted to eliminate the Sunday school superintendent as an *ex officio* member of the local board of administration. General regulations concerning this office are given in 815. The duties and powers of the Sunday school superintendent shall be:

(1) To have executive supervision of the Sunday school, administering its affairs in keeping with the provisions of 887.

(2) To consult with the pastor and the Sunday school committee, if there is such (903), on all major decisions.

(3) To promote interest in and attendance at the school.

(4) To have immediate supervision of each session of the school, seeing that each department and class has the necessary leaders and that order is maintained.

(5) To counsel with the teachers about their work.

(6) To conduct the assembly periods, unless such are assigned to departmental supervisors and to maintain variety and interest in the assembly periods.

(7) To make a full report of statistics and general information to the local board of administration quarterly, to the local church conference at each regular session and to the General Department of Sunday School and Discipleship Ministries and the district Sunday school secretary as required (cf. 895).

**890. Director of Discipleship.** If a church seeks to provide a comprehensive approach to discipleship, including both Sunday school and small groups, upon vote of the local church conference it may elect a director of discipleship in place of a Sunday school superintendent. The director of discipleship will assume the Sunday school superintendent's responsibilities as outlined in 889, plus assume full responsibility to administer and coordinate weekday small groups under the direction of the pastor and local board of administration, seeking to provide a fully coordinated approach in local church Christian education and discipleship.

**895. Sunday School Secretary.** The local board of administration shall, at the time of its annual election (782:22; 825), elect from nominations submitted by the local board of Christian education (875; 880:7), a Sunday school secretary, to serve for one year or until a successor is elected. The Sunday school secretary shall keep complete and accurate minutes of all sessions of the Sunday school committee, maintain complete records of enrollment, attendance, absentees, visitors and such other items as shall be required, and assist the pastor and the Sunday school superintendent in the preparation of reports involving Sunday school statistics. The local board of Christian education shall appoint such assistants as the Sunday school secretary shall require.

**898. Sunday School Treasurer**. The local board of administration may, at the time of its annual election (782:22; 825), elect from nominations submitted by the local board of Christian education (875; 880:7), a Sunday school treasurer, to serve for one year or until a successor is elected. Or the local board of administration may recommend, and the local church conference order, that the Sunday school funds be received by the local church treasurer as part of a common treasury. If there is a separate Sunday school treasurer elected, that person shall receive, hold and disburse the Sunday school funds as ordered by the local board of administration, reporting concerning all receipts and expenditures to the local board of administration monthly, and to each regular session of the local church conference. All general church and district funds raised by the Sunday school shall be transferred to the local church treasurer for forwarding to the proper destination (842:1).

**900. Sunday School Departmental Supervisors.** The local board of administration may, at the time of its annual election (782:22; 825), elect from nominations submitted by the local board of Christian education (875; 880:7) a supervisor for each department (cf. 913). The departmental supervisor shall assist the Sunday school superintendent, being responsible for the general operation of the department including the assembly period of the department, and the immediate supervision of each session of the department (cf. 889:4). The local board of Christian education shall appoint such other departmental officers as may be needed.

**903. Sunday School Committee.** The immediate administration of the Sunday school may be vested in a Sunday school committee, subject to the approval of and correlated with the plans of the local board of Christian education. It shall be composed of the Sunday school superintendent as chair, the pastor (or if the pastor prefers, the associate or assistant pastor), assistant superintendent, secretary (who shall serve as secretary of the committee), treasurer and the departmental supervisors.

**906. Sunday School Teachers.** The local board of administration shall, at the time of its annual election (782:22; 825), elect from nominations submitted by the local board of Christian education (875; 880:7) such Sunday school teachers and assistants as are needed, to serve for one year or until their successors are elected.

**910. Amenability.** General regulations covering the amenability, removal and filling of vacancies for Sunday school officers, departmental supervisors and teachers elected by the local board of administration are found in 825. All others appointed by the local board of Christian education are amenable to the local board of Christian education and can be replaced as it sees fit.

### c. Organization

**913.** Guidelines for organization of Sunday school shall be provided through the *General Board Policy for Sunday School and Discipleship Ministries* and the standard adopted by the General Board and promoted through the General Department of Sunday School and Discipleship Ministries.

## 3. Christian Youth Clubs International

**915.** Each local church may maintain a local chapter of Christian Youth Clubs International (920; cf. 1489).

**920. The local CYCI chapter shall be organized as follows:**

(1) **Local CYCI Staff.** The local board of administration shall, at the time of its annual election (782:22; 825), elect from nominations submitted by the local board of Christian education (875; 880:7) a local CYCI director, to serve for one year or until a successor is elected. The local CYCI director shall be chair of the CYCI committee (880:8; 920:2). General regulations concerning this office are given in 825. The local CYCI director shall seek to qualify as quickly as possible for certification by the General Department of Youth as a local director. All other CYCI workers, including age-level directors and squadron leaders, shall be appointed by the local board of Christian education, shall be amenable to it, and may be replaced by it as it deems necessary.

(2) **Local CYCI Committee.** The local CYCI shall be administered by a CYCI committee, consisting of the local CYCI director as chair and of others appointed by the local board of Christian education (880:8). The work of the CYCI committee shall be subject to the approval of and correlated with the

plans of the local board of Christian education. General regulations governing membership on this committee are given in 825.

(3) **Correlation.** Whenever it is impractical for a local church to maintain CYCI and Wesleyan Kids for Missions (950) separately, the local board of administration may authorize the CYCI to make full use of the WKFM program of missionary education and promotion, and to channel missionary dues and offerings as if they were WKFM funds (7335:2).

### 4. Wesleyan Youth

**922.** Each local church may maintain a local chapter of Wesleyan Youth (7500-7545).

### 5. Young Adults International

**924.** Each local church may maintain a local chapter of Young Adults International (7700-7745).

### 6. Local Educational Director

**926.** The local board of administration may, at the time of its annual election (782:22; 825), elect a local educational director, to serve for one year or until a successor is elected. General regulations concerning this office are given in 825. The local education director shall promote the interests of the general educational institutions within the area, in keeping with the programs of the General Department of Education and the Ministry, the officials of the schools and the district educational director, and shall recruit students from the local church constituency for the schools.

### 7. Literature Secretary

**928.** The local board of administration may, at the time of its annual election (782:22; 825), elect a literature secretary, to serve for one year or until a successor is elected. General regulations concerning this office are given in 825. The literature secretary shall be assigned such duties as the local board of administration shall determine, such as the handling and distribution of Sunday school literature, the management of a church and/or Sunday school library and the promoting of the interests of the Wesleyan Publishing House. (Cf. 840.)

## G. Missions and Evangelism

### 1. Local Director of Missions

**930.** The local board of administration may, at the time of its annual election (782:22; 825), elect a local director of missions, to serve for one year or until a successor is elected. General regulations concerning this office are given in 825. The local director of missions shall assist the pastor in promoting the work of world missions, in keeping with the policies and programs of the General Department of World Missions, the district conference and district board of administration and the district director of world missions.

### 2. Local Director of Evangelism

**935.** The local board of administration may at the time of its annual election (782:22; 825) elect a local director of evangelism to serve for one year or until a successor is elected. General regulations concerning this office are given in 825. The local director of evangelism shall assist the pastor in promoting the work of evangelism in the local church in accordance with the mission of The Wesleyan Church (100) and in cooperation with the district director of evangelism and church growth (1426). The local director of evangelism shall also assist the pastor in the follow-up and discipling of new Christians, in the recruiting and training of workers for visitation evangelism and in the administration of evangelism and follow-up programs.

### 3. Wesleyan Men

**940.** Each local church may maintain a chapter of Wesleyan Men (7100-7135).

### 4. Wesleyan Women

**945.** Each local church may maintain a local chapter of Wesleyan Women (7306-7330).

### 5. Wesleyan Kids for Missions

**950.** Each local church may maintain a local Wesleyan Kids for Missions (7330:7; 7335).

### 6. Committee on Missions

**955.** The local board of administration may establish a committee on missions, composed of the pastor, the local director of missions, the president of Wesleyan Men or a representative of the men's group, the director of Wesleyan Women, the coordinator of Wesleyan Kids for Missions and such other members as the local board of administration shall elect. General regulations governing the elected membership on this committee are given in 825. The local board of administration shall name the chair of the committee, and the committee shall choose its own vice-chair and director.

**958.** The local board of administration shall assign such duties to the committee on missions as it deems best, including any or all of the following:

(1) To promote the interests of Wesleyan world missions, in keeping with the programs of the General Department of World Missions and the district director of world missions.

(2) To coordinate all missionary promotion and fund raising of the local church and its various departments and auxiliaries.

(3) To carry out all programs of missionary education authorized and assigned by the local board of Christian education.

(4) To make recommendations to the local board of administration concerning missionary conventions and services.

(5) To nominate, for election by the local board of administration, such standing or special subcommittees as the local board of administration shall approve, with a member of the committee as chair of each.

### 7. Committee on Evangelism

**960.** The local board of administration may establish a committee on evangelism, composed of the pastor, the local director of evangelism and such other members as the local board of administration shall elect. General regulations concerning membership on the committee are given in 825. The local board of administration shall assign such duties to the committee on evangelism as it deems best, including any or all of the following:

(1) To promote the work of evangelism through the local church in accordance with the mission of The Wesleyan Church (100).

(2) To organize, in cooperation with the pastor, the calling and visitation programs of the church.

(3) To organize, in cooperation with the pastor, follow-up and discipleship programs for new converts.

(4) To provide for and oversee, in cooperation with the local Christian education board, the training of workers for outreach evangelism and discipleship ministries.

(5) To make recommendations to the local board of administration concerning evangelistic services and to assist in promotion and conducting of such efforts.

(6) To alert the church to its wider responsibilities in meeting social and material needs of its community as such needs are discovered through its calling and discipling ministries.

(7) To promote extension projects carried on by the local church.

### H. Lay Delegates to District Conference

**965.** The local church conference, at one of its officially announced sessions, shall elect by ballot (cf. 820-823), from among its covenant members, the number of lay delegates to the district conference assigned by the district board of administration and a sufficient number of alternate delegates who shall serve for the regular annual session and for any reconvened session. General regulations covering this office are given in 815 and in 1100-1109.

### I. Judicial Committees

**970.** The local board of administration shall elect, when it deems it necessary and in accord with the regulations of the Judiciary, a committee of investigation (5100:1-4; 5250-5278) or a local judicial committee (5115). Complete regulations concerning the qualifications, procedures and duties of such committees are given in 5100-5115 (cf. 5250-5347).

# PART III

# DISTRICT CHURCH GOVERNMENT

## Chapter I

## DISTRICT ORGANIZATION

### A. Definition

**1000.** A district is a grouping of churches created by the authority of the General Conference, within which the churches, ministers and members of The Wesleyan Church are organized according to *The Discipline* and are under its governing authority (317).

### B. Developing District

**1003. Purpose.** New work, or other work which does not meet the requirements for a provisional district (1025), shall be provided for by establishing a developing district.

**1006. Authorization.** The establishment of a developing district may be authorized by the General Conference (1590:11), upon recommendation of the General Board, or, in the interim of General Conference sessions, by the General Board. The authorizing act shall define the boundaries and assign an official name to the developing district. Any proposed boundaries that will alter the bounds of an established district in the interim of General Conference sessions must have the approval of such a district and shall be effected as required in 1060-1065 (cf. 1655:33).

**1009. Jurisdiction.** A developing district shall be under the jurisdiction of the General Department of Evangelism and Church Growth and shall be organized and administered by the General Director of Evangelism and Church Growth in accord with *The Discipline*, the *Policy of the General Board for Evangelism and Church Growth* and other directives from the General Board or its Executive Board (1655:26). The General Director of Evangelism and Church Growth shall be responsible for developing the work as rapidly as possible, in harmony with the missionary objectives of The Wesleyan Church (2200), to the status of a provisional district (1025).

**1012. Organization.** The superintendent, other officers and assigned workers shall be appointed by and the granting of ordination and commissioning and issuing of licenses shall be voted by the Board of General Superintendents, for which recommendations shall be submitted by the General Director of Evangelism and Church Growth.

**1015. General Conference Representation**. The developing district shall be represented in the General Conference by the General Director of Evangelism and Church Growth, and by the superintendent of the developing district as a nonvoting member (1503:2).

### C. Provisional District

#### 1. Authorization

**1020. Authorization.** A provisional district is created by the General Conference, upon recommendation of the General Board (1590:11), or, in the interim of General Conference sessions, by the General Board. The authorizing act shall define the boundaries of the provisional district and assign to it an official name. Any proposed boundaries that will alter the existing bounds of an established district in the interim of General Conference sessions must have the approval of such district and shall be effected as required in 1060-1065 (cf. 1655:33).

**1025. Requirements.** The minimum requirements for a provisional district are:

(1) A minimum of five churches and 200 covenant members.

(2) A sufficient number of ordained ministers for a district board of administration (1203).

(3) The holding of all property in trust for The Wesleyan Church as required in 4610, or steps taken to accomplish the same (4590-4630; 4650-4780; 4800-4820).

(4) A recommendation by the General Director of Evangelism and Church Growth for recognition as a provisional district.

#### 2. Organization and Government

**1028. Jurisdiction.** A provisional district shall be under the jurisdiction of the General Department of Evangelism and Church Growth, and shall be supervised by the General Director of Evangelism and Church Growth in accord with *The Discipline*, the *Policy of the General Board for Evangelism and Church Growth* and any other directives of the General Board or its Executive Board (1655:26; 1785:2). The General Director of Evangelism and Church Growth shall be responsible for the developing of a provisional district to meet the requirements of an established district as soon as possible (1036; 4105).

**1030. Organization.** A provisional district shall be organized in the same manner as an established district as set forth in *The Discipline*, insofar as possible, but with the following restrictions on its duties and powers:

(1) **District Superintendent.** The district superintendent of a provisional district shall be elected by the district conference (cf. 1180:31; 1303). The Board of General Superintendents may, however, at its discretion, present one or more nominations, from which the district conference shall elect the district superintendent (1935:8, 10). The provisional district superintendent shall confer with the General Director of Evangelism and Church Growth concerning the important plans of the district, including the location of property, the erection of buildings and financial matters (cf. 1030:3). No property within a provisional district may be received, transferred, bought or sold without the written permission of the General Director of Evangelism and Church Growth.

(2) **District Officers, Boards and Committees.** A provisional district shall first be concerned with the election of its district officials (1255) and district board of administration (1203). Other district departmental officers, boards and committees shall be established as qualified personnel are available. It shall be the goal of the officials of a provisional district, in cooperation with the General Director of Evangelism and Church Growth (1028), to meet the requirements for a complete district organization as soon as possible (1038).

(3) **Amenability.** The minutes of the provisional district conference and its district board of administration shall be reviewed by the General Director of Evangelism and Church Growth.

### 3. General Conference Representation

**1032.** The district superintendent and a lay delegate, elected by ballot and by majority vote, shall be the representatives of a provisional district to the General Conference (1503:1a; 1506).

### 4. Reclassification

**1034.** Whenever a provisional district falls below the minimum requirements in 1025, it may be reclassified as a developing district by the General Conference (1590:11), or, in the interim of its sessions, by the General Board (1655:24), upon recommendation from the Board of General Superintendents.

### 5. Constitutional Language

**1035.** Wherever the term "mission district" appears in *The Discipline*, including the constitutional section, it shall be read and interpreted according to the paragraphs relating to provisional districts herein (1020-1034).

## D. Established District

### 1. Authorization

**1036.** An established district is created by the General Conference (317; 1590:10), upon recommendation by the General Board, or, in the interim of General Conference sessions, may be created by the General Board, subject to the approval of the next General Conference (1655:24, 34; 1920:22). The authorizing act shall define the boundaries of the district and assign to it an official name.

**1038.** The minimum requirements for an established district are:

(1) Twenty churches.

(2) Seven hundred fifty covenant members

(3) The holding of all property in trust for The Wesleyan Church as required in 4610, or steps taken to accomplish the same (4590-4630; 4650-4880; cf. 4140).

(4) A reasonable degree of spiritual, organizational and financial stability.

(5) A recommendation by the Board of General Superintendents in concurrence with the General Director of Evangelism and Church Growth (1920:22).

### 2. Organizing Conference

**1040.** When an established district has been authorized (1036), an organizing session of the district conference shall be convened by the General Superintendent over the district or another designated General Superintendent (1920:17). The presiding General Superintendent shall declare it to be an established district of The Wesleyan Church, vested with all the authority and power as properly belong to it according to *The Discipline*. After such has been declared, the district conference shall proceed to do business and elect its officials.

### 3. Reclassification

**1042.** If a district no longer meets one or more of the requirements for an established district (1038), it may be reclassified as a provisional district by the General Conference (1590:11), or the General Board.

**1045.** An established district, by a vote of its district conference, may petition the General Board for reclassification as a provisional district if it falls below the requirements for an established district (1038). The General Board shall have authority to reclassify it as a provisional district and place it under the jurisdiction of the General Department of Evangelism and Church Growth (1038; 1655:33-34; 1935:8, 14).

### 4. Amenability

**1050.** An established district is amenable to the General Conference and to the General Board. It may be placed under discipline for cause as set forth in the Judiciary (5218-5240; cf. 360:3e).

## E. Merger or Realignment of Districts

**1060.** The General Conference shall have the authority to approve the merger or division of districts or the realignment of any district boundaries (317). Negotiations for such a merger, division or realignment of districts shall be under the supervision of the Board of General Superintendents who shall work with representatives appointed for such a purpose by the General Board and the districts concerned (cf. 1655:33).

**1065.** Whenever each district conference involved in a merger, division or other realignment of districts shall approve the proposed plan, the General Board shall have the authority to grant final approval in the interim of General Conference sessions (cf. 1935:14; 1655:33).

# Chapter II

# DISTRICT CONFERENCE

### A. Function

**1075.** A district conference is the chief governing body of a district, exercising such powers as are delegated to it in the Constitution and by the General Conference as set forth in *The Discipline* of The Wesleyan Church.

### B. Membership

#### 1. Plan of Representation

**1080.** The district conference, as required by the Constitution (317), shall be composed of an equal number of ministers and lay members as voting members, and other nonvoting members as listed herewith.

##### a. Voting Members

**1083. Ministers.** The ministerial voting members of the district conference are those who meet the following requirements:

(1) Ordained ministers under appointment (1240:I:A:1-7), retired (1240:I:B; 3370), on reserve (1240:I:C; 3360) or on educational leave (1240:I:D; 3350:1).

(2) Licensed ministers who are ordained ministers-elect (317).

(3) Commissioned or licensed ministers who are pastors or full-time associate or assistant pastors of churches in that district (317; 1240:II:A; 1240:III:A; 3059; 3030).

(4) Ministerial members of the district board of administration who are not voting members by some other right (317).

(5) Ordained ministers (including licensed ministers who are ordained ministers elect) who have applied for transfer to another district but whose processes of transfer out of the district are yet incomplete.

**1086. Laity.** The lay members of the district conference with voting rights are those elected as delegates by the churches or circuits of that district (315:7; 317; 1100-1109) and the lay members of the district board of administration (317). The total number of lay members with voting rights shall be equal to the total number of ministerial voting members as set forth in 1100:1. Each established church or circuit is entitled to a minimum of one lay delegate as its constitutional right (315:7; cf. 503), and, according to its number of covenant members, to additional lay delegates allotted by the district board of administration (1100:1-5). A developing church which is judged to be qualified may be allotted one lay delegate (510:5; 1100:2; 1103).

### b. Nonvoting Members

**1090.** The nonvoting members of the district conference, with a voice but without a vote, are (cf. 317):

(1) Ordained ministers without appointment (1240:I:E; 3380).

(2) Ordained ministers in process of transfer (3104; 3390).

(3) Commissioned or licensed ministers who are not voting members of the district conference as listed in 1083:2-4, including those in process of transfer (3104).

(4) Ministerial students (3015:3b; 3350:2).

(5) Commissioned and licensed special workers (1240:V:A,B,C; 3460-3470).

(6) Commissioned lay missionaries (1240:V:D).

(7) Supply pastors (1240:V:E; 3260:4).

(8) District presidents of Wesleyan Men (7165:2) and Wesleyan Youth (7575:2k), and district director of Wesleyan Women (7370:2), district coordinator of Wesleyan Kids for Missions (7370:7) and district directors of Christian Youth Clubs International (1489) and Young Adults International (1494).

(9) Ordained ministers, commissioned ministers and licensed ministers whose process of transfer into the district are pending completion.

## 2. Forfeiture of Representation

**1095.** A local church or circuit which is under discipline as provided for in the Judiciary shall forfeit all rights to representation by a lay delegate in the district conference (315:7; 317; 5185-5195).

## 3. The Election of Lay Delegates

**1100. Allotment.** The district board of administration shall assign to each church or circuit the specific number of lay delegates which it shall elect as its representatives to the district conference, in keeping with the provision in 1086 for the total number of lay delegates and subject to the following regulations:

(1) The district board of administration shall first determine the total number of lay delegates required for the next session of the district

conference (1086) which shall equal the number of ministerial voting members eligible at the time such determination is made (cf. 1083:1-5).

(2) One lay delegate shall first be allotted to each pastoral charge (315:7; 528:3; 317; 503), including any developing churches deemed qualified (510:5; 1086).

(3) One shall be subtracted from the number needed to balance the ministerial vote for each lay member of the district board of administration.

(4) The number of lay delegates yet required for the next district conference shall be allotted to the pastoral charges according to a ratio of representation. In fixing the ratio of representation, only the covenant members as listed on the statistical report of the preceding district conference, shall be considered. The district board of administration shall establish the ratio of representation and apply it in such a manner as to assign the exact number of delegates to be elected by each pastoral charge.

(5) The district shall promptly notify each pastor of the exact number of lay delegates allotted to that particular pastoral charge,.

**1103. Election.** The lay delegates to the district conference shall be elected at any duly called session of the local church conference or circuit conference, by ballot, and by a majority vote of those covenant members present and voting (823; 965). In the case of a developing church, election shall be by the local advisory council, subject to approval by the district superintendent (510:3,5). A person accepting election as a delegate has an obligation to attend faithfully the entire district conference session, unless hindered by unforeseen and justifiable circumstances. The local church secretary shall promptly forward a certified list of the elected lay delegates to the district secretary.

**1106. Alternate Delegates.** A sufficient number of alternate lay delegates having the same qualifications (1109) shall be elected in the same manner and at the same session as the delegates (1103), and shall fill any vacancies in the order of their election. Whenever an alternate delegate is required to serve, the pastor or local church secretary shall certify this appointment to the district secretary.

**1109. Qualifications.** A lay delegate must be a covenant member and in good standing of the pastoral charge represented, both at the time of election and at the time of the district conference. An ordained, commissioned or licensed minister may not be elected or serve as a lay delegate.

### C. Sessions

**1112. Annual Session.** The district conference shall meet annually at a place chosen by the district board of administration and at a time as decided upon by the Board of General Superintendents in cooperation with the district board of administration (1233:5; 1920:20). The district secretary shall notify in writing all ministerial voting members, pastoral charges and nonvoting members of the time and the place not less than sixty days before the scheduled opening. Whenever an emergency shall require a change in the plans adopted, the district board of administration may declare that such an emergency exists and authorize the necessary changes.

**1115. Reconvened Session.** The district conference may be reconvened at any time during the year by a two-thirds majority vote of the district board of administration and the approval of the Board of General Superintendents (1920:20). A reconvened session shall also be ordered by the district board of administration when requested to do so by the General Board, its Executive Board, or the Board of General Superintendents. The district board of administration shall designate the place and, in cooperation with the General Superintendents, fix the date, which shall be not less than thirty days after the call shall be issued. The district shall notify in writing all ministerial voting members, pastoral charges and nonvoting members of the time, place and purpose of the reconvened session. The district conference shall have the same rights and powers in a reconvened session as in the annual session.

## D. Organization and Procedure

### 1. Officers

**1120. The Chair.** A General Superintendent, or a representative appointed by a General Superintendent, shall preside over the district conference, assisted by the district superintendent in the manner provided for in the Constitution (350:3). When neither the General Superintendent nor the appointed representative is present, the district superintendent shall preside or take the responsibility for the same. If none of the foregoing is present, the district conference shall elect from among its ordained ministers a chair pro tem.

**1123. The Secretary**. The district secretary shall be the secretary of the district conference *ex officio*. The district secretary shall accurately record the proceedings and preserve them in permanent form as prescribed by *The Discipline* (cf. 1178), and perform any other duties as shall be required by the district conference.

### 2. Procedure

**1126. Rights.** The rights of the district conference are declared in the Constitution (323:1-10; 325; 327; 350:3; 360:3c, e; 375:2, 4, 6; 385).

**1129. Quorum.** A majority of all the ministerial voting members and lay delegates of the district conference (1083-1086) shall constitute a quorum for the transaction of business.

**1132. Delegates.** Once a delegate has been seated at the annual district conference, an alternate delegate cannot thereafter be seated in place of the previously seated delegate.

**1135. Voting (317).** The ministerial and lay members of the district conference shall deliberate and transact business as one body. However, on the final vote on any question, one-fourth of the members may call for a divided vote. The house shall then be divided, and the ministerial and lay members shall vote separately, with a majority vote of each branch required to pass the question on which the division has been called.

**1138. Rules of Order.** District conference business shall be conducted according to the current edition of *Robert's Rules of Order, Newly Revised,* except when otherwise ordered by *The Discipline* (cf. 1156).

**1141. Suspension of Rules**. The district conference may by two-thirds vote suspend any rules of order for a certain item of business, provided such a suspension does not contravene *The Discipline* or other General Conference legislation.

**1144. Appeals on Questions of Order.** The chair shall decide all questions of order, subject to an appeal to the district conference body. If any matter is ruled out of order by the chair on the basis that it is unconstitutional or in violation of *The Discipline*, the decision of the chair may be appealed by any member of the district conference. If the appeal is seconded, the chair shall clearly state the question and the reasons for the decision, and the one moving the appeal shall state the reasons for the appeal. The vote shall then be taken without debate. A two-thirds vote of the district conference, present and voting, shall be required to overrule the decision of the chair. If the chair is overruled, the action of the district conference shall be suspended until a ruling shall be given by the Board of General Superintendents as provided for in 1920:24.

**1147. Legislation.** Rules and resolutions adopted by a district conference shall continue in force until amended or rescinded, unless such actions are by nature temporary or unless an action of the district conference is declared unconstitutional or contrary to *The Discipline* as set forth in 1920:24 and 5440:3 (cf. 323:6).

### 3. Resolutions

**1150. Resolutions.** Resolutions may be submitted to the district conference by a local church conference, a circuit conference, the district board of administration, the annual district convention of Wesleyan Men Wesleyan Women, Wesleyan Youth or Young Adults International, a district board or committee concerning the work assigned to it, or any three voting members of the district conference with their signatures.

**1153. Memorials.** All resolutions intended for eventual recommendation by the district conference to the General Conference, including changes in *The Discipline* and any other proposals, shall be designated as "memorials" (1557-1560). Anyone authorized to submit a resolution may also submit a memorial to be passed upon by the district conference.

**1156. Procedure.** All resolutions shall be submitted as directed by the district conference and within a time limit as set by the district conference. The appropriate district conference committee (cf. 1168:1) shall be responsible to review each resolution or memorial as to its origin (1150), clarity, relationship to *The Discipline* and other existing legislation of the General Conference or district conference, and shall report them out to the district conference together with their recommendations. A properly submitted resolution cannot be withheld from the conference body by a committee unless withdrawn by its authors or declared out of order by the chair of the district conference as contravening *The Discipline* (1935:9). The committee chair shall present any resolutions in question to the district conference chair for a ruling before presenting them on the conference floor. The district conference may by a two-thirds vote suspend the requirement that a resolution must first be reviewed by a committee (cf. 1168:1) and immediately proceed to consider and vote upon said resolution.

### 4. Committees

**1159.** The district conference shall have such committees as are required by *The Discipline*, and may create and define the duties of such other committees as are deemed necessary.

#### a. District Conference Action Committee

**1165.** A district conference may establish a district conference action committee (1180:9) that shall perform the functions of a resolutions committee. It shall consist of the district superintendent, the district treasurer and from three to nine other members elected by the conference with due consideration for lay representation (cf. 1175:2). The district conference may delegate the election of the committee members to the district board of administration. The district superintendent shall be the chair or shall appoint another to serve instead, and the committee shall elect a secretary and other officers as deemed necessary.

**1168.** The duties of the district conference action committee are:

(1) To receive all resolutions and memorials for the district conference, to review them, and to report them to the district conference with the committee's recommendation except as provided for in 1233:8 (1150-1156).

(2) To conduct and report on any research or investigation regarding the merits of proposed district legislation as requested by the district conference or district board of administration, or as deemed necessary by the committee.

(3) To assign members of the committee to study, prepare and plan any phase of the committee's work and report back to the committee.

(4) To review the standing rules of the district in order to make recommendations to the district conference concerning the alignment of such rules with General Conference legislation, and concerning any other necessary amendments (1180:5).

(5) To provide, if possible, all delegates to the district conference with copies of resolutions or memorials, properly classified, at least ten days before the opening of the district conference.

### b. District Conference Nominating Committee

**1172.** Each district may have a district conference nominating committee consisting of the district superintendent as chair, and two or more ministers and an equal number of lay members elected by the district conference (1180:10). The elected members of the nominating committee shall not succeed themselves and may not be reelected until after a lapse of one year. The committee shall organize itself. It shall serve for one year and shall meet as called by the chair.

**1175.** The duties of this committee shall be determined by the district conference and may include such as the following:

(1) To present nominations for the district secretary, district treasurer (see 1335), members-at-large on the district board of administration, and each elected delegate to the General Conference.

(2) To present nominations for each of the following in accord with the requirements and regulations for each as set forth in *The Discipline*, and in keeping with the provisions of *The Discipline* for various options in combining responsibilities or referring the power of nomination or election

to other bodies: the district conference action committee (1165), the district building committee (1345), the district statistical committee (1350), the district director for Church periodicals (1355), the district director of evangelism and church growth (1426), the district director of world missions (1429), the district Sunday school director (1483), the district director of leadership training (1486), the district director of CYCI (1489).

(3) To present any other nominations as shall be requested by the district conference.

### 5. The District Conference Journal

**1178.** The district conference journal shall contain the complete and accurate record of the proceedings of the district conference, prepared by the district secretary who shall have the duty:

(1) To have it certified by an editing committee or by the district superintendent.

(2) To arrange the journal as far as possible according to the table of contents and general format prepared by the General Secretary and approved by the General Board.

(3) To see that it contains a complete directory for the district as set forth in 1332:8.

(4) To annually deliver to the General Secretary copies of the district journal in such quantities as needed for the offices in The International Center.

## E. Duties and Powers

**1180.** The duties and powers of the district conference as set forth in the Constitution (cf. 1126) and as authorized by the General Conference are:

### Relating to the Constitution

(1) To propose an amendment to the Constitution, by a two-thirds vote, to be submitted to the General Conference as a memorial (385; 1560; 1590:1) or to propose an amendment to the Constitution to be submitted first to the other district conferences (385; 1590:2).

(2) To vote on the ratification of an amendment to the Constitution adopted by the General Conference (385; 1590:1); and to vote on a proposed amendment to the Constitution originating in another district conference (385; 1590:2).

### Relating to the General Conference

(3) To adopt memorials to the General Conference for proposed changes in *The Discipline* or for other legislation (1153; 1557-1560; 1565).

(4) To elect delegates to the General Conference as set forth in 1503-1526 (cf. 1175:1).

(5) To review all standing rules of the district and bring them into harmony with the Constitution, other provisions of *The Discipline* as currently revised and amended and with other General Conference legislation (323:6; 1168:4).

(6) To request a special session of the General Conference in concurrence with two-thirds of the district conferences (330:2; 1532).

### Relating to the District Conference

(7) To receive the appointed general representative to preside over the district conference whenever a General Superintendent is not present (350:3; 1920:21).

(8) To receive a report concerning the interests and progress of the denomination from the General Superintendent presiding over the district conference, or if a General Superintendent is not present, from the general representative (1920:20).

(9) To authorize, if desired, a district conference action committee, designate its number of members and provide for the election of the members as set forth in 1165.

(10) To authorize, if desired, a district conference nominating committee, designate its number of members, elect such members and determine its duties as set forth in 1172-1175.

(11) Space reserved.

### Relating to District Administration

(12) To take charge of all ordained, commissioned or licensed ministers, ministerial students, commissioned and licensed special workers, missions, developing churches, pastoral charges, auxiliary organizations (cf. 1233:24; 7365:2) and other district work within its bounds, except when the district is under discipline (360:3c, e), and except for those members of the district who are elected as general officials (1800), missionaries appointed under the General Department of World Missions (2272) and others who are amenable only to the General Board for their official duties (323:1; 360:2; 5150; 5203).

(13) To receive a report concerning their official duties from the following: the district superintendent (1310:26), the assistant district

superintendent (if any, 1323:6), the district treasurer (1337:8), the leaders of all district departments and auxiliaries, and any others as desired by the district conference.

(14) To consider the numerical and financial progress of the district by receiving a complete statistical and financial report as compiled and submitted by the district statistical committee (1352:1-3).

(15) To take such actions and adopt such rules as it shall judge necessary to promote the interests and prosperity of The Wesleyan Church within the bounds of the district, and to amend or rescind the same, provided that it shall not add to or take from any provision of the Constitution or other provisions of *The Discipline*, and provided that any three members may appeal an action of the district conference as set forth in 323:6 (cf. 1920:24).

(16) To adopt financial plans which will provide for the support of the district work, and for the payment of the district obligation for the United Stewardship Fund (2015:1), assigning to each church its share of these obligations (2015:2; cf. 1233:10).

(17) Space reserved.

(18) To determine the dates for the district fiscal year, which shall be binding on all churches, boards, committees and organizations within the district for the keeping of records and reports.

(19) To authorize employment of the assistant district superintendent (1320) as a full time official, if desired, and further to define any duties in addition to those required by *The Discipline* (1323-1327).

(20) To create, if so desired, a camp meeting board and define its duties or to delegate this to the district board of administration.

(21) To authorize the incorporation of the district as provided for in 4100-4150. After such incorporation, the district board of administration shall carry out the will of the district conference concerning the holding of district and local church property (cf. 4680), and shall have power, on its own resolution, to acquire, purchase, manage, sell, exchange, mortgage, deed in trust, pledge, rent, lease and convey any property, real, personal, or mixed, as may be necessary or convenient for the purpose of the corporation.

(22) To elect, in states where local laws prohibit such incorporation, or where the law requires the property to be held by trustees, a district board of trustees from among the members of the district board of administration, which shall carry out the will of the district conference concerning the holding of district and local church property (cf. 4680), and which shall carry out its duties as set forth in 1365 (cf. 4500-4630; 4800-4880).

(23) To delegate any of its duties not restricted to the district conference by the Constitution.

**Relating to Churches, Ministers, and Lay Workers**

(24) To authorize the establishing of a mission (537), a developing church (510), a church (518), a circuit (525), the reclassification of a church as a developing church (518:5; cf. 1233:29), to declare a church as discontinued or abandoned (4730) and to hear a report from the district superintendent of the organization of new churches (520:6; 1310:14); to grant in concurrence with the General Board prior approval to a local church conference for post-secondary education in terms of an institute, junior college or college-level programs (655:18; 1655:35).

(25) To determine the boundaries of each pastoral charge within the district (323:5; 1233:9c; 4750).

(26) To receive and pass upon the recommendations of the district board of administration concerning the pastoral agreements, appointments and district conference relations, as follows (1233:9):

(a) To approve the pastoral agreements entered into between the pastoral charges and the ministers, or to alter such an agreement, or to veto the action of the pastoral charge and appoint another pastor, provided that any such alteration or veto shall be for reasons as set forth in the Constitution, and shall be voted on as a separate action by the district conference (323:1-2; 697).

(b) To appoint a pastor to those pastoral charges not yet supplied at the time of the district conference or whenever requested to do so by a local church (708) or to delegate such appointment to the district board of administration, and to employ a qualified person as a supply pastor when deemed necessary (3260).

(c) To appoint each minister to the proper category of service or other appointment (3250-3391), appointing each ordained minister not included on the appointed list (1240:I:A) to the proper district conference relation as retired, on reserve, on educational leave, without appointment (1240:I:B-E) or in process of transfer (3104); appointing each commissioned or licensed minister to the proper category of service (1240:II:A-B; 1240:III:A-B; 3255-3391) or in the process of transfer (3104); to license as ministerial students those persons so qualified (1240:IV; 3015:1); and to appoint as commissioned or licensed special workers, designating their particular ministry (3450-3480), those who have been granted the proper commissions and licenses (1240:V:A-C) or to list them as in process of transfer (1240:V:B), and to appoint commissioned lay missionaries.

(27) Space reserved.

(28) To elect to ordination or for commissioning as a minister, a candidate the district conference deems qualified (3070), after receiving a report from the district board of ministerial development (1390:5) which shall be acted upon as a separate item of business.

(29) To grant a license, commission, recognition or restoration, in keeping with the requirements of *The Discipline*, after receiving the report and recommendations from the district board of ministerial development (1390:5), as follows:

(a) A recognition as ordained minister in process of transfer to an ordained minister being received from another denomination (3104), and a recognition as an ordained minister of The Wesleyan Church in full standing when all requirements have been met (3104:4-5).

(b) A district ministerial license, the granting of which shall become effective when the person receives appointment as set forth in 3033:7 and 3040:3 (cf. 1180:26c; 1233:9).

(c) A recognition of a commissioned or licensed minister being received from another denomination as in process of transfer (3104) and a recognition of such commissioned or licensed ministers in full standing when all requirements are met (3104).

(d) A license as a ministerial student for those who are qualified (3015:1; 3350).

(e) A license or commission as special worker, designating the particular ministry (3450-3480), or a recognition of a commissioned special worker or the equivalent thereof in process of transfer from another denomination, and subsequent recognition as a commissioned special worker in full standing when all requirements have been met (3470).

(f) A commission as lay missionary (3490).

(g) Any other license or commission as shall be authorized by *The Discipline*.

(h) The restoration of ordination, commission or license as set forth in 3120-3145; 3480 (cf. 1390:4).

(30) To receive and pass on a written annual service report, through the district board of ministerial development as set forth in 1390:7-9, from each ordained, commissioned and licensed minister, ministerial student and commissioned and licensed special worker; to receive an explanation from the district board of ministerial development relative to each person whose report has been found unsatisfactory, and to vote on the continuation of such person for appointment which shall require a two-thirds vote of confidence for approval (1390:9).

**Relating to the Election of Officials and Committees**

(31) To elect, by ballot and by majority vote, an ordained minister to the office of district superintendent for a term of two years (cf. 1303:1-2; 1935:10). Reelection thereafter shall be for a term of four years.

(32) To authorize, if so desired, election by the district board of administration of an ordained minister as assistant district superintendent (1320).

(33) To elect, by ballot and by majority vote, a district secretary (1330; cf. 1175:1), a district treasurer (1335; cf. 1175:1) or, if deemed advisable, a district secretary-treasurer and members-at-large of the district board of administration (1203-1206). The district conference may authorize the district board of administration to appoint a district treasurer (1335).

(34) To designate, if it so desires, the ordained ministers of the district board of ministerial development as the council of ordination (1405; cf. 1233:37).

(35) To elect the following or to delegate election to the district board of administration:

(a) One or more ordained ministers and an equal number of lay members to the building committee;
(b) The district statistical committee;
(c) District director of church periodicals;
(d) District director of evangelism and church growth;
(e) District director of world missions.

(36) Space reserved.

(37) To employ, if desired, or to authorize the district board of administration to employ a district director of Christian education (1460); and to assign the duties of the various district directors of Christian education agencies to the district director of Christian education as desired (1463:3; 1483; 1486; 1489; 1492; 1494; 1496).

(38) To elect (cf. 1175:2), whenever such duties have not been assigned to a district director of Christian education (cf. 1180:37), a district Sunday school director (1483), district director of leadership training, if desired (1486), and a district director of CYCI (1489). The district conference may authorize the district board of administration to appoint a district Sunday school director (1233:19; 1483).

(39) To elect a district board of review as set forth in paragraph 1370 (cf. 1175:2; 5159).

**Relating to Church Law and the Judiciary**

(40) To request, by a two-thirds majority vote, a ruling on a point of Wesleyan Church law or an interpretation of *The Discipline* from the Board of General Superintendents (1920:24a); and to appeal, by a two-thirds majority vote, such a ruling to the General Board of Review (1920:24c; 5440:3).

(41) To appeal, by a two-thirds majority vote, a decision of the Board of General Superintendents on the legality of an action by the district conference, a district board or committee or a district official, to the General Board of Review (375:2; 1920:24; 5440:3; cf. 323:6). All appeals must be filed in the office of the General Secretary within sixty days after the date of the official decision on the matter.

(42) To adopt, by a two-thirds majority vote, a complaint against the General Conference or another district and order its presentation to the General Board of Review for settlement (375:4,6; 5440:5-6); and to adopt such a complaint, by a majority vote, against the General Board to be presented to the General Board of Review for settlement (5440:5; cf. 323:10).

(43) To appeal, by a two-thirds majority vote, a judgment of the General Board of Review to the General Conference for final settlement (5445; cf. 323:10; 380). All appeals must be filed in the office of the General Secretary within sixty days after the date of the official decision on the matter.

(44) To exercise judicial powers according to the provisions of the Judiciary (5000-5070; 5150-5195; 5250-5370).

# Chapter III

# DISTRICT BOARD OF ADMINISTRATION

## A. Function

**1200.** The district board of administration carries out the will of the district conference, promotes the interests of The Wesleyan Church within the district and serves as the chief governing body of the district in the interim of district conference sessions.

## B. Membership

**1203. Composition.** The district board of administration is composed of the district superintendent, the assistant district superintendent (if any), the district secretary, the district treasurer and members-at-large according to the size of the district:

(1) When a district has fewer than fifty churches, the district conference shall elect at least five members-at-large to the district board of administration, making a total board of not fewer than eight members, elected so that at least three are lay members (cf. 1203:3).

(2) When a district has fifty or more churches, the district conference shall elect at least seven members-at-large to the district board of administration, making a total of not fewer than ten members, elected so that at least four are lay members (cf. 1203:3).

(3) Whenever a district conference chooses to elect more than the minimum number of members-at-large to its district board of administration, due regard shall be given to elect a proportionate number of lay members.

**1206. Regulations for a Member-at-Large.** Each member-at-large of a district board of administration shall be a covenant member of a local Wesleyan church within the district of service, both at the time of election and throughout the tenure of membership. A ministerial member-at-large shall be chosen from among the ordained ministers of the district. The term of office shall be for one year, and the member-at-large shall serve from the close of the district conference at which elected until the close of the next regular session of the district conference or until a successor is elected and qualified. Regulations governing the amenability of a member-at-large of the district board of administration and the declaring and filling of a vacancy in such office are the same as those for district officials set forth in 1265 and 1272 (cf. 1233:27a).

## C. Sessions

**1209. Organizing Sessions.** The district board of administration shall meet immediately after the close of the district conference for an organizing session:

(1) To care for any business delegated to it by the district conference which requires immediate attention.

(2) To appoint a district treasurer (1335), when such appointment has been authorized by the district conference (1180:33).

(3) To elect those departmental officers and members of boards or committees and to elect or ratify the election of those officers of auxiliaries, whose terms expire at the time of the district board's organizing session (cf. 1233:19).

(4) To make plans for the year and to care for any other business as deemed necessary.

**1212. Regular Sessions.** The district board of administration shall meet at such time and place as it shall determine, provided that it shall meet at least once each quarter.

**1215. Special Sessions.** The district board of administration may authorize special sessions as it deems necessary, or it may be called into special session by the district superintendent or in the event of an emergency when the district superintendent is unable to act, by the assistant district superintendent, if any, or the area general superintendent or the area general superintendent's representative. A special session shall also be called when requested by the General Board or its Executive Board, or the Board of General Superintendents. All members shall be notified at least one week in advance of a special session, except when all are able to meet on shorter notice.

**1218. Evaluation Sessions.** The area general superintendent shall, with the district board of administration, evaluate periodically the service of and financial provision for the district superintendent. The method and extent of such evaluation shall be determined by the Board of General Superintendents with special attention focused on those responsibilities that are most likely to contribute to future outreach and growth to the glory of God.

## D. Organization and Procedures

**1221. Chair.** The district superintendent shall preside as chair over the district board of administration. The assistant district superintendent, if any, shall preside in the absence of the district superintendent or when requested to do so by the district superintendent. If neither is present, the board shall elect from among its members a chair pro tem.

**1224. Secretary.** The district secretary is the secretary of the district board of administration by virtue of this office.

**1227. Quorum.** A majority of all members of the board shall constitute a quorum.

**1230. Voting.** A majority of those present and voting shall be sufficient except for those matters for which a larger majority is required by *The Discipline* or by legal or corporate requirements.

## E. Duties and Powers

**1233.** The duties and powers of the district board of administration are:

### General Duties

(1) To serve as the chief governing body of the district in the interim of district conference sessions, caring for all the interests of The Wesleyan Church within the bounds of the district in accord with *The Discipline*.

(2) To promote the interests of the general departments and educational institutions of The Wesleyan Church; to encourage their support and to receive their representatives.

(3) To be responsible within the district for the promotion of world missions and general evangelism and church growth (1410).

### Related to the District Conference

(4) To carry out the plans and objectives of the district conference.

(5) To cooperate with the Board of General Superintendents in fixing the date for the annual session of the district conference so that a General Superintendent may preside (1112; 1920:19).

(6) To call for a reconvened session of the district conference by a two-thirds majority vote of all members of the district board of administration, subject to the approval of the Board of General Superintendents (1920:19), and to call for a reconvened session when requested to do so by the General Board (1115) or its Executive Board. or the Board of General Superintendents.

(7) To allot to each church or circuit of the district the number of lay delegates it shall elect to the district conference (1100).

(8) To submit resolutions directly to the district conference that will provide for a more efficient administration, better correlation and advancement of the district work and to submit proposed memorials to the General Conference (1557; cf. 1180:3).

(9) To serve the district conference as a committee on pastoral relations and ministerial appointments, being responsible:

(a) To review all pastoral agreements between churches and ministers of the district (cf. 690-722).

(b) To receive a report from the district board of ministerial development concerning matters related to district conference appointments and relations as set forth in 1390:10.

(c) To submit to the district conference a comprehensive report covering all the churches and ministers of the district: recommending any necessary changes in the boundaries of the pastoral charges or in the classification of churches (1180:24-25; cf. 4720-4750); recommending the appointment of pastors for all churches for the coming year (cf. 510:1), including the approval, alteration or veto of pastoral agreements already made by the churches and ministers (323:2), and the appointment of pastors or the delegation of responsibility for such appointment for churches otherwise without pastors (1180:26) and recommending the appointment and/or classification of all other ordained ministers (3075:5), commissioned or licensed ministers, special workers and the licensing of ministerial students as set forth in 1180:26 and 1240 (cf. 3015:1).

(10) To carry out the following duties concerning the United Stewardship Fund (2000-2045): to submit a recommendation to the district conference for the raising of the district obligation and the apportioning to each church of its share of the district obligation (2015; cf. 1337:6), unless the district conference shall delegate this to another committee (cf. 1165-1168); to approve adjustments in United Stewardship Fund assessments due to building projects as set forth in 2005:2; to administer the district plan for raising the district obligation and to see that such obligation is paid in full (2015:3).

### Duties Relating to District Officers, Committees and Auxiliaries

(11) To have the general oversight of all district officials (1255), district departmental officers (1275), boards, committees, employees, auxiliary organizations of the district; to approve their plans and to coordinate their work; and to see that the work is administered according to *The Discipline* and the directives of the district conference. (cf. 1265-1272; 1285-1292; 1337:8; 1384; 1410; 7150; 7155:4; 7160:4,6; 7165:6; 7360; 7365:4; 7370:5,7; 7370:7; 7560; 7565:1d, 3; 7575:3d; 7770:6; 7785.)

(12) To divide the district into zones and determine the boundaries thereof, which shall be the same for all district organizations.

(13) To incorporate the district, when so authorized by the district conference (1180:21), as provided for in 4100-4150; to serve as the board of directors of such corporation; and to have power on its own resolution to acquire, purchase, manage, sell, exchange, mortgage, deed in trust, pledge, rent, lease and convey any property, real, personal or mixed, as may be necessary or convenient for the purpose of the corporation, and to exercise its corporate powers in accord with the provisions of *The Discipline* (4100-4150; 4500-4630; 4660; 4680; 4800-4880).

(14) To carry out, whenever the district is not incorporated, such duties, and to exercise such authority over district property and other legal affairs as set forth in 4500-4630 and 4800-4880.

(15) To provide for the preservation and security of all district records and archives, directing the district superintendent (1310:11; 4760), the district secretary (1332:6-7), the secretary of the district board of ministerial development (1387) and any others, concerning the care of the records placed in their custody.

(16) Space reserved.

(17) To adopt an annual budget of income and expense for the district; to set the salaries, allowances and related matters for the district officials and district departmental officers; to promote the raising of district funds in keeping with the plans of the district conference (1180:16); to direct the district treasurer in the handling and disbursement of such funds (1337:3); and to have the district treasurer bonded and to set the amount of such bond, the expense for which shall be paid by the district.

(18) To employ an auditor when so authorized by the district conference and to assign the duties (1340); to direct an audit of the records and funds in the custody of the district treasurer, the district treasurers of the auxiliary organizations or any other treasurers of the district, whenever such is deemed necessary (1337:7; 7165:5; 7370:6-7; 7575:3d).

(19) To appoint a district treasurer when so authorized by the district conference (1335) and to elect such district departmental officers and members of the district boards or committees as required by *The Discipline* or delegated to it by the district conference (cf. 1165; 1180:20, 33, 38; 1233:37; 1245; 1340; 1345; 1350; 1355; 1416; 1426; 1429; 1430; 1440; 1446; 1460; 1471; 5175:1; 7160:4; 7365:4,6; 7585:5; 7770:4); to elect members of the district board of ministerial development in keeping with the requirements for that board and to ratify the appointment of the chair if the district superintendent chooses not to serve (1378-1381).

(20) To serve as or to establish a separate district board of evangelism and church growth as set forth in 1413-1423, taking a special interest in and responsibility for developing, supervising and promoting an aggressive

program of district evangelism and church growth, and to cooperate in such endeavor with the General Superintendent over the district and the General Director of Evangelism and Church Growth (1935:11; 2208:1).

(21) To serve as or to establish a separate district board of Christian education as set forth in 1440-1443; to elect a chair and such members as may be decided upon (1443); to approve its plans and to assign such duties as desired (1452; 1455:9).

(22) To employ, when so authorized by the district conference (1180:37), a district director of Christian education (1460), who shall be nominated by the district board of Christian education (1455:7); and to assign duties to such a director (1463:1-9).

(23) To approve the time and place for the district Wesleyan Men convention to approve the nominations submitted by the Wesleyan Men nominating committee for the district Wesleyan Men president or to make other nominations as desired (7160:4); to ratify the election of district Wesleyan Men officers to approve all plans and actions of the district Wesleyan Men convention and the district Wesleyan Men executive committee.

(24) To approve the time and place of the district conventions of Wesleyan Women, Wesleyan Youth and Young Adults International to recommend to the district conference the enlargement of the membership of the WW convention, to approve the nominations for the district director of WW, the district president of WY and the district director of Young Adults International or to make other nominations as desired and to ratify the election of the other district officers, and to approve the plans of the district conventions and the executive committees of WW, WY and YAI as provided in their respective constitutions.

(25) To elect four ordained ministers and three lay members as members of the district board of review, and to elect two ordained ministers and two lay members to serve as alternates and to fill vacancies as set forth in 5159.

(26) To request a ruling on a point of church law or an interpretation of *The Discipline* from the Board of General Superintendents and to appeal the same to the Board of Review (1920:24a; cf. 5440:6); and to request assistance from the General Board or its Executive Board, through the General Superintendent, when deemed necessary.

(27) To remove for cause or whenever the best interests of the Church and the district so require:

(a) Any of its own members, with the exception of the district superintendent (cf. 1307), by a two-thirds majority vote of all members, and to fill such vacancies for the unexpired term (1206; 1265; 1272).

(b) Any departmental officer (1275), member of a board, committee or other agency of the district or the district officers of an auxiliary organization, by a majority vote and to fill such vacancies for the unexpired term(1292).

### Related to Churches and Ministers

(28) To organize and supervise all pastoral charges of the district in accord with *The Discipline* and other district directives so that each one may be an effective unit of The Wesleyan Church; to guard carefully the spiritual life and general welfare of all the churches; to plan and conduct conventions, institutes or seminars for pastors and other workers in the district, promoting such for the purpose of spiritual refreshment, leadership development, greater efficiency and a more united effort within the district and the general church (cf. 1935:13).

(29) To authorize the establishment of a mission (537; 655:15), a developing church (510) and a church (518) and to receive a report from the district superintendent on the effecting of such organizations (520:6); to reclassify an established church as a developing church when its number of covenant members drops to ten or fewer (518:5); and to declare a church as discontinued or abandoned (1180:24; 4730).

(30) To receive the report of the district superintendent concerning the actions of the local advisory council of each developing church (510:3).

(31) To approve all pastoral agreements and make all ministerial appointments in the interim of district conference sessions, subject to the final approval of the district conference (715; 722:3).

(32) To approve in writing the proposal of a local church conference for the acquisition, purchase, sale, mortgage, transfer or other disposal of real property in accord with the provisions in 4700-4780 (cf. 4000-4070), after first receiving a written report and recommendation from the district building committee when such is required as set forth in 1345; to advise, or appoint an investment committee to advise, a local board of administration when a local church has received an out-of-pattern contribution with value equal to or exceeding the total contributions of the preceding year (cf. 782:34); to authorize the incorporation of a local church in keeping with 4000 (cf. 655:14; 4010:6); to approve the name of a new church or name change or adaptation requested by a developing or established church.

(33) To supervise and coordinate the merger of two or more churches and to establish the procedures for such mergers. The plans for merger initiated by the local board or boards of administration must be submitted for consideration and approval to the district board of administration before presenting the proposals to the local church conference for consideration and vote.

(34) To approve the plans of a local board of administration for the establishment of a day care and/or day school, and after its establishment to approve any significant change in mission, facilities or finances (cf. 655:19; 782:34-35; 2305).

(35) To take charge of any complaints or accusations against a local church or circuit within the district and to carry out disciplinary proceedings as deemed necessary in accord with the Judiciary (5185; cf. 5162:2, 4); to intervene and protect the property rights of The Wesleyan Church and the district as set forth in 4010:6; 4770; 4840:6; and to authorize the district superintendent to call for an affirmation of loyalty and to reorganize a local church as set forth in 5190.

(36) To grant temporary recognition (cf. 1390:3) to ordained ministers, commissioned ministers, licensed ministers and commissioned special workers or persons with equivalent standing, from other denominations, as being in process of transfer, subject to the action of the next district conference (1180:29a, d, e; 1310:25; STET).

(37) To appoint the desired number of ordained ministers as a council of ordination (1405), except when the district conference shall designate the ordained ministers on the district board of ministerial development as the council of ordination (1180:34; 1390:6); and, in case of emergency, in the interim of district conference sessions, to elect to ordination a candidate recommended by the district board of ministerial development (3070:5).

(38) To consider and pass on the proposed resignation by, or a proposed vote on, a pastor after the renewal of the call, when such is considered before the term of service expires or in the interim of quadrennial reviews (720:2); or to remove a pastor by a two-thirds majority vote of all members of the district board of administration in keeping with the provisions of 712; 722:3; 1310:19; and to appoint a supply pastor, if necessary, until another pastor has been obtained (715); or to remove a supply pastor by a majority vote if deemed necessary (3260:5).

(39) To take charge of judicial proceedings, the ordering of investigation (5278) or trial, for any ordained minister, commissioned minister, licensed minister, ministerial student, commissioned or licensed special worker or other worker under the jurisdiction of the district (5150), in accord with the provisions of the Judiciary (5170-5180).

(40) To represent the district, in the interim of district conference sessions, in judicial proceedings over matters of controversy between the district and other local, district or general units or agencies (323:10; cf. 5440:5b).

### F. The Listing of District Conference Relations and Appointments

**1240.** The ordained ministers, commissioned ministers, licensed ministers, ministerial students, commissioned special workers, licensed special workers, commissioned lay missionaries and supply pastors of the district shall be listed in the following order as appointed by the district conference (1180:26; cf. 1233:9). This listing shall be included in the district conference journal (1178) as an official district directory and shall be used for that portion of the district conference roll call.

#### I. Ordained Ministers

A. **APPOINTED ORDAINED MINISTERS** (3250-3390).

1. **District Service.**
The district superintendent and other ordained ministers in full-time service of the district in a ministerial capacity (3320; cf. 1327; 1460).
2. **Pastoral and Local Service.**
   a. Ordained ministers appointed as pastors, associate or assistant pastors, within the district (3255).
   b. Ordained ministers on loan to other districts of The Wesleyan Church for service as supply pastors (3100:2; 3260:1).
   c. Ordained ministers appointed to serve in a local church Christian education program (3310:2).
3. **Evangelistic Service.**
   a. Associate general evangelists. Ordained ministers appointed as associate general evangelists (3270; 3280).
   b. General evangelists. Ordained ministers appointed as general evangelists (3270; 3275; 3285:1)
   c. Reserve evangelists. Ordained ministers appointed as reserve evangelists (3270; 3275; 3285:2).
4. **Denominational Service.**
   a. Ordained ministers elected by the General Conference or General Board as general officials (1800; cf. 3320).
   b. Ordained ministers employed at the International Center, or those elected or employed by the board of directors of a general subsidiary corporation other than an educational institution, for full-time general church service in a ministerial capacity as set forth in 3320.
   c. Ordained ministers appointed by the General Board for service in a ministerial capacity as missionaries or workers

under the General Departments of Evangelism and Church Growth or World Missions as set forth in 3300.

d. Ordained ministers employed to serve in a ministerial capacity on the administrative staff or faculty of a general educational institution of The Wesleyan Church (2365) or one of the seminaries approved by the Wesleyan Seminary Foundation (2382).

5. **Chaplains** (3330).
Ordained ministers approved by the Committee on Chaplains and commissioned by the government as military chaplains, or employed as full-time professional institutional chaplains.

6. **Interchurch Service** (3335).
Ordained ministers employed in a ministerial capacity in interchurch service, serving with an educational, evangelistic or missionary organization not directly related to The Wesleyan Church, provided such service is approved by the district conference.

7. **Special Service** (3345).
Ordained ministers serving in active ministry not otherwise provided for, if such service is approved by the district conference.

8. **Affiliate Church Pastor** (3346; 7910).
Ordained ministers appointed by the district conference to service on staff of an affiliate church.

B. **RETIRED ORDAINED MINISTERS** (3370).
Ordained ministers retired because of age or incapacitated by infirmity, provided they were either on the appointed list, on reserve or on educational leave at the time of such incapacitation or retirement.

C. **RESERVE ORDAINED MINISTERS** (3360).
Ordained ministers available for but without appointment. An ordained minister who remains on reserve for two consecutive years shall be automatically transferred to the list of ordained ministers without appointment unless continued on reserve by vote of the district conference.

D. **ORDAINED MINISTERS ON EDUCATIONAL LEAVE** (3350:1).
Ordained ministers enrolled in a seminary or other graduate school for advanced training for church service.

E. **ORDAINED MINISTERS WITHOUT APPOINTMENT** (3380).

1. Ordained ministers not available for appointment.
2. Ordained ministers employed in other than a ministerial capacity by the general church (3320), by a general educational institution or one of the seminaries connected with the Wesleyan Seminary Foundation (3310) or in interchurch service (3335).

3. Ordained ministers not otherwise listed.

F. **ORDAINED MINISTERS IN PROCESS OF DISTRICT TRANSFER**

Ordained ministers receiving appointment by the district conference to 1240:I:A, B, C or D but whose process of transfer between districts of The Wesleyan Church are not yet completed.

1. The receiving district shall list the ordained minister under the appropriate category of service, followed by the notation, "Pending Completion of District Transfer." The minister shall be a non-voting member of this district until completion of the transfer (1090:9).
2. The sending district shall list the ordained minister as having "Applied for District Transfer." The ordained minister shall be a voting member of the sending district until completion of the district transfer (3100:1; 1083:5).

G. **ORDAINED MINISTERS IN PROCESS OF DENOMINATIONAL TRANSFER** (3104; 3390).

Ordained ministers from another denomination who have been granted recognition as ordained ministers in process of transfer (1180:29a; cf. 1390:3; 3104).

## II. Commissioned Ministers

A. **PASTORS** (3255).

Commissioned ministers appointed as pastors or as full-time associate or assistant pastors of Wesleyan churches in that district (317; 1083:3).

B. **OTHER APPOINTMENTS**

Commissioned ministers appointed to service in a local church Christian education program (3310:2) or in a ministerial capacity to district, denominational or interchurch service (3250; 3300; 3320; 3335).

C. **COMMISSIONED MINISTERS WITHOUT APPOINTMENT** (3380)

1. Commissioned ministers not available for appointment.
2. Commissioned ministers employed in other than a ministerial capacity by the general church (3320), by a general educational institution or one of the seminaries connected with the Wesleyan Seminary Foundation (3310) or in interchurch service (3335).

D. **IN PROCESS OF DISTRICT TRANSFER.**

Commissioned ministers receiving appointment by the district conference to 1240:II:A or B but whose processes of transfer from another district of The Wesleyan Church are not yet completed.

1. The receiving district shall list the commissioned minister under the appropriate category of service, followed by the notation, "Pending Completion of District Transfer." The commissioned minister shall

be a non-voting member of this district until completion of the transfer (3100:1).

2. The sending district shall list the commissioned minister as having "Applied for District Transfer." The commissioned minister shall remain a non-voting member of the sending district until completion of the transfer (1083:3).

E. **IN PROCESS OF DENOMINATIONAL TRANSFER.**
Commissioned ministers or their equivalent from other denominations who have been granted recognition as commissioned ministers in process of transfer (3104).

F. **RETIRED COMMISSIONED MINISTERS** (3371)
Commissioned ministers retired because of age or incapacitated by infirmity, provided they were either on the appointed list, on reserve or on educational leave at the time of such incapacitation or retirement.

## III. Licensed Ministers

A. **PASTORS** (3255).
Licensed ministers appointed as pastors or as full-time associate or assistant pastors of Wesleyan churches in that district (317; 1083:3).

B. **OTHER APPOINTMENTS.**
Licensed ministers appointed to service in a local church Christian education program (3310:2) or in a ministerial capacity to district, denominational or interchurch service (3250; 3300; 3320; 3335).

C. **IN PROCESS OF DISTRICT TRANSFER.**
Licensed ministers receiving appointment by the district conference to 1240:III:A or B but whose processes of transfer from another district of The Wesleyan Church are not yet completed.

1. The receiving district shall list the licensed minister under the appropriate category of service, followed by the notation, "Pending Completion of District Transfer." The licensed minister shall be a non-voting member of this district until completion of the transfer (3100:1).
2. The sending district shall list the licensed minister as "Applied for District Transfer." Unless a licensed minister is an ordained minister-elect, said minister shall remain a non-voting member of the sending district until completion of the district transfer (1083:2, 3).

D. **IN PROCESS OF DENOMINATIONAL TRANSFER.**
Licensed ministers or their equivalent from other denominations who have been granted recognition as licensed ministers in process of transfer (3104).

### IV. Ministerial Students

Those approved by the district conference to be licensed as ministerial students as set forth in 3015:1.

### V. Lay Workers

A. **COMMISSIONED SPECIAL WORKERS** (3450; 3470).
List by specific category such as director of music, director of Christian education, youth director, song evangelist, chalk artist, children's worker, lay evangelist, social worker or spouse in ministry.

B. **COMMISSIONED SPECIAL WORKERS IN PROCESS OF TRANSFER** (3450; 3470).
List by specific category (refer to 1240:V:A).

C. **LICENSED SPECIAL WORKERS** (3450; 3460).
List by specific category (refer to 1240:V:A).

D. **COMMISSIONED LAY MISSIONARIES** (3490).

E. **SUPPLY PASTORS** (3260).

### G. Executive Committee

**1245.** A district board of administration with nine or more members may establish an executive committee which shall consist of the executive officers of the district board of administration. Additional members may be elected upon the recommendation of the district superintendent. The executive committee may act for the district board of administration as that board shall authorize.

# Chapter IV

# DISTRICT OFFICERS AND COMMITTEES

## A. List of District Officers, Boards and Committees

**1250.** The following summarizes for quick reference the various officers, boards and committees of the district:

(1) The district *shall* have:
administration, board of (1200-1233)
auditing committee or auditor (1340)
building committee (1345)
Christian Youth Clubs International director (1489)
delegates to General Conference (1032; 1180:4; 1503-1526)
evangelism and church growth director (1426)
ministerial development, board of (1375-1390)
ordination council (1405)
review, board of (1370; 5159-5167)
secretary (1330-1332)
statistical committee (1350-1352)
Sunday school director (1483)
superintendent (1300-1310)
treasurer (1335-1337)
world missions director (1429)

(2) The district *may* have:
assistant superintendent (1320-1327)
camp meeting board (1180:20)
Christian education, board of (1440-1455)
Christian education director (1460-1463)
Church periodicals director (1355)
conference action committee (1165-1168)
conference journal editing committee (1178:1)
conference nominating committee (1172-1175)
educational director (1496)
executive committee of the district board of administration (1245)
evangelism and church growth, board of (1413-1423)
judicial committee (5175)

leadership training director (1486)
secretary-treasurer (1180:33)
Sunday school committee (1468-1480)
trustees, board of (1180:22; 1360; 1365; 4855)
world missions, board of (1430-1435)

(3) The district *may* have the following auxiliary officers and committees:
Wesleyan Men officers and committees (7155:3; 7160-7165)
Wesleyan Women officers and committees (7365:3; 7370-7375)
Wesleyan Youth officers and committees (7560; 7565-7575; 7585)
Young Adults International officers and committees (7765; 7770)
Wesleyan Kids for Missions coordinator (7370:7)

### B. District Officials

**1255. Identification.** The district officials include the district superintendent, the assistant district superintendent, if any, the district secretary and the district treasurer. They are elected by the district conference (with the possible exception of the district treasurer, (1335; 1180:33), and assistant district superintendent, (1320) by ballot and by majority vote, and are *ex officio* members of the district board of administration (1180:31-33; cf. 1203).

**1258. Qualifications.** A district official other than the district superintendent (cf. 1303:1) must be, at the time of election and throughout the term of service, a covenant member of a local Wesleyan church within the district and, if a minister, a ministerial member of the district where service is rendered (cf. 1272).

**1262. Term of Office.** District officials other than the district superintendent (cf. 1303:2) shall be elected for a term of one year. All district officials shall assume office at the close of the district conference session at which they are elected and shall serve until the close of the district conference marking the end of their term or until their successors are elected and qualified with the possible exception of the district treasurer, (1335; 1180:33).

**1265. Amenability.** A district official shall administer the respective office according to ***The Discipline***, and as directed by the General Conference, the General Board, the district conference and the district board of administration. District officials other than the district superintendent shall serve under the general supervision of the district superintendent, shall be amenable to the district board of administration and may be removed for cause or when the best interests of The Wesleyan Church and the district so require, upon a two-thirds majority vote of all members of the district board of administration (1233:27a). The amenability of the district superintendent is set forth in 1307 (cf. 323:1).

**1268. Reports.** A district official shall report to each session of the district conference concerning all official duties (1180:13) and to the district board of administration as may be required.

**1272. Vacancies.** The office of a district official may become vacant by death, by cessation of membership in a local Wesleyan church within the district, by resignation, by removal (1265) or in the case of a minister, by ceasing to be a ministerial member of the district. In all cases other than that of the district superintendent (1303:7), the filling of a vacancy in the office of a district official until the next session of the district conference shall be by a majority vote of all members of the district board of administration (1233:27a).

### C. District Departmental Officers and Committees

**1275. Identification.** District departmental officers include the district director for Church periodicals (1355), the district director of evangelism and church growth (1426), the district director of world missions (1429), the district director of Christian education (1460), the district Sunday school director (1483), the district director of leadership training (1486), the district director of CYCI (1489), district director of YAI (1494) and the district educational director (1496). All district departmental officers and members of district boards (other than the district board of administration, cf. 1206) and committees are subject to the regulations as set forth herewith in 1275-1292. (Regulations governing the auxiliaries are set forth in their respective constitutions.)

**1278. Qualifications.** A district departmental officer or member of a district board or committee (1275) must be a covenant member of a local Wesleyan church within the district at the time of election, with the exception of ordained ministers appointed to denominational service, and if a minister, a ministerial member of the district (cf. 1292).

**1282. Term of Office.** A district departmental officer or member of a district board or committee (1275) shall be elected to serve for a term of one year, unless otherwise stated in *The Discipline*. The district departmental officer or member of a district board or committee shall assume office at the close of the district conference session at which elected or, whenever elected by a district board, at the time of the election and shall serve until the close of the next regular session of the district conference.

**1285. Amenability.** All district departmental officers and members of district boards or committees (1275) shall carry out their duties according to

*The Discipline* and other directives of the general church or district. They shall serve under the general supervision of the district superintendent and shall be amenable to the district board of administration. They may be removed by the district board of administration, by a majority vote, for cause or when the best interests of The Wesleyan Church and the district so require (1233:27b).

**1288. Reports.** A district departmental officer shall report to the district conference as required by *The Discipline* or by the district conference (1180:13), and shall make other reports to the board or committee under which service is performed, the district board of administration or the district superintendent as may be requested.

**1292. Vacancies.** The office of a district departmental officer or membership on a district board or committee (1275) may become vacant by death, by cessation of membership in a local Wesleyan church within the district, by resignation, by removal (1285) or in the case of a minister, by ceasing to be a ministerial member of the district, or in the case of a minister serving under the special provision of paragraph 1278, by discontinuing the appointment to denominational service. A vacancy may be declared and filled for the unexpired term by the district board of administration, by a majority vote.

# Chapter V

# DISTRICT ADMINISTRATION

### A. District Superintendent

**1300. Function.** The district superintendent is to be the spiritual and administrative leader of the district.

**1303. Qualifications and Tenure.** The regulations for a district superintendent are (cf. 1255-1272):

(1) **Election.** The district superintendent shall be elected by the district conference, by ballot and by majority vote, from among the ordained ministers of The Wesleyan Church (1180:31; cf. 1935:10). If the district superintendent is elected from outside the membership of the electing district, the district superintendent shall immediately arrange for the transfer of local and district membership.

(2) **Term of Office.** The initial election of a district superintendent shall be for a term of two years. Reelection thereafter shall be for a term of four years or an extended period (cf. 1262). The salary of a district superintendent shall continue for one month beyond the date for the termination of service.

(3) **Reelection.** Unless a district superintendent whose term is expiring shall give notice to the area General Superintendent and district board of administration no less than 90 days prior to district conference the district superintendent shall be considered available. The only exception is that the Board of General Superintendents, after consultation with and a majority vote by the district board of administration requesting procedural intervention, may declare that reelection by a "yes/no" vote shall not occur but that the nomination process in *Discipline* 1303:8 must be followed. In all other cases a vote shall be taken by "yes/no" ballot and in keeping with all other provisions for such an election. When an incumbent district superintendent does not receive a majority vote on the initial "yes/no" ballot for reelection, the provision of 1303:8 for the special committee on nominations shall become effective.

(4) **Term of Reelection.** One of the following alternative procedures shall be followed:

(a) A vote for a four-year renewal of the call shall be taken. If the vote on a four-year renewal of the call is favorable, the district board of administration, after consulting with the district superintendent and upon approval of the area General Superintendent, may then recommend to the district conference that a ballot vote be taken to renew the call for an extended period.

(b) Or, prior to the vote on renewing the call, the district board of administration, after consultation with the district superintendent and upon approval of the area General Superintendent, shall recommend to the district conference a specific call for four years or an extended call.

(5) **Special Regulations for Extended Call.** The General Superintendent shall review the call relationship with the district board of administration at least quadrennially. At the evaluation, the district board of administration shall either reaffirm by majority vote the extended call or shall, in consultation with the General Superintendent, announce a vote of the district conference for affirmation of continuing the call.

(6) **Ex Officio Duties.** The district superintendent is a ministerial member of the General Conference (325; 1503:1a), vice-chair of the district conference (350:3; 1120), chair of the district board of administration (1203; 1221), chair of the district board of ministerial development unless electing to appoint another to serve (1381), chair of the district board of evangelism and church growth unless electing to appoint another to serve (1416), chair of the district building committee (1345), chair of the district conference action committee when such is authorized (1165), unless electing to appoint another to serve, chair of the district conference nominating committee when such is authorized (1172) and an *ex officio* member of the district conventions and the district executive committees of Wesleyan Men (7155:2; 7160:1), Wesleyan Women (7365:1; 7375:1), Wesleyan Youth (7565:1; 7585:3a) and Young Adults International (7765:2; 7770:2, 4).

(7) **Vacancy.** Whenever the office of superintendent is vacated other than at district conference, the district board of administration, in consultation with the area General Superintendent, shall appoint an acting superintendent to serve until the next annual session of the district conference.

(8) **Special District Committee for Nominations.** Whenever a vacancy has resulted in the appointment of an acting superintendent, or whenever a district superintendent shall announce unavailability for continued service, a special district committee for nominations shall be formed with the area General Superintendent as chair, comprised of the members of the district board of administration, or by persons they choose. The special district committee for nominations shall screen and select persons believed to have the qualities needed for the office of district superintendent and present one or more nominees to the district conference session. The district conference shall elect in accordance with 1303:1, and shall not be limited to the persons nominated by the special committee on nominations.

**1307. Amenability.** The district superintendent is amenable, as provided in the Constitution, to the General Board for official duties and to the district conference for both official duties and moral character (323:1). The district superintendent may be removed from office by the General Board, by a two-thirds majority vote of all its members, for cause or whenever the General Board deems it necessary for the best interests of the Church and the preservation of the district (1655:36, 39a).

**1310. Duties.** The district superintendent shall administer this office in accord with *The Discipline* and any other official directives from the General Conference, the General Board, the Board of General Superintendents, the district conference and the district board of administration. The duties of the district superintendent are (cf. 1300; 1303:6):

### General

(1) To have the oversight of the Church within the district, endeavoring to lead the district forward in the fulfillment of the mission of The Wesleyan Church (100-105).

(2) To give special attention to the initiation and promotion of an aggressive program of evangelism and church growth, as approved by the district conference or the district board of administration (cf. 537; 510; 518; 1233:3, 19; 1413).

(3) To carry on a spiritual and inspirational ministry, teaching the people concerning the doctrines, purposes and programs of The Wesleyan Church, and promoting the interests of all the general departments and the district.

(4) To cooperate with the General Superintendent over the district (cf. 1935:8), the General Board and its Executive Board in the oversight of the district work and, in matters of district evangelism and church growth, with the General Director of Evangelism and Church Growth (1935:11; cf. 1233:3, 20; 1413).

(5) To assist the General Superintendent in presiding over the district conference, and to assist the representative appointed by the General Superintendent when the General Superintendent is unable to be present. If neither the General Superintendent nor a representative appointed by the General Superintendent is present, it is the duty of the district superintendent to preside or to take responsibility for the same (350:3; 1120).

### District Administration

(6) To be the chair of the district board of administration (1203; 1221), and to submit recommendations to the district board of administration that

will provide for a more efficient administration, correlation and advancement of the district work.

(7) To be the chair of the district board of ministerial development, or to appoint another to serve instead, subject to ratification by the district board of administration (1381); to be the chair of the district building committee (1345), to be the chair of the district conference action committee, when such a committee has been authorized, or to appoint the chair (1165), and to be the chair of the district conference nominating committee when such has been authorized (1172).

(8) To exercise administrative supervision over all district officials, departmental officers, boards (cf. 1416; 1452; 1496), committees, auxiliary organizations (cf. 7150; 7165:2; 7350; 7370:2, 7; 7565; 7770:1), missions, developing churches, churches, circuits, ministers and other workers (cf. 3260:2) of the district with the exception of those who are amenable only to the General Board for their official duties (323:1; 1180:12), and to see that the plans and policies of the general church and district are carried out.

(9) To meet with any district board, committee, auxiliary organization or other district agency at the discretion of the district superintendent, and make such recommendations as deemed advisable; and to counsel with the various officers, directors, employees and others serving the district concerning their work.

(10) To serve as an *ex officio* member of the district executive committees of Wesleyan Men, Wesleyan Women, Wesleyan Youth and Young Adults International (7160:1; 7365:1; 7565:1; 7770:1).

(11) To examine all written instruments and legal papers for the conveyance of property acquired by local churches (4700:5) or the district and to approve them as to their conformity with the requirements of *The Discipline* (4590-4880; cf. 4000-4070), the inclusion of the proper trust clause (4610), and conformity to local laws (4510); and to have the custody, under the direction of the district board of administration, of property and legal records for both the district and the local churches as provided for in 4760.

### Local Churches

(12) To visit, or to appoint the assistant district superintendent, if any, or other representative to visit, each church in the district at least once a year, or according to a schedule of visits approved by the district board of administration, making careful inquiry into the progress and administration of the church and seeking to advance its spiritual life, and to preserve a written report of such visits in the district office for future reference and for the successor in office.

(13) To investigate carefully concerning the support of pastors and to advise and encourage the local churches to provide for their adequate support.

(14) To recommend that the district board of administration authorize the establishment of a mission (537), a developing church (510), a church (518), the reclassification of a church (518:1); and to preside over the organization of an established church or appoint a representative to do so (520), and to report the organization of new churches to the district board of administration and to the district conference (520:6).

(15) To supervise and promote the development of a developing church, approving the reception of members (510:2; cf. 5100:2), appointing the local advisory council in cooperation with the pastor (510:3), and approving the plans of the pastor and the local advisory council in the interim of sessions of the district board of administration (510:3).

(16) To approve the date for the regular session of a local church conference (630:1-2), to preside over a local church conference whenever present (635), to convene, when deemed advisable, a local board of administration or a local church conference and preside over the same (633:1; 712; 722:2-3; 773) and carry out any other provisions for a local board of administration or conference as prescribed in *The Discipline*.

(17) To counsel with a local board of administration for the securing of a pastor (705:1-3), providing it with specific recommendations and names, and to carry out the provisions of *The Discipline* concerning the call, the renewal of a call, the review and termination of an extended call, the resignation and release of a pastor from the pastoral agreement and other matters pertaining to pastoral relations for the pastoral charges under district care (633:3; 692:2; 705:1-3; 710; 712; 718-722; 773).

(18) To approve the transfer of any ordained minister or commissioned or licensed minister from another district, in concurrence with the General Superintendent (313:6; 705:3; 1935:16; 3100:1) and, when objecting to such a transfer, to state any reasons if requested to do so.

(19) To recommend the removal of a pastor to the district board of administration, whenever the best interests of the church involved demand it, and to recommend to the district board of administration the appointment of a supply, if necessary, until another pastor has been obtained (712; 715; 722:3; 1233:31).

(20) To perform all the functions of a pastor for a local church within the district when such church is without a pastor, or to recommend to the district board of administration the appointment of a supply pastor until the local church obtains a pastor (1233:30, 38).

(21) To approve the employment of an evangelist or workers of another denomination for revivals or other meetings by a local church or any district

organization and, when objecting to such employment, to state any reasons if requested to do so (725:19; 782:17).

**Ministers**

(22) To counsel with the pastors, ministers and special workers under district care, giving special attention to the encouragement and guidance of candidates for the ministry.

(23) To be responsible, if the General Superintendent is absent, and if the representative appointed by the General Superintendent is absent (3091), for leading the Council of Ordination (1405) in conducting the ritual of ordination (3070:6; 5750-5792), and the ritual of commissioning a minister (5800-5845), a special worker (3470; 5855) and a lay missionary (3490; 5855); to sign with the district secretary such certificates, licenses or other official forms, as are required of this office and issued to such persons as are authorized by the district conference; to have charge of services for the installation of pastors (5905).

(24) To request any special reports from the pastors, ministers and churches that will facilitate oversight of the district.

(25) To approve in writing the temporary service of an ordained minister in a district other than the one in which membership is held (3100:2); to grant a letter of transfer or standing to any ordained, licensed or commissioned worker in good standing of the district (6440; 6460); to instruct the district secretary to enroll as a member of the district a minister who transfers from another district in the manner prescribed by *The Discipline* (313:6; 3100:1; 6440-6450), and to order the enrollment of a ministerial student or special worker so transferring (3015:3c, 5d; 3480; 6440-6450); and to guide a minister or special worker from another denomination seeking recognition and membership in The Wesleyan Church (3104; 3470; cf. 3117).

**Reports**

(26) To report annually to the district conference concerning official duties and personal ministry (1180:13), and to submit other reports to the General Board or its Executive Board, the Board of General Superintendents and the district board of administration as required; to counsel with the area General Superintendent at least once a year concerning the plans and objectives for the district, reporting to the General Superintendent on the activities of the district and progress toward its objectives during the past year (cf. 1935:8).

### Judicial

(27) To receive any complaint or accusation against any person or local unit under the jurisdiction of the district (5115:4; 5150:1-5; 5170:1, 3; 5185:1-2), and to give such complaint or accusation prompt and careful attention as required in the Judiciary (5170:1; 5185:1-2), and to refer any matter requiring official investigation or judicial proceedings to the district board of administration for disposition (1233:33, 36; cf. 5180:2; 5190).

(28) To forward to the General Secretary the credentials of a minister when such have been surrendered or removed by judicial process (1951; 3100:4; 3127; 5180:2).

## B. Assistant District Superintendent

**1320.** A district may have an assistant district superintendent as determined by majority vote of the district conference. In those districts where the district conference has voted to have an assistant district superintendent, the office shall be filled from among the ordained ministers of the district (1180:32) upon nomination by the district superintendent and election by the district board of administration. The qualifications, term of office, amenability and other regulations are those of a district official as set forth in 1255-1272.

**1323.** The duties of the assistant district superintendent, if any, are:

(1) To serve as member and vice-chair of the district board of administration, presiding over the board whenever the district superintendent is not present or when appointed to do so by the district superintendent (1221).

(2) To convene the district board of administration in times of emergency when the district superintendent is not able to act (1215).

(3) To serve as member of the district board of ministerial development (1378).

(4) To assist the district superintendent and to serve as a representative of the district superintendent to local churches or district organizations as the superintendent may request.

(5) To perform such other duties as may be required by the district conference or the district board of administration.

(6) To report annually to the district conference concerning all official duties (1180:13), and to the district board of administration as required.

**1327.** A district conference may choose to have the assistant district superintendent, if any, as a full-time district official, and shall further define the duties of the assistant district superintendent in addition to those set forth in *The Discipline*.

### C. District Secretary

**1330.** The district secretary shall be elected by the district conference by ballot and by majority vote (1180:33; cf. 1175:1). The qualifications, term of office, amenability and other regulations are those of a district official as defined in 1255-1272.

**1332.** The duties of the district secretary are:

(1) To be the secretary of the district conference, recording accurately and completely the proceedings of each session and forwarding sufficient copies to the General Secretary for distribution to the general offices and departments (cf. 1178:4).

(2) To serve as a member and as the secretary of the district board of administration (1203; 1224), recording accurately and completely the proceedings of each session and preserving them in permanent form, forwarding a copy of the minutes of each session to each member of the board and to the General Superintendent over the district.

(3) To issue official notices and communications from the district conference and from the district board of administration; and to keep permanent file copies of all correspondence, reports and other records.

(4) To issue and sign all certificates, licenses and other official forms as properly authorized by the district and as prescribed for a district secretary by the General Conference or General Board (1310:23).

(5) To forward promptly to the General Secretary: the statistical and financial reports of the district conference as may be required by the General Board; a certified list of the General Conference delegates, and the certification of an alternate when a delegate is unable to attend (1512-1518); a copy of each memorial adopted for presentation to the General Conference; a copy of the official district directory for inclusion in the denominational directory, and of each change in the directory as it occurs (1332:8); and to cooperate in forwarding other information to the General Secretary as the General Secretary may request.

(6) To be the custodian of the official district records and archives, except as otherwise provided for in *The Discipline* (1387; 4760), including the records of the district statistical committee (1352:3) and all district judicial committees (5159; 5175:4), and to be instructed by the district board of administration as to the exercise of such custody (1233:15).

(7) To receive an official copy of the minutes of each board, committee, auxiliary organization or other district agency, and to preserve them in the district archives.

(8) To maintain a complete and current district directory, listing the district officials, each district board or committee with the names of its members and officers, the district departmental officers (1275), the names

and addresses of each ordained minister, commissioned minister, licensed minister, ministerial student, commissioned and licensed special worker and commissioned lay missionary, the address of each mission, developing church, church, circuit and parsonage within the bounds of the district, and other information as desired (cf. 1240).

(9) To aid in collecting books, documents, photographs or other historical materials for the historical archives of the denomination in cooperation with the General Secretary (1948).

(10) To notify all churches and ministerial members of the district of the time and place of the next regular session of the district conference at least sixty days in advance (1112), and to notify them of any reconvened sessions as directed by the district board of administration (1115).

(11) To perform such other duties as may be required by the district conference or the district board of administration and as pertain to this office.

### D. District Treasurer

**1335.** The district treasurer shall be elected by the district conference, by ballot and by majority vote (1175:1; 1180:33), unless the district conference by prior action has voted to authorize the district board of administration to appoint the district treasurer. If the district conference authorizes the district board of administration to appoint the district treasurer, said appointment shall take place at the organizing session of the district board of administration immediately after the rise of the annual district conference (1209:2). The district treasurer shall serve as an ex officio member of the district board of administration and shall be a voting member of the district conference. Said treasurer's qualifications, term of office, amenability and other regulations are those of a district official as defined in 1255-1272.

**1337.** The duties of a district treasurer are:

(1) To serve as a member of the district board of administration (1203), and, when such has been authorized, as a member of the district conference action committee (1165).

(2) To be bonded to the amount set by the district board of administration, the cost of which shall be paid by the district (1233:17).

(3) To have custody of all district funds, unless otherwise provided for by *The Discipline*; to receive, record, hold and disburse such funds in keeping with the financial plans of the General Conference and the district conference and as directed by the district board of administration.

(4) To receive, record, and hold all USF funds for the general church raised within the district and to remit such funds monthly to the General Treasurer on the approved forms.

(5) To serve as a district director of stewardship, promoting stewardship and storehouse tithing on the district level, in cooperation with the general director of stewardship.

(6) To prepare and submit to the district board of administration, or to another committee if such has been designated by the district conference, a recommended plan to provide for the raising of the district obligation to the United Stewardship Fund, designating the amount to be assigned to each local church as its share of the district obligation, in accord with the regulations for the United Stewardship Fund (2015); which plan, as approved by the proper board or committee, shall be presented to the district conference for adoption (1180:16; 1233:10; cf. 1165-1168); and to promptly notify the General Treasurer of the district USF obligation on forms provided by the General Treasurer (cf. 2015:2).

(7) To submit all records and funds for an annual audit, after the close of the fiscal year, as provided for in 1340, and at any other time as may be requested by the district board of administration (1233:18).

(8) To submit a complete financial report of all funds administered or attended to by the district treasurer, to each regular session of the district conference (1180:13); to submit reports to the district board of administration (1233:11), the district superintendent and the General Treasurer as they may require.

(9) To perform such other duties as may be required by the district conference or the district board of administration and as pertain to this office.

### E. District Auditing Committee

**1340.** The district board of administration shall provide for the auditing of all district treasurers' books annually, either by an elected district auditing committee, or by employing a certified public accountant, chartered accountant or public accountant. Audits shall be conducted on the records and funds of the district treasurer (1337:8) and all other treasurers of district boards or agencies having custody of district funds. The audit reports shall be submitted to the district board of administration for adoption. After appropriate review, the district board of administration may submit the reports to the district conference or the respective district conventions of the auxiliaries as information. The district auditing committee, certified public accountant, chartered accountant or public accountant may perform such other duties as may be required by the district conference or the district board of administration.

### F. District Building Committee

**1345.** There shall be a district building committee elected by the district conference (1180:35a; cf. 1175:2), unless the district conference shall delegate the election to the district board of administration. The committee shall consist of the district superintendent as chair, and one or more ordained ministers as desired with an equal number of lay members. The elected members should be persons who are capable and experienced in property transactions and the construction of buildings. General regulations governing the membership of this committee are given in 1275-1292. The duties of the district building committee are:

(1) To investigate the proposed sites for local church buildings, parsonages or other units, in order to ascertain that such properties are properly located in the community to be served and adequate in size for future expansion and parking facilities; to consider also the plans and requirements of any metropolitan or urban planning commission, if such an agency exists; to consider also the financial plans and liabilities to be incurred; to act upon the proposal of the local church and to report its findings and recommendations in writing both to the district board of administration and the local church (cf. 4700-4720).

(2) To consider the proposal of a local church, on behalf of the church or a subsidiary of the church (655:13) for the:

(a) Purchase of land;

(b) Purchase of land and buildings;

(c) Construction of a new building;

(d) Addition to or remodeling of a building when the consequent costs are anticipated to be ten percent or more of the value of the current building.

(3) To advise the local church in detail concerning the architectural plans; to consider carefully the financial liability and the plans of the local church for meeting such liabilities; and to report its findings and recommendations in writing to the local church and the district board of administration (1233:32; cf. 4700-4720).

### G. District Statistical Committee

**1350.** Each district conference shall elect a district statistical committee of the desired number (1180:35b; cf. 1175:2), or the district conference may delegate this responsibility to the district board of administration. General regulations for the membership of this committee are given in 1275-1292.

**1352.** The duties of the district statistical committee are:

(1) To receive, on behalf of the district conference, complete annual statistical and financial reports from such persons, units and agencies as the General Board shall designate, on forms approved by the Board of General Superintendents (1920:16) and made available by the General Secretary; and to compile and submit to the district conference a comprehensive statistical and financial report for the district as a whole.

(2) To report to the district board of administration the name of each person who fails to submit the report in the proper manner and at the appointed time.

(3) To submit, after the committee has finished its work, all reports and records to the district secretary for filing.

### H. District Director of Church Periodicals

**1355.** Each district conference may elect a district director of Church periodicals, or the district conference may delegate this responsibility to the district board of administration. The qualifications, term of office, amenability and other regulations are those of a district departmental official as defined in 1275-1292. The duties of the district director of Church periodicals are:

(1) To secure and maintain the names and addresses of the local directors of Church periodicals.

(2) To assist the pastor and the local director of Church periodicals in securing subscriptions.

(3) To assist the editors of the Church periodicals in securing subscriptions.

(4) To submit an annual report of official activities to the district conference, a copy of which shall be forwarded to the General Director of Communications (1180:13).

### I. District Board of Trustees

**1360.** The district conference of each established district shall be incorporated or shall cause a corporation to be formed and maintained to facilitate the management of its legal and corporate affairs as set forth in 4100-4150. In places where local laws prohibit such incorporation, or where the local laws require property to be held by trustees, the district conference may elect from among the members of the district board of administration the members of the district board of trustees in such number as desired (1180:22; cf. 4855). The district trustees shall hold office until their term expires as members of the district board of administration and until their successors are elected and qualified. The district board of trustees shall be amenable to the district board of administration (cf. 4840). A district trustee may be removed from office by a two-thirds majority vote of all the members of the district board of administration whenever it is deemed necessary for the best interests of The Wesleyan Church and the district or whenever a trustee shall refuse to carry out the directions of the district board of administration, except when such directions are contrary to local laws or to *The Discipline* (1206; 1233:27a; 1265; 4540). The office of a district trustee may also become vacant by death, cessation of membership in The Wesleyan Church or cessation of membership on the district board of administration. A vacancy on the district board of trustees shall be filled for the unexpired term by a majority vote of all the members of the district board of administration (1206; 1233:27a; 1272).

**1365.** The district board of trustees shall administer its duties in accord with *The Discipline* (4500-4630; 4830-4880), and as directed by the district board of administration. Its duties are:

(1) To hold all district property, and such local property as may be held by the district (4660; 4680), in trust for The Wesleyan Church as set forth in 4830 (cf. 323:8).

(2) To attend to all legal matters pertaining to the district transactions for the purchase, sale, encumbrance, transfer or other disposal of property, as ordered by the district board of administration (cf. 4840).

(3) To fulfill such other duties as pertain to their office as trustees and as may be assigned to them by the district board of administration.

### J. District Board of Review

**1370.** Each established district shall have a district board of review, which shall consist of four ordained ministers and three lay members elected annually by the district board of administration (1233:25; 5159). Two ordained ministers and two lay members shall also be elected at the same time to serve as alternates and to fill vacancies in the order of their election (5159). The district board of review serves as an appellate body for lay members and local churches and has original jurisdiction over charges or complaints proffered against local churches. The duties and powers of the district board of review are set forth in the Judiciary (5159-5162). General regulations governing the members of the district board of review are set forth in 1275-1292.

# Chapter VI

## DISTRICT MINISTERIAL SUPERVISION

### A. District Board of Ministerial Development

**1375. Function.** There shall be a district board of ministerial development which shall be responsible for the examination and recommendation to the district conference of all candidates for ordination, license, commission, ministerial study, restoration or transfer from another denomination.

**1378. Membership.** The board shall consist of the district superintendent, the assistant district superintendent, if any, and, in addition, the district board of administration shall elect as many additional members as deemed sufficient. At least two members shall be from among the laity, and the ministerial members shall be ordained. The term of office for the elected members shall be for three years, with the election so arranged that approximately one third shall be elected each year. General regulations for the members of this board are defined in 1275-1292.

**1381. Organization.** The district superintendent shall be the chair unless electing to appoint another to serve instead, with such appointment subject to ratification by the district board of administration. The board shall annually elect a vice-chair and a secretary. The board may divide into smaller groups and apportion the work among them as deemed necessary, provided that all recommendations of the board to the district conference shall be adopted by the full board.

**1384. Sessions.** The board shall be convened by the chair in sufficient time before the opening of the district conference to enable the board to complete its work in a careful and thorough manner, and shall meet at other times as deemed necessary upon the call of the chair.

**1387. Records.** The secretary of the district board of ministerial development shall keep suitable and permanent records which shall be the property of the district and shall be preserved as directed by the district superintendent and the district board of administration. The secretary of the board shall keep:

(1) A correct and complete journal of the proceedings of the board meetings, an official copy of which shall be submitted to the district secretary for permanent filing (1332:7).

(2) A record of the ministerial studies and training of each licentiate and ministerial student, including the work done in a university, college, theological school or by correspondence with the Ministerial Study Course

Agency. A record of all credits earned shall be recorded at least once each year in cooperation with the Ministerial Study Course Agency as set forth in 2388:1, and shall be available to the board in considering its recommendations to the district conference.

(3) A personnel record of each ordained, licensed or commissioned member of the district, on forms as authorized by the General Board, including: important personal and family information; educational qualifications; ministerial service including pastoral and other district appointments, offices held and credentials issued by the district. Whenever a letter of transfer is granted, a transcript of the personnel record shall be provided, if requested, but the record shall remain in the permanent files of the district.

**1390. Duties.** The duties of the district board of ministerial development shall be:

### Related to Ordination, Commissions, Licenses and Ministerial Students

(1) To examine carefully (cf. 1935:15) each candidate for election by the district conference to ordination or election to a commissioned minister's status, the granting of a district ministerial license, a license as a ministerial student, a commission or license as special worker, a commission as a lay missionary and any other commission or license as may be authorized by *The Discipline*: The examination shall include an interview with each candidate, making such investigation as is deemed necessary to affirm the individual's:

(a) Personal experience of salvation and entire sanctification;

(b) Full commitment to the Articles of Religion, Membership Commitments, Elementary Principles and polity of The Wesleyan Church and acceptance of its authority;

(c) Evidence of having the qualifications for the ministry to which the candidate feels called as set forth in *The Discipline*;

and shall result in recommendations to the district conference for those whom the district board of ministerial development judges to be qualified for said ministry (cf. 1381; 1390:5).

(2) To consider each person recommended by a local church conference (655:8) or circuit conference (528:2) or local board of administration (655:8) for the granting of a license as a ministerial student (1240:IV; 3015:1) and to recommend to the district conference for such license those who are deemed worthy (1180:29b, c; cf. 3350:2); to encourage all such ministerial students to enroll for ministerial training in an approved school of The Wesleyan Church (2365; 2382); to supervise and counsel them,

keeping a record of their ministerial studies (1387:2) and cooperating with the director of the Ministerial Study Course Agency in supervising those enrolled in courses under the Agency (2388; cf. 3170-3210).

(3) To consider and examine any person who desires to be received into the district from another denomination, and to be recognized as an ordained, commissioned or licensed minister or commissioned special worker and to recommend to the district conference for reception as in process of transfer, and subsequently for recognition as in full standing, only such a person as it deems properly qualified according to *The Discipline* (cf. 3104, 3470); and, in the interim of district conference sessions, to make such recommendation to the district board of administration (1233:36).

(4) To consider and examine any person applying for restoration of ordination, commission or license and to recommend to the district conference only such a person as it deems properly qualified according to *The Discipline* (cf. 3120-3148; 3480).

(5) To present to the district conference, as a separate report, a recommendation for the election of a candidate to ordination as an ordained minister (1180:28; cf. 3070.5) or commission as a minister (3059) or the reinstatement or restoration of ministerial credentials and to present to the district conference a combined report of all other recommendations concerning the commissioning, licensing, and recognition of ministers and special workers and the licensing of ministerial students (1180:29; 3015:1).

(6) To serve, with the exception of the lay members, and when so designated by the district conference (1180:34; cf. 1233:37), as a council of ordination (1405); and to perform such other duties as may be assigned by the district conference.

### Related to the Annual Service Reports

(7) To receive, on behalf of the district conference, a written annual service report (1402) from each ordained, commissioned or licensed minister, ministerial student, and commissioned or licensed special worker; to review such reports and pass on each one as follows (cf. 1180:30):

(a) A report which shows that the work has been done according to *The Discipline* and that the annual statistical report (1352:1) has been properly submitted shall be marked as approved and returned to the person submitting it (cf. 1390:9).

(b) A report in which there are unsatisfactory answers, or which shows that the work has not been done according to *The Discipline*, or that the annual statistical report (1352:1) has not been properly submitted, shall be reviewed with the person submitting the report. If reasons for such irregularities are not satisfactory to the district board of ministerial development, the report shall be marked as unsatisfactory and returned to the person submitting it (cf. 1390:9).

(8) To investigate the reason for the failure to submit an annual service report on the part of those persons required to do so (1402; 3015:4), and to take appropriate action as set forth in 3040:1; 3059:4c; 3089:3; 3460; and 3470.

(9) To present a report (cf. 1381) to the district conference concerning the results of the examination of the annual service reports, listing all members of the district responsible to submit such reports as to whether their reports were approved, unsatisfactory or not received. The district board of ministerial development shall report to the district conference concerning a person whose annual service report has been found unsatisfactory (1390:7b) and it shall require a two-thirds vote of confidence by the district conference to approve such a person for continued appointment.

**Related to Appointments and District Conference Relations**

(10) To submit reports to the district board of administration concerning the following matters related to district conference appointments and relations: The results of the examination of the annual service reports (1390:8-9); the availability for appointment, and any desired changes in appointment or district conference relations, as recorded on the annual service reports; those persons qualified for a district ministerial license, the granting of which shall become effective upon their appointment (1180:26c, 29b; 1233:9; cf. 3033:7; 3040:3); those other persons qualified for a license, commission, reception from another district or denomination or restoration (1180:26, 29; 1233:9).

**Related to Ministerial Development**

(11) To cooperate with the district superintendent (1310:22) and the district board of administration (1233:28) in providing opportunities for the personal and professional growth of ministers within the district. The activities of the district boards of ministerial development may include individual or group interviews, assessments, growth contracts, seminars or other means of assisting ministers to achieve their full potential for ministry.

### B. Annual Service Reports

**1402. Annual Service Reports.** The district conference shall receive an annual service report from each ordained minister, commissioned minister, licensed minister, ministerial student and commissioned or licensed special worker on forms authorized by the Board of General Superintendents (1920:16) and made available by the General Secretary. Pastors or senior pastors shall submit the "Pastor's Annual Service Report." Associate and assistant pastors shall submit the "Associate/Assistant Pastor's Annual Service Report." Other ordained ministers and commissioned or licensed ministers shall submit the "Minister's Annual Service Report." Special workers shall submit the "Lay Worker's Annual Service Report." Ministerial students shall submit the "Ministerial Student's Annual Service Report." All such reports shall be submitted to the district board of ministerial development, serving on behalf of the district conference, as directed by the district board of administration or the district superintendent (1390:7-9).

### C. Council of Ordination

**1405.** Each district shall provide for a Council of Ordination to assist the General Superintendent (1935:15; 5752), or, in the absence of the General Superintendent the representative appointed by the General Superintendent (3091), or in the absence of the appointed representative, the district superintendent (1310:23), in carrying out the will of the district conference for the ordination of ministers (3070:6; 5750-5792) and the commissioning of ministers (5805), special workers (5850) and lay missionaries (5850). The Council of Ordination may consist of the desired number of ordained ministers appointed by the district board of administration (1233:37), or the district conference may designate the ordained ministers of the district board of ministerial development as the Council of Ordination (1180:34; 1390:6). The Council of Ordination will be responsible to plan the ordination and/or commissioning services.

## Chapter VII

## DISTRICT MISSIONS AND EVANGELISM

### A. District Coordination of Missions and Evangelism

**1410.** The district board of administration shall be responsible within the district for the promotion of world missions, general and district evangelism and church growth and the coordination of Wesleyan Men and Wesleyan Women on the district level as set forth in *The Discipline* (1233:3, 20-24).

### B. District Board of Evangelism and Church Growth

**1413. Function.** The district board of administration shall serve as or shall establish a district board of evangelism and church growth to aid the district superintendent and the district board of administration in developing, supervising and promoting an aggressive program of district evangelism and church growth (1233:20; 1310:2).

**1416. Membership.** If a separate district board of evangelism and church growth is established, it shall have as its chair the district superintendent (cf. 1310:2), unless the district superintendent shall appoint another to serve instead, with such appointment subject to ratification by the district board of administration. In addition to the chair, the board shall consist of two or more ordained ministers and an equal number of lay members elected by the district board of administration who are especially concerned and qualified for this phase of the church's mission. In addition, the district director of evangelism and church growth shall serve as an *ex officio* member (1426). The term of office for the elected members shall be for two years, with the election so arranged that approximately one-half shall be elected each year. Other than the chair, the board shall elect its own officers. General regulations governing the members of this board are set forth in 1275-1292.

**1420. Sessions.** The district board of evangelism and church growth shall meet soon after the close of the district conference to make plans for the year and shall meet for regular sessions as it shall decide or the district board of administration shall order. Special sessions may be called by the chair as needed.

**1423. Duties.** The duties of the district board of evangelism and church growth shall be:

(1) To study potential fields for district extension work and report on and make recommendations to the district board of administration concerning the same.

(2) To stimulate interest in district evangelism and church growth throughout the district to help raise the funds needed for the district church growth program.

(3) To make recommendations to the district board of administration concerning the establishment of a mission, developing church or church, the appointment of pastors for the same, and real estate transactions and building projects connected with church growth projects (cf. 1233:29, 31-32).

(4) To assume direct supervision of the district church growth program or a specific church growth project to the extent delegated by the district board of administration.

(5) To perform other duties as may be required by the district board of administration in the interest of district evangelism and church growth.

### C. District Director of Evangelism and Church Growth

**1426.** A district director of evangelism and church growth shall be elected by the district conference (1180:35; cf. 1175:2), unless the district conference by prior action has voted to authorize the district board of administration to appoint the district director of evangelism and church growth, and is an *ex officio* member of the district board of evangelism and church growth (1416). The term of office, amenability and other requirements as a district departmental officer are set forth in 1275-1292. The duties of the district director of evangelism and church growth are:

(1) To report the election or appointment promptly to the General Director of Evangelism and Church Growth and to cooperate with the General Director of Evangelism and Church Growth in promoting the interests of general evangelism and church growth; and likewise to promote the interests of the district program of evangelism and church growth.

(2) To make a general plan of activities for the year and submit it to the district board of administration for approval.

(3) To assist the district superintendent in arranging for deputational work within the district by representatives of the General Department of Evangelism and Church Growth.

(4) To assist the district superintendent in planning and conducting special services in the interests of general or district evangelism and church growth at the district conference or campmeeting; to arrange for promotional displays and the distribution of literature at district or zone meetings.

(5) To assist pastors in promoting evangelism and church growth in the local churches.

(6) To promote membership in the Church Builders' Club.

(7) To keep a record of activities, reports and correspondence and to submit it to the successor in office.

(8) To submit an annual report of official activities to the district conference (1180:13), including a financial report of expenses and a report of what has been accomplished in the district for general and district evangelism and church growth, a copy of which shall be forwarded to the General Director of Evangelism and Church Growth; and to submit other reports as may be requested (cf. 1288).

(9) To perform other duties in the interest of general and district evangelism and church growth as may be required by the district conference, the district board of administration or the district board of evangelism and church growth.

### D. District Director of World Missions

**1429.** A district director of world missions shall be elected by the district conference (1180:35; cf. 1175:2), unless the district conference by prior action has voted to authorize the district board of administration to appoint the district director of world missions. The term of office, amenability and other requirements as a district departmental officer are set forth in 1275-1292. The duties of the district director of world missions are:

(1) To report the election or appointment promptly to the General Director of World Missions and to cooperate with the General Director of World Missions in promoting an interest in and a burden for world missions outreach within the district.

(2) To make a general plan of activities for the year and submit it to the district board of administration for approval (cf. 1410).

(3) To assist the district superintendent in arranging for deputational work within the district by representatives of the General Department of World Missions.

(4) To assist the district superintendent in planning and conducting special services in the interests of world missions at the district conference or campmeeting; to arrange for promotional displays and the distribution of literature at district or zone meetings.

(5) To assist pastors in planning for world missions conventions and in promoting world missions in the local church.

(6) To keep a record of all activities, reports and correspondence and to submit this to the successor in office.

(7) To submit an annual report of official activities to the district conference (1180:13), including a financial report of expenses and a report of what has been accomplished by the district for world missions, a copy of

which shall be forwarded to the General Director of World Missions; and to submit other reports as may be requested (cf. 1288).

(8) To perform other duties in the interest of world missions outreach as may be requested by the district conference or the district board of administration.

### E. District Board of World Missions

**1430. Function**. The district board of administration shall serve as or shall establish a district board of world missions to aid the district board of administration in developing, supervising and promoting an aggressive program of district participation in The Wesleyan Church's program of world evangelism.

**1432. Membership**. If a separate district board of world missions is established, it shall have as its chair the district superintendent, unless the district superintendent shall appoint a chair subject to ratification by the district board of administration. In addition to the chair, an equal number of ordained ministers and lay members shall be elected to two-year terms, with terms so arranged that approximately one-half shall be elected each year. The district board of administration shall determine the size of the board. The district director of world missions, district director of Wesleyan Women and the district president of Wesleyan Men shall be *ex officio* members. General regulations governing the membership of this board are set forth in 1275-1292.

**1434. Sessions**. The district board of world missions shall meet soon after the close of the district conference to make plans for the year and shall meet for regular sessions as deemed necessary or as directed by the district board of administration. Special sessions may be called by the chair as needed.

**1435. Duties**. The district board of world missions is amenable to the district board of administration in fulfilling the following duties:

(1) To develop yearly and long-range plans for the promotion of world missions within the district.

(2) To stimulate interest in and increase awareness of Wesleyan World Missions throughout the district.

(3) To build a strong prayer base for world missions.

(4) To promote increased financial support of world missions.

(5) To assist pastors in developing local church programs for promotion of and participation in missions.

(6) To emphasize the call to missions service and encourage those in preparation for such service.

(7) To perform other duties as may be required by the district board of administration in the interest of world missions.

### F. District President of Wesleyan Men

**1437.** The district president of Wesleyan Men (7165:2) is a nonvoting member of the district conference unless he is a voting member by some other right (1090:8). He shall submit all plans for Wesleyan Men to the district board of administration for approval (1233:23). In the interim of district board of administration sessions, such plans may be approved by the district superintendent. He shall endeavor to guide the district activities of Wesleyan Men toward soul-winning, service, stewardship and fellowship in a coordinated effort to forward the district program.

### G. District Director of Wesleyan Women

**1439.** The district director of Wesleyan Women is a nonvoting member of the district conference (7370:2) unless she is a voting member by some other right (1090:8). She shall submit all district plans for Wesleyan Women to the district board of administration for approval (1233:24). In the interim of district board of administration sessions, such plans may be approved by the district superintendent. She shall endeavor to guide the district activities of Wesleyan Women into soul-winning, evangelism, pioneer work and concern for world outreach in a coordinated effort to forward the district program.

# Chapter VIII

# DISTRICT CHRISTIAN EDUCATION

## A. District Board of Christian Education

**1440. Function.** The district board of administration shall serve as or shall establish a district board of Christian education, which shall endeavor to develop, supervise, correlate and promote a comprehensive district program of Christian education, viewing Christian education as a total process, dealing with the whole person, aiming at a fully coordinated educational program in harmony with the objectives for Christian education as set forth in 2300:1-7 (cf. 1233:21).

**1443. Membership.** If a separate district board of Christian education is established, it shall have as its chair a person elected by the district board of administration. General regulations governing other members of this board are set forth in 1275-1292. Additional members shall be chosen in one of the following ways:

(1) **Supervision Option.** The district board of administration shall elect two or more ordained ministers and an equal number of lay members to serve with the chair as the district board of Christian education.

(2) **Coordination Option.** The district board of Christian education shall consist of the chair elected by the district board of administration (1233:21), the district director of Christian education (1460), the district director of Sunday schools (1483), the district director of leadership training (1486), the district director of Christian Youth Clubs International (1489), the district president of Wesleyan Youth (1492; 7565:1a), the district director of Young Adults International (1494; 7770:1), the district president of Wesleyan Men (7165:2), the district director of Wesleyan Women (7370:2), the district coordinator of Wesleyan Kids for Missions (7370:7), the district educational director (1496) and such members-at-large as the district board of administration shall elect.

**1446. Organization.** The district board of administration shall elect a chair of the district board of Christian education. The board shall otherwise organize itself, elect its own officers, and may elect an executive committee for ad interim business (cf. 1440).

**1449. Sessions.** The district board of Christian education shall meet soon after the close of the district conference to make plans for the year and shall meet for regular sessions as it shall determine, provided that not less than two sessions shall be held each year. Special sessions may be called by the chair as deemed necessary.

**1452. Amenability.** The district board of Christian education shall be an advisory and coordinating body, and shall be amenable to the district board of administration. All plans of the board shall be approved by the district board of administration (1233:21) or, in the interim of its sessions, by the district superintendent (1310:8), before their implementation.

**1455. Duties.** The duties and powers of the district board of Christian education are:

(1) To develop, supervise and coordinate the work of Christian education within the district; to review and coordinate plans of each director and agency, including the district director of Christian education, the district Sunday school committee, the district Sunday school director, the district director of leadership training, the district WY president, the district director of CYCI, the district director of YAI, the district educational director and others that may be appointed for Christian education activities in the district, which shall subsequently be submitted to the district board of administration for approval (cf. 1452).

(2) To receive reports from the various district directors and secretaries of the board and to advise them concerning their work, assisting each district agency to maintain an effective program for its particular phase of Christian education.

(3) To advise and assist the district directors in implementing the plans and programs of the general departments which they represent within the district.

(4) To be responsible for the planning and supervision of the summer camps for children and youth; to submit detailed plans for such camps to the district board of administration for their approval; and to carry out the approved plans.

(5) To promote the interests of the educational institutions of The Wesleyan Church, particularly the general educational institutions in the area of which the district is a part, and to see that they are represented in the various youth camps and conventions as deemed appropriate.

(6) To present recommendations to the district board of administration and to the district conference for the growth of the work through the various ministries of Christian education, and for the financial plans and other interests of the work under their care.

(7) To nominate a district director of Christian education as set forth in 1460; to define the duties of the district director of Christian education in addition to what is set forth in *The Discipline* and to supervise the activities of the district director of Christian Education.

(8) To nominate to the district board of administration the members-at-large for the district Sunday school committee (1471; cf. 1233:19).

(9) To perform such other duties related to Christian education as are assigned by the district conference or the district board of administration.

### B. District Director of Christian Education

**1460.** The district conference may employ or may authorize the district board of administration to employ a district director of Christian education (1180:37) who shall in the latter case be nominated by the district board of Christian education (1233:22; 1455:7). The term of office, amenability and other regulations as a district departmental officer are set forth in 1275-1292, except that when the district director of Christian education is employed by the district board of administration that board shall have authority to determine the term of office.

**1463.** The duties of a district director of Christian education shall be (cf. 1460):

(1) To promptly report the election to the General Director of Sunday School and Discipleship Ministries, the General Director of Youth and the General Director of Education and the Ministry, and to cooperate with them in implementing and promoting the policies and programs of the general departments within the district.

(2) To serve as the executive secretary of the district board of Christian education, if so appointed by the district board of administration (cf. 1440-1443), helping to coordinate the total program of Christian education within the district, and serving as a resource person in advising and assisting the various educational leaders in their particular phase of the work.

(3) To assume, as assigned by the district conference (1180:37), the duties of the district director of leadership training, the district Sunday school director, the district CYCI director, the district director of YAI, the district educational director and the promotional duties of the district WY president.

(4) To visit the churches of the district in such order and manner as the district superintendent shall approve, assisting pastors, Sunday school superintendents, CYCI directors, WY presidents and other educational leaders.

(5) To serve as director of the summer camping program to the extent recommended by the district board of Christian education and approved by the district board of administration (cf. 1455:4).

(6) To promote the interests of the general educational institutions within the area, helping to recruit students and to promote the raising of funds.

(7) To submit an annual report of official activities to the district conference (1180:13), including a financial report of expenses and a report of what has been accomplished by the district for Christian education, a copy of

which shall be forwarded to the General Directors of Sunday School and Discipleship Ministries, Youth, and Education and the Ministry; and to submit other reports as may be requested (cf. 1288).

(8) To keep a file of correspondence and other records, and to submit the same to the successor in office.

(9) To perform other duties in the interests of Christian education as may be assigned by the district conference, the district board of administration or the district board of Christian education.

### C. District Sunday School Committee

**1468. Function.** The district Sunday school committee is responsible for those phases of Christian education within the bounds of the district as assigned to the General Department of Sunday School and Discipleship Ministries in 2305, with particular emphasis on the Sunday school work and leadership training.

**1471. Membership.** Each district may have a district Sunday school committee which shall be composed of the district Sunday school director as chair (1483), the district director of leadership training (if any, 1486) and from one to three additional members-at-large as decided upon and elected by the district board of administration (1209:3; cf. 1233:19; 1455:8). Whenever the duties of either the district director of leadership training or the district Sunday school director are assigned to the district director of Christian education (1463:3), the district director of Christian education shall be an *ex officio* member of the Sunday school committee. General regulations for the members of the Sunday school committee are set forth in 1275-1292.

**1474. Organization.** The district Sunday school director shall be the chair, and the committee shall elect a recording secretary who shall record the proceedings of committee meetings (cf. 1332:7) and keep a permanent file of records and reports. The committee may also elect a vice-chair and a treasurer, if deemed necessary.

**1477. Amenability.** The district Sunday school committee shall be amenable to the district board of Christian education and through that board to the district board of administration, in all matters of district organization and program. All committee plans shall be submitted to the district board of Christian education for review and coordination, and subsequently to the district board of administration for approval (cf. 1452). In matters pertaining to Sunday school organization, philosophy, curriculum and objectives the committee shall carry out their work in accord with *The Discipline* and the directives of the General Department of Sunday School and Discipleship Ministries.

**1480. Duties.** The duties of the district Sunday school committee are:

(1) To promote and encourage the Sunday school work of the district, seeking to carry out the objectives of The Wesleyan Church for Christian education as set forth in 2300:1-7 (cf. 1468).

(2) To emphasize evangelism and soul-winning in the Sunday schools, seeking the conversion of every scholar and their enrollment in the church and promoting outreach through the establishing of branch Sunday schools.

(3) To implement the plans and policies of the General Department of Sunday School and Discipleship Ministries and to assist pastors and Sunday school superintendents in doing the same.

(4) To make recommendations to the district board of Christian education for a more efficient administration, correlation and advancement of Sunday school work (cf. 1468).

(5) To see that a Sunday school has been organized in each church, and to assist each Sunday school to meet the approved standard of achievement.

(6) To plan for Sunday school and leadership training rallies, conventions, institutes or workshops on a district, zone or local level; to arrange for special services or promotional displays at zone or district meetings; submitting all such plans to the district board of Christian education for review and coordination, and subsequently to the district board of administration for approval (cf. 1452).

(7) To assist pastors and local Sunday school officers in the organization of leadership training classes and programs.

(8) To submit recommendations for Sunday school work, including the financial plans for Sunday school promotion, to the district board of Christian education for review and coordination, and subsequently to the district board of administration for approval (cf. 1452).

(9) To encourage the use of The Wesleyan Church curriculum materials.

(10) To perform other duties in harmony with its responsibility as may be assigned to it by the district conference, the district board of administration or the district board of Christian education.

### D. District Director of Sunday Schools

**1483.** A district director of Sunday schools shall be elected by the district conference (1180:38; cf. 1175:2), or these duties shall be assigned to the district director of Christian education (1180:37; 1463:3), unless the district conference by prior action has voted to authorize the district board of administration (1180:38) to appoint the district director of Sunday schools. The district director of Sunday schools shall be chair of the district Sunday school committee. The term of office, amenability and other regulations as a district departmental officer are set forth in 1275-1292. The duties of the district director of Sunday schools are:

(1) To promptly report the election or appointment to the General Director of Sunday School and Discipleship Ministries and to cooperate with the General Director of Sunday School and Discipleship Ministries in implementing and promoting the plans and policies of the General Department of Sunday School and Discipleship Ministries within the district.

(2) To serve as chair of the district Sunday school committee, providing leadership to the committee for the Sunday school work of the district; to present all plans and recommendations of the committee to the district board of Christian education for review and coordination (1455:1), and subsequently to the district board of administration for approval (cf. 1452).

(3) To cooperate with and assist the pastors and local Sunday school superintendents in the organization and advancement of their Sunday schools according to the approved standard and in reaching the goals set by the general church and the district conference.

(4) To keep a file of correspondence and other records and to submit it to the successor in office.

(5) To submit an annual report to the district conference (1180:13) concerning official activities, the work of the district Sunday school committee and a complete statistical report for the Sunday schools; and to submit other reports as may be requested (cf. 1288).

(6) To increase the personal qualifications and capacity for Sunday school and Christian education work by attending denominational and other approved Sunday school conventions, conferences and seminars, and through correspondence courses, and periodicals as time permits and opportunity affords.

(7) To conduct any special Sunday school services or programs, or to arrange for promotional displays at the district conference, campmeeting and other district gatherings.

(8) To give leadership to the district program of family ministries and the coordination of local church family ministries in cooperation with the program of the General Department of Sunday School and Discipleship Ministries.

(9) To perform such other duties in harmony with the other responsibilities of this office, as may be assigned by the district conference, the district board of administration or the district board of Christian education (cf. 1486).

## E. District Director of Leadership Training

**1486.** A district conference may elect a district director of leadership training (1180:38; cf. 1175:2), or the district conference may assign these duties to the district director of Christian education (1180:37; 1463:3). If the district does not have a district director of Christian education and also chooses not to have a district director of leadership training, the duties of the district director of leadership training shall be assigned by the district conference to the district Sunday school director (1483:9). The district director of leadership training shall be a member of the district Sunday school committee (1471). The term of office, amenability and other regulations as a district departmental officer are set forth in 1275-1292. The duties of the district director of leadership training are:

(1) To be responsible for the district program of leadership training under the General Department of Sunday School and Discipleship Ministries; to report at once after the election to the General Director of Sunday School and Discipleship Ministries and to cooperate with the General Director of Sunday School and Discipleship Ministries in the implementation and promotion of leadership training within the district.

(2) To be certified as a director of leadership training.

(3) To formulate plans with the district Sunday school committee for leadership training rallies, institutes, conventions or seminars on a district, zone or local church level; and to submit such plans to the district board of Christian education for review and coordination (1455:1) and subsequently to the district board of administration for approval (cf. 1452).

(4) To assist pastors and local church directors of Christian education in conducting classes or setting up effective programs of leadership training in the local church.

(5) To keep a permanent record of correspondence and other plans and to submit them to the successor in office.

(6) To conduct any special services or to arrange for promotional displays on leadership training at the district conference, campmeeting and other district gatherings.

(7) To submit an annual report to the district conference (1180:13) regarding all official activities and the progress of leadership training within the district, including a statistical report; and to submit other reports as may be requested (cf. 1288).

(8) To perform such other duties, in harmony with the other responsibilities of this office, as may be assigned by the district conference, the district board of administration or the district board of Christian education.

## F. District Director of Christian Youth Clubs International

**1489.** There shall be a district director of Christian Youth Clubs International elected by the district conference (1180:38; cf. 1175:2), or these duties shall be assigned to the district director of Christian education (1180:37; 1463:3). The district director of CYCI shall be a nonvoting member of the district conference (1090:8). The term of service, amenability and other regulations as a district departmental officer are set forth in 1275-1292. The duties of the district director of CYCI are:

(1) To promptly report the election to the General Director of CYCI, and to cooperate with the General Director of CYCI in developing and promoting the program and policies for children and youth under the CYCI organization within the district.

(2) To serve as a member of the district board of Christian education, if so appointed by the district board of administration (cf. 1443); and to work with that board for a coordinated program of all the various phases of Christian education throughout the district (cf. 1452; 1455:1).

(3) To work with pastors and local CYCI directors in establishing and maintaining effective CYCI organizations; and to help pastors and local workers to become certified as CYCI directors.

(4) To be responsible for CYCI district rallies and CYCI activities or events or to arrange for promotional displays, at the district conference, campmeeting, summer camps and other district gatherings.

(5) To submit an annual report to the district conference (1180:13) regarding official activities and the progress of CYCI in the district, including a statistical report; and to submit other reports as may be requested (cf. 1288).

(6) To perform such other duties related to CYCI as may be assigned by the district conference, the district board of administration or the district board of Christian education.

## G. District President of Wesleyan Youth

**1492.** There may be a district president of Wesleyan Youth who shall be a nonvoting member of the district conference unless the district president of Wesleyan Youth is a voting member by some other right (1090:8; 7565:1a; 7575:2k). The district president of Wesleyan Youth shall coordinate all plans for WY with the district board of Christian education and submit them to the district board of administration for approval. In the interim of district board of administration sessions, such plans may be approved by the district superintendent. The district president of Wesleyan Youth shall endeavor to guide the district activities of WY in accord with the purpose and mission of

WY (7505), and in a coordinated effort to forward the district program of Christian education.

### H. District Director of Young Adults International

**1494.** The Young Adults International district director is elected by the annual YAI district convention as set forth in 7770:4 and is a nonvoting member of the district conference unless the Young Adults International district director is a voting member by some other right (1090:8). The YAI constitutions are set forth in paragraphs 7700 through 7840.

### I. District Educational Director

**1496.** The district educational director may be appointed by the district superintendent after discussing potential candidates with the president(s) of the educational institution(s) serving that district's educational area, or the district board of administration may assign such duties to a district director of Christian education (1180:37, 38). The district educational director's term of office, amenability and other regulations as a district departmental officer are set forth in 1275-1292. The duties of the district educational director are:

(1) To promptly report the election to the General Director of Education and the Ministry and to cooperate with the General Director of Education and the Ministry in promoting the interests of the educational institutions of The Wesleyan Church, and particularly the general educational institutions in the area of which the district is a part.

(2) To assist the district superintendent and to cooperate with the general educational institutions within the area to which the district is assigned in formulating plans for deputational work within the district (cf. 2050:3), submitting all plans to the district superintendent for approval.

(3) To represent the educational institutions, or to arrange for such representation, at the summer camps, conventions and other appropriate occasions, including promotional displays and the distribution of literature, as directed by the district board of Christian education and approved by the officers in charge of the meetings.

(4) To assist the district superintendent in planning and conducting special services for promoting the interests of the general educational institutions during the district conference, campmeeting and other district gatherings, arranging for promotional displays and the distribution of literature if desired, and cooperating with representatives of the educational institutions in such plans.

(5) To encourage young people to attend the schools of The Wesleyan Church, notifying such institutions of any prospective students and encouraging all pastors to do the same.

(6) To submit an annual report to the district conference (1180:13) concerning all official activities and the support given by the district for the general educational institutions, including the number of students enrolled in the educational institutions of The Wesleyan Church; and to submit other reports as may be requested (cf. 1288).

(7) To perform such other duties in harmony with the other responsibilities of this office, as may be assigned by the district conference, the district board of administration or the district board of Christian education.

# PART IV

# GENERAL CHURCH GOVERNMENT

## Chapter I

## GENERAL CONFERENCE

### A. Function

**1500.** The General Conference is the supreme governing body of The Wesleyan Church. The basic provisions, powers and restrictions of this body are set forth in the Constitution (325-360).

### B. Membership

### 1. Plan of Representation

**1503.** The General Conference shall be composed of voting and nonvoting members as follows:

#### Voting Members

(1) The voting members shall consist of an equal number of ordained ministers and lay members of The Wesleyan Church (325):

(a) The district superintendent of each district and provisional district and a lay delegate elected at the same time and in the same manner as the other delegates (1512-1526).

(b) One ministerial and one lay delegate elected by an established district for every seven hundred fifty covenant members and major fraction thereof. The district superintendent and the lay delegate elected (1503:1a) shall be the representatives for the first seven hundred fifty covenant members.

(c) The general officials of the Church as defined in 1800, the General Superintendents Emeriti, members of the General Board who are not voting members by some other right, the presidents of the general educational institutions (2365), the general directors of Hephzibah Children's Home, Wesleyan Investment Foundation, Wesleyan Native

American Ministries, Wesleyan Women and the Wesleyan Pension Fund, and such delegates-at-large as shall be necessary to maintain parity between ordained ministers and lay members (1508-1510).

(d) Voting delegates from units under the General Department of World Missions according to a plan approved by the General Board (325; 1655:31).

**Nonvoting Members**

(2) The following when they are not voting members by some other right shall be seated as nonvoting members when present at the General Conference session: former General Superintendents, superintendents of developing districts (1015), the general directors of Wesleyan Medical Fellowship, Wesleyan Men, executive secretaries or directors of subsidiary corporations and missionary directors and such nonvoting delegates from units under the General Department of World Missions as provided for by the General Board (325; 1655:31).

**2. Forfeiture of Representation**

**1506.** A district or provisional district which has been placed under discipline as provided for in the Judiciary (5218-5230), shall forfeit all rights to any representation in the General Conference (323:9). The delegates, including the district superintendent and any delegate-at-large from that district, shall not be recognized or seated until the district or provisional district they represent is officially reinstated (5225).

**3. Election of Delegates**

**a. Delegates-at-Large**

**1508.** The election of delegates-at-large shall be arranged for by the recommendation of the General Secretary and the approval of the General Board in accordance with the following regulations:

(1) The parity of equal ministerial and lay membership in the General Conference shall be maintained (325; 360:3b).

(2) The established districts shall be considered in alphabetical order, and each eligible district in turn shall be appointed to elect one delegate-at-large. A provisional district shall not be eligible to elect a delegate-at-large.

**1510.** The General Board shall act upon the recommendation of the General Secretary in one of its sessions consistent with the provisions of paragraph 1512. The delegates-at-large shall be elected by the appointed districts at the same time and in the same manner as the other General Conference delegates (1512-1526).

### b. Delegates

**1512.** The delegates to the General Conference shall be elected by the district conference, by ballot and by majority vote, at its last annual session preceding the General Conference. When the last annual session is within sixty days of the opening date of the General Conference, the district conference may elect its delegates at the previous annual session. The statistical report for the annual session of the district conference at which the delegates are elected shall be used for determining the number of covenant members, and consequently, the number of General Conference delegates (1503:1b). A certified list of all delegates to the General Conference shall be promptly forwarded by the district secretary to the General Secretary (1332:5).

**1514.** A person accepting election as a delegate is obligated to attend faithfully the entire General Conference session, unless hindered by unforeseen and justifiable circumstances. (Cf. 1541.)

### c. Alternate Delegates

**1516.** Each district conference shall also at the same session (1512) elect by ballot and by majority vote a sufficient number of alternate ministerial and lay delegates, not to exceed the number of delegates. Such alternates shall meet the same qualifications as the delegates (1520-1526) and shall fill vacancies in the order of their election (cf. 1332:5).

**1518.** Whenever the district superintendent, who is an *ex officio* member of the General Conference (1503:1a), is unable to attend, the place of the district superintendent shall be filled by the assistant district superintendent. If the assistant district superintendent is an elected delegate to the General Conference, the place of the assistant district superintendent shall then be filled like any other vacancy by an alternate ministerial delegate.

## 4. Qualifications of Delegates

### a. Ministerial Delegates

**1520.** A ministerial delegate must be an ordained minister who is a member of the district represented, both at the time of election and at the time of the General Conference (327:2).

**1522.** Whenever ministerial delegate-elect shall transfer membership to another district, the right to represent the district shall be vacated and an alternate ministerial delegate shall be certified (1332:5; 1516).

### b. Lay Delegates

**1524.** A lay delegate must be a lay person who is a covenant member of a local church in the district represented, both at the time of election and at the time of the General Conference (327:3).

**1526.** Whenever a lay delegate-elect shall cease to meet the requirements in 1524, the right to represent the district shall be vacated and an alternate lay delegate shall be certified (1516).

## C. Sessions

### 1. Regular Sessions

**1528.** The General Conference shall meet quadrennially, in the spring season at a place, date and hour determined by the General Board (330:1; 1655:3).

**1530.** Whenever an emergency shall require a change in the plans of the General Conference for the time of the next regular session, the General Board may, by a two-thirds vote, declare that such an emergency exists and authorize the necessary changes (cf. 330:1; 1655:4-5).

### 2. Special Sessions

**1532.** A special session of the General Conference shall be called by the Board of General Superintendents (1920:7) whenever authorized to do so by a two-thirds vote of the General Board (1655:5), or when requested to do so by two-thirds of the established district conferences (330:2; 1180:6). The time and place for the special session shall be decided by the General Board (1655:5), or, in the interim of its sessions, by the Executive Board. The time shall always be later than the next session of each district conference (330:2).

**1534.** Any duly called special session of the General Conference shall have full authority to transact any item of business which may be transacted at a regular session.

## D. Organization and Procedure

### 1. Officers

**1536. The Presidency** (332). The General Superintendents shall preside over the General Conference in such order as they shall determine (1920:6). When no General Superintendent is present, the General Conference shall elect by ballot an ordained minister as president pro tem.

**1539. The Secretary** (334). The General Secretary shall be the secretary of the General Conference. The General Secretary shall accurately record the proceedings, preserve them in permanent form, and perform any other such duties as shall be required by the General Conference (1948; 1951).

### 2. Procedure

**1541. Delegates.** Once a delegate has been seated at the General Conference, an alternate delegate cannot thereafter be seated in place of the seated delegate (cf. 1514).

**1543. Quorum** (336). A majority of all the delegates elected by the districts shall constitute a quorum for the transaction of business. A smaller number shall have the authority to adjourn from time to time until a quorum is obtained.

**1545. Voting** (338). The ministerial and lay delegates shall deliberate in the sessions of the General Conference as one body. However, upon the final vote on any question, except proposed amendments to the Constitution (200-385) on a call of one-fourth of the members, the house shall divide so that ministerial and lay delegates shall vote separately. It shall require a majority vote of each branch to pass any question upon which the division has been called.

**1547. Rules of Order.** General Conference business shall be conducted according to the current edition of *Robert's Rules of Order, Newly Revised,* except when formally suspended by the General Conference or when other procedures are required by *The Discipline* (360:1).

**1550. Appeals on Questions of Order.** The chair shall decide all questions of order, subject to an appeal to the General Conference. In case of such an appeal, the vote shall be taken without debate, except that the chair may state the grounds of the decision, and the appellant may state the grounds of the appeal.

**1553. Suspension of Rules.** The General Conference may suspend for a particular session any statutory law (155) set forth in *The Discipline* governing the procedures of the General Conference by a two-thirds majority vote.

### 3. Memorials

**1557.** Memorials to the General Conference, including proposed changes in *The Discipline* other than the Constitution (200-385), may be submitted by a district conference, a district board of administration, the General Board, a General Conference committee, the governing board of an educational or benevolent institution, the governing board of a subsidiary corporation, the general executive committee of an auxiliary organization or any ten members of the General Conference.

**1560.** Memorials proposing an amendment to the Constitution (200-385) may be submitted to the General Conference only by a district conference by a two-thirds vote (1180:1) or by the General Board (1655:6).

### 4. Committees

**1563.** The General Conference shall have such committees as it may deem necessary. The committees shall be nominated by the General Board, unless ordered otherwise in *The Discipline* or by the General Conference, and elected by the General Conference.

#### a. Committee on Memorials

**1565.** The General Board shall serve as the Committee on Memorials. It shall be the duty of the Committee on Memorials to receive all memorials for the General Conference, classify them, pass on each of them and submit such memorials to the General Conference, together with the committee's recommendation, and in such order as the committee shall determine. All memorials received no later than November 1 of the year prior to the General Conference shall be classified and printed for distribution to the General Conference delegates no later than sixty days before the opening date of the General Conference. Any memorial received by the Committee on Memorials after November 1 shall only be presented to the General Conference if it is recommended for adoption by the Committee on Memorials and if the General Conference votes to hear it..

#### b. General Conference Planning Committee

**1570.** The General Secretary, General Treasurer and four other persons elected by the General Board at least one year before the convening of a regular session of the General Conference, shall constitute a General Conference Planning Committee.

**1573.** The General Conference Planning Committee shall be responsible to arrange all necessary matters for the General Conference such as the lodging, meals, exhibits, space allotments and whatever else may be necessary for the convenience and efficiency of the General Conference. They shall have the authority to carry out this responsibility and to enter into any necessary contracts, subject to the approval of the General Board or, in the interim of its sessions, the Executive Board.

**1576.** The General Conference Planning Committee, together with the Board of General Superintendents, shall formulate a program for the General Conference, including any worship services, and other special features, all of which shall be subject to the approval of the General Board or, in the interim of its sessions, the Executive Board.

### c. Committee on Special Nominations

**1580.** The General Board shall serve as the Committee on Special Nominations (1655:6). The duties of this committee shall be:

(1) To present to the General Conference one or more nominations for each of the general officials elected by the General Conference. In the event an incumbent is not nominated, the committee shall normally present two or more nominations for that office. The general officials involved are: The General Secretary, the General Director of Sunday School and Discipleship Ministries, the General Director of Evangelism and Church Growth, the General Director of Education and the Ministry, the General Director of World Missions and the General Director of Youth.

(2) To present nominations for the members of the Board of Review (1590:19; 5400:3).

(3) To present such other nominations or fulfill such duties as may be assigned to them by the General Conference.

### d. General Conference Editing Committee

**1585.** The General Conference Editing Committee shall be elected by the General Board and shall be responsible for editing *The Discipline*, the *General Conference Journal* and any other item assigned by the General Conference or the General Board. It shall consult with the Board of General Superintendents on matters of interpretation and shall be amenable to the General Board. All recommendations concerning the dedication of the *General Conference Journal* shall be referred to the General Board which shall determine the matter and instruct the committee accordingly.

### e. Duties and Powers

**1590.** The duties, powers and restrictions of the General Conference are set forth in the Constitution (325-360), and as hereinafter provided:

#### The Essentials and the Constitution

(1) To vote on an amendment to the Essentials (cf. 125).

(2) To propose an amendment to the Constitution (200-385) by a two-thirds vote, subject to ratification by two-thirds of all the members of the several district conferences, present and voting (385; 1180:1; 1560; 1920:28); to ratify, by a two-thirds vote, an amendment to the Constitution, which has originated in a district conference and has been approved by a two-thirds vote of all the members of the several district conferences, present and voting (385; 1180:2; 1560; 1920:28). When the voting is completed, the Board of General Superintendents shall canvass the vote; and when the amendment has received the required majority, they shall declare it effective as constitutional law (385; 1920:28).

(3) To request, by a vote of one-fifth of its members, present and voting, a judgment from the Board of Review as to the constitutionality of an action of the General Conference (375:1); and to overrule such a judgment by a two-thirds majority of those present and voting (380).

#### General Legislation

(4) To have full power in keeping with the Constitution (135; 145) and by majority vote to enact statutory law (155) and to adopt ritual (175) for *The Discipline* and to adopt other rules and regulations for the Church, all of which shall be the chief authority for the North American General Conference of The Wesleyan Church and its subordinate units (cf. 2550); to ratify amendments to the Charter of the Wesleyan World Fellowship (see Appendix A) or to authorize the General Board to approve such amendments in the interim of General Conferences.

(5) To authorize a corporation to be formed and maintained for The Wesleyan Church to facilitate the management of its legal and corporate affairs (4200); and to approve its articles of incorporation and bylaws and any or all amendments thereto, by a two-thirds vote (4270).

(6) To authorize the incorporation of any agency, institution, board organization or other similar body, as a subsidiary corporation of The Wesleyan Church (4300), and to approve the articles of incorporation and bylaws, and any amendments thereto, for such a subsidiary corporation (4300-

4320). In the interim of General Conferences, this authority shall be vested in the General Board (1655:34; 4300; cf. 2362).

(7) To receive reports of the spiritual, numerical and financial condition of The Wesleyan Church, worldwide, including reports concerning their official duties from the general officials and others designated by the General Conference (cf. 1800; 1840; 1920:10; 1976; 2308; 2321; 2341; 7195:2; 7420).

(8) To adopt plans for the advancement of the Church in all phases of its ministry, including the financial plans for the general church (cf. 1995-2050).

(9) To define in a general way the duties of the general officials, subject to the additional definition of their duties by the General Board in the interim of General Conference sessions. (1845)

(10) To organize the work in the United States and Canada into districts and to determine their boundaries, for which a recommendation shall be received from the General Board (317; 1036; 1655:33; 2400-2403); to authorize the establishing of a general conference as set forth in 2610.

(11) To authorize the establishing of a developing district (1006) or a provisional district (1020); to reclassify a provisional district (1034) or an established district (1042-1045).

(12) To group the districts into representative areas (2430-2445) to serve for the election of area representatives to the General Board and as the area divisions of Wesleyan Men, Wesleyan Women, Wesleyan Youth and Young Adults International, for which a recommendation shall be received from the General Board (cf. 1655:13).

(13) To authorize the establishment, merger or dissolution of any educational or benevolent institution for the general church or an area of the same; to define the purpose and adopt any regulations deemed necessary for the government of such institutions (cf. 2362).

(14) To determine the boundaries of the educational areas in such a way as to provide an equitable distribution of the membership and financial strength of the Church among the approved schools, for which a recommendation shall be received from the General Board (2365-2371; 2450-2470; cf. 1655:13).

(15) To designate a criterion of parliamentary procedure for itself and other representative or official bodies of The Wesleyan Church as desired (360:1).

### Elections

(16) To elect by ballot and by majority vote, from among the ordained ministers of The Wesleyan Church three General Superintendents (1900-

1909). The first ballot for election of General Superintendents shall be a "yes/no" ballot for incumbent General Superintendents available for reelection. Any vacancies remaining after the first ballot shall be filled by using unprinted ballots until elections are completed.

(17) To elect the following general officials by ballot and by majority vote, from one or more nominees for each office presented by the Committee on Special Nominations (1580:1) and any additional nominations from the floor of the General Conference: the General Secretary, the General Director of Sunday School and Discipleship Ministries, the General Director of Evangelism and Church Growth, the General Director of Education and the Ministry, the General Director of World Missions and the General Director of Youth.

(18) To elect by majority vote three ordained ministers and three lay members from each of the representative areas (2430-2445) as members of the General Board (1605:2), who shall be nominated by an area caucus. Area caucuses shall be held simultaneously at a time decided upon by the General Conference, for each of which a chair shall be appointed by the presiding officer. In an area caucus, the delegates of each district and provisional district which comprise the representative area shall nominate three ordained ministers and three lay members of that area, by ballot and by majority vote, as their area representatives on the General Board.

(19) To elect by majority vote, from nominees submitted by the Committee on Special Nominations or made from the floor, five ordained ministers and four lay members as members of the Board of Review, and four ordained ministers and three lay members as alternate members (cf. 1580:2; 5400-5405).

(20) To confer the title General Superintendent Emeritus upon a former General Superintendent when recommended by the General Board (1945).

## Judiciary

(21) To place an established district under discipline for cause, as set forth in the Judiciary, and to authorize the General Board to appoint a General Superintendent or other general official to take charge of the district as provided for in the Constitution (360:3c; 5218-5240).

(22) To hear and determine appeals from decisions of the Board of Review, and to overrule such decisions by a two-thirds majority vote (380; 5445).

(23) To receive a report from the Board of General Superintendents of their rulings on points of church law, interpretations of *The Discipline* and rulings on the legality of district actions; to sustain, modify or annul such rulings, in whole or in part (1920:24-26).

(24) To exercise authority in matters of judicial discipline as set forth in the Judiciary (5200; 5440:5c).

# Chapter II

# GENERAL BOARD

## A. Name and Function

**1600.** The General Board of Administration referred to in the Constitution shall in practice be referred to under the title "General Board." The General Board carries out the will of the General Conference, promotes the interests of The Wesleyan Church and serves as its chief governing body in the interim of General Conference sessions (340).

## B. Membership

**1605.** The General Board is composed of General Superintendents and area representatives:

(1) **General Superintendents.** The General Superintendents are members of the General Board by virtue of their office.

(2) **Area Representatives.** Three ordained ministers and three lay members shall be elected by the General Conference from each representative area to serve as members of the General Board (340:1; 1590:18; 2430-2445. In order to accomplish broad representation when electing area representatives to the General Board, it is recommended that no more than two persons be elected from any one district. They shall serve from the close of the session at which they are elected until the close of the succeeding General Conference and until their successors are elected and qualified. Whenever an area representative shall transfer residence or membership outside the area represented, the General Board shall declare the office vacant and shall fill the vacancy in such a manner as to maintain the representation provided for herewith. An area representative, who is not a voting member of the General Conference by some other right, is a voting member of the General Conference by virtue of membership on the General Board (1503:1c).

## C. Sessions

**1610. Organizing Session.** The General Board shall meet immediately after the adjournment of the General Conference for an organizing session:

(1) To organize by electing officers and committees, as required by *The Discipline*, the General Conference, the articles and bylaws of the several corporations, or the policies and bylaws of the General Board.

(2) To care for any business assigned to it by the General Conference which requires immediate attention.

(3) To elect the Executive Board as provided in 1755.

(4) To care for any other necessary business.

**1615. Regular Session.** The General Board shall meet annually or semiannually at a time and place it shall designate or as fixed in its bylaws. The Executive Board may change the time and place by a two-thirds vote if circumstances so require (1785:1). Notice of all sessions shall be published by the General Secretary in the official church publication and sent in writing to all members at least four weeks in advance.

**1620. Special Session.** A special session may be ordered by the General Board, the Executive Board (1785:1) or the Board of General Superintendents (1920:7). All members shall be notified at least ten days before the convening of a special session (cf. 1615).

**1625. Evaluation Session.** Periodically, either during regular sessions or in a session called specifically for self-evaluation, the General Board shall consider its priorities, review the distribution of its time and evaluate the effectiveness of its efforts, using the duties and powers listed in *The Discipline* as a guide. The method and extent of such evaluation shall be determined by the General Board, but special attention should be focused on those responsibilities that are most likely to contribute to future outreach and growth to the glory of God.

## D. Organization and Procedure

**1630. Chair.** The General Board shall elect quadrennially, at its organizing session, from among the General Superintendents and on a rotating basis, a chair (1935:1) and a vice-chair for terms of equal length during the quadrennium.

**1635. Secretary.** The General Secretary is secretary of the General Board *ex officio* (cf. 1951).

**1640. Quorum.** A majority of all the members of the General Board shall constitute a quorum.

**1645. Voting.** A majority vote of those present and voting shall be sufficient except for those matters for which a larger majority is required by *The Discipline* (1530; 1532; 1655:5, 10, 15, 17, 18, 20, 22, 39:a, 39:b, 43; 4300; 5212:1; 5225), by legal or corporate requirements or by the policies and regulations of the General Board.

**1650. Bylaws.** The General Board shall adopt its own bylaws and perfect all plans necessary for the performance of its own duties, in harmony with *The Discipline* and the instructions of the General Conference.

### e. Duties and Powers

**1655.** The General Board shall serve as the chief governing body of The Wesleyan Church in the interim of General Conference sessions, caring for and promoting the general interests of the Church, with these specific duties and powers:

#### Related to Leadership

(1) To join the General Superintendents and general officers in strategic planning, helping to define mission, vision, core values, and strategies, and to measure the denomination's progress in fulfilling its mission and vision.

(2) To engage in an ongoing review of the denominational structures, maintaining openness to needed changes, and making appropriate recommendations to the General Conference.

#### Related to General Conference

(3) To select the place and determine the day and the hour at which regular sessions of the General Conference shall convene, provided that the day and the hour are within the spring season (cf. 330:1; 1528).

(4) To declare that an emergency exists requiring a change in the time of General Conference, and subsequently to alter the same (330:1; 1530).

(5) To authorize by a two-thirds vote a special session of the General Conference, and to set by majority vote the time and place of such special session (330:2; 1532).

(6) To serve as the General Conference Committee on Memorials (1565) and the Committee on Special Nominations (1580).

(7) To originate recommendations and memorials to the General Conference, including proposed amendments to the Constitution (1557-1560).

(8) To instruct the General Conference Editing Committee concerning the dedication, if any, of the *General Conference Journal* (1585).

(9) To care for any business delegated to the General Board by the General Conference.

### Related to the General Board

(10) To fill, for the unexpired term, vacancies occurring among the general officials (1800; 1850) or the area representatives of the General Board (1605:2), by a two-thirds majority of the members of the General Board present and voting or by a majority of all the members of the General Board, whichever is greater (1850), in such a manner as to fulfill all the requirements for such offices and positions (1605:2; 1800-1810; 1903).

(11) To elect by majority vote, from among the area representatives of its own membership, three ordained ministers and three lay members to be members of the Executive Board (1755).

(12) To refer such matters to the Executive Board as shall be deemed wise (1785); to review such actions of the Executive Board as are not final (1785:2, 6); and to receive and act upon its recommendations.

### Related to the Church in General

(13) To recommend to the General Conference the number of representative areas and the boundaries of such areas for the election of representatives to the General Board (1590:12); to approve the boundaries of the administrative areas and to assign the General Superintendents to their respective administrative areas as set forth in 1915; to recommend to the General Conference the assignment of the districts to educational areas for the support of the educational institutions (1590:14) and in the interim of General Conference sessions to assign new districts to the proper area (2450).

### Related to Corporations

(14) To serve as the board of directors of The Wesleyan Church Corporation and its precedent corporations (4230); to appoint committees from among its own members and to delegate to such committees the exercise of such powers in the interim of its sessions as it shall deem wise.

(15) To buy, own, hold, manage, mortgage, sell, convey, donate or otherwise acquire, encumber and dispose of any general church property, whether real, personal or mixed, in keeping with the trust provisions given in 4920 and to buy, sell or lease any denominational headquarters site (by whatever name it shall be called) by a two-thirds majority of the members of the General Board present and voting, except that property for which other provision is made in the articles and bylaws of subsidiary corporations, and to provide for the proper care and maintenance of such property.

(16) To elect an Assistant Secretary for The Wesleyan Church Corporation and all precedent corporations.

(17) To carry out the instructions of the General Conference relative to the incorporation of any agency, institution, board organization or other similar body (1590:6); or, in the interim of General Conference sessions, to authorize the establishment of such a corporation by a two-thirds majority vote and to care for such corporation matters as the approval and amendment of articles and bylaws, all in keeping with the provisions of *The Discipline* (cf.2358-2362; 4300-4320; 4425).

(18) To elect by majority vote all except the *ex officio* members of all other general church boards; to be or to elect all boards of trustees, directors or managers of subsidiary corporations, including all approved benevolent institutions, and to exercise such control and direction of said subsidiary corporations and related agencies as is provided for in *The Discipline* (cf. 2358-2362; 4300-4320), and in their several articles of incorporation and bylaws; and to remove a member of any such board, for cause or when the best interests of the Church so require, by a majority vote of all the members of the General Board (cf. 5215), and to fill all vacancies.

(19) To direct an annual audit, and at other times as deemed necessary, of all corporations, general offices, departments, agencies, auxiliaries and institutions of the Church, and to take any action required by the findings of such audit (cf. 4320:7).

(20) To have the authority to negotiate and arbitrate legal and temporal matters in cases of dispute involving the general church without resort to the courts when the General Board, by a two-thirds vote, deems such procedure necessary; provided, however, that the emergency authority hereby granted shall not be construed to modify or rescind any of the provisions of *The Discipline* of The Wesleyan Church with reference to the prescribed conveyance of church property; and further provided, that this authority to negotiate and arbitrate shall not be a limit on the power or authority to resort to litigation in the courts when such procedure is deemed advisable.

### Related to General Offices and Departments

(21) To direct the general officials and those elected by the General Board in their work, in keeping with the provisions of *The Discipline* (cf. 1830), and assigning to them such special duties as shall be deemed necessary (cf. 1590:9); to receive reports annually and as needed from the general officials and such others as *The Discipline* or the General Board shall require (cf. 1840; 1920:10; 4320:8; 7195:2; 7420:2), and to set the salaries and allowances of all general officials (1800) and of those elected by the General Board.

(22) To adopt a comprehensive budget for each of the general offices, departments, agencies and auxiliaries (1880) and apportion the USF-

Educational Institutions Fund among the general educational interests; to determine the obligation to the United Stewardship Fund of churches within developing districts; and, in the interim of General Conference sessions, to designate those interests which will share in the benefits of the USF-General Fund, and to alter the percentage of the USF-General Fund, in case of emergency, by a two-thirds majority vote of all the members of the General Board (2005:2).

(23) To request the Board of General Superintendents to rule on points of Church law and interpretations of *The Discipline* as set forth in 1920:24, to receive reports from the Board of General Superintendents on all such rulings as a matter of information, and to appeal any such ruling to the Board of Review (375:2; 1920:24c; 5440:3). All appeals must be filed in the office of the General Secretary within sixty days after the date of the official decision on the matter.

(24) To receive and act upon the recommendations of the Board of General Superintendents (1920:8).

(25) To recommend at the discretion of the General Board that the General Conference confer the title, General Superintendent Emeritus, upon a former General Superintendent (1590:20; 1945).

(26) To adopt official policies for the general offices, departments, agencies, auxiliaries and institutions of the Church, in keeping with the provisions of *The Discipline*, defining the duties of the various executive officers.

(27) To employ the General Treasurer (1970); to receive, hold, borrow for, loan and appropriate all general church funds, in accordance with the financial plans adopted by the General Conference, through the General Treasurer, in the execution of its lawful purpose, subject to the limitations imposed by *The Discipline*, the articles and bylaws of the several corporations, and the specific provisions of trust agreements; to have the General Treasurer bonded and to set the amount of such bond (cf. 1976).

(28) To employ a General Director of Estate and Gift Planning (2070-2075).

(29) To define the duties and designate the additional members of the General Administrative Council (1990).

(30) To employ the General Publisher (2155) and to oversee the publishing operations of the Church

(31) To authorize adaptation of the church name for units of The Wesleyan Church when necessary (80; 205; 340:2); to approve a Discipline for each unit under the General Department of World Missions in keeping with 340:2; and to provide for the General Conference representation of units under the General Department of World Missions (325; 1503:1-2).

(32) To employ a General Director of Communications (2110).

**Related to Districts**

(33) To make recommendation to the General Conference for the establishment or alteration of district boundaries (1590:10); and to approve the merger, division or other realignment of districts when each district conference involved has approved the plan (1065).

(34) To authorize the incorporation of a provisional district (4105); to approve the articles of incorporation and bylaws for the incorporation of a district, and all amendments to the same (4110); and to exercise such control and direction of said district corporations as is set forth in 4120:3, 6, 9; 4250; 4870.

(35) To grant in concurrence with the respective district conference prior approval to a local church conference for post-secondary education in terms of an institute or of junior college or college-level programs (655:18; 1180:24).

**Related to Judiciary**

(36) To exercise administrative and judicial discipline in accordance with the Constitution and as set forth in the Judiciary over officers elected by the General Conference including the general officials of the Church (360:2) and the area representatives of the General Board (340:1), over those elected or employed by the General Board (323:1), over districts (360:3c) and over district superintendents (323:1; 360:2; cf. 5203-5240).

(37) To refer charges against the moral character of a minister under its jurisdiction to the district in which ministerial membership is held (323:1; 360:2), and charges against the moral character of a lay member under its jurisdiction to the local church where membership is held; and to receive a copy of the official record of any subsequent investigation or trial from the judicatory involved immediately after such is conducted (cf.5115:4; 5175:4; 5203; 5212).

(38) To hear and determine any charges alleging an administrative offense in relation to official duties filed against a person under its jurisdiction and to administer discipline as it deems necessary and proper (cf. 5203; 5212).

(39) To remove from office any person under its jurisdiction whenever the best interests and preservation of the Church or the disabling physical or mental health of the person require it, subject to the following conditions:

(a) To remove from office a general official elected by the General Conference (1800:1a, b), or to remove from General Board membership an area representative, or to remove from office a district superintendent shall require a two-thirds majority vote of all the members of the General Board (5212:1).

(b) To remove from office a person elected or employed by the General Board (1800:2) shall require a majority vote of all the members of the General Board (5212:2).

(40) To file charges with the General Board of Review against a district for an offense as set forth in 5070 (cf. 375:6; 5218-5220; 5440:5).

(41) To administer discipline to a district which has been found guilty by the proper judicatory as set forth in the Judiciary (5218-5240).

(42) To take whatever steps are necessary to preserve the interests of the Church within the bounds of a district under discipline.

(43) To end the state of discipline for a district, by a majority vote of all the members of the General Board, when the offense has been removed to the satisfaction of said majority (cf. 5225), or to authorize the reorganization of a district (5235-5240).

(44) To adopt additional rules of judicial procedure for such matters as evidence, testimony and other technicalities as set forth in 5250.

## F. The Executive Board

### 1. Function

**1750.** The Executive Board carries out the will of the General Board, serving as necessary in the interim of General Board sessions.

### 2. Membership

**1755.** The Executive Board shall be composed of the General Superintendents and three ordained ministers and three lay members to be elected from among the area representatives by the General Board. They shall serve from the close of the session at which they are elected until the close of the next session of the General Conference or until their successors are elected and qualified. Whenever an area representative on the Executive Board ceases to be a member of the General Board, the General Board shall declare the office vacant and shall fill the vacancy in such a manner as to maintain the representation provided for herewith.

### 3. Sessions

**1760.** The Executive Board shall meet immediately prior to each meeting of the General Board and at other times and places as it may determine or upon the call of the chair.

### 4. Organization

**1765. Chair.** The chair and vice-chair of the General Board shall serve as chair and vice-chair, respectively, of the Executive Board.

**1770. Secretary.** The General Secretary of The Wesleyan Church shall serve as secretary of the Executive Board by virtue of office but shall not be a member nor have the right to vote.

**1775. Quorum.** A majority of all members of the Executive Board shall constitute a quorum.

**1780. Voting.** A majority vote of all those present and voting shall be sufficient except for those matters for which a larger majority is required by *The Discipline*, by legal or corporate requirements, or by the policies and regulations of the General Board.

### 5. Duties, Powers and Restrictions

**1785.** In the interim of General Board sessions, the Executive Board shall exercise such powers and have such duties as may be assigned to it by *The Discipline* or by the General Board, including the power:

(1) To transact all business referred to it by the General Board; to change the time and place of a regular session of the General Board if circumstances require it (1615); and to order a special session of the General Board if deemed necessary (1620).

(2) To transact any and all other business the General Board may transact except that the Executive Board shall not make recommendations directly to the General Conference, nor take final action on the adoption of the annual budgets (1655:22) nor the amending of General Board policies (1655), nor transact any business which requires more than a simple majority vote of the General Board (cf. 1530; 1532; 1655:5, 10 15, 17, 18, 20, 22, 39:a, 39:b, 43; 4300; 5212:1; 5225).

(3) To provide overall correlation of commissions, corporate societies, departments, agencies, auxiliaries and institutions in planning and carrying out programs adopted by the General Conference and the General Board.

(4) To serve as the members of the budget committee with the General Treasurer serving as a non-voting member of that committee.

(5) To require reports from all such officers as it shall designate and to consult with and give direction to the same.

(6) To receive from the Board of General Superintendents annually a detailed report on its evaluation of the performance of the general officers (1800) and other executives heading the various offices, departments, agencies and auxiliaries (cf. 1880).

(7) To take emergency action by a two-thirds majority vote of all the members of the Executive Board, suspending from office a person under the jurisdiction of the General Board (1655:36), pending the action of the General Board. In the case of a general official (1800), no more than thirty days shall elapse from the time such suspension is effected until the General Board shall review the matter, either through a regular or special session.

(8) To appoint such subcommittees as it shall deem wise, and to delegate duties and powers to the same.

**1790.** Minutes of the Executive Board meetings shall be forwarded promptly by the General Secretary to all members of the General Board for their information and review.

### G. Task Forces

**1793. Task Force on Public Morals and Social Concerns.** The General Board shall determine the manner of election of two general officers and five other persons who shall serve with the chair of the General Board as the Task Force on Public Morals and Social Concerns (1920:13), which task force shall meet at least annually for its work; cultivate the Church's awareness of its responsibility to raise a standard for social righteousness; issue guidance through the denominational periodical and other such means; be a voice for the Church in matters of public morals and social concerns; utilize the services of a department, agency and auxiliary when such relate to issues; seek correlation of such units by the General Administrative Council; and report to the General Board and the General Conference.

### H. Conflict of Laws

**1796. Generally.** In the event of a conflict between provisions of *The Discipline* relating to church administration at the local, district or general level and applicable local laws, such provisions of *The Discipline* may be modified to the extent deemed necessary to comply with such local laws, by utilizing the approval process hereinafter specified; provided, however, that this clause shall not be construed to give the consent of The Wesleyan Church (or any component part or affiliated entity thereof) to the regulation of its affairs by any civil authority where such regulation would violate: (1) Any of the Essentials of the Church (cf. 2500:3); (2) The rights of the Church or its members to freedom of religion, freedom of association, freedom of speech or other civil rights; (3) Separation of church and state, in the sense of excessive entanglement of the civil authority in the affairs of the Church; or (4) The rights of the Church to define its religious doctrines and membership requirements, to prescribe its rituals, and otherwise to maintain its polity on matters such as ordination, sacraments, religious beliefs and practice, requirements for employment by the Church (or its component parts or affiliated entities) or any other similar matters deemed by the Church to be central to the identity, faith, doctrine and practice of the Church.

**1797. Approval Process.**

(1) **Local level.** If the conflict which arises relates to church administration at the local level, no modification shall be effective until approved by the district board of administration and the General Board.

(2) **District level.** If the conflict which arises relates to church administration at the district level, no modification shall be effective until approved by the Board of General Superintendents and the General Board.

(3) **General level.** If the conflict which arises relates to church administration at the general level, no modification shall be effective until approved by the Board of General Superintendents and the General Board.

**1798. Record of Permitted Changes.** The General Secretary shall maintain a record of any change which has been approved under the foregoing procedure, and shall notify an affected local, district or general entity when the process of approving a change relevant to that entity has been approved.

**1799. Report to General Conference.** All modifications approved under the foregoing procedure shall be reported to the next subsequent General Conference. If a modification approved under the foregoing procedure is unacceptable to the General Conference, it may, by resolution, identify the respects in which the modification is unacceptable, and direct the General Board to formulate an alternative plan which is consistent with the instructions of the General Conference.

# Chapter III

## GENERAL OFFICIALS OF THE CHURCH

**1800. Identification.** The general officials of the Church are those general officers which are designated as follows:

(1) **Elected by the General Conference:**

(a) The General Superintendents (1590:16).

(b) The General Secretary, the General Director of Sunday School and Discipleship Ministries, the General Director of Evangelism and Church Growth, the General Director of Education and the Ministry, the General Director of World Missions and the General Director of Youth (1580:1; 1590:17).

(2) **Elected by the General Board**—the General Treasurer (1655:27), the General Publisher (1655:30), the General Director of Communications (1655:32), and the General Director of Estate and Gift Planning (1655:28).

**1810. Qualifications**. A general official must be a covenant member of The Wesleyan Church at the time of election; and if at any time a general official ceases to be a covenant member, the office shall be declared vacant as provided for in 1850.

**1820. Term of Office.** The General Superintendents, the General Secretary and the General Directors listed above, (1800:1a, b) shall be elected by the General Conference (1580:1; 1590:16-17) for a term of four years, and shall serve from the close of that session until the close of the next regular session of the General Conference or until their successors are elected and qualified. A special session of the General Conference may, however, declare that the term is ended and order a new election. The General Treasurer, the General Publisher, the General Director of Communications and the General Director of Estate and Gift Planning shall be elected by the General Board for a term determined by the General Board. The salary of a retiring general official shall continue one month beyond the date of termination of service.

**1830. Amenability.** The general officials are amenable to the General Board for their official conduct, and to their districts for their moral character (323:1; 360:2). They are subject to direction from the General Conference, the General Board and its Executive Board. They may be removed from office for cause or when the best interests of the Church or the disabling physical or mental health of the official so requires. The removal from office of those general officials elected by the General Conference (1800:1a, b) shall require a two-thirds majority vote of all members of the General Board (1655:39a; 5212:1). The removal from office of those general officials that are elected or employed by the General Board (1800:2) shall require a majority vote of all members of the General Board (1655:39b; 5212:2).

**1840. Reports.** The general officials shall report to each session of the General Conference concerning their official duties, annually to the General Board concerning their official duties and personal ministry, and at other times as required by the General Conference, the General Board or the Executive Board.

**1845. International Center Structure.** The number and nature of general offices and departments and the assignments of the general officials of The Wesleyan Church may be adjusted in times of exigency by a two-thirds majority vote of the members of the General Board present and voting, or a majority of all members of the General Board, whichever is greater.

**1850. Vacancies.** The office of a general official may become vacant by death, by cessation of membership in The Wesleyan Church, by resignation from office or by removal (1830). In all cases, except as provided for in 1845, the vacancy shall be filled by a two-thirds majority vote of the members of the General Board present and voting, or by a majority vote of all the members of the General Board, whichever is greater (1655:10).

**1860. Church and District Membership.** An ordained minister who serves as a general official may hold ministerial membership in any district, and church membership in any local church. The responsibilities to the general church shall take precedence over responsibilities to the district and local church (323:1; 360:2).

**1870. Residence.** The general officials shall reside in or near the place where the general headquarters of The Wesleyan Church is located.

**1880. Official Listing.** The official listing of the offices, departments, agencies, auxiliaries, subsidiary corporations, benevolent and educational institutions of the general church is:

*Offices*

Office of Estate and Gift Planning
Office of the General Secretary
Office of the General Superintendents
Office of the General Treasurer

*Departments*

General Department of Communications
General Department of Education and the Ministry
General Department of Evangelism and Church Growth
General Department of Sunday School and Discipleship Ministries
General Department of World Missions
General Department of Youth

*Agency*

Wesleyan Publishing House

*Auxiliaries*

Wesleyan Medical Fellowship
Wesleyan Men
Wesleyan Women
Wesleyan Kids for Missions
Wesleyan Youth
Young Adults International

*Subsidiary Corporations*

Wesleyan Indian Ministries, Inc.
Wesleyan Investment Foundation, Inc.
Wesleyan Pension Fund, Inc.

*Benevolent Institution*
(Subsidiary Corporation)

Hephzibah Children's Home, Macon, Georgia

*Educational Institutions*
(Subsidiary Corporations)

Bethany Bible College, Sussex, New Brunswick
Houghton College, Houghton, New York
Indiana Wesleyan University, Marion, Indiana
Oklahoma Wesleyan University, Bartlesville, Oklahoma
Southern Wesleyan University, Central, South Carolina

# Chapter IV

# GENERAL ADMINISTRATION

## A. General Superintendents

### 1. Function

**1900.** The General Superintendents are to be considered as the general spiritual and administrative leaders of the Church (350:1).

### 2. General Regulations

**1903.** A General Superintendent is elected, from among the ordained ministers of The Wesleyan Church, by the General Conference as a general official of the Church (325; 350:1; 1590:16), and is an *ex officio* member of the General Conference (1503:1c), the General Board (1605:1), the Executive Board (1755) and the General Administrative Council (1990).

**1906.** The General Superintendents together shall serve the entire Church and, individually, each shall have specific charge over the administrative area to which assigned by the General Board.

**1909.** The term of service, amenability and other regulations for a General Superintendent are those set forth for a general official in 1800-1870.

### 3. The Board of General Superintendents

#### a. Organization

**1912.** The General Superintendents shall organize themselves as a Board of General Superintendents, and shall assign any particular work to the members thereof as desired, unless otherwise provided for in *The Discipline*. An official copy of the minutes of the Board of General Superintendents shall be filed with the official records of the Church, at least annually.

#### b. Administrative Areas

**1915.** The supervisory responsibilities of the General Superintendents (1920:17-23; 1935:4-7) shall be provided for by grouping the districts and world missions fields into administrative areas. The boundaries of the administrative areas and the assignment of the General Superintendents to the areas shall be recommended by the Board of General Superintendents and decided upon by the General Board (1655:13) in keeping with the following regulations:

(1) The number of administrative areas shall be equal to the number of General Superintendents so that a General Superintendent may be assigned to each area.

(2) The entire geographical area of The Wesleyan Church shall be divided as equitably as possible among the administrative areas. Each district, provisional district, developing district and world missions field or area shall be assigned to one of the administrative areas.

(3) Each of the general offices, departments, agencies, auxiliaries, subsidiary corporations, benevolent and educational institutions and any other units of the general church shall also be assigned to one of the General Superintendents along with the assigned administrative area.

(4) The assignment of a General Superintendent to an administrative area shall be for the term of four years, coinciding with the term of office, or until the close of the next General Conference, provided that no General Superintendent shall be assigned to an area twice before having served each of the other areas.

### c. Duties of the Board of General Superintendents

**1920.** The General Superintendents shall devote their full time to supervising, coordinating and promoting the various branches of The Wesleyan Church. Their duties are:

#### Leadership of the Church

(1) To provide spiritual and administrative leadership for The Wesleyan Church.

(2) To encourage soul winning and evangelism in all of its phases.

(3) To carry on a spiritual and inspirational ministry, both verbal and written, teaching the doctrines and furthering the spiritual purposes of the Church, as the need demands and the opportunity affords.

#### Administration of the General Church

(4) To review, advise and approve speakers, musicians and/or resource persons of denominationally sponsored, authorized and/or related conventions and programs.

(5) To exercise general administrative supervision over The Wesleyan Church, in harmony with *The Discipline* and to see that the plans and policies of the Church are carried out; to submit annually to the Executive Board

detailed reports on the performance evaluation of the general officials and other executives heading the various offices, departments, agencies and auxiliaries (1785:5; cf. 1880).

(6) To preside over the General Conference in such order as they themselves shall determine.

(7) To issue the call for a special session of the General Conference (1532), or a special session of the General Board (1620).

(8) To make recommendations to the General Board and the Executive Board concerning any part of the Church in order to provide for a more efficient administration, a proper correlation or the advancement of the work.

(9) To arrange, in cooperation with the General Director of World Missions (2261) for the visit of a General Superintendent to each field or area under the General Department of World Missions during the quadrennium, and for additional visits as authorized by the General Board or the Executive Board (cf. 1655:21); and during such visits to inspect the work, preside over the various councils and conferences and carry out such duties as are defined in the *Policy of the General Board for World Missions*.

(10) To report, jointly and individually, to each session of the General Conference concerning their official duties (1590:7); to report annually, jointly and individually, to the General Board concerning their official duties, personal ministry and the goals, objectives and plans of the Board of General Superintendents for The Wesleyan Church (cf. 1655:21, 24).

(11) To prepare an annual budget of expense for coordination with the other administrative offices.

(12) To appoint fraternal delegates and representatives for The Wesleyan Church to other denominations or religious organizations unless otherwise provided for by the General Conference or the General Board.

(13) To be represented on the Task Force on Public Morals and Social Concerns through its chair (cf. 1793).

(14) To carry out such special assignments as the General Conference, the General Board and the Executive Board may assign from time to time.

(15) To direct the General Secretary in serving as the executive secretary to the Board of General Superintendents, defining the duties as desired.

(16) To approve all general church report blanks and forms, certificates and credentials not provided for by the General Conference which are submitted by the General Secretary.

**Supervision of the Administrative Areas**

(17) To provide for an administrative area during the temporary absence of the assigned General Superintendent from the country or in an emergency,

and to assign a General Superintendent to any special duties outside of the assigned area when it is deemed necessary to do so.

(18) To plan and conduct, jointly or individually, leadership conferences or seminars on an administrative area level for the inspiration, unity and greater effectiveness of Church leaders.

(19) To provide for an exchange of ministry by the General Superintendents in the various administrative areas, if desired.

(20) To arrange the dates for the district conferences, in consultation with each district board of administration (1233:5), so that a General Superintendent may preside (350:3), and to assign a General Superintendent, whenever necessary, to preside over a district conference outside of the assigned administrative area; to approve a reconvened session of a district conference (1115).

(21) To appoint a general official as a general church representative to a district conference whenever a General Superintendent is unable to attend (350:3).

(22) To recommend a provisional district for the status of an established district to the General Board, in concurrence with the General Director of Evangelism and Church Growth (cf. 1038).

(23) To counsel with district leaders and make recommendations for the advancement of the district work.

### Interpretation of Church Law

(24) To rule on points of Church law and interpretations of *The Discipline* for The Wesleyan Church when properly requested to do so or whenever deemed necessary for the proper administration of the Church:

(a) A request for such a ruling shall be submitted, in writing, by the following for the work under their jurisdiction: the General Board, the Executive Board (1785), a general official, the governing board of an institution or subsidiary corporation, a district conference (1180:40) or a district board of administration (1233:26).

(b) A majority vote of all members of the Board of General Superintendents shall be required for the approval of any ruling or interpretation of *The Discipline*.

(c) A ruling of the Board of General Superintendents may be appealed to the Board of Review by the party submitting the original request or by the General Board (375:2; 1180:40; 5440:3). All appeals must be filed in the office of the General Secretary within sixty days after the date of the official decision on the matter.

(25) To rule on the legality of an official action by a district conference, any district board or committee, or a district official as follows: Any three or

more members of The Wesleyan Church within a district or provisional district may request such a ruling and shall submit their petition in writing, signed by each petitioner (323:6). The Board of General Superintendents, by a majority vote of all its members, shall decide if the official act in question, in whole or in part, is deemed properly taken according to the Constitution (200-385), or other provisions of *The Discipline* (cf. 155-185). If the action is ruled as contravening the Constitution, or other provisions of *The Discipline*, it shall be null and void. Appeals from the decision of the Board of General Superintendents may be made by the petitioners or the district board of administration to the General Board of Review (375:2).

(26) To submit a report of all rulings on points of law, interpretations of *The Discipline* or other judicial acts, to the next session of the General Board or its Executive Board for their information, and to the next session of the General Conference for review and approval (1590:23). Upon approval of the General Conference, such rulings become the law of the Church. A record of such rulings shall be inserted in a special section of *The Discipline* as follows:

> The General Superintendents on (date) officially interpreted and the General Conference on (date) sustained (GC- ), thereby authorizing this provision to mean: (insert the ruling)

(27) To request a ruling from the Board of Review on the constitutionality of an act of the General Conference (375:1), the legality of an act of any general church board (375:3) and the legality of any issues arising between a district and the General Conference (375:6).

(28) To canvas the vote taken by the several district conferences on an amendment to the Constitution originating in the General Conference and, when the amendment has received the required majority, to declare it effective as constitutional law (1590:2).

### 4. Duties of a General Superintendent

**1935.** In addition to the duties as a member of the Board of General Superintendents, a General Superintendent shall be responsible:

#### General Supervision

(1) To preside over the General Board and the Executive Board, when elected to such duty by the General Board on a rotating basis, and to call for a special session of the Executive Board when serving as its chair (1760; cf. 5115:4; 5175:4; 5212:1; 5220).

(2) To perform such duties as may be properly assigned by the General Board (1655:21), the Executive Board (1785) or the Board of General Superintendents (1912).

(3) To counsel with the general officials and the executive officers under direct supervision, and to see that such executives administer their work in harmony with *The Discipline*, the respective Policy of the General Board and any other directives from the General Conference, the General Board or its Executive Board.

**Area Supervision**

(4) To travel throughout the administrative area to which assigned (1915), giving such spiritual leadership and inspirational ministry as the need demands and the opportunity affords.

(5) To visit annually and conduct an administrative survey of each educational and benevolent institution, or any other agency or organization of The Wesleyan Church in the administrative area to which assigned; when any such institution or organization is under the General Department of Evangelism and Church Growth, the General Department of World Missions or the General Department of Education and the Ministry, the General Superintendent shall consult with and arrange for the visit with the general official having jurisdiction over it; to approve the bylaws (4350:2) and, as needed, review the records and minutes of affiliate corporations within the area of supervision (4350: 7, 9); to exercise care lest any adjunct entity create the impression of being a part of any entity of The Wesleyan Church (4370:5).

(6) To meet with any governing board, district board of administration, committee or other official body, at the discretion of the General Superintendent, and make those recommendations deemed necessary to uphold *The Discipline* and carry out the directives of the General Conference (350:4), the General Board (1655) or its Executive Board (1785).

(7) To fulfill such special official duties in other administrative areas as may be assigned by the General Board (1655), the Executive Board (1785) or the Board of General Superintendents (1912).

**District Supervision**

(8) To exercise general supervision, within the assigned area, over each district, provisional district and developing district and the work of its superintendent (1920:22), and to counsel with the General Director of Evangelism and Church Growth whenever a provisional district or developing district is concerned; to schedule and conduct a minimum of one personal conference each year with each district superintendent in the assigned area, counseling the district superintendent regarding plans and objectives of the district for the year and receiving reports of activities and progress toward objectives during the past year (1310:26); to meet periodically with each

district board of administration to evaluate the service of and financial provision for the district superintendent (1218).

(9) To rule on questions of order which arise during the proceedings of a district conference as set forth in 1144.

(10) To present, for their consideration, one or more nominations for district superintendent to a district conference, when requested to do so by the district conference; to counsel a district board of administration in the appointment of an acting district superintendent (1303:7); to chair the special nominating committee named to select nominees for the office of district superintendent (1303:8); and to have charge of the service of installation of a district superintendent (5930).

(11) To work closely with the district officials in promoting evangelism and formulating plans for pioneer work and church growth (1233:3; 1310:4).

(12) To encourage and promote special efforts in each district to raise the district obligation for the United Stewardship Fund (2015:1) and the district budget in full, and to encourage the support of world missions.

(13) To encourage each district board of administration to plan and conduct conventions, institutes or seminars for pastors and other workers in the district, promoting such for the purpose of spiritual refreshment, leadership development, greater efficiency and a more united effort within the district and general church (1233:28).

(14) To recommend to the General Board or the General Conference the reclassifying of an established district as a provisional district (1042-1045) when it fails to meet the minimum requirements for an established district (1038) and appears to be making insufficient progress toward again meeting those requirements.

(15) To preside over the ordination of ministers (3070:6; 5750-5792), the commissioning of ministers (3059:1e; 5800) and lay workers (5855) or lay missionaries when present (1310:23; 1405), and to deliver the address or, if absent, to appoint a representative to preside over the ordination service and deliver the address and to sign all credentials, certificates and other forms incidental to this office.

(16) To approve the transfer of any ordained, commissioned or licensed minister into a district (1915), in concurrence with the district superintendent of that district (313:6; 705:3; 1310:18; cf. 3100:1); to approve the reception of a minister from another denomination (3104).

(17) To consult with a district board of administration concerning the purchase, location, encumbrance, sale, transfer or other disposition of real property used for district purposes such as a district parsonage, headquarters or campground (cf. 4150; 4840:1); to receive from each district superintendent property conveyance reports on approved forms (1310:11;

1920:16); and to approve the purchase, conveyance or mortgage of any local or district property of a district placed under discipline (4870; 5344).

### Judicial Supervision

(18) To carry out judicial responsibilities as set forth in 3136; 3139; 3142; 5170; 5175; 5212:1-2; 5218; 5235.

(19) To certify that the disciplinary requirements have been met for the restoration of a minister and to forward such request and certification to the General Secretary.

## 5. General Superintendent Emeritus

**1945.** The General Conference, upon recommendation of the General Board (1655:25), may confer the title of General Superintendent Emeritus upon a former General Superintendent, provided the former General Superintendent shall have served as a General Superintendent for two or more quadrennia and shall have reached the sixty-fifth birthday, or shall have become disabled (cf. 1590:20). It is understood that the tenure of the emeritus relation is for life. A General Superintendent Emeritus is a voting member of the General Conference (1503:1c).

## B. The General Secretary

**1948. Function.** The General Secretary has custody of the official records and archives and is responsible for legal work, statistics, directory and public relations for the general church.

**1951 Office.** The General Secretary is elected by the General Conference as a general official (334; 360:2; 1539; 1580:1; 1590:17; 1800), and is an *ex officio* member of the General Conference (1503:1c) and the General Administrative Council (1990). The General Secretary is amenable to the General Board, serves as a nonvoting resource person to the board, and is under the supervision of a General Superintendent (1915:3; 1935:3). The General Secretary serves as recording secretary to the General Board and the Executive Board (1770). The General Secretary shall exercise leadership in this office in keeping with *The Discipline*, the *Policy of the General Board for the General Secretary*, and other directives as may be given by the General Conference, the General Board or its Executive Board. The term of service and other regulations for this office are provided for in 1810-1870.

### C. The General Treasurer

**1970. Function.** The General Treasurer has custody of the general church funds and accounting records and is responsible for assigned fiscal management.

**1976. Duties.** The General Treasurer is employed by the General Board as a general official (1800:2), and is an *ex officio* member of the General Conference (1503:1c) and the General Administrative Council (1990). The General Treasurer is amenable to he General Board, serves as a nonvoting resource person to the board, and is under the supervision of a General Superintendent (1915:3; 1935:3). The General Treasurer shall exercise leadership in this office in keeping with *The Discipline*, the *Policy of the General Board for the General Treasurer*, and other directives as may be given by the General Conference, the General Board or its Executive Board. The term of service and other regulations for this office are provided for in 1810-1870.

### D. General Administrative Council

**1990.** The general officials (1800) and any officer of similar rank elected by the General Board shall be *ex officio* members of the General Administrative Council with responsibility for interdepartmental cooperation. The General Board may designate other members as are necessary to represent all departments, offices, auxiliaries, agencies, and subsidiary corporations in the headquarters operation (cf.1880). All members of the General Administrative Council shall be available to attend the meetings of the General Board except for executive sessions, and shall be invited to speak to any issue.

### E. General Church Financial Plan

#### 1. Summary

**1995.** The financial plan for the general church shall consist of the United Stewardship Fund, special offerings and planned gifts:

(1) **United Stewardship Fund** shall be established and administered as set forth in 2000 through 2045.

(2) **Special offerings** shall be authorized and administered as set forth in 2050 and shall provide support for world missions, supplementary support for general evangelism and church growth and the general educational institutions and support for such other purposes as may be authorized by the General Conference or the General Board.

(3) **Planned gifts** shall be promoted by the General Director of Estate and Gift Planning as set forth in 2075, and the funds shall be administered by the General Treasurer.

## 2. United Stewardship Fund

### a. Definition

**2000. The United Stewardship Fund** is a unified budget for the financial support of designated general church interests and the general educational institutions. It shall consist of two parts:

(1) **The USF-General Fund** shall provide support for general church administration, general benevolent institutions, ministerial training and other general church ministries as set forth in 2035.

(2) **The USF-Educational Institutions Fund** shall provide support for the approved general educational institutions as listed in 2365 and in a manner as set forth in 2040 (cf. 2377).

### b. Basis

**2005.** The USF-General Fund and the USF-Educational Institutions Fund shall be determined annually by a percentage (2005:2) of the base income of all churches for the previous fiscal year which shall be computed in the following manner (cf. 2005:3):

**(1) Base Income.** The base income shall be the total income of a local church and all of its departments for the previous fiscal year less money received (cf. 2005:3a):

(a) By loans (borrowed money).

(b) From the sale, rental or lease of property.

(c) From general or district church growth funds.

(d) By a bequest through a will.

(e) For Wesleyan World Missions and Wesleyan Native American Ministries.

(f) For the Easter offering to the General Department of Evangelism and Church Growth, the Heart-of-Missions offering, the Wesleyan Hour annual offering and the Hephzibah Children's Home offerings.

(g) As investment earnings.

(h) From day care centers, day schools, retirement homes, nursing homes and such enterprises (cf. 782:35).

(i) For youth attendance at general or regional Wesleyan youth conventions.

(j) From designated funds for major building projects as approved by the district board of administration (2005:3b).

**(2) Percentage.** The percentage for determining the USF-General Fund and a separate percentage for determining the USF-Educational Institutions Fund, shall be fixed by the General Conference (1590:8). The percentage in each case shall be applied to the assessable income as defined in 2005:1 except as provided for in 2005:3. In the event of an emergency during the interim of General Conference sessions, the General Board may alter the percentage of the USF-General Fund by a two-thirds majority vote of all its members (1655:22).

**(3) Exceptions and Adjustments**

(a) **Assessment Limits and Maximum**. All churches shall be subject to full assessment on all assessable income up to $500,000. Above that level, there shall be a graduated reduction in the percentage applied. For that portion of a church's assessable income between $500,000 and $1,000,000, there shall be a reduction of one in the total percentage divided proportionately between the USF-General Fund and the USF-Educational Institutions Fund. For that portion between $1,000,000 and $2,000,000 there shall be a reduction of two in the total percentage divided proportionately between the two funds. For that portion that exceeds $2,000,000 there shall be no assessments. The percentage in each case shall be applied to the same base income as defined in 2005:1 subject to the exceptions and adjustments set forth in 2005:3b-e.

(b) **Building Project Adjustment**. Whenever a local church engages in a major building project (1345:2) and fund drive which has been granted district board of administration approval, the involved local church's base income figure shall be reduced by the amount of designated funds received for the approved project.

(c) **Mother Church Exception**. For the first year following the planting of a daughter church, the mother church shall pay the USF assessments based upon the base income (cf. 2005:1) received in the mother church during that first year.

(d) **New Church Plant Adjustment**. Whenever a district plants a new church, the USF obligation for that church shall be phased in over the first five years of its operation in the following manner: For the first year of operation, there will be no obligation; for the second year the assessment will be set at 25 percent of the regular assessment; for the third year at 50 percent; for the fourth year at 75 percent; and for the fifth year at 100 percent.

(e) **Developing Church Adjustment**. Whenever a developing church is deemed to be under financial duress by the district board of administration, that board may subtract up to $25,000 from the USF base income used to calculate the USF obligation.

### c. District and Local Regulations

**2015. District Responsibility.** Each district and provisional district, with the exception of the work under the General Department of World Missions, shall be responsible to raise its share of the United Stewardship Fund, including the USF-General Fund and the USF-Educational Institutions Fund, in accord with the following regulations:

(1) **District Obligation.** The obligation of a district or provisional district shall be an amount equal to the designated percentage of the total base income, as defined in 2005:1-2, of all developing churches and churches of the district, subject to such exceptions and adjustments as are indicated in 2005:3. When this amount has been paid in full to the General Treasurer, for both the USF-General Fund and the USF-Educational Institutions Fund, a district has met its obligation to the United Stewardship Fund. The computations for the district obligation shall be based on the financial reports of the local churches as compiled by the district statistical committee (1352:1), prior to the annual district conference.

(2) **District Apportionment.** The district conference shall apportion its total obligation among the local churches under its jurisdiction by assigning an amount to each as its share of the USF-General Fund and the USF-Educational Institutions Fund respectively, under whatever plan the district conference shall adopt after receiving a recommendation from the district board of administration, or other special committee as assigned by the district conference (1233:10; 1337:6; cf. 1165-1168). The district secretary shall officially notify each pastor within two weeks after the close of the district conference session of the amount assigned to that local church. The district treasurer shall promptly notify the General Treasurer of the district USF obligation on forms provided by the General Treasurer (1337:6).

(3) **District Administration.** The district board of administration shall be responsible to administer the district plan for raising the United Stewardship Fund and shall be responsible to see that the district obligation is paid in full for both the USF-General Fund and USF-Educational Institutions Fund (1233:10). All USF money received by the district treasurer shall be remitted monthly to the General Treasurer on the approved forms.

**2025. Local Church Responsibility**. The pastor and the local board of administration shall be responsible for the faithful collection of the amount assigned by the district to their church, and shall raise it on the undivided plan. The local church treasurer shall forward all money received for the USF-General Fund and the USF-Educational Institutions Fund monthly to the district treasurer (cf. 842:4). A local church has met its obligation to the United Stewardship Fund when it has paid in full to the district treasurer the amounts assigned to it by the district for both the USF-General Fund and the USF-Educational Institutions Fund. In a developing church, the pastor and the local advisory council shall have the responsibility for raising the United Stewardship Fund.

**2030. Developing District Responsibility.** The obligation of a developing district, or of the churches within a developing district, to the United Stewardship Fund shall be determined by the General Board (1655:22). The assigned obligation shall be raised by the superintendent of the developing district, under the direction of the General Director of Evangelism and Church Growth and in accord with the *Policy of the General Board for Evangelism and Church Growth.*

### d. General Church Regulations

**2035. USF-General Fund, Beneficiaries and Apportionment.** The USF-General Fund shall provide support for general church departments and ministries and be apportioned among them as follows:

(1) Beneficiaries. The designated beneficiaries to receive support from the USF-General Fund are: the administrative offices of the General Superintendents, the General Secretary and the General Treasurer; the General Department of Evangelism and Church Growth; the General Department of Sunday School and Discipleship Ministries; the General Department of Youth; the General Department of Education and the Ministry; the General Department of Communications; the General Office of Estate and Gift Planning; and such other benevolent institutions, offices or agencies of the general church as the General Conference or the General Board shall designate from time to time.

(2) **Apportionment.** The apportioning of the USF-General Fund among the designated beneficiaries (2035:1) shall be determined annually by the General Board.

**2040. USF-Educational Institutions Fund, Beneficiaries and Apportionment.** The USF-Educational Institutions Fund shall provide support for general educational institutions and general ministerial education, and shall be apportioned among them as follows:

(1) **Beneficiaries.** The beneficiaries receiving support from the USF-Educational Institutions Fund shall include the general educational institutions (both those currently listed in 2365 and those formerly so listed for which there are ongoing fiscal obligations), approved programs for subsidizing ministerial training, the Wesleyan Seminary Foundation (2382) and the Ministerial Study Course Agency (2385-2388).

(2) **Apportionment.** The General Board shall determine the apportionment of the USF-Educational Institutions Fund among the beneficiaries listed in 2040:1.

**2045. General Promotion and Administration.** The General Director of Estate and Gift Planning shall promote the raising of the United Stewardship Fund as general director of stewardship. The General Treasurer shall cooperate with the General Director of Estate and Gift Planning in such promotion and shall administer the USF funds as provided for in *The Discipline* and as directed by the General Board (1976).

## 3. Special Offerings

**2050. Special offerings**, in addition to the United Stewardship Fund for the support of general church ministries and world outreach of The Wesleyan Church, shall include the following offerings and other such offerings as shall be authorized by the General Board. No agency, department, institution, organization or similar body of The Wesleyan Church may solicit offerings or present financial appeals without the approval of the General Board.

(1) **World Missions Support.** The General Department of World Missions shall not be included in the United Stewardship Fund, but shall be supported by the November self-denial offering, funds raised through deputational work and other solicitations, money raised by the auxiliary organizations, and other offerings specified for world missions.

(2) **Thanksgiving, Easter and September Offerings.** Two special offerings, apart from and in addition to the United Stewardship Fund, shall be received annually throughout the Church: a November self-denial offering for world missions and an Easter offering for general evangelism and church growth. In addition each local church is urged to receive an offering for the support of the Wesleyan Hour in the month of September. Such an offering should be received as close to the last Sunday of September as possible, in order to coincide with the anniversary celebration of the Wesleyan Hour.

(3) **Solicited Offerings.** The General Department of World Missions, the General Department of Evangelism and Church Growth and the general educational institutions shall raise financial support for the work under their care by sending representatives to visit the districts, local churches, members and constituency of the Church. District and local officials shall receive them and cooperate in their work. Offerings received shall be used as designated and shall be in addition to and apart from United Stewardship Fund, and shall be remitted promptly through the regular channels. The General Department of World Missions shall not engage in deputational work within the week prior to Easter, and the General Department of Evangelism and Church Growth shall not do deputational work within the week prior to Thanksgiving

or on the Sunday following Thanksgiving. Exception to the above may be made with the approval of the General Directors of Evangelism and Church Growth and World Missions. An educational institution shall do its deputational work in the manner decided upon in the plans for such institutions approved by the General Board.

(4) **Auxiliary Organizations.** The Wesleyan Medical Fellowship, Wesleyan Men, Wesleyan Women, Wesleyan Youth and Young Adults International shall raise financial support for approved projects in accord with their respective constitutions and subject to the general oversight of the General Board.

(5) **Other Contributions.** Other offerings, contributions, bequests and donations shall be used as specified by the donor and may be forwarded through the regular channels to the General Treasurer. Those individuals who prefer to contact the General Director of Estate and Gift Planning (2075) or a general department or institution concerning annuities, bequests and other special contributions may do so.

### 5. Office of Estate and Gift Planning

**2070. Function**. The General Director of Estate and Gift Planning shall develop, promote and administer an estate and gift planning service for the general church.

**2075. Office.** The General Director of Estate and Gift Planning is employed by the General Board as a general official (1800:2), and is an *ex officio* member of the General Conference (1503:1c) and the General Administrative Council (1990). The General Director of Estate and Gift Planning is amenable to the General Board, serves as a nonvoting resource person to the board, and is under the supervision of a General Superintendent (1915:3; 1935:3). The General Director of Estate and Gift Planning shall exercise leadership in this office in keeping with *The Discipline*, the *Policy of the General Board for Estate and Gift Planning*, and other directives as may be given by the General Conference, the General Board or its Executive Board. The term of service and other regulations for this office are provided for in 1810-1870).

## Chapter V

# GENERAL PUBLICATIONS AND COMMUNICATIONS

### A. Objectives

**2100.** The objectives of the general publications and communications program of The Wesleyan Church shall be to facilitate the spread and advancement of scriptural holiness and to promote the witness and outreach of The Wesleyan Church through the various media of mass communications in a world becoming increasingly literate, by providing doctrinally sound and spiritually effective periodicals, curriculum materials, books, tracts and other similar materials and promoting their distribution and use. All publications and communications of the Church shall be in harmony with its Articles of Religion, Membership Commitments and Elementary Principles.

### B. General Department of Communications

#### 1. Function

**2105.** The General Department of Communications is responsible for the literary content and form of the official church publication and all other general church publications assigned to it by the General Conference or the General Board, and for ministry through other forms of media, as so assigned.

#### 2. The General Director of Communications

**2110.** The General Director of Communications is employed by the General Board as a general official (1800:2), and is an *ex officio* member of the General Conference (1503:1c) and the General Administrative Council (1990). The General Director of Communications is amenable to the General Board, serves as a nonvoting resource person to the board, and is under the supervision of a General Superintendent (1915:3; 1935:3). The General Director of Communications shall exercise leadership in this office in keeping with *The Discipline*, the *Policy of the General Board for Communications*, and other directives as may be given by the General Conference, the General Board or its Executive Board. The term of service and other regulations for this office are provided for in 1810-1870.

### 3. Book Committee

**2135.** The Book Committee shall consist of the General Director of Communications as chair, the General Director's supervising General Superintendent and the General Publisher. Other qualified persons may be employed for evaluating and appraising specialized manuscripts at the discretion of the chair.

**2140.** The Book Committee shall assist the General Director in the work as denominational editor. No book or other manuscript, other than curriculum materials or publications of the general offices, departments, agencies, auxiliaries and institutions, shall be published by the Wesleyan Publishing House, without the approval of the Book Committee.

## C. Departmental Publications

**2145.** Each general office, department, agency, auxiliary or institution may produce such publications as the General Board shall approve (1655:30). If such a publication becomes competitive with other publications, the body authorized by the General Board shall resolve the issue.

## D. Wesleyan Publishing House

### 1. Function

**2150.** The Wesleyan Publishing House is responsible for the production, sale and distribution of such general publications of The Wesleyan Church as the General Conference or the General Board shall assign, and for the sale and distribution of such other religious literature and materials as the General Board shall direct.

### 2. The General Publisher

**2155.** The General Publisher is employed by the General Board as a general official (1800:2), and is an *ex officio* member of the General Conference (1503:1c) and the General Administrative Council (1990). The General Publisher is amenable to the General Board, serves as a nonvoting resource person to the board, and is under the supervision of a General Superintendent (1915:3; 1935:3). The General Publisher shall exercise leadership in the Wesleyan Publishing House in keeping with *The Discipline*, the *Policy of the General Board for the General Publisher*, and other directives as may be given by the General Conference, the General Board or its Executive Board. The term of service and other regulations for this office are provided for in 1810-1870.

### 3. Committee on Management of the Wesleyan Publishing House

**2180.** The Committee on Management of the Wesleyan Publishing House shall consist of the General Publisher as chair, and of four to six persons experienced in the field of business administration subject to the approval of the General Administrative Council.

**2185.** The Committee on Management of the Wesleyan Publishing House shall serve as an advisory committee to the General Publisher in the management of the Wesleyan Publishing House, especially in seeking the most economical means of securing the production of the Church's literature.

# Chapter VI

# GENERAL MISSIONS AND EVANGELISM

## A. Objectives

**2200.** The ultimate objective of The Wesleyan Church is to fulfill the Great Commission of the Lord Jesus Christ by sharing with all mankind the good news and glorious experience of full salvation. To this end, The Wesleyan Church, through its General Department of Evangelism and Church Growth and General Department of World Missions, shall endeavor:

(1) To evangelize the nations of earth, seeking the salvation of the individual and the entire sanctification of believers as the primary responsibility of all missionary work.

(2) To gather the converts into churches and enlist them in the work of God's kingdom.

(3) To place well-qualified and Spirit-filled pastors over the churches, giving special emphasis to the training of workers and leaders for the church.

(4) To share the benefits of the gospel, and to facilitate evangelistic work through specialized ministries such as medical, educational, literary and benevolent work.

(5) To promote, in accordance with scriptural and indigenous principles, the growth and development of the churches in each field or area to a church body that is spiritually mature, well organized, financially responsible and missionary minded, and that can assume its place in The Wesleyan Church.

## B. General Department of Evangelism and Church Growth

### 1. Function

**2205.** The General Department of Evangelism and Church Growth is responsible for carrying out the missionary objectives of The Wesleyan Church (2200) within the borders of the United States and Canada, and in such other places as shall be assigned to it by the General Conference or the General Board.

### 2. Divisions

**2208.** The ministries of the General Department of Evangelism and Church Growth are threefold:

(1) **The division of general church growth,** involving the development, promotion and supervision of an aggressive program of church growth through evangelistic and missionary work, both in cooperation with the established districts (1233:3; 1310:2, 4) and in new or undeveloped areas provided for in the plan for developing districts and provisional districts (cf. 1003-1034).

(2) **The division of special ministries,** involving the missionary outreach of The Wesleyan Church in the United States and Canada among foreign language and racial minorities, including such as the Native Americans, the Jews, the blind and other minority groups requiring a specialized ministry, as authorized by the General Board. This work may be carried on directly by the department or through the districts and local churches, and does not preclude the districts and local churches from exercising their privilege and duty of evangelizing and ministering to the needs of minorities in their own territories.

(3) **The division of general evangelism,** involving the promotion of soul-winning concern and evangelism in all of its forms and phases, the correlation of the ministries of the general evangelists (cf. 3280-3285) and commissioned special workers (cf. 3470), and the provision of a service agency for such workers.

### 3. The General Director of Evangelism and Church Growth

**2212.** The General Director of Evangelism ad Church Growth is elected by the General Conference as a general official (360:2; 1580:1; 1590:17; 1800), and is an *ex officio* member of the General Conference (1503:1c) and the General Administrative Council (1990). The General Director of Evangelism and Church Growth is amenable to the General Board, serves as a nonvoting resource person to the board, and is under the supervision of a General Superintendent (1915:3; 1935:3). The General Director of Evangelism and Church Growth shall exercise leadership in this department in keeping with *The Discipline*, the *Policy of the General Board for Evangelism and Church Growth*, and other directives as may be given by the General Conference, the General Board, or its Executive Board. The term of service and other regulations for this office are provided for in 1810-1870.

### 4. Church Builders' Club

**2236.** The Church Builders' Club shall provide for church growth by enlisting voluntary donors who pledge to answer calls for aiding the establishment of new works. The General Director of Evangelism and Church

Growth shall be responsible to manage the Church Builders' Club as directed by the General Board.

### 5. Wesleyan Native American Ministries

**2239.** The work among the native Americans in the United States and Canada shall be organized as Wesleyan Native American Ministries, including all chapels, churches, institutions or other work among the native American people, as assigned by the General Board.

**2242.** Wesleyan Native American Ministries shall be incorporated as Wesleyan Indian Ministries and shall be governed by a board of directors as follows:

(1) **Composition.** The board of directors shall consist of the General Director of Evangelism and Church Growth as chair, the General Director of Wesleyan Native American Ministries and other members-at-large as determined in number and elected by the General Board, for which nominations shall be submitted by the General Director of Evangelism and Church Growth (cf. 1655:18). Each director must be a covenant member of The Wesleyan Church and shall serve for four years.

(2) **Amenability.** The board of directors shall be amenable to the General Board (1655:18; 1655:39b).

(3) **Duties.** The board of directors of Wesleyan Native American Ministries shall:

(a) Govern and coordinate all phases of the work in accord with *The Discipline*, the *Policy of the General Board for Evangelism and Church Growth*, the articles of incorporation and the bylaws.

(b) Promote and develop evangelistic, educational, benevolent and church growth work among the Native American peoples of the United States and Canada in those areas approved by the General Board (2208:2) and in harmony with the missionary objectives (2200).

(c) Adopt financial plans for the work of Wesleyan Native American Ministries.

(d) Employ teachers, missionaries, Christian workers and other personnel as deemed necessary, and dismiss the same.

(e) Acquire, own, hold, use, lease, mortgage, pledge, sell, convey or otherwise dispose of property, real, personal or mixed, tangible or intangible, in the name of the corporation and in trust for The Wesleyan Church, and exercise any or all other powers as set forth in the articles of incorporation and bylaws.

(f) Recommend to the General Board any plans for organizing the workers and churches under Wesleyan Native American Ministries into developing districts, provisional districts and established districts.

## 6. Other Workers

**2244. Missionaries Appointed To Serve Under The Wesleyan Native American Mission.** A missionary appointed to serve the Wesleyan Native American Mission under the jurisdiction of the General Department of Evangelism and Church Growth may retain membership in the local church and district as of the time of appointment. The missionary shall also relate to the Wesleyan Native American church where assigned and shall hold active membership therein.

**2246. Developing District Pastor or Other Worker.** A pastor or other worker duly appointed to serve in a developing district under the jurisdiction of the General Department of Evangelism and Church Growth may retain membership in a local church and district during the time of appointment to serve in a developing district. The pastor or other worker shall also relate to the developing district where assigned and shall hold membership as set forth in *The Discipline* and according to the *Policy of the General Board for Evangelism and Church Growth*. The pastor or other worker shall be amenable for conduct and performance to the proper authorities in the developing district in which service is rendered, to the General Director of Evangelism and Church Growth and to the General Board as set forth in the Judiciary and the *Policy of the General Board for Evangelism and Church Growth*.

## 7. Program of Evangelism

**2248. Executive Director of Evangelism.**

(1) **General Regulations.** There may be an Executive Director of Evangelism who shall be elected by the General Board from one or more nominations submitted by the General Director of Evangelism and Church Growth. The Executive Director of Evangelism shall serve for a term designated by the General Board or until a successor is chosen. The Executive Director of Evangelism shall be an *ex officio* member of the Council on Evangelism (2254:1). The Executive Director of Evangelism shall be amenable to the General Director of Evangelism and Church Growth for the conduct of the office, and may be removed from office for cause or when the best interests of the Church so require by a majority vote of all the members of the General Board (1655:39b).

(2) **Duties.** The Executive Director of Evangelism shall administer the office in keeping with *The Discipline*, the *Policy of the General Board for Evangelism and Church Growth* and as directed by the General Director of Evangelism and Church Growth. The Executive Director of Evangelism shall be responsible:

(a) To assist the General Director of Evangelism and Church Growth in promoting interest in soul-winning and evangelism in all of its forms and phases, and in promoting the interests of general evangelism (2208:3).

(b) To serve as a member of the Council on Evangelism (2254:1).

(c) To act as consultant to all church organizations in evangelistic methods.

(d) To create literature on evangelism including inspirational and promotional materials, and study guides and training programs.

(e) To plan and coordinate conventions and united meetings on evangelism.

(f) To correlate the work of the general evangelists, providing through this office a service agency for general evangelists and special workers (cf. 2208:3).

(g) To aid districts and local churches, as they may request and as time may permit, in initiating evangelistic ventures, and to provide standardized promotional materials for such ventures.

(h) To carry out such other duties as may be assigned by the General Board.

**2254. Council on Evangelism.**

(1) **Membership.** The Council on Evangelism shall consist of the General Director of Evangelism and Church Growth as chair, the Executive Director of Evangelism (2248:2b), and two members from each administrative area. The area representatives shall be nominated by the General Director of Evangelism and Church Growth, and shall be elected as provided by the General Board.

(2) **Duties.** The Council on Evangelism shall serve as an advisory body to the General Director of Evangelism and Church Growth and to the Executive Director of Evangelism in promoting an aggressive program of evangelism on the general, district and local levels.

(3) **Additional Regulations.** Further regulations for the Council on Evangelism shall be provided by the General Board.

### C. General Department of World Missions

#### 1. Function

**2258.** The General Department of World Missions is responsible for carrying out the missionary objectives of The Wesleyan Church (2200) in those fields and areas beyond the national borders of United States and Canada as approved by the General Conference or the General Board.

## 2. The General Director of World Missions

**2261.** The General Director of World Missions is elected by the General Conference as a general official (360:2; 1580:1; 1590:17; 1800), and is an *ex officio* member of the General Conference (1503:1c) and the General Administrative Council (1990). The General Director of World Missions is amenable to the General Board, serves as a nonvoting resource person to the board, and is under the supervision of a General Superintendent (1915:3; 1935:3). The General Director of World Missions shall exercise leadership in this department in keeping with *The Discipline*, the *Policy of the General Board for World Missions*, and other directives as may be given by the General Conference, the General Board or its Executive Board. The term of service and other regulations for this office are provided for in 1810-1870)

## 3. Missionaries

**2272.** A missionary or other worker duly appointed to serve under the General Department of World Missions may retain membership in the local church and district where membership is held as of the time of appointment by the General Board. The missionary or other worker shall also relate to the national church where assigned and shall hold membership as set forth in *The Discipline* or other regulations adopted for the particular field to which assigned and according to the *Policy of the General Board for World Missions*. The missionary or other worker shall be amenable for all conduct to the proper authorities on the field or area of service, the General Director of World Missions and the General Board as set forth in the Judiciary and the *Policy of the General Board for World Missions*.

## 4. Organization of Mission Units

**2275.** Mission units under the General Department of World Missions shall be organized on four levels:

(1) A **developing district** shall be a unit which does not meet the requirements for a provisional district.

(2) A **provisional district** shall be a unit with a minimum of five churches, two hundred covenant members, and a sufficient number of ordained ministers for a district board of administration.

(3) An **established district** shall be a unit with a minimum of twenty churches and seven hundred fifty covenant members.

(4) A **national or regional conference** shall be a unit with two or more provisional or established districts.

**2278.** Mission units under the General Department of World Missions shall be entitled to send delegates to the North American General Conference on a plan of representation determined by the General Board (325).

**2281. Membership Rights.** In keeping with the Statement of Relationship contained in the Essentials (see the Charter of the Wesleyan World Fellowship), members of units under the General Department of World Missions have the right to transfer membership not only among local Wesleyan churches but also from one unit under the department to any other unit under the department, or to districts within the United States or Canada (2550), subject to 297:5.

**2284. Transfer of Ministers.** The transfer of ministerial credentials from one unit under the General Department of World Missions to any other unit under the department, or to any district of the United States or Canada may be effected with the understanding that consideration must be given to differences in requirements for licensing and ordination of ministers as provided for in the various books of discipline of units worldwide.

**2287. Eligibility for Holding Office.** As outlined in 2500:5, units under the General Department of World Missions are expected to adopt, subject to the approval of the General Board, a discipline or other similar document for the administration of the churches within their boundaries. While the right to be elected to office is worldwide, the right to hold office shall be exercised within the administrative jurisdiction of each book of discipline.

# Chapter VII

## GENERAL CHRISTIAN EDUCATION

### A. Objectives

**2300.** The ultimate objective of Christian education within The Wesleyan Church is to declare the truth of full salvation through Christ as recorded in the Holy Scriptures, and to guide sinful, fallen men and women to experience the crises of conversion and entire sanctification, dynamic service to God and humanity, and continuous growth unto the fullness of the stature of Christ. To accomplish this, Wesleyan Christian education will endeavor:

(1) To help each person to recognize the Bible as the inspired Word of God, and to know, believe and obey its teachings.

(2) To help each person to recognize the need of salvation and of God's provision for it through Christ's death and resurrection, and to lead each person to experience the new birth through repentance and faith in Jesus Christ.

(3) To help each convert to recognize the need for cleansing from the carnal nature and for the sanctifying and empowering presence of the Holy Spirit, and to experience the crisis of entire sanctification through consecration and faith.

(4) To help each believer to relate to the Church as the body of Christ, encouraging each believer to become a member of the local church and to find a place of service within it.

(5) To instruct each person in the fundamentals of the faith, in the history of the Christian church, the importance of the Reformation and the Wesleyan movement, the history of The Wesleyan Church, its precedent bodies and its missionary outreach, warning each person against the false doctrines of the age and equipping each as a witness for the Lord.

(6) To help each person to develop a Christian interpretation of life and of the universe, enabling each person to see God's sovereign purpose at work, and training each person to be a good steward of the talents, time, opportunities and material goods with which God has entrusted each person.

(7) To encourage each person to grow toward spiritual maturity in Christ Jesus, demonstrating Christian attitudes and actions in every relationship of life.

## B. General Department of Sunday School and Discipleship Ministries

### 1. Function

**2305.** The General Department of Sunday School and Discipleship Ministries is responsible, on the general level, to carry out the objectives of The Wesleyan Church for Christian Education (2300) in such phases as Sunday schools, vacation Bible schools, leadership training, membership training, children's church, weekday church schools and day care centers, released time classes, music ministries and the promotion of Christian family life.

### 2. The General Director of Sunday School and Discipleship Ministries

**2308.** The General Director of Sunday School and Discipleship Ministries is elected by the General Conference as a general official (360:2; 1580:1; 1590:17; 1800), and is an *ex officio* member of the General Conference (1503:1c) and the General Administrative Council (1990). The General Director of Sunday School and Discipleship Ministries is amenable to the General Board, serves as a nonvoting resource person to the board, and is under the supervision of a General Superintendent (1915:3; 1935:3). The General Director of Sunday School and Discipleship Ministries shall exercise leadership in this department in keeping with *The Discipline*, the *Policy of the General Board for Sunday School and Discipleship Ministries*, and other directives as may be given by the General Conference, the General Board or its Executive Board. The term of service and other regulations for this office are provided in 1810-1870.

## C. General Department of Youth

### 1. Function

**2315.** The General Department of Youth is responsible for carrying out The Wesleyan Church's objectives for Christian education (2300) as they relate to the youth ministries of the Church, represents the interests of youth to the Church and serves as the Church's resource agency for youth-related concerns.

## 2. Divisions

**2318.** The ministries of the General Department of Youth are threefold:

(1) **The division of Christian Youth Clubs International** (CYCI), a program of training, activity and fellowship for children through grade six (cf. 915-920; 1489).

(2) **The division of Wesleyan Youth** on general, district and local levels, known organizationally as Wesleyan Youth (WY). Full details concerning the operation of WY are given in 7500-7650.

(3) **The division of young adult ministries** through which The Wesleyan Church maintains contact with its youth in their post-high school years, including Young Adults International and persons in the armed forces and on college campuses, and seeks to win and hold them to Christ and the Church, and trains them for effective witness in their immediate environment and in their future service within the Church (924: 1494).

## 3. The General Director of Youth

**2321.** The General Director of Youth is elected by the General Conference as a general official (360:2; 1580:1; 1590:17; 1800), and is an *ex officio* member of the General Conference (1503:1c) and the General Administrative Council (1990). The General Director of Youth is amenable to the General Board, serves as a nonvoting resource person to the board, and is under the supervision of a General Superintendent (1915:3; 1935:3). The General Director of youth shall exercise leadership in this department in keeping with *The Discipline*, the *Policy of the General Board for the General Department of Youth* and other directives as may be given by the General Conference, the General Board or its Executive Board. The term of service and other regulations for this office are provided in 1810-1870.

## 4. General WY Executive Committee

**2332.** The general Wesleyan Youth executive committee shall be composed of the General Director of Youth as chair (7625) and the area WY directors (7630). The area WY directors shall be elected as provided by the General Board. Vacancies shall be filled as provided by the General Board.

**2335.** The general WY executive committee shall serve as an advisory body to the General Director of Youth concerning Wesleyan Youth and shall have other duties as set forth in 7625:2. All plans of the committee shall be subject to the approval of the General Board (7625:2).

## D. General Department of Education and the Ministry

### 1. Function

**2338.** The General Department of Education and the Ministry is responsible for coordinating the implementation of The Wesleyan Church's objectives for Christian education (2300) as they relate to the training of Christian ministers, missionaries and educators on the study course, college and seminary levels, the development of youth in higher education for various fields of service, and continuing education and career development for the ministers of The Wesleyan Church.

### 2. The General Director of Education and the Ministry

**2341.** The General Director of Education and the Ministry is elected by the General Conference as a general official (360:2; 1580:1; 1590:17; 1800), is an *ex officio* member of the General Conference (1503:1c) and the General Administrative Council (1990), and is a member and the executive secretary of both the Committee on Chaplains (2395) and the Wesleyan Educational Council (2355). The General Director of Education and the Ministry is amenable to the General Board, serves as a nonvoting resource person to the board, and is under the supervision of a General Superintendent (1915:3; 1935:3). The General Director of Education and the Ministry shall exercise leadership in this department in keeping with *The Discipline*, the *Policy of the General Board for Education and the Ministry*, and other directives as may be given by the General Conference, the General Board or its Executive Board. The term of service and other regulations for this office are provided in 1810-1870.

### 3. Wesleyan Educational Council

**2355.** The Wesleyan Educational Council shall consist of the General Director of Education and the Ministry, who shall serve as its executive secretary (2341), and the president and chair of the board of trustees for each general educational institution (2365). The Council shall serve as an advisory body to the General Director of Education and the Ministry.

## E. Educational Institutions

### 1. Ownership and Control

#### a. Basic Principles

**2358.** The educational institutions of The Wesleyan Church shall be governed in harmony with these principles:

(1) All schools, in fulfilling the mission of The Wesleyan Church, shall seek to produce Christian workers and committed lay members for the church of Jesus Christ. The Church recognizes that more than one type of educational institution will be needed. Some institutions will devote themselves primarily to the preparation of full-time Christian workers for the Church. Some colleges, recognizing the God-given mandate to explore and bring under dominion the whole range of knowledge for the glory of God and the good of mankind (Gen. 1:26-28; 9:1-7; Matt. 6:10; 1 Cor. 3:21b-23; 2 Cor. 10:5; 1 Tim. 4:4-5), will offer a Christian liberal arts program. Some students will use such a curriculum as training for full-time, church-related vocations or as a foundation for graduate training for such vocations; some to prepare for other vocations in which they have been called to serve Christ, His church and His world.

(2) The Church and all its schools shall work in the closest harmony. In its legislative assemblies, the Church defines its faith. In its classrooms, the Church studies, expounds and defends its faith. In the congregation, the Church worships its Lord and proclaims its faith. To safeguard the doctrinal purity of the Church, it shall be required that all schools maintain and promote the doctrinal position of the Church as set forth in its Articles of Religion, Covenant Membership Commitments and Elementary Principles. Any person employed on the administrative staff or faculty of an educational institution of The Wesleyan Church must affirm adherence to the doctrine of entire sanctification and other doctrines of The Wesleyan Church as set forth in the Articles of Religion.

(3) In establishing its educational institutions, and in guiding their life and work, The Wesleyan Church seeks to provide the highest possible quality of Christian education for its own constituents and for other persons who wish to study under its auspices without regard to race, national origin or sex (265:11; 360:3d).

### b. Lines of Authority

**2362.** Ultimate authority over the educational institutions of The Wesleyan Church rests with the General Conference (cf. 1590:13). In practice this authority is delegated to the General Board and consists of the following:

(1) Authority, by two-thirds vote, to establish, merge or dissolve an educational institution, or to enter into a cooperative agreement with other persons/groups of like theological and behavioral commitment in the ownership and operation of an educational institution.

(2) Authority to provide for and deal with all matters pertaining to charters and bylaws.

(3) Provision for boards of control in keeping with 340:2.

(4) The adoption and revision of such *Standards of the General Board for Educational Institutions* as the General Board shall deem to be wise.

(5) The General Board is not empowered or authorized to contravene, override or set aside a decision of a college board of trustees except as is provided and specifically stated in 2362:1-4.

## 2. General Educational Institutions and Curricula Offerings

**2365.** The general educational institutions of The Wesleyan Church and their curricula offerings are:

(1) Bethany Bible College, Sussex, New Brunswick, Canada: two-year terminal and transfer degree curricula; four-year Bible and Christian Ministries curricula (cf. 2368).

(2) Houghton College, Houghton, New York: two-year terminal and transfer degree curricula; four-year liberal arts and professional curricula (cf. 2368)

(3) Indiana Wesleyan University, Marion, Indiana: two-year terminal and transfer degree curricula; four-year liberal arts and professional curricula; professional curricula leading to master's degrees (cf. 2368)

(4) Oklahoma Wesleyan University, Bartlesville, Oklahoma: two-year terminal and transfer degree curricula; four-year liberal arts and professional curricula (cf. 2368).

(5) Southern Wesleyan University, Central, South Carolina: two-year terminal and transfer degree curricula; four-year liberal arts and professional curricula; professional curricula leading to master's degrees (cf. 2368).

**2368.** Each of the four-year colleges shall maintain a curriculum which satisfies the educational requirements for ordination as an ordained minister by The Wesleyan Church.

### 3. Educational Areas

**2371.** The established districts, provisional districts and developing districts of The Wesleyan Church in the United States and Canada shall be divided into four educational areas (1590:14), corresponding in general with the four representative areas of the Church, and in general with the regional accreditation associations serving the area in which the schools are located. The boundaries of the educational areas are given in 2455-2470.

**2374.** Each general educational institution shall be considered as serving all the districts of the area or areas to which it is assigned.

### 4. Financial Support

**2377.** The financial support of the general educational institutions of The Wesleyan Church shall be provided for as follows:

(1) **The United Stewardship Fund-General Fund** (2035). The USF-General Fund shall include provision for the General Department of Education and the Ministry (2338), and the Wesleyan Educational Council (2355).

(2) **The United Stewardship Fund-Educational Institutions Fund** (2040). The USF-Educational Institutions Fund shall provide for the support of the approved general educational institutions (cf. 2365; 2450-2470), the Ministerial Study Course Agency (2385-2388), the Wesleyan Seminary Foundation (2382) and the subsidizing of ministerial training (cf. 2035:1).

(3) **Special Offerings.** Each general educational institution shall supplement its income through deputational work, solicitations and special offerings (cf. 2050:3).

## F. Educational Agencies

### 1. Wesleyan Seminary Foundation

**2382.** The Wesleyan Seminary Foundation is the Church agency providing for the advanced training of Wesleyan ministers. Its connection with a particular institution, the official agreement between The Wesleyan Church and the institution, and consequent policies and programs shall be determined as provided by the General Board. The Foundation shall be under the direction of the General Director of Education and the Ministry.

## 2. Ministerial Study Course Agency

**2385.** Ministerial training within The Wesleyan Church will ordinarily take place in one of the approved educational institutions. However, for those persons whose circumstances make such institutional education impossible in whole or in part, the General Department of Education and the Ministry shall provide correspondence courses of study. The correspondence courses shall also be open to others who wish to prepare for Christian service. (Cf. 3200-3210.)

**2388.** The Ministerial Study Course Agency shall be maintained at the denominational headquarters to centralize and standardize the keeping of records on all students for the various ministries recognized by The Wesleyan Church and the administering of the correspondence study courses for those ministries (3200-3210). It shall be directed by the General Director of Education and the Ministry. The duties of the General Director of Education and the Ministry in this connection shall be:

(1) To maintain records on all students for the various ministries recognized by The Wesleyan Church, whether enrolled in educational institutions or in correspondence courses (3170:1-3), and including students of the lay minister's course of study (3210:4; 3420), commissioned minister's course of study (3059:1b; 3210:3); the pre-ordination course of study (3040:2; 3051:1; 3070:3; 3210:1), the courses of study for specialized ministries (3210:2), and the special worker's courses of study (3210:5; 3460-3470). The records shall include transcripts, grades, courses finished and current standing. The Agency shall exchange needed information with the educational institutions and the local and district boards directing the students, issuing an annual report concerning progress for the year and current standing to each student, a similar report on each student of the lay minister's course of study to the local board of administration of the local church where membership is held, and a similar report on each student recognized by the district to the home district board of ministerial development prior to the session of the district conference (cf. 1387:2; 1390:2; 3040:2; 3460).

(2) To provide a correspondence course for each course required in each course of study, securing the services of a qualified instructor and approving the choice of textbooks and study plans, providing for the registration of students properly authorized to use the correspondence courses (cf. 3170:3), and providing study guides and instructions as well as examinations which shall be administered through an ordained minister whenever possible (cf. 3200).

(3) To provide suitable transcripts and to issue certificates upon the satisfactory completion of the work assigned (cf. 6410).

(4) To evaluate any training taken outside the institutions and agencies of The Wesleyan Church by a student for one of the ministries recognized by The Wesleyan Church, to judge the equivalence of such outside training to the appropriate course of study, and to report any conclusions and recommendations to the appropriate local boards of administration or district board of ministerial development (3070:3; 3104:4; 3170:4; 3470).

### G. Committee on Chaplains

**2395.** The Committee on Chaplains shall include the General Director of Education and the Ministry as its executive secretary, with other members to be selected as provided by the General Board.

# Chapter VIII

# BOUNDARIES

## A. District Boundaries

**2400.** The boundaries of an established district, provisional district or developing district shall be defined by the General Conference or, in the interim of its sessions, by the General Board as set forth in 317; 1006; 1020; 1034; 1036; 1042-1045; 1060-1065; 1590:10-11; 1655:33.

**2403.** The boundaries of the districts in the United States and Canada are:

(1) The **Atlantic District** shall include the Atlantic Provinces (New Brunswick, Newfoundland and Labrador, Nova Scotia, and Prince Edward Island) and the State of Maine.

(2) The **Central Canada District** shall include the provinces of Ontario and Quebec.

(3) The **Central New York District** shall include those portions of the states of New York and Pennsylvania in an area bounded as follows: beginning at the northernmost point of Jefferson County, New York, on the St. Lawrence River, and continuing southeastward along the northern boundaries of Jefferson, Lewis and Herkimer Counties to the eastern boundary of Herkimer County, thence south along the eastern boundary of Herkimer County to the southwest corner of Hamilton County, thence southwest in a direct line to the easternmost point of Madison County, thence south along the western boundaries of Otsego and Delaware Counties to the Pennsylvania state line, thence including that part of Wayne County, Pennsylvania, which is north of Routes 106 and 6, thence west to include Susquehanna, Bradford and Tioga Counties in Pennsylvania, thence west on the New York state line and north to include that part of the state of New York which is east of the Western New York District.

(4) The **Chesapeake District** shall include the District of Columbia; the states of Delaware and Maryland; and shall include the Northampton, Accomack, Prince William, Loundon, Faquier, Fairfax, Stafford, and Arlington counties, and the cities of Alexandria and Falls Church, in the state of Virginia, but with the exception of the Aldersgate Wesleyan Church of Falls Church, Virginia.

(5) The **Colorado-Nebraska District** shall include the states of Colorado and Nebraska.

(6) The **Dakota District** shall include the states of North Dakota, South Dakota, Montana, Wyoming, and Alaska.

(7) The **East Michigan District** shall include that part of the state of Michigan which is east of the following boundary: beginning from the northwest corner of Tuscola County at Saginaw Bay, thence south along the western boundary of Tuscola County to Genesee County, thence west and south along the boundary of Genesee County to Livingston County, thence west and south along the boundary of Livingston County and continuing south along the western boundary of Washtenaw County to Lenawee County, thence west and south along the Lenawee County line to the Ohio state line, except the church in Hudson; and shall include the church in Lennon, Michigan and the Detroit Avenue church in Toledo, Ohio.

(8) The **Eastern New York/New England District** shall include that part of the state of New York which is north and east of the Central New York District, bounded on the south by a line beginning on the New York-New Jersey state line at the Hudson River and continuing eastward to the southwestern corner of Connecticut; and shall include the states of New Hampshire, Vermont, Massachusetts, Connecticut and Rhode Island.

(9) The **Florida District** shall include the state of Florida.

(10) The **Greater Ohio** District shall include the state of Ohio, and shall include the churches in Paden City, South Parkersburg and Weirton, West Virginia.

(11) The **Illinois District** shall include the state of Illinois.

(12) The **Indiana Central District** shall include that part of the state of Indiana which is south of the northern boundaries of Benton, White, Carroll, Howard, Madison, Delaware and Randolph Counties; north of the northern boundaries of Vigo, Clay, Owen, Morgan, Johnson, Rush, Fayette and Union Counties and north of U. S. Highway 40 in Hancock County.

(13) The **Indiana North District** shall include that part of the state of Indiana which is north of the northern boundaries of the following counties: Benton, White, Carroll, Howard, Madison, Delaware and Randolph.

(14) The **Indiana South District** shall include that part of the state of Indiana which is south of the northern boundaries of Vigo, Clay, Owen, Morgan, Johnson, Rush, Fayette and Union Counties, and south of U.S. Highway 40 in Hancock County.

(15) The **Iowa-Minnesota District** shall include the states of Iowa and Minnesota.

(16) The **Kansas District** shall include the state of Kansas.

(17) The **Kentucky District** shall include the state of Kentucky.

(18) The **North Carolina East District** shall include that part of the state of North Carolina which is east of the following boundary: beginning at the Virginia-North Carolina state line, following State Road 87 south to Reidsville, thence south on U.S. 29 to Greensboro, thence southwest on Interstate 85 to Salisbury, thence south on U.S. 52 to Wadesboro, thence east on U.S. 74 to

Laurinburg, thence south on U.S. 15 and U.S. 401 to the South Carolina state line, with the exception of the Midway church near Randleman and Peele's Chapel near Hamlet, and shall include the church and the camp meeting facility in Kernersville, North Carolina.

(19) The **North Carolina West District** shall include that part of the state of North Carolina which is west of the following boundary: beginning at the Virginia-North Carolina state line, follow State Road 87 south to Reidsville, thence south on U.S. 29 to Greensboro, thence southwest on Interstate 85 to Salisbury, thence south on U.S. 52 to Wadesboro, thence east on U.S. 74 to Laurinburg, thence south on U.S. 15 and U.S. 401 to the South Carolina state line, with the exception of the church and camp meeting facility in Kernersville, and with the further exception of Macon and Jackson Counties but including that portion of the Cherokee Indian Reservation in Jackson County beginning at a point one-quarter mile from Cherokee, North Carolina, on the Jackson and Swain County line on the Soco Gap Road and running directly southeast to Sheep Rock Mountain, and then following the southern watershed of Soco Creek to Water Rock Knob in Haywood County; and shall include the Midway church near Randleman, Peele's Chapel near Hamlet; and shall include the following churches in South Carolina: Clover, York and Rock Hill (York County); Prevatt's Chapel, Fletcher's Chapel and Bennettsville (Marlboro County).

(20) The **North Michigan District** shall include that part of the state of Michigan which is north and west of the following boundary: beginning at the northwest corner of Ottawa County at Lake Michigan, thence east in a straight line to the northwestern corner of Ionia County, thence east along the northern boundaries of Ionia, Clinton and Shiawassee Counties to the western boundary of Genesee County, then north and east along the Genesee County line to the eastern boundary of Saginaw County, thence north along the eastern boundaries of Saginaw and Bay Counties to Saginaw Bay, except the Rockford church.

(21) The **Northwest District** shall include the states of Idaho, Oregon and Washington.

(22) The **Pacific Southwest District** shall include the states of Arizona, California, Hawaii, Nevada, New Mexico and Utah.

(23) The **Penn-Jersey District** shall include that part of the states of Pennsylvania, New Jersey and New York in an area bounded as follows: beginning on the Pennsylvania-Maryland state line at U.S. 15, thence northward on U.S. 15 to the southern boundary of Tioga County, thence east along the southern boundaries of Tioga, Bradford and Susquehanna Counties to the western boundary of Wayne County at Forest City, thence eastward across Wayne County on Routes 106 and 6 to Narrowsburg, thence southeast along the New York State line to the Hudson River, thence east to the

southwestern corner of Connecticut, thence eastward to include Long Island, thence southward to include all of New Jersey, thence westward along the Pennsylvania-Maryland state line to U.S. 15.

(24) The **South Carolina District** shall include the state of South Carolina except the Clover, Rock Hill and York churches in York County and the Prevatt's Chapel, Fletcher's Chapel and Bennettsville churches in Marlboro County; and shall include Jackson and Macon Counties in the state of North Carolina, except the part of the Cherokee Indian Reservation in Jackson County assigned to the North Carolina West District.

(25) The **South Coastal District** shall include the state of Alabama, the state of Georgia with the exception of the churches in LaFayette and Rossville, and the state of Mississippi.

(26) The **Tennessee District** shall include the state of Tennessee, and shall include the churches in LaFayette and Rossville, Georgia.

(27) The **Texas-Louisiana District** shall include the states of Texas and Louisiana.

(28) The **Tri-State District** shall include the states of Arkansas, Missouri and Oklahoma.

(29) The **Virginia District** shall include the state of Virginia except the counties of Prince William, Loudoun, Fauquier, Fairfax, Stafford, Arlington, Northampton, Accomack and the cities of Alexandria and Falls Church; and shall include the Aldersgate Wesleyan Church in Falls Church, Virginia and the Aspen Hill Wesleyan Church in Rockville, Maryland.

(30) The **Wesleyan Native American Developing District** shall include the churches under the supervision of Wesleyan Native American Ministries.

(31) The **West Michigan District** shall include that part of the state of Michigan which is south and west of the following boundary line: beginning at the northwest corner of Ottawa County at Lake Michigan, thence east in a straight line to the northwestern corner of Ionia County, thence east along the northern boundaries of Ionia, Clinton and Shiawassee Counties to the western boundary of Genesee County, thence south along the western boundaries of Genesee, Livingston, Washtenaw and Lenawee Counties to the Ohio state line, except the church in Lennon, Michigan; and shall include the churches in Hudson and Rockford, Michigan.

(32) The **West Virginia District** shall include the state of West Virginia except the churches in South Parkersburg, Paden City and Weirton, belonging to the Greater Ohio District.

(33) The **Western New York District** shall include that part of the states of New York and Pennsylvania in an area bounded as follows: beginning on Lake Ontario at the northwest corner of Monroe County, thence south and east along the western boundary of Monroe County to the Genesee River, thence southward following said river in the direction to include Mount

Morris, thence southeast along the canal to the village of Dansville, thence along the boundary between Steuben and Allegany Counties to the Pennsylvania state line, thence west along the New York state line to the southwest corner of Chautauqua County, thence north along the western boundary of Chautauqua County to Lake Erie; thence following the New York state line along Lake Erie, Niagara River and Lake Ontario to the point of beginning; and shall include Potter and McKean Counties in the state of Pennsylvania.

(34) The **Western Pennsylvania District** shall include that part of the state of Pennsylvania in an area bounded as follows: beginning at the southwestern corner of Pennsylvania, thence north to Lake Erie, thence east along Lake Erie to the New York state line, thence south and east along the New York state line to the western boundary of McKean County, thence south on the western boundary of McKean County, thence east along the southern boundaries of McKean, Potter and Tioga Counties to U.S. 15, thence south on U.S. 15 to the Pennsylvania-Maryland state line, thence west on the Pennsylvania state line to the point of beginning.

(35) The **Wisconsin District** shall include the state of Wisconsin.

### B. Representative Area Boundaries

**2430.** The NORTH CENTRAL REPRESENTATIVE AREA shall include the East Michigan, Greater Ohio, Illinois, Indiana Central, Indiana North, Indiana South, North Michigan, West Michigan and Wisconsin Districts.

**2435.** The NORTHEASTERN REPRESENTATIVE AREA shall include the Atlantic, Central Canada, Central New York, Chesapeake, Eastern New York/New England, Penn-Jersey, Western New York and Western Pennsylvania Districts.

**2440.** The SOUTHERN REPRESENTATIVE AREA shall include Florida, Kentucky, North Carolina East, North Carolina West, South Carolina, South Coastal, Tennessee, Virginia and West Virginia Districts.

**2445.** The WESTERN REPRESENTATIVE AREA shall include the Colorado-Nebraska, Dakota, Iowa-Minnesota, Kansas, Northwest, Pacific Southwest, Texas-Louisiana and Tri-State Districts and the Wesleyan Native American Developing District.

### C. Educational Area Boundaries

**2450.** The merger of districts and of educational institutions between sessions of the General Conference may lead to changes in the educational area boundaries, which changes may be made by the General Board (cf. 1655:13).

**2455.** The NORTH CENTRAL EDUCATIONAL AREA shall be served by Indiana Wesleyan University and Bethany Bible College, and shall include the districts of the North Central Representative Area (cf. 2430).

**2460.** The NORTHEASTERN EDUCATIONAL AREA shall be served by Houghton College and Bethany Bible College, and shall include the districts of the Northeastern Representative Area (cf. 2435).

**2465.** The SOUTHERN EDUCATIONAL AREA shall be served by Southern Wesleyan University and Bethany Bible College, and shall include the districts of the Southern Representative Area (cf. 2440).

**2470.** The WESTERN EDUCATIONAL AREA shall be served by Oklahoma Wesleyan University and Bethany Bible College, and shall include the districts of the Western Representative Area (cf. 2445).

### D. Administrative Area Boundaries

**2475.** The boundaries of the administrative areas are determined by the General Board upon the recommendation of the Board of General Superintendents (cf. 1655:13; 1915), and are given here as a matter of information.

**2480.** The EASTERN ADMINISTRATIVE AREA shall include the Atlantic, Central Canada, Central New York, Chesapeake, Eastern New York/New England, North Carolina East, North Carolina West, Penn-Jersey, Virginia, Western New York and Western Pennsylvania Districts and Albania, Bosnia/Croatia, British Isles, Czech Republic, Germany, Karis People, Liberia, Mozambique, Russia, Sierra Leone, Southern Africa, and Zambia.

**2485.** The SOUTH/CENTRAL ADMINISTRATIVE AREA shall include Florida, Greater Ohio, Illinois, Indiana Central, Indiana North, Indiana South, Kentucky, South Carolina, South Coastal, Tennessee, and West Virginia Districts and Australia, Bougainville, Caribbean Provisional General Conference, Haiti, India Central, India East, India West, Mongolia, Myanmar, Nepal, Pakistan, Papua New Guinea, Puerto Rico, and Sri Lanka.

**2490.** The WEST/CENTRAL ADMINISTRATIVE AREA shall include Colorado-Nebraska, Dakota, East Michigan, Iowa-Minnesota, Kansas, North Michigan, Northwest, Pacific Southwest, Texas-Louisiana, Tri-State, West Michigan, Wisconsin Districts, and Wesleyan Native American Developing District and Brazil, Cambodia, Chile, Colombia, Costa Rica, Cuba, Dominican Republic, Guatemala, Guyana, Honduras, Indonesia, Japan, Korea, Korea Yeon Hap, Mexico, Nicaragua, Panama, Peru, Philippines GC, Suriname.

# PART V

# WORLD ORGANIZATION

## Chapter I

## BASIC PRINCIPLES

**2500.** The Wesleyan Church, in the fulfillment of its mission to spread scriptural holiness throughout the world (100-105), recognizes the following as basic principles for its worldwide organization:

(1) The missionary objectives of The Wesleyan Church, as set forth in 2200, call for dynamic worldwide evangelism, resulting in the planting of local churches, which in turn develop into national church structures in the host countries or regions, each of which should become a partner in world evangelism as a unit of The Wesleyan Church worldwide.

(2) Such national churches shall be organized as developing districts, provisional districts, established districts and national or regional conferences as set forth in 2275. As they increase in spiritual, numerical, financial and organizational strength and maturity, they may become general conferences as set forth in 2610.

(3) The Essentials is a statement of faith, practice and relationship which serves as a unifying bond for all units of The Wesleyan Church around the world. This statement is incorporated in the Charter of the Wesleyan World Fellowship (see Appendix A) (cf. 125) and no unit of The Wesleyan Church may contravene any of the provisions of the Essentials in the development of its own book of discipline or in establishing church structures and practice.

(4) The church in each field or area under the General Department of World Missions shall endeavor to establish its own pattern of government, since it is recognized that variations in local conditions, cultural patterns, governmental regulations and other factors require local adaptations in the organizational structure of the church.

(5) The organization and government of the various units under the General Department of World Missions shall be set forth in the *Policy of the General Board for World Missions* and a book of discipline or a supplement to *The Discipline* shall be approved by the General Board for each unit (205; 340:2; 1655:26).

(6) It shall not be the purpose of The Wesleyan Church to keep units under the General Department of World Missions dependent on the parent body, but to develop strong churches that are aggressive in assuming responsibility for progress and growth in their own countries or regions as well as having the vision of participating in the missionary objectives of The Wesleyan Church worldwide.

# Chapter II

# GENERAL CONFERENCES

**2550.** The North American General Conference shall be composed of the established, provisional and developing districts in the United States and Canada, all of which are governed by the North American *Discipline*. The regional/national conferences, established districts and developing areas under the North American General Department of World Missions (2275), all of which are governed by their own disciplines as approved by the General Board (2500:5), shall also be represented in the North American General Conference according to a plan approved by the General Board (325; 1655:26).

**2560.** The Philippine General Conference shall be composed of all developing districts, provisional districts and established districts in the Philippines and Indonesia and such other units as it shall receive.

### A. General Conference

**2610.** A national or regional conference may be advanced to the status of a general conference by the authority of the North American General Conference (1590:10) when it meets the following requirements:

(1) An effective church organization on the local, district and/or general levels.

(2) Effective programs for the nurture and training of members, new converts, children, young people and lay workers.

(3) An effective program for ministerial training.

(4) Evidence of responsible stewardship of life and possessions, including the proper management of funds and the provision for the support of its own pastors, workers and officers.

(5) A definite program of evangelism, church extension and missionary outreach on an indigenous basis.

(6) A discipline approved by the General Board (1655:26).

(7) The existence of a property-holding body, or more than one such body, if required by local laws.

(8) Acceptance of the Essentials of The Wesleyan Church.

(9) A recommendation for such status from the General Director of World Missions.

(10) A recommendation for such status from the General Board (cf. 1655:26).

## B. General Conference Interrelations

**2630.** The relationships between general conferences shall be supervised by the General Council of the Wesleyan World Fellowship and the International Board of Review as set forth in the Charter of the Wesleyan World Fellowship (see Appendix A).

**2640.** The unity of The Wesleyan Church worldwide is to be recognized and maintained through the relationships provided in the Charter of the Wesleyan World Fellowship (see Appendix A). The North American General Conference shall relate to all other general conferences as outlined in the Charter, including the recognition of the right of members and ministers to transfer membership and/or credentials between general conferences, subject to the same approval as that provided for transfers between its own local churches and districts (6730).

## Chapter III

## WESLEYAN WORLD FELLOWSHIP

**2650.** There shall be a Wesleyan World Fellowship for the purpose of promoting worldwide holiness evangelism in keeping with the mission of The Wesleyan Church (100-105), the coordinating of the activities of The Wesleyan Church worldwide, the promoting of a closer fellowship and mutual understanding, and the providing of a means for joint planning and cooperative action among all areas and general conferences of The Wesleyan Church.

**2660.** The Wesleyan World Fellowship shall consist of those bodies which have originated in or which have affiliated with The Wesleyan Church which adhere to the Essentials of The Wesleyan Church and other provisions of its Charter.

**2670.** The Wesleyan World Fellowship shall function through its general council composed of representatives from each general conference and each mission unit functioning under a missions department. The number of representatives from each unit shall be determined according to the number of members, with due regard to the principle of lay representation.

**2680.** The Wesleyan World Fellowship shall be organized and governed in accord with its Charter (see Appendix A).

# PART VI

# MINISTRY

## Chapter I

## MINISTERIAL ORDERS AND REGULATIONS

### A. Meaning of Ministry

**3000.** Ministry in the Christian context means service. It is a term which has been lifted out of the commonplace through the modeling of the Lord Jesus Christ, who is identified in both the Old and New Testaments as the Servant or Minister of God and man. His service involved His humiliation in the incarnation, His self-forgetful teaching and healing activity, and His shameful suffering and death on the cross for the redemption of the human race. Our Lord also chose this term to characterize the activity of His followers in obedience to His commands and mission. He called all members of His body to a general or corporate ministry which would glorify Him, edify the church and evangelize the world. And He made such possible through imparting to each believer one or more gifts of the Spirit (1 Cor. 12:7-27) in order that each member might participate in the work of the ministry and contribute to the growth and development of the whole body (Eph. 4:11-16).

### B. Qualifications and Call of the Specialized Minister

**3003.** While God, through the ministry of the Holy Spirit, assigns to each believer a part in the general or corporate ministry of the church, He also calls some to a specialized or representative type of ministry. As Christ called unto Him whom He would, chose and ordained His twelve apostles "that they should be with him, and that he might send them forth to preach" (Mark 3:14), so He still calls and sends forth His messengers to be servants of the servants who make up the whole church. And as the Holy Spirit impresses this call upon the individual involved, He also confirms the call through the Church. It is the responsibility of the Church both to recognize and endorse God's call, providing for the training and employment of those He selects, and to respect the office of the specialized ministry by refusing its exercise to those not called of God. The Church's endorsement may be limited to a probationary period, taking the form of a license, or it may be granted on a more permanent basis, taking the form of commissioning or ordination.

**3006.** The Wesleyan Church believes that four marks will concur in the person whom God has called: grace, gifts, fruit and an abiding sense of a divine call. All candidates for ministerial license, commission or ordination shall be examined concerning each of these marks:

(1) As to grace, are they converted? are they entirely sanctified? are they manifesting the fruit of the Spirit? are they worthy examples to the church and to the world?

(2) As to gifts, are they able to think clearly? to understand and communicate clearly matters related to salvation? to speak persuasively? to practice loving care? to provide leadership?

(3) As to fruit, have any been truly convicted of sin and converted to God through their ministry? and have believers been edified?

(4) As to an abiding sense of a divine call, can they testify to a continuing and increasing conviction that they have been chosen by God for a specialized and representative ministry?

**3012.** Any person sustaining a marriage relation contrary to the Scriptures and the Covenant Membership Commitments (265:5; 410:6; 3108; 3136) shall be ineligible for licensing, commissioning or ordination in The Wesleyan Church.

## C. Ministerial Student

**3015.** Those pursuing ministerial studies under the direction of the district board of ministerial development shall include those licensed as ministerial students as follows:

(1) **Ministerial Student.** A covenant member of The Wesleyan Church who confesses a call to be a minister (cf. 3000-3006) may be granted a license as a ministerial student by meeting the following requirements in order:

(a) Membership in a local Wesleyan church within the district granting the license.

(b) Recommendation from the local church conference or the local board of administration (655:8) to the district conference for license as a ministerial student.

(c) Readiness to pursue studies with all diligence until completed, to prepare for ordination, and to give oneself wholly to the ministry in The Wesleyan Church when studies are completed..

(d) Examination by the district board of ministerial development (1390:2) relative to qualifications for ministry (cf. 3000-3006) including a personal religious experience, ministerial call and evidence thereof, and its recommendation to the district conference for the granting of the license (1390:5).

(e) Enrollment in the Ministerial Study Course Agency and in a program of ministerial education approved by the district board of ministerial development.

(f) Recommendation by the district board of administration for appointment as a ministerial student (3350:2) and its adoption by the district conference (1180:26c; 1233:9c; 1390:2).

(g) Issuance and signing of the license by the district superintendent and the district secretary (6260).

(2) **Renewing a License for a Ministerial Student.** The license for a ministerial student may be renewed annually by meeting the following requirements:

(a) The reports from both the ministerial student and the Ministerial Study Course Agency show that progress has been made in the course of study.

(b) The ministerial student shows readiness to continue studies in preparation for ordination in The Wesleyan Church (3350:2) or, for one having just completed the course of study, to take an appointment within the coming year.

(c) The proper reports have been made (3015:4).

(3) **Rights of a Ministerial Student.** As long as a ministerial student qualifies for and receives a license the student shall have the right:

(a) To preach the gospel.

(b) To be a nonvoting member of the district conference (1090:4).

(c) To transfer from one district to another (3015:5d); the district superintendent shall send a letter directly to the district superintendent of the district to which the student is transferring and the student shall continue to be considered a member of the former district until a reply has been received from the latter district that the student has been duly received as a member of a local church within the district and has been duly enrolled as a ministerial student by the district.

(d) To have recourse, even if under discipline, to a proper court of jurisdiction in any matters involving complaint against character or ministerial conduct and to appeal the decision of such a court (302:4; 313:7; 5150; 5170-5180).

(4) **Duties of a Ministerial Student.** A person holding a license as a ministerial student shall be responsible to report annually to the district board of ministerial development concerning progress in studies (1390:2) and service (1390:7); and to report to the district superintendent and the board of ministerial development at other times as required.

(5) **Regulations for a Ministerial Student.**

(a) A ministerial student is amenable to the district which grants the license, and the license may be revoked between sessions of the district conference by judicial process as set forth in 5170-5180.

(b) A ministerial student's credentials shall consist of the license, signed annually by the district superintendent and the district secretary (6260), and an annual pocket certificate of standing, issued and signed by the district secretary (6430).

(c) A ministerial student from another denomination will need to qualify for such license in The Wesleyan Church as set forth in 3015:1.

(d) A ministerial student, when transferring district membership (cf. 3015:3c; 3100:1), in addition to a letter of transfer, shall be supplied by the district superintendent and the district board of ministerial development with a properly attested statement of standing in the ministerial study course.

## D. Licensed Minister

**3030. Identification.** A licensed minister is one whose ministerial calling and gifts have been formally recognized by a district conference, through the granting of a ministerial license which serves as authorization for and appointment to actual service in the ministry, subject to supervision and evaluation, as a step toward ordination. A licensed minister may be a former ministerial student who has qualified for and been appointed to regular service in one of the categories listed in 3250-3345.

**3033. Granting a District Ministerial License.** A covenant member of The Wesleyan Church who confesses a call of God to be a minister (cf. 3000-3006), may be granted a district ministerial license by meeting the following requirements in order:

(1) Membership in a local Wesleyan church within the district granting the license.

(2) Satisfactory service as a ministerial student in The Wesleyan Church for at least one year.

(3) Certificate from the Ministerial Study Course Agency showing completion of the courses adopted as being prerequisites for licensing (6410; cf. 3170:1-4; 3210).

(4) Recommendation from the local church conference to the district conference for a district ministerial license (655:8).

(5) Readiness to accept the district conference's appointment to active service in one of the categories listed in 3250-3335; to pursue the studies with all diligence until completed; to prepare for ordination; and to give oneself wholly to the ministry.

(6) Examination by the district board of ministerial development (1390:1) relative to the qualifications for the ministry and for a district ministerial license (cf. 3000-3006; 3033:1-5), including a personal religious experience, ministerial call and evidence thereof, matters of education, doctrine and practice, and circumstances of personal, family and business life which bear upon the ministry; and subsequent recommendation by the district board of ministerial development to the district conference for the granting of a district ministerial license (1390:5).

(7) Recommendation by the district board of administration for immediate appointment to one of the categories of service listed in 3250-3335.

(8) Adoption by the district conference of the separate recommendations of the district board of ministerial development (3033:6) and of the district board of administration (3033:7).

(9) Issuance and signing of the license by the district superintendent and the district secretary (6260; cf. 1310:23; 1332:4).

**3040. Renewing a District Ministerial License.** A district ministerial license is effective for one year only, and authority to carry on the office and work of a minister under such a license shall cease unless it is renewed annually by the district conference until such time as the holder of the license is commissioned or ordained to the ministry. A minister may be granted renewal of the ministerial license by meeting the following requirements:

(1) Satisfactory service under a previous appointment, including loyalty to and compliance with the rules of The Wesleyan Church and of the district, and including the proper filing of reports. If a licensed minister fails to file the annual service report (1402), unless such failure is due to illness, injury or a similar emergency, the license shall not be renewed (cf. 1390:8).

(2) Confirmation through the annual report of the Ministerial Study Course Agency that the minister has completed at least two courses in the pre-ordination study course (3210:1). The pre-ordination study course must be completed within seven years of service under a ministerial license. The ministerial license shall not be renewed beyond the seventh year (cf. 3059).

(3) Agreement to continue under district appointment to one of the categories of service listed in 3250-3335 or for one having completed the course of study for ordination, to take an appointment, within the coming conference year.

**3044. Rights of Licensed Minister.** As long as a minister qualifies for and receives a district ministerial license, the minister shall have the right (cf. 313):

(1) To preach the gospel (313:1), and, when appointed as a pastor or full-time associate or assistant pastor of a Wesleyan church, to administer

baptism and the Lord's Supper, to perform all parts of divine worship, and to solemnize the rite of matrimony wherever local laws will permit.

(2) To contract the pastoral relationship with local Wesleyan churches subject to the approval of the district conference and other regulations of *The Discipline* (313:3; 323:1-2).

(3) To enjoy, if appointed as a pastor, the use for religious meetings of the church building or buildings of the pastoral charge to which assigned by the district conference (313:4); and to serve the assigned pastoral charge without interference by unauthorized activities of another minister of The Wesleyan Church (313:5; cf. 3114-3117).

(4) To be a voting member of the district conference if an ordained minister-elect or if the pastor or a full-time associate/assistant pastor of a Wesleyan church in that district (317; 1083:2-4). To be a nonvoting member if otherwise classified or appointed (1090:3). To be eligible for election to any office not restricted to ordained ministers or lay persons.

(5) To transfer in the manner prescribed by *The Discipline* from one district to another, subject to the concurrence of the district superintendent and the General Superintendent over the district into which transfer is sought (313:6; cf. 3055:3; 3097; 3100:1).

(6) To have recourse, even if under discipline, to a proper court of jurisdiction in any matters involving complaint against character or ministerial conduct and to appeal the decision of such court (313:7; 5150; 5170-5180).

**3051. Duties of a Licensed Minister.** A person holding a district ministerial license shall be responsible:

(1) To enroll in the pre-ordination study course (3210:1) under the Ministerial Study Course Agency and the district board of ministerial development, and to pursue the study course with all diligence until completed, either through a program of ministerial training at one of the Wesleyan educational institutions, or through correspondence courses from the Ministerial Study Course Agency (cf. 3200).

(2) To serve the district faithfully under whatever appointment is received, seeking to complete the service requirements for ordination as quickly as possible.

(3) To report annually to the district conference on the appropriate service report form (cf. 1402; 3040:1), and to the district superintendent and the board of ministerial development as required (cf. 725:32).

**3055. Regulations for a Licensed Minister.**

(1) A licensed minister is amenable to the district which grants the license, and the license may be revoked between sessions of the district conference by judicial process as set forth in 5170-5180.

(2) A licensed minister's credentials shall consist of the license, signed annually by the district superintendent and the district secretary (3033:9;

6260), and an annual pocket certificate of standing, issued and signed by the district secretary (6430).

(3) A licensed minister, when transferring district membership (cf. 3100:1), in addition to a letter of transfer, shall be supplied by the district superintendent and the district board of ministerial development with a properly attested statement of standing in the pre-ordination study course and a record of service under the appointment of the district conference.

### E. Commissioned Minister

**3059. Identification.** A commissioned minister is one who may have demonstrated calling, gifts and usefulness, who has responded to the call to ministry, yet after counsel with an agreement by the district board of ministerial development, has chosen not to pursue full ministerial development as an ordained minister, and has been separated to the service of Christ by the vote of a district conference and by a commissioning service and thus has been invested with those functions of the Christian ministry essential to this level of service. The commissioned minister shall be subject to the following regulations:

(1) **Qualifications for Commissioning.** A licensed minister of The Wesleyan Church who has an abiding conviction of God's call to be a minister (cf. 3000-3006) may be commissioned as a minister by meeting the following requirements in order:

(a) Forty years of age or older at the time of receiving a license as a ministerial student or a person who because of aptitude or other extenuating circumstances is approved by the district board of administration.

(b) Satisfactory service as a licensed minister with appointment by the district for a minimum of two years.

(c) Certification from the Ministerial Study Course Agency that the commissioned minister's course of study or its equivalent has been completed (3210:3). The commissioned minister's course of study must be completed within six years of service under a ministerial license. The ministerial license shall not be renewed beyond the sixth year.

(d) Recommendation of the district board of ministerial development after consultation with the district board of administration (cf. 3059:1).

(e) Election by the district conference by a majority vote to a commissioned minister's status (1180:28, 29).

(f) Public service of commissioning (5800), in which the minister shall witness to a Christian experience, conviction of a divine call to the ministry, commitment to the doctrines and practices of The Wesleyan

Church, and loyalty to The Wesleyan Church, after which the minister shall be separated to the Christian ministry through the laying on of hands in the person of the General Superintendent (if present, cf. 1935:15), or the representative appointed by the General Superintendent (1935:15; 3091); the district superintendent (1310:23) and a Council of Ordination (1405).

(g) Issuance and signing of a commission certificate by the General Superintendent over the district, the district superintendent and the district secretary (6280).

(2) **Rights of a Commissioned Minister.** As long as a commissioned minister maintains spiritual life, moral character and faithful ministry, and is neither under discipline nor expelled from the ministry, the minister shall have the right (313):

(a) To preach the gospel and to administer baptism and the Lord's Supper, to perform all parts of divine worship, and to solemnize the rite of matrimony wherever local laws will permit (313:1).

(b) To be eligible for election to any office not restricted to ordained ministers or lay persons. The commissioned minister shall not be eligible for election as district superintendent, assistant district superintendent, member-at-large on the district board of administration, member of the district board of ministerial development, nor as a delegate to General Conference.

(c) To contract the pastoral relationship with local Wesleyan churches subject to the approval of the district conference and other regulations of *The Discipline* (313:3; 323:1-2).

(d) To enjoy, if appointed as a pastor, the use for religious meetings of the church building or buildings of the pastoral charge to which appointed by the district conference (313:4); and to serve the pastoral charge without interference by unauthorized activities of another minister of The Wesleyan Church (313:5; cf. 3114-3117).

(e) To be a voting member of the district conference if pastoring a Wesleyan church or serving as a full-time associate or assistant pastor of a Wesleyan church (317; 1083:3), or a nonvoting member of the district conference if appointed to some other category of service or in the process of transfer (317; 1090:3).

(f) To transfer in the manner prescribed by *The Discipline* from one district to another, subject to the concurrence of the district superintendent and the General Superintendent over the district into which transfer is sought (313:6; 3097; 3100:1).

(g) To have recourse, even if under discipline, to a proper court of jurisdiction in any matters involving complaint against character or ministerial conduct and to appeal the decision of such court (313:7; 5150; 5170-5180).

(3) **Duties of a Commissioned Minister.** A commissioned minister shall be responsible:

(a) To be devoted without reservation to the Christian ministry, following the leadership of the Holy Spirit and the appointment of the district conference in determining and occupying this field of service.

(b) To report annually to the district conference on the appropriate service report form (cf. 1402; 3059:4c), and to the district superintendent as required (cf. 725:32).

(c) To voluntarily file all credentials with the district superintendent if service in one of the categories of ministry listed in 3250-3335 ceases for four or more consecutive years (cf. 3124); this does not apply to those listed under 3370-3371.

(d) To voluntarily surrender credentials if guilty of an offense which would disqualify from service as a commissioned minister (cf. 3127; 3130-3133).

(4) **Regulations for a Commissioned Minister.**

(a) A commissioned minister is amenable to the district where membership is held, and may be deposed from the ministry and ordered to surrender credentials by judicial process as set forth in 5170-5180.

(b) A commissioned minister's credentials shall consist of the commission certificate (6280) and an annual pocket certificate of standing, issued and signed by the district secretary (6430).

(c) A commissioned minister who fails to file the annual service report (1402) for two successive years, shall be notified by the district board of ministerial development, and requested to report at the next session of the district conference. One who then fails to report shall be declared withdrawn from the district, and this name shall be so entered upon the minutes of the district conference.

(d) When a commissioned minister surrenders the commission certificate after acknowledging guilt for an offense (3059:3d), or is ordered to surrender it after due judicial process (5180:4), it shall be lawful to publish such fact in the official church publication.

### F. Ordained Minister

**3067. Identification.** An ordained minister is a minister whose calling, gifts and usefulness have been demonstrated and enhanced by proper training and experience, and who has been separated to the service of Christ by the vote of a district conference and by the solemn act of ordination (5750-5792), and thus has been fully invested with all the functions of the Christian ministry.

**3070. Qualifications for Ordination.** A licensed minister of The Wesleyan Church who has an abiding conviction of God's call to be a minister (cf. 3000-3006) may be ordained by meeting the following requirements in order:

(1) Covenant membership in a local Wesleyan church within the district granting ordination.

(2) Satisfactory service for two years subsequent to completion of the pre-ordination study course, except for those who have been under appointment and supervision during the years spent completing said course of study. This service must be full-time (as determined by the district board of ministerial development) in one of the categories of service listed in 3250-3335. At least one year must have been in The Wesleyan Church within the district in which ordination is to take place except as hereinafter provided. In case of a ministerial student graduating from a three-year divinity course at an approved seminary the service requirement is for one year. If ordination is to be in a district other than the one in which the service requirement was met, the district board of ministerial development of the appointing district must recommend the student to the ordaining district.

(3) Certificate from the Ministerial Study Course Agency showing completion of the pre-ordination course of study or of its equivalent (6410; cf. 3170:4; 3210:1).

(4) Examination by the district board of ministerial development relative to qualifications for the ministry and for ordination (cf. 3000-3006; 3070:1-3), including a personal religious experience, ministerial call and evidence thereof, matters of education, doctrine and practice, particularly a personal commitment without reservation to each of the Articles of Religion and the Membership Commitments and loyalty to The Wesleyan Church, and circumstances of personal, family and business life which bear upon the ministry; and a subsequent report by the district board of ministerial development to the district conference (1390:1, 5).

(5) Election by the district conference to ordained minister's orders (1180:28). In case of an emergency, a candidate who has been recommended by the district board of ministerial development may be elected to ordained minister's orders by the district board of administration in the interim of the sessions of the district conference (1233:37).

(6) Public service of ordination (3091; 5750-5792), in which the minister shall witness to a Christian experience, affirm conviction of a divine call to the ministry, commitment to the doctrines and principles of The Wesleyan Church, and loyalty to The Wesleyan Church, after which the minister shall be separated to the Christian ministry by the Church through

the laying on of hands in the person of the General Superintendent (if present, cf. 1935:15), or the representative appointed by the General Superintendent (1935:15; 3091), the district superintendent (1310:23) and a council of ordination (1405).

(7) Issuance and signing of a certificate of ordination by the General Superintendent, district superintendent and district secretary (6300).

(8) The Board of General Superintendents, by unanimous vote and after consultation with the district board of ministerial development of the involved district, may postpone the intended ordination of any candidate and/or refer the same to the district board of ministerial development for further consideration.

**3075 Rights of an Ordained Minister.** An ordained minister who maintains spiritual life, moral character and faithful ministry, and is neither under discipline nor expelled from the ministry shall have the right (cf. 313):

(1) To preach the gospel and to administer baptism and the Lord's Supper, to perform all parts of divine worship and to solemnize the rite of matrimony (313:1).

(2) To be eligible for election to any office in the Church for which ordained ministers are eligible (313:2).

(3) To contract the pastoral relationship with local Wesleyan churches subject to the other provisions of *The Discipline* (313:3).

(4) To enjoy, if appointed as a pastor, the use for religious meetings of the church building or buildings of the pastoral charge to which assigned by the district conference (313:4); and to serve the assigned pastoral charge without interference by unauthorized activities of another minister of The Wesleyan Church (313:5; cf. 3114-3117).

(5) To be a voting member of the district conference if under appointment, retired, on reserve, on educational leave or a member of the district board of administration (317; 1083:1; 1240:I:A-D) and a nonvoting member if without appointment or in the process of transfer (1090:1-2); and to have these conference relations changed only after careful investigation by the district board of administration, and interview if possible (1233:9c).

(6) To transfer in the manner prescribed by *The Discipline* from one district to another, subject to the concurrence of the district superintendent and the General Superintendent over the district into which transfer is sought (313:6; cf. 3100:1).

(7) To have recourse, even if under discipline, to a proper court of jurisdiction in any matters involving complaint against character or ministerial conduct and to appeal the decision of such court (313:7; 5150; 5170-5180).

**3085. Duties of an Ordained Minister.** An ordained minister shall be responsible:

(1) To be devoted without reservation to the Christian ministry, following the leadership of the Holy Spirit and the appointment of the district conference in determining and occupying a field of service.

(2) To report annually to the district conference on the appropriate service report form (cf. 1402; 3089:3), and to the district superintendent as required (cf. 725:32).

(3) To voluntarily file all credentials with the district superintendent if service in one of the categories of ministry listed in 3250-3346 ceases for four or more consecutive years (cf. 3124); this does not apply to those given other ministerial listings set forth in 3350:1; 3360; 3370.

(4) To voluntarily surrender credentials if guilty of an offense which would disqualify one for service as an ordained minister (cf. 3124; 3127-3148; 5180).

**3089. Regulations for an Ordained Minister.**

(1) An ordained minister is amenable to the district where membership is held, and may be deposed from the ministry and ordered to surrender credentials by judicial process as set forth in 5170-5180.

(2) An ordained minister's credentials shall consist of the certificate of ordination (3070:7; 6300), and an annual pocket certificate of standing, issued and signed by the district secretary (6430).

(3) An ordained minister who fails to file the annual service report (1402) for two successive years, shall be notified by the district board of ministerial development, and requested to report at the next session of the district conference. If no report is filed at that time the district shall declare the minister withdrawn and shall record the action upon the minutes of the district conference.

(4) When an ordained minister surrenders the certificate of ordination because guilty of an offense (3085:4), or is ordered to surrender it after due judicial process (5180:4), it shall be lawful to publish such fact in the columns of the official church publication.

**3091. Ordination Service.** The public service of ordination shall be presided over by the General Superintendent or a representative appointed by the General Superintendent. The service shall be planned by the district superintendent and the Council of Ordination; the time and place shall be subject to the approval of the General Superintendent. The General Superintendent shall deliver the ordination sermon except when delegating that responsibility to another. The rituals of commissioning ministers, special workers, and lay missionaries may be blended with the ordination service or may be conducted separately. The laying on of hands shall be by the General Superintendent (or the representative appointed by the General Superintendent), the district superintendent, the Council of Ordination and such other ministers as they shall invite.

## G. General Regulations for Ordained Ministers and Commissioned or Licensed Ministers

### 1. Special Advice to Ministers

**3093.** John Wesley's "Rules of a Helper" have perhaps never been excelled as counsel to ministers, whether young or old. These "Rules" are, in part, as follows:

(1) Be diligent. Never be unemployed a moment, never be triflingly employed, never while away time; spend no more time at any place than is strictly necessary.

(2) Be serious. Let your motto be, "Holiness unto the Lord." Avoid all lightness, jesting and foolish talking.

(3) Believe evil of no one without good evidence; unless you see it done, take heed how you credit it. Put the best construction on everything. The judge is always supposed to be on the prisoner's side.

(4) Speak evil of no one, else your word especially would eat as doth a canker. Keep your thoughts within your own breast till you come to the person concerned.

(5) Tell every one under your care what you think wrong in his conduct and temper, and that lovingly and plainly as soon as may be: else it will fester in your heart. Make all haste to cast the fire out of your bosom.

(6) Avoid all affectation. A preacher of the gospel is the servant of all.

(7) Be ashamed of nothing but sin. Let your industry, as well as your humility, commend itself to all.

(8) Be punctual: do everything exactly at the time.

(9) Do not mend the rules, but keep them; not for wrath but for conscience' sake.

(10) You have nothing to do but to save souls; therefore spend and be spent in this work; and go always not only to those that desire you, but to those who need you most.

### 2. Membership of Ministers

**3097. Local Church Membership.** Each Wesleyan minister, whether ordained, commissioned or licensed, must be a covenant member of a local Wesleyan church (310). If serving as a pastor, membership is automatically transferred to the church of service (578:2). If serving in some capacity other than that of a pastor, the holding and transfer of local church membership shall occur in the same manner as a lay member. A commissioned or licensed minister must be a covenant member of a local Wesleyan church within the district where appointed or licensed. An ordained minister may be a covenant member of a local Wesleyan church outside the district where ministerial membership is held except when regulations governing a particular appointment or office prohibit such (cf. 578:2; 1258; 1278). In recognition of the undesigned but inherent potential to create divided loyalties or undermine the strengths of new pastoral leadership, ministers should be discouraged from remaining in the congregation or community immediately following pastoral service in that place. If a minister leaves a pastoral assignment to accept appointment to another service category or to begin retirement and, for such reason as a prior home purchase and/or no other Wesleyan church in the community, feels it necessary to retain membership and worship in the church where pastoral leadership was just terminated, it is recommended that said former pastor shall not accept appointment to the local board of administration.

**3100. District Membership.** An ordained or commissioned minister shall be a member of the district where appointed to service (cf. 3059:4), and each licensed minister a member of the district which issues the license (cf. 3015:3b; 3044:4; 3075:5). The ordained, commissioned, or licensed minister's district membership shall be subject to the following regulations:

(1) If a minister desires to accept a pastoral call from a church within the bounds of another district, or if a minister not serving as a pastor desires to transfer ministerial membership to another district, the minister must first obtain the written permission of the General Superintendent and the district superintendent over the district into which transfer is desired (313:6; 1310:18; 1935:16). When such has been obtained, the minister shall ask the district superintendent for a letter of transfer (6440; cf. 1310:25) to be sent directly to the district superintendent of the district into which transfer is desired (cf. 3055:3). The minister shall continue to be considered as a member of the former district until a reply has been received from the district to which application has been made stating that the minister has been duly enrolled as a member of the district conference (6450; cf. 1310:25). To avoid dual listings, ministers receiving appointment by the receiving district conference prior to completion of enrollment shall be listed in that district conference journal as an ordained, commissioned or licensed minister Pending Approval of District Change (1240:II:D; 1240:III:C).

(2) In an emergency, an ordained minister may serve as supply pastor of a church located within the bounds of a district other than the one in which ministerial membership is held (cf.3260:1), provided that such an arrangement has the written approval of the superintendent of each district involved (1310:25), and does not continue beyond the next session of the district conference in which membership is held without the consent of the district conference.

(3) If a minister so requests, the district superintendent may grant a letter of standing (6460;cf.1310:25), which shall immediately terminate ministerial membership in The Wesleyan Church (cf. 3126). Such a letter of standing shall be valid for one year from the date of issuance in the case of an ordained minister, or until the next session of the district conference from which withdrawn in the case of a commissioned or licensed minister.

(4) If a minister joins another denomination or, in writing, declares withdrawal from the Church, said action shall immediately terminate ministerial membership in The Wesleyan Church (cf. 3124), upon recommendation of the district superintendent to the district board of administration.

(5) If a minister leaves for parts unknown or fails to submit the annual service report (1402; 3059:4c; 3089:3), the district board of administration may recommend and the district conference may order that the minister be declared withdrawn (cf. 3040; 3120; 3124). (cf. 5180:2; 5235-5240.)

(6) No letters of transfer or standing shall be granted to any minister by a district superintendent until satisfactory evidence is given by the applicant that no outstanding debts are unprovided for, and that the minister has honorably withdrawn from the contract for service with the church or district.

### 3. Reception of Ministers from Another Denomination

**3104. Reception of a Minister from Another Denomination.** An ordained minister from another denomination, or a minister from another denomination who has been ordained to deacon's orders or who has been licensed or authorized in some manner equivalent to the commissioning or licensing of a Wesleyan minister by a district conference, may seek reception into The Wesleyan Church as an ordained minister or commissioned or licensed minister, as the case may justify (1233:36) according to the following procedure:

(1) The applicant shall present a letter of standing or photocopy of ministerial credentials and photocopies of transcripts or other records of ministerial training to the district superintendent (1310:25). If the district superintendent is favorable to initiating steps which might lead to the applicant's transfer, the superintendent shall forward copies of these documents to the Ministerial Study Course Agency.

(2) The district superintendent shall assist the applicant in applying for the approval of the area General Superintendent (1935:16) for reception as a minister in process of transfer.

(3) The applicant shall be examined by the district board of ministerial development relative to Christian experience, call and qualifications for the

ministry as given in 3000-3006 (cf. 3059:1; 3070:4), and to the nature of ordination, commission or license.

(4) If the district board of ministerial development so recommends (1390:3), the district conference may appoint the applicant as an ordained minister in process of transfer (1180:29a; cf. 1240:I:G; 3390; cf. 3067), a commissioned minister in process of transfer (1240:II:E; 3059; 3391) or a licensed minister in process of transfer (1240:III:D; 3391), which relation shall continue for one year unless the district conference shall by vote extend it. While serving under this relation, the applicant is a nonvoting member of the district conference (1090:2, 3), may serve as a supply pastor (3260), and shall seek to satisfy any requirements in ministerial training, particularly in Wesleyan doctrine, history and polity. If at any time the district board of administration shall determine that it is not in the best interests of the district to continue the relation, they may by majority vote terminate the relation and any supply assignment, and thus dismiss the applicant from all ministerial relations to The Wesleyan Church. An ordained minister in the process of transfer shall have authority to administer the sacraments and perform marriages, while serving as a supply pastor (3260:2).

(5) If the year of service is satisfactory and all requirements in ministerial training have been met as evidenced by the certification of the Ministerial Study Course Agency, the district board of ministerial development, after consultation with and approval of the area General Superintendent, may recommend to the district conference that the applicant be recognized as an ordained minister or commissioned or licensed minister of The Wesleyan Church and be received as a ministerial member of the district (1390:3). If the transferring minister has not previously joined a local Wesleyan church within the district, this must be done prior to the vote by the district conference receiving the applicant as a ministerial member of the district. If an ordained minister in process of transfer faces extensive additional academic requirements, and age or other extenuating circumstances make it doubtful to the applicant and the district board of ministerial development that such requirements can be met, the district board of ministerial development may authorize the applicant to qualify for commissioned minister's status and proceed accordingly (cf. 3059).

(6) When an ordained minister or commissioned minister has been received, a proper certificate validating the ordination or commission shall be signed and issued (6320). For the licensed minister, a license shall be issued (6260).

### 4. Minister and Marriage

**3108.** Any minister who enters into a marriage relation contrary to the Scriptures, and to those expositions of Scripture as set forth in the Membership Commitments (265:5; cf. 410:6), after having been ordained, commissioned or licensed, shall be dismissed from ministerial standing, provided that guilt shall be established in accord with the judicial processes set forth in *The Discipline* (5170-5180).

**3111.** In performing marriages, Wesleyan ministers shall not unite in marriage any person who is divorced, unless such divorce and remarriage is in keeping with the Scriptures and the Covenant Membership Commitments (265:5). In carrying out this duty, the minister shall be guided by the principles set forth in 410:6.

**3112.** In performing marriages, Wesleyan ministers shall not unite in marriage persons of the same sex.

### 5. Relationship to Other Ministers and Churches

**3114.** Each minister of The Wesleyan Church shall respect the rights of each other minister within the field of labor, and shall not interfere with the work of, nor influence anyone against any pastor, district official or other minister of The Wesleyan Church (cf. 313:5). In the event of any such violation of ministerial ethics, the aggrieved person may file a complaint with the district superintendent (5170; cf. 5050:2, 4).

**3117.** If a Wesleyan minister shall engage to serve another denomination, or an interdenominational or independent work, as a pastor or in some other regular capacity, except by permission of the district conference, or in the interim of its sessions, by permission of the district board of administration, the district board of administration may recommend and the district conference may order that the minister be declared withdrawn. If serving within the territory of a district other than the one to which the minister belongs, the minister must have not only the permission of the district in which membership is held, but also the permission of the district superintendent over the territory where labor is proposed (1310:25). An ordained minister serving outside The Wesleyan Church with the permission of the district in which membership is held shall be placed either on the appointed list in the category of interchurch service (3335) or special service (3345) or listed as an ordained minister without appointment (3380).

### 6. Reinstatement of Ministers

**3120.** If a licensed minister or ministerial student ceases to be licensed or is declared withdrawn from the district conference, and was neither under charges nor under discipline, the minister may at a later time again be recommended by the local church conference and qualify for and be granted a district license.

**3124.** An ordained minister or commissioned minister who has voluntarily filed credentials with the district superintendent (3059:3c; 3085:3), or who has taken a letter of standing and has not used the same within the prescribed time (3100:3), or who has been declared withdrawn when neither under charges nor under discipline (cf. 3059:4c; 3089:3; 3100:4; 3117; 5240), may be reinstated in the office of an ordained minister or commissioned minister in The Wesleyan Church, if such is approved by the district board of ministerial development and district board of administration of the district in which ministerial membership is sought, and if such reinstatement is approved by the area General Superintendent.

### 7. Restoration of Ministers

**3127.** If an ordained minister or commissioned minister, because of guilt in an offense which disqualifies the minister from being an ordained minister or commissioned minister, has either voluntarily surrendered ministerial credentials (3059:3d; 3085:4) or been required to surrender them, the credentials shall be forwarded to the General Secretary, to be filed and preserved.

**3130.** The district in which the disqualified person is a member shall take initiative to express its desire for and commitment to the restoration of that person, with God's help, to a holy life and relationship. If the disqualified person expresses a repentant spirit and a desire to reestablish ministerial calling, practice and credentials with The Wesleyan Church, the district may, when appropriate, initiate a process which potentially could lead to ministerial restoration.

**3133.** An ordained, commissioned or licensed minister, or ministerial student, who has been expelled from the ministry of The Wesleyan Church, either through voluntary surrender of credentials because of guilt (3059:3d; 3085:4) or through judicial process and disciplinary action, other than that considered in 3124, may be restored to the office and work of a minister in The Wesleyan Church, provided that the minister shall have shown evidence of repentance and amendment of life, and provided that such is approved by the district conference from which withdrawn, or in the interim of its sessions, by the district board of administration, and if such is recommended by the district board of ministerial development of the district in which ministerial membership is sought, and if such restoration is voted by the district conference in which membership is sought. In the case of immorality or crime, to which the minister has confessed guilt or for which guilt was declared by judicial process, such restoration may be accomplished only with the additional approval of the General Board (3142).

**3136.** The district and the involved person, under the direction of and subject to the approval of the area General Superintendent, shall develop a specific plan and process of restoration, communication and assessment. The plan shall follow guidelines established by the General Board. The plan shall not be initiated until the involved person has fully conformed with the requirements of 5180:4. Once the plan is initiated, a record of progress shall be maintained by the district superintendent and the district board of ministerial development, with regular reports to the area General Superintendent, and reports to the district board of administration as requested.

**3139.** If adequate progress is observed and restoration criteria are met, and if a mutual desire of ministerial restoration is expressed by the person, the district officials and their General Superintendent, then steps may be taken for restoration of credentials and, subsequently, opportunity for ministerial assignment. Based on such an approved program of spiritual restoration, the restoration of ministerial credentials could possibly occur after three years.

**3142.** When a request for restoration of a minister in a case such as that described in 3133 has received the approval of the appropriate local and district bodies, it shall be processed as follows:

(1) The request shall be directed to the area General Superintendent who shall ascertain if indeed all required district actions have been taken.

(2) The area General Superintendent shall review the entire matter and make recommendations for or against restoration to the Board of General Superintendents.

(3) The Board of General Superintendents shall then either recommend for or against restoration in presenting the matter to the General Board.

**3145.** In no case shall a minister who has been restored and then falls again be considered for restoration.

**3148.** An ordained, commissioned or licensed minister, or ministerial student who has been disqualified for the ministry through a marriage contrary to the Scriptures and the Membership Commitments (265:5), shall not be restored to the office and work of a minister as long as both the minister's former and latter spouse are living, and then only if the minister has manifested repentance and been approved, recommended and voted restoration by the various bodies designated in 3124.

# Chapter II

# MINISTERIAL EDUCATION

## A. Priority of Ministerial Education

**3150.** The importance of the training of the Christian minister has been evident ever since Christ gave the name of "disciples" or "learners" to His first preachers, and ever since the aging Paul provided for successive classes of ministerial students by admonishing Timothy, "The things that thou hast heard of me among many witnesses, the same commit thou to faithful men, who shall be able to teach others also" (2 Tim. 2:2). Such training becomes even more urgent in an age when the thirst for knowledge is almost universal, when human knowledge is multiplying, and when formal education on the highest level is becoming the normal pattern for a large segment of society. The Wesleyan Church gives priority in its organization and its educational institutions to the training of its youth for the Christian ministry and related fields of labor (cf. 2358:1). The Church expects each person who answers the call to preach to prepare thoroughly for this ministry and to continue this ministry devoted to being an able dispenser of divine wisdom.

## B. Administration of Ministerial Education

**3160.** The administration of ministerial education in The Wesleyan Church involves both general and district bodies, officers and agencies. The General Conference adopts the overall framework for ministerial training and establishes the various agencies and schools responsible to carry out the work (1590:4, 9, 13; 2362). The General Board provides the frame work for adopting the basic courses of study and coordinating the total program (1655:21, 26; 3200-3210). The General Director of Education and the Ministry promotes the enlistment and preparation of candidates for the ministry, and directs the Ministerial Study Course Agency, which maintains records on all ministerial students in The Wesleyan Church and administers the correspondence courses (2341; 2385-2388). The various colleges and the Wesleyan Seminary Foundation adapt the basic study courses to their use, and enroll candidates for the ministry in classroom preparation. The district board of ministerial development has a part in recognizing potential ministers, in encouraging and guiding them in their training, and in administering the oral examination to a candidate prior to recommendation for ordination or commission (1390:1; 3059:1c; 3070:4).

## C. Types of Ministerial Education

### 1. Programs of Study

**3170.** The following programs of study are open to the candidates in meeting the educational requirements for becoming an ordained minister in The Wesleyan Church.

(1) **Seminary.** It consists of graduation from a four-year course of study at one of the institutions of higher education of The Wesleyan Church, plus graduation from a three-year divinity course under the Wesleyan Seminary Foundation (cf.3170:4). This is recommended as the most adequate academic preparation for the Wesleyan minister. Graduation from a three-year divinity course at an approved seminary reduces the period of service required before ordination (cf. 3070:2). One-year and two-year master's degrees in ministerial preparation are not as adequate as the standard three-year divinity course, but may be combined with undergraduate courses to meet academic requirements for ordination.

(2) **College/University.** It consists of graduation from one of the institutions of higher education of The Wesleyan Church, involving the completion of a minimum of four years' work and covering the authorized ministerial study courses (3200; 3210:1-3). This is recommended as the minimum academic preparation for becoming an ordained minister in The Wesleyan Church.

(3) **Correspondence.** It is recognized that some individuals are converted late in life, and hear God's call to the ministry after the normal time for education has passed and family responsibilities make attendance at an institution of higher education extremely difficult. In such cases, a district board of ministerial development may grant special permission to a candidate for the ministry to secure part of the training through correspondence courses administered by the Ministerial Study Course Agency. These courses will of necessity concentrate on the specialized subjects needed for the ministry, and the district board of ministerial development shall encourage such candidates to secure training in the more general educational subjects in formal class settings (cf. 3210:1). (cf. 1390:2.)

(4) **Training Outside The Wesleyan Church.** Some candidates for the ministry will have secured some or all of their higher education outside the institutions and agencies of The Wesleyan Church. In such a case, the district board of ministerial development shall forward copies of transcripts or other records of study to the Ministerial Study Course Agency so that it can carefully evaluate such work in terms of its equivalence to the ministerial courses of study of The Wesleyan Church, giving particular attention to the candidate's qualifications in the areas of Wesleyan doctrine, history and polity (2388:4;

3033:3; 3059:1b; 3070:3; 3104:2). Subsequent to each evaluation and the report of the Ministerial Study Course Agency, the district board of ministerial development shall have the right to require additional work until it and the Agency are fully satisfied that all requirements for the Wesleyan ministry have been met. (cf. 1390:2.)

### 2. Courses of Study

**3200.** The General Director of Education and the Ministry shall develop (2341) courses of study for pre-ordination, specialized ministries, commissioned ministers and special lay ministries. Each course of study shall be composed of a number of courses, each course being implemented by a college or seminary course of two or more hours, or by a correspondence course involving the use of a study guide issued by the Ministerial Study Course Agency, the intensive study of one or more textbooks plus collateral reading, and other pertinent study assigned by the Agency, and an examination prepared by the Ministerial Study Course Agency and taken in the presence of an ordained minister. No credit shall be given for any correspondence course in which the final grade is less than passing.

**3210.** The following courses of study shall be provided:

(1) **Pre-ordination Course of Study.** It shall require as a prerequisite a high school diploma or its equivalent. It shall consist of four years of college and/or seminary-level work, and shall cover necessary general education courses as well as the full range of ministerial training subjects—biblical, historical, theological and practical, including courses in Wesleyan doctrine, history and polity.

(2) **Courses of Study for Specialized Ministries.** These shall consist of special adaptations of the pre-ordination study course (3210:1) for those who are called to the work of minister of music, minister of Christian education or others as deemed necessary.

(3) **Commissioned Minister's Course of Study.** It shall consist of two years of college-level work, and shall incorporate biblical, historical, theological and practical courses, including courses in Wesleyan doctrine, history and polity.

(4) **Lay Minister's Course of Study.** It shall consist of one year of college-level work, and shall include courses in Wesleyan doctrine, the history of The Wesleyan Church, the polity of The Wesleyan Church, including a study of *The Discipline* and other basic ministerial subjects.

(5) **Special Workers' Courses of Study.** These shall be designed to prepare lay members for special fields of service, such as director of music, director of Christian education, evangelistic singer, chalk artist, children's worker, spouse in ministry, lay evangelist and social worker. Such study

courses shall consist of two years of college-level work, and shall include courses in Wesleyan doctrine, history and polity, and such other subjects as are pertinent.

### 3. Continuing Education

**3240.** The General Director of Education and the Ministry shall adopt within structure provided by the General Board varying programs of continuing education for the ordained ministers, ordained ministers' spouses, commissioned ministers and spouses and commissioned special workers of The Wesleyan Church (2341).

# Chapter III

## MINISTERIAL APPOINTMENTS

### A. Categories of Service

**3250.** While The Wesleyan Church recognizes only two levels of ministry which in and of themselves have a degree of permanency, that of ordained minister and that of commissioned minister, it also recognizes that the ordained minister, commissioned minister or licensed minister preparing for ordination may serve the Church in various capacities. Christ has called some to be "apostles, some to be prophets, some to be evangelists, and some to be pastors and teachers, to prepare God's people for works of service, so that the body of Christ may be built up" (Eph. 4:11-12, NIV). The Church recognizes the following categories of service to which a district conference may appoint an ordained minister, or, as circumstances warrant, a commissioned or licensed minister (1180:26): pastor (3255-3260); evangelist (3270-3285); missionary (3300); educator (3310); administrator (3320); chaplain (3320; cf. 3330); interchurch service (3335); special service (3345); and affiliate church pastor (3346). Service within these categories that qualifies as being "in a ministerial capacity" would include that service for which ministerial training is required or greatly desired. The General Board adopts guidelines for each category which will aid district boards in identifying the kinds of service which are considered to be "in a ministerial capacity."

#### 1. Pastors

**3255. Regular Pastoral Service.** The pastoral office is defined in 675. In The Wesleyan Church, pastoral service includes the pastor of a church (735), an associate pastor (738) and an assistant pastor, who may specialize in such ways as minister of Christian education, minister of music, minister of visitation or minister of youth (741). An ordained minister appointed by a district conference to any of these levels of pastoral service in connection with a Wesleyan church, developing church or mission shall be placed on the appointed list (cf. 1240:I:A:2); a commissioned or licensed minister appointed as pastor or full-time associate or assistant pastor of a Wesleyan church shall be a voting member of the district conference (317;1083:3;1240:II:A; 1240:III:A; 3044:4; 3059:2e).

**3260. Supply Pastors.** A district conference (503; 1180:26b; 1240:V:E), or, in the interim of its sessions, the district superintendent and the district board of administration (1233:31,38;1310:19-20) shall have the power to appoint a supply pastor, who shall serve subject to the following regulations:

(1) A supply pastor may be a Wesleyan ordained minister or commissioned or licensed minister serving under some other appointment or an ordained minister on loan from one district to another (cf. 503; 1240:I:A:2b; 3100:2), a commissioned or licensed special worker (3460-3470), a minister in process of transfer from another denomination (3104), a minister who belongs to another denomination, a ministerial student, a lay minister or a lay member.

(2) A supply pastor shall be appointed temporarily to fill the pulpit and to provide a spiritual ministry, but shall not have authority to administer the sacraments or to perform marriages unless that authority adheres on some other basis, and shall not perform the administrative function of the pastor except in filing of reports unless authorized to do so by the district superintendent (cf. 1310:8, 20). If a supply pastor is serving a congregation isolated from Wesleyan ministers, making it difficult to provide for administration of the sacraments (725:6), the district superintendent may grant the supply pastor special authorization to administer them.

(3) A supply pastor's church membership shall not be automatically transferred to the church of service.

(4) A supply pastor shall be granted a certificate of authorization to supply on the form provided in 6240, and shall be a nonvoting member of the district conference unless qualifying as a voting member by some other right (1090:7).

(5) A supply pastor may be removed or replaced at any time by the district board of administration (1233:38; 1310:19, 20; cf. 5150:4).

## 2. Evangelists

**3270. Functions.** An evangelist is an ordained minister or commissioned or licensed minister who devotes time to traveling and preaching the gospel without any specific pastoral assignment, and who is authorized by the Church to promote revivals and to spread the gospel of Jesus Christ abroad in the land. The Wesleyan Church recognizes three levels of evangelistic service to which a district conference may appoint ministers: associate general evangelist, general evangelist and reserve evangelist.

**3275. Examination.** Before appointment as an evangelist, the candidate shall be examined carefully by the district board of ministerial development relative to personal Christian experience, full personal commitment to and support of the Articles of Religion and Covenant Membership Commitments, to the government, institutions and best interests of The Wesleyan Church, gifts and aptitudes for the work of an evangelist, and the intention to devote time to the work of evangelism.

**3280. Associate General Evangelist.** An associate general evangelist is an ordained minister, commissioned minister or licensed minister appointed by a district to serve in the field of evangelism. An ordained minister so appointed shall be placed upon the appointed list (cf.1240:I:A:3a). A commissioned or licensed minister so appointed shall be listed under "B. Other Appointments" (1240:II:B; 1240:III:B) and is a nonvoting member of the district conference (1090:3). To receive such an appointment, the minister must devote a major portion of time to do the work of evangelism. Those entering the field of evangelism will serve in this category for at least two years. To be continued in this appointment the minister must conduct at least 40 services devoted to evangelism each year after the first year of appointment.

**3285. General Evangelist.** A general evangelist is an ordained minister appointed by a district conference to the field of evangelism and recommended for service to the church. An ordained minister so appointed shall be placed on the appointed list (cf. 1240:I:A:3b). Appointment as general evangelist is subject to the following conditions and procedures:

(1) Upon completion of two years of service as an associate general evangelist, the district board of administration may recommend that person to the district conference as a general evangelist. The two-year requirement may be waived if, in the judgment of the district board of administration and the district conference, an ordained minister is uniquely qualified to serve the general church in this capacity. Endorsement of the district conference, the General Superintendent who relates to the General Department of Evangelism and Church Growth and the General Director of Evangelism and Church Growth shall be required for appointment as a General Evangelist. Upon approval for appointment to the category of general evangelist a certificate of such appointment shall be issued and signed by the district superintendent, the district secretary (cf. 6340) and the General Director of Evangelism and Church Growth.

(2) Appointment and certification as a general evangelist shall only be continued in subsequent years if the evangelist reports to the district conference at least 80 services each year devoted to evangelism. At the time this requirement is not met, the general evangelist shall be reclassified as an associate general evangelist or reserve evangelist.

**3286. Reserve Evangelist.** An ordained minister who due to age or physical disability is limited in activities may be appointed as a reserve evangelist (cf. 1240:I:A:3c). Appointment and certification as a reserve evangelist shall be by the district. To qualify for renewal of the appointment, the reserve evangelist shall be required to conduct a satisfactory level of evangelistic service each year as determined by the district board of ministerial development.

**3295. Evangelistic Reports.** Each associate general or general evangelist shall file an annual service/statistical report with the district statistical committee, the district board of ministerial standing and the General Department of Evangelism and Church Growth on forms approved by the Board of General Superintendents (1920:16) and made available by the General Secretary.

### 3. Missionaries

**3300.** When an ordained or licensed minister has been appointed by the General Board to serve in a ministerial capacity under the General Department of World Missions or under the General Department of Evangelism and Church Growth, the district conference shall list the minister as if it had made the appointment. An ordained minister so appointed shall be placed upon the appointed list (1240:I:A:4c). A commissioned or licensed minister so serving shall be a nonvoting member of the district conference and shall be listed under "Other Appointments" (cf. 1090:3; 1240:II:B; 1240:III:B). (Cf. 2272.)

### 4. Educators/Itinerant Bible Teachers

**3310.** Ordained, commissioned or licensed ministers may serve as educators in educational institutions, or itinerant Bible teaching ministers to local churches and districts, and be appointed as follows:

(1) When an ordained, commissioned or licensed minister has been employed to serve in a ministerial capacity on the administrative staff or faculty of one of the general educational institutions of The Wesleyan Church, or of one of the seminaries approved by The Wesleyan Seminary Foundation, the district conference shall list the minister as if it had made the appointment. An ordained minister so serving shall be placed upon the appointed list (cf. 1240:I:A:4d) and shall be a voting member of the district conference (1083:1). A commissioned or licensed minister so serving shall be a nonvoting member of the district conference (1090:3).

(2) An ordained, commissioned or licensed minister may be employed in a ministerial capacity in a special Christian education program of a local Wesleyan church, subject to review by the district board of administration and appointment by the district conference (1180:26;1233:9). An ordained minister so appointed shall be placed upon the appointed list (1240:I:A:2c). A commissioned or licensed minister so serving shall be a nonvoting member of

the district conference and shall be listed under "Other Appointments" (cf. 1090:3; 1240:II:B; 1240:III:B).

(3) When an ordained, commissioned or licensed minister devotes time to traveling and teaching in local churches and districts without a specific or pastoral assignment, the minister shall be recognized as an itinerant Bible teacher subject to recommendation and appointment by the district conference of which the minister is a member. An ordained minister so appointed shall be placed on the appointed list (1240:I:A), and shall be a voting member of the district conference. A commissioned or licensed minister so appointed shall be a non-voting member of the district conference and shall be listed under "other appointments" (1240:II:B or 1240:III:B) as is appropriate.

### 5. Administrators

**3320.** When an ordained minister has been elected by the General Conference as a general official (1800), or an ordained, commissioned or licensed minister has been employed at the International Center, or elected or employed by the board of directors of a general subsidiary corporation other than an educational institution, to serve the general church in a ministerial capacity, or an ordained minister has been elected by the district conference as district superintendent or full-time assistant district superintendent, or an ordained, commissioned or licensed minister has been elected or employed for full-time service of the district in a ministerial capacity, the district conference shall list the minister as if it had made the appointment. An ordained minister serving in this manner shall be placed on the appointed list (cf. 1240:I:A:1, 4a, b), and a commissioned or licensed minister so serving shall be a nonvoting member of the district conference and shall be listed under either "Commissioned" or "Licensed Ministers, Other Appointments" (cf. 1090:3; 1240:II:B). Any ordained or commissioned minister employed by the general church in other than a ministerial capacity shall be placed on the appropriate list of ministers without appointment (cf. 1240:I:E; 1240:II:C).

### 6. Chaplains

**3330.** When an ordained minister has been approved by the Committee on Chaplains and commissioned by the government as a military chaplain, or employed as a full-time professional institutional chaplain, the district conference shall list the chaplain as if it had made the appointment. An ordained minister serving in this capacity shall be placed on the appointed list (cf. 1240:I:A:7).

### 7. Ministers Engaged in Interchurch Service

**3335.** An ordained minister employed in a ministerial capacity as an officer in a church-related organization serving The Wesleyan Church, or approved upon careful evaluation of the district conference to serve with an educational institution, evangelistic or missionary organization not directly related to The Wesleyan Church shall be appointed to interchurch service and shall be listed by the district as an appointed ordained minister (cf. 1240:I:A:6). A commissioned or licensed minister so appointed shall be a nonvoting member of the district conference and shall be listed under "Other Appointments" (cf. 1240:II:B; 1240:III:B).

### 8. Ministers Engaged in Special Service

**3345.** An ordained minister serving in active service not otherwise provided for shall be appointed to special service, if such service is approved by the district conference and shall be listed by the district as an appointed ordained minister (1240:I:A:7).

### 9. Affiliate Church Pastor

**3346.** An ordained Wesleyan minister appointed by the district conference to serve on staff of an affiliate church shall be listed by the district as a minister appointed to affiliate church pastor (cf. 7910; 1240:1:A:8).

## B. Other Assignments

### 1. Students

**3350.** The district conference may list ordained ministers and others pursuing ministerial studies in keeping with these regulations:

(1) **Ordained Minister on Educational Leave.** An ordained minister without other appointment who enrolls in a seminary or other graduate school for advanced training for church service shall be listed as an "ordained minister on educational leave" (1240:I:D). An ordained minister so appointed shall be a voting member of the district conference (1083:1).

(2) **Ministerial Student.** A student engaged in full-time study in preparation for ordination, either by enrolling in the four-year or five-year ministerial or pre-ministerial course of a Wesleyan educational institution, or in an approved theological seminary or other approved graduate-level program of theological education, or by pursuing full-time study in the Ministerial Study Course Agency either by correspondence or by work in a

college along with correspondence, if the student meets all other qualifications (3015:1), may be granted a license and appointed by the district conference as a ministerial student (3015:1). The ministerial student shall be a nonvoting member of the district conference (1090:4).

### 2. Reserve Ministers

**3360.** An ordained minister on reserve is one available for appointment but left without one (1240:I:C). The ordained minister on reserve shall be a voting member of the district conference (317; 1083:1). An ordained minister remaining on reserve for two consecutive years without definite appointment shall be automatically transferred to the list of ordained ministers without appointment (3380) unless continued on reserve by the district conference (1180:26c).

### 3. Retired Ministers

**3370. Ordained Ministers.** An ordained minister who is retired because of age or incapacitated by infirmity, and who was on either the appointed list, on reserve or on educational leave at the time of retirement or incapacitation, shall be placed on the retired list (1240:I:B). A retired ordained minister shall be a voting member of the district conference (317; 1083:1). When special circumstances are present, the district conference may place an ordained minister without appointment on the retired list.

**3371. Commissioned Ministers.** A commissioned minister who is retired shall be a nonvoting member of the district conference (1083:3; 3059).

### 4. Ministers Without Appointment

**3380.** An ordained or commissioned minister in active service outside The Wesleyan Church with the consent of the district conference but who is not eligible for inclusion in 3345 or 3350:1, or an ordained or commissioned minister who is not available for appointment, or an ordained or commissioned minister who is not otherwise provided for in the appointed, reserve, educational leave or retired lists shall be placed on the appropriate list of ordained or commissioned ministers without appointment (1240:I:E; 1240:II:C). An ordained or commissioned minister without appointment shall be a nonvoting member of the district conference (1090:1, 3).

## 5. Ministers in Process of Transfer From Another Denomination

**3390. Ordained Ministers.** An ordained minister seeking to be received into The Wesleyan Church from another denomination shall be listed by the district conference for the first year and until all deficiencies in educational or service requirements are cared for as an ordained minister in process of transfer (cf. 1240:I:G; 3104; 3170:4). An ordained minister in process of transfer shall be a nonvoting member of the district conference (1090:2).

**3391. Other Ministers.** A commissioned or licensed minister or ordained deacon seeking to be received into The Wesleyan Church from another denomination shall be listed by the district conference for the first year and until all deficiencies in educational requirements are cared for as a commissioned or licensed minister in process of transfer (cf. 3104). A commissioned or licensed minister in process of transfer shall be a nonvoting member of the district conference (1090:3).

# Chapter IV

# SPECIAL LAY MINISTRIES

## A. Lay Minister

**3400. Identification.** A lay minister is a lay member of The Wesleyan Church whom the local church conference, or the local board of administration if so delegated, has licensed to preach or serve (655:7), under the pastor's direction and as opportunity affords (725:28), thus providing for the employment and development of gifts and usefulness.

**3410. Granting a Lay Minister's License.** A covenant member of a local Wesleyan church who applies for a license as a lay minister or who is presented as a candidate for such license by the pastor shall be examined by the local board of administration. If the local board of administration is satisfied that the candidate shows promise of the proper gifts and usefulness, it shall recommend to the local church conference the granting of a license (782:19), unless the local church conference has delegated such authority to the local board of administration. When the license has been authorized (650:6; 655:7), the pastor and local church secretary shall issue the license on the approved form (6200; cf. 725:28; 830:3).

**3420. Renewing a Lay Minister's License.** A lay minister's license is effective for one year only, and authority to preach or serve under such a license shall cease unless it is renewed annually by the authorized body. The authorized body may renew the license if its holder has served satisfactorily under the pastor's direction, if personal gifts and graces give promise of continued usefulness, and if the annual report of the Ministerial Study Course Agency shows that the lay minister has completed two courses in the study course for lay ministers (3210:4) during the year, or if the lay minister holds a certificate from the Ministerial Study Course Agency showing that the study course has been completed.

**3430. Duties of a Lay Minister.** A person holding a lay minister's license shall be responsible:

(1) To enroll in the course of study for lay ministers under the Ministerial Study Course Agency (3210:4), and to pursue it with all diligence until completed, either through a program of ministerial training at one of the Wesleyan educational institutions or through correspondence courses from the Ministerial Study Course Agency. Any training taken outside The Wesleyan Church shall be carefully evaluated by the Ministerial Study Course Agency which shall have authority to determine to what extent it may be credited toward the prescribed study course (3170:4).

(2) To assist the pastor as directed (725:28), preaching as often as opportunity affords, including the holding of evangelistic services in neighboring churches with the pastor's approval or serving in other ways befitting the lay minister's gifts and local needs.

(3) To report the progress of studies and the nature and extent of labors to the pastor and the local board of administration as they shall require (782:4) and to the local church conference annually (650:5; 655:5).

**3440. Regulations for a Lay Minister.**

(1) A lay minister has no authority to solemnize marriages or to administer the sacraments, except as provided for in 3260:2, nor any vote in the local board of administration nor in the district conference unless elected thereto.

(2) A lay minister is amenable to the local church conference, and the license may be revoked by the authorized body for cause or when the best interests of the church so require (655:7; 782:19).

(3) A lay minister who transfers membership may also ask for a letter of standing as a lay minister (6220), and present it to the pastor of the church to which transfer is sought for consideration by the local board of administration there in issuing a new license.

## B. Special Worker

**3450. Function.** A special worker is a lay person with a sense of divine leading to serve the Church as a director of music, director of Christian education, youth director, song evangelist, chalk artist, children's worker, spouse in ministry, lay evangelist, social worker or in some other special capacity, and who has been authorized to carry on such work by a district conference.

**3460. Licensed Special Worker.** A covenant member of The Wesleyan Church may be granted a special worker's license by the district conference (1180:29e) provided that the candidate has been recommended for such license by the local church conference, or by the local board of administration if so delegated (655:8; cf. 782:20), that the candidate promises to pursue the course of study for the particular field of service (3210:5), and that the candidate has been recommended for such license by the district board of ministerial development after careful examination concerning Christian experience, gifts, calling and experience in the particular field of service (1390:5). The license shall be issued and signed by the district superintendent and district secretary (6360; cf. 1310:23; 1332:4). The license may be renewed annually by continued qualification as above, if the candidate completes two courses in the course of study as attested by the Ministerial Study Course Agency, and if service is satisfactory, including the proper filing of reports. If a licensed special worker fails to file the annual service report (1402), unless such failure is due to illness, injury or a similar emergency, the license shall not be renewed (cf. 1390:8). The licensed special worker shall be amenable to the district (1233:38), and the license may be revoked between sessions of the district conference by judicial process as set forth in 5170-5203. A person from another denomination holding a district license as a special worker or its equivalent may be received into The Wesleyan Church subject to the regulations which govern the reception of a minister (3104).

**3470. Commissioned Special Worker.** A licensed special worker may be commissioned by the district conference provided that the worker has completed the course of study (3210:5) or its equivalent (3170:4) as certified by the Ministerial Study Course Agency (6410), has served satisfactorily under a district special worker's license for at least two years, and has been recommended for commissioning by the district board of ministerial development after careful examination concerning Christian experience, gifts, calling and experience in the particular field of service (1390:5). The commissioning shall include the affirmative vote of the district conference (1180:29e), a solemn act of consecration as set forth in 5855 (cf. 1405; 3091), and the issuance of a commission signed by the General Superintendent over the district, the district superintendent and the district secretary (6380; cf. 1310:23; 1332:4; 1935:15). The commission shall be continuous until such time as the worker ceases to be active in the particular field of service and files the commission with the district superintendent, or unless deprived of the commission by judicial process (5170-5180). A commissioned special worker who fails to file the annual service report (1402) for two successive years, shall be notified by the district board of ministerial development and requested to report at the next session of the district conference. A commissioned special worker who then fails to report, shall be declared withdrawn from the district, and the special worker's name shall be so entered upon the minutes of the district conference (cf. 1390:8). A person from another denomination holding a commission as a special worker or its equivalent may be received into The Wesleyan Church subject to the regulations which govern the reception of an ordained minister (1233:36; 1390:3; 3104).

**3480. General Regulations for Special Workers.** A licensed or commissioned special worker shall be a covenant member of a local church within the district which authorizes the service, and shall serve under the direction of the pastor, or upon the call of local churches, or under a district or general agency, as the case may be. The special worker shall be a nonvoting member of the district conference (1090:5), and shall report annually to the district conference (1390:7). The special worker may be granted a letter of transfer or standing (6440-6460). The license or commission of a special worker may only be restored in keeping with the provisions of 3127-3148.

### C. Lay Missionary

**3490.** A lay member who has been appointed to service under the General Department of World Missions, or under the General Department of Evangelism and Church Growth, shall be commissioned by the district conference (1180:29f) as a lay missionary. The commissioning shall include a solemn act of consecration as set forth in 5855 (cf. 1405; 3091), and the issuance of a commission signed by the General Superintendent who relates to the involved department, the district superintendent and the district secretary (6400; cf. 1310:23; 1332:4; 1935:15). The commission shall be continuous with the period of service. The missionary shall be a nonvoting member of the district conference (1090:6). The missionary shall be amenable in keeping with the provisions of 2272.

# PART VII

# CORPORATIONS

## Chapter I

## LOCAL CHURCH CORPORATIONS

### A. Authorization

**4000.** A local church within an established district may be incorporated (cf. 655:14) when so authorized by the district board of administration (1233:32), and when in the opinion of the district board of administration it is deemed necessary for the issuing of bonds, the securing of commercial loans or some other special reason. The incorporation of a local church within a developing district or provisional district may be authorized when deemed necessary by the General Director of Evangelism and Church Growth.

**4005.** The articles of incorporation and bylaws for the incorporation of a local church shall be according to the standard provisions in 4010, any other pertinent requirements of *The Discipline*, the requirements of local laws as advised by competent legal authority, and shall be approved in writing by the authorizing district board of administration or official (4000).

### B. Standard Provisions

**4010.** The standard provisions for the incorporation of a local Wesleyan church are as follows, provided that whenever such standard provisions shall conflict with the local laws under which the incorporation is effected, such provisions shall be deemed to be modified to the extent necessary to conform with such local laws (4510).

(1) The name of the corporation shall be: "__________ (name or place) Wesleyan Church, Inc."

(2) The primary purposes for which the corporation is formed shall be religious, benevolent, charitable and educational in keeping with the purposes of The Wesleyan Church as set forth in its *Discipline* (cf. 100-105; 200; 2200; 2300), and shall not be for the pecuniary gain or profit to the

members thereof, and especially, to purchase, hold in trust for the benefit and use of the members and ministers of The Wesleyan Church, manage, encumber, sell, transfer or otherwise dispose of property, real, personal or mixed, as may be necessary or convenient for the purposes of the corporation; to acquire or erect and maintain buildings for the worship of God, the use and occupancy of its ministers, Christian education, and other purposes in keeping with the doctrines and principles of The Wesleyan Church; to receive, manage and hold in trust for members and ministers of The Wesleyan Church, any and all donations, bequests and devises of any kind or character that may be given, bequeathed or conveyed to the local church or to the trustees of the local church as such, and to administer the same and income therefrom in accordance with the directions of the donor, trustor or testator; provided that any and all of the foregoing purposes shall be carried out in conformity with the provisions of *The Discipline* of The Wesleyan Church as legislated and declared from time to time (cf. 4040).

(3) The corporation shall be subject to The Wesleyan Church, its duly elected officials and its rules and regulations as set forth in its *Discipline* from time to time and as otherwise legislated and declared in keeping with said *Discipline*.

(4) The bylaws of the corporation shall include *The Discipline* of The Wesleyan Church as legislated and declared from time to time; and no other bylaws shall be adopted that are inconsistent with the provisions of said *Discipline* (4005).

(5) The term for which the corporation is to exist is perpetual.

(6) If the corporation shall be dissolved or become inactive, or whenever the board of directors (4010:7) shall cease to function or cease to be amenable to The Wesleyan Church as set forth in the Judiciary (5070; 5185-5190), any or all assets of the corporation shall inure to the district of which the local church is a member, and the district board of administration shall be authorized and empowered to carry on the function of said board of directors (1233:32, 35).

(7) The directors of the corporation shall be the members of the local board of trustees as set forth in *The Discipline* (cf. 850-859; 4500-4780), who shall carry out the directions of the local church conference (655:13) and the local board of administration (782:27) as set forth in *The Discipline*. A member of the board of directors shall not be personally liable for the debts, liabilities or obligations of the corporation.

(8) The members of the corporation shall be the covenant members of the local church, or such other body as local laws may require, provided that each voting member of the corporate body shall be a covenant member of The Wesleyan Church.

### C. Ownership

**4030.** All grants, conveyances, devises, gifts, transfers and assignments made of any property, real, personal or mixed, to or for an incorporated local church shall be held by and/or *conveyed and transferred to the corporate body in its corporate name,* in trust for the use and benefit of such local church and The Wesleyan Church, and subject to *The Discipline*, regulations and appointments of said Church as from time to time legislated and declared. Every instrument or conveyance of real property shall contain the trust clause as set forth in 4610 (cf. 4690) and shall be approved by the district superintendent as being in conformity with the requirements of *The Discipline* (1310:11).

### D. Acquisition, Sale, Transfer or Mortgage of Property

**4040.** An incorporated local church shall acquire, purchase, sell, mortgage, transfer or otherwise dispose of real property subject to the following authorization and conditions:

(1) A resolution authorizing the proposed action shall be recommended by the local board of administration (782:31) and passed by the local church conference (655:13) in corporate session, or such other corporate body as local laws may require and as set forth in the articles of incorporation and bylaws of the local church corporation, with the members thereof acting in their capacity as members of the corporate body, by a majority vote of those present and voting, at any regular or special session duly called for such purpose (630:1-2; 633:1), provided that notice of such intended action shall be given to the covenant members of the local church through announcement from the pulpit in two regular services, the first of which shall be at least one week prior to the meeting at which the action shall be presented, and in the church bulletin, when such is available (cf. 633:1), and through such other notice as may be required by local laws or by the bylaws of the local church corporation.

(2) The district building committee shall study the proposal of the local church whenever the purchase of property, the construction or remodeling of buildings or other work of the committee is involved as set forth in 1345, and shall give its written recommendation to the district board of administration and the local church.

(3) The written approval of the district board of administration as stated in 1233:32 shall be necessary and shall be affixed to the written instrument involved.

(4) The resolution authorizing such proposed action shall direct and authorize the corporation's board of directors (4010:7) to take all necessary steps to carry out the action so authorized, and to cause to be executed, as hereinafter provided, any necessary contract, deed, bill of sale, mortgage or other written instrument.

(5) The board of directors of the local church corporation (4010:7) shall take such action and adopt such resolutions as may be necessary or required to carry out the proposal as approved, provided that such shall be in conformity with *The Discipline* and as required by local laws (4510).

(6) The chair of the board of directors (4010:7), or another designated director shall submit all written instruments of conveyance and title for the acquisition of property to the district superintendent for the approval of the district superintendent as to their conformity with *The Discipline* as stated in 1310:11 and shall see that permanent legal and property records are properly stored as required in 4760.

### E. Other Regulations

**4060.** An incorporated local church and/or its board of directors (4010:7) may not divert property from the ownership and use of The Wesleyan Church and is subject to other regulations concerning local church property as set forth in *The Discipline* in 4500-4630, 4700-4780, and any other pertinent provisions.

**4070.** The proceeds from the sale of any real property by an incorporated local church shall only be used for the purchase or improvement of property for that local church, unless otherwise authorized by the district board of administration as set forth in 4720-4730 (cf. 1233:32).

## Chapter II

## DISTRICT CORPORATIONS

### A. Authorization

**4100.** Except where prohibited by state or provincial law, the district conference of each established district shall be incorporated or shall cause a corporation to be formed and maintained as a subsidiary corporation of The Wesleyan Church (1180:21; 4310) such as will enable it to receive, hold in trust, encumber, sell, transfer and otherwise dispose of district property and such local property as may be held by the district (cf. 323:8; 4660-4680; 4730-4750; 4770-4780), and to facilitate the management of its legal and corporate affairs in such manner as may be directed by the district conference (1180:21) from time to time and according to *The Discipline* (4590). In places where such incorporation is prohibited by law, or where the law requires the property to be held by trustees, the legal affairs of the district shall be administered as set forth in 4830-4880.

**4105.** A provisional district may be incorporated when so recommended by the General Director of Evangelism and Church Growth and authorized by the General Board (1655:34) or its Executive Board, and such incorporation shall be according to the standard provisions for an established district (4120).

**4110.** The articles of incorporation and bylaws for the incorporation of a district, and any amendments thereto, shall be according to the standard provisions in 4120 and any other pertinent requirements as set forth in *The Discipline*, and shall be subject to the approval of the General Board (1655:34).

### B. Standard Provisions

**4120.** The standard provisions for the incorporation of a district of The Wesleyan Church shall be as listed herewith, provided that when such standard provisions shall conflict with local laws under which the incorporation is effected, said standard provisions shall be deemed to be modified to the extent required by the local laws (4510):

(1) The name of the corporation shall be: "___________ (official district name) District of The Wesleyan Church, Inc."

(2) The primary purposes for which the corporation is formed shall be religious, benevolent, charitable and educational in keeping with the

purposes of The Wesleyan Church as set forth in its *Discipline* (cf. 100-105; 200; 2200; 2300), and shall not be for the pecuniary gain of the members thereof, and especially shall be to acquire, purchase, manage, sell, exchange, mortgage, deed in trust, pledge, rent, lease, and convey any property, real, personal or mixed, as may be necessary or convenient for the purposes of the corporation; provided that all such property shall be held in trust, in the corporate name, for the benefit and use of the members and ministers of The Wesleyan Church as set forth in 4140; to acquire or erect and maintain buildings for the worship of God, the use and occupancy of its ministers, Christian education and other activities that are in harmony with the doctrines and purposes of The Wesleyan Church; to receive and hold in trust for the benefit and use of the members and ministers of The Wesleyan Church any and all donations, bequests and devises of any kind or character, real, personal or mixed, that may be given, devised, bequeathed or conveyed to the district, or to the district board of trustees as such, for any purpose consistent with the purposes of the corporation and to administer the same in accordance with the direction of the donor, trustor or testator; and in addition to have all other powers as are expressly or impliedly given to said corporation by the laws under which it is incorporated when such do not contravene the provisions of *The Discipline*.

(3) The corporation shall be subject to The Wesleyan Church, its duly elected officials and its rules and regulations as set forth in *The Discipline* as legislated and declared from time to time and as otherwise directed by the General Conference (1590:4) and the General Board (1655:34); and shall not have authority to divert property from the ownership or use of The Wesleyan Church and its duly elected officials (cf. 4870-4880).

(4) The bylaws of the corporation shall include *The Discipline* of The Wesleyan Church as legislated and declared from time to time, and no bylaws shall be adopted that are inconsistent with the provisions of said *Discipline* (4110).

(5) The term for which the corporation is to exist is perpetual.

(6) The district board of administration, duly constituted and organized as required in 1203-1230, shall be the board of directors of the district corporation (1233:13), shall exercise its corporate powers, shall carry out the duties assigned to the district board of administration in *The Discipline* in all matters relating to property in 4830-4840 and any other provisions. It shall carry out the directions of the district conference (1180:22; 1233:14), and, in the interim of its sessions, shall have power to act on its own resolution to acquire, purchase, sell, exchange, mortgage, deed in trust, pledge, rent, lease and convey any property, real, personal or mixed, as may be deemed necessary or convenient for the purpose of the district and so to order the district board of trustees (1360-1365; 4855), provided that in transactions

concerning real property used for district purposes, such as a district parsonage for the district superintendent, district headquarters or district campground, the district board of administration shall consult with the General Superintendent over the district (1935:17), and further provided that said district board of administration shall be subject to the general regulations concerning property as set forth in 4500-4630. The district board of administration of an incorporated district, acting as its board of directors, may authorize and direct the district corporation to guarantee in writing any note, mortgage, contract or any other evidence of indebtedness, of any local church of said district. The district board of administration shall be amenable to the district conference, the General Board and the General Conference (cf. 4870-4880). A director shall not be personally liable for the debts, liabilities or obligations of the corporation.

(7) The board of directors (4120:6) shall be authorized and empowered to institute all necessary legal and equitable actions in the name of the district corporation to protect the interests and rights of The Wesleyan Church within the bounds of the district, including all matters relating to property and the rights to property, whether arising by gift, devise or otherwise, for all property held by the district corporation and all property held by local churches, circuits, or other agencies within the bounds of the district.

(8) The members of the corporation shall be the members of the district conference as constituted and organized in 1080-1109, or such other body as local laws may require, provided that all voting members of the corporate body shall be covenant members of The Wesleyan Church.

(9) In the event the corporation shall be dissolved, or become inactive, or whenever the board of directors (4120:6) shall cease to function, any and all assets of the corporation shall inure to The Wesleyan Church Corporation (4200), and the General Board, in the name of The Wesleyan Church Corporation, shall carry on the functions of the corporation and exercise its corporate powers and shall be authorized to institute any necessary legal or equitable actions to preserve the interests and rights of the district and of The Wesleyan Church (1655:34).

### C. Ownership

**4140.** All grants, conveyances, devises, gifts, transfers and assignments made of any property, real, personal or mixed, to or for an incorporated district shall be held by and/or conveyed and transferred to the corporate body in its corporate name, in trust for the use and benefit of the members and ministers of The Wesleyan Church and of such district and subject to *The Discipline*, regulations and appointments of said Church, as from time to time legislated and declared. Every instrument or conveyance of real property shall contain the trust clause as set forth in 4610 (cf. 323:8).

### D. Other Regulations

**4150.** The members (4120:8) and/or board of directors (4120:6) of a district corporation shall not have authority to divert any property from the ownership and use of The Wesleyan Church and its duly elected officials, and said members and/or board of directors are subject to the regulations concerning property held by a district as set forth in *The Discipline* (cf. 4870-4880; 5235). The board of directors of a district corporation shall consult with the General Superintendent over the district concerning transactions involving real property used for district purposes such as a district parsonage, headquarters or campgrounds (1935:17; cf. 4840:1).

# Chapter III

## THE WESLEYAN CHURCH CORPORATION

### A. Name and Purpose

**4200.** The General Conference shall cause a corporation to be formed and maintained for The Wesleyan Church such as will enable it to receive, own, encumber, sell, transfer and otherwise dispose of property, and such as will facilitate the management of its legal and corporate affairs as may be directed by the General Conference from time to time (1590:5). Said corporation shall be known and incorporated under the name of The Wesleyan Church Corporation.

### B. Board of Directors

**4210.** The General Board, duly constituted as required by *The Discipline* (1605-1650), shall be and constitute the board of directors of The Wesleyan Church Corporation and of each of its precedent corporations as listed in 4230. The corporate powers, business and other affairs of the Corporation shall be exercised, conducted and controlled by its board of directors in accord with its articles of incorporation and bylaws, *The Discipline* of The Wesleyan Church as from time to time amended, and any other directives of the General Conference (1655:9, 14), and the laws of the several states (4510). The Executive Board, duly constituted as required by *The Discipline* (1750-1790), shall be the executive committee of said board of directors and shall exercise its powers and authority in the interim of its sessions except for that business which requires more than a simple majority of said board (1785:2), shall carry out such duties as are required of it by the board of directors, and shall be subject at all times to the control of said board of directors (cf. 1750; 1785). The board of directors shall be authorized to appoint committees from among its own members and to delegate its corporate powers to such committees as it may deem wise in the interim of its sessions, all as may be permitted by the corporation laws of the state of Indiana.

### C. Officers

**4220.** The president, vice-president and other officers of the Corporation shall be elected by the board of directors, with the exception of the General

Secretary who shall be the secretary of the Corporation and the General Treasurer who shall be the treasurer of the Corporation (1976). All officers shall serve as set forth in the bylaws.

### D. Precedent Corporations

**4230.** The Wesleyan Church Corporation shall receive and administer new trusts and funds, and so far as may be legal, shall be the legal and ecclesiastical successor in trust and carry out the functions of "The Pilgrim Holiness Church Corporation," an Indiana corporation, "The Pilgrim Holiness Church Corporation," a Michigan corporation, "The Wesleyan Methodist Church of America," a New York corporation, "The Wesleyan Methodist Publishing Association of America," a New York corporation, "The Wesleyan Educational Society," a New York corporation, "The Missionary Society of the Wesleyan Methodist Church of America," a New York corporation, "The Woman's Missionary Society of the Wesleyan Methodist Church of America, Inc.," a New York corporation, "The Missionary Bands of the World," an Indiana corporation and "The Pentecost Bands of the World," an Illinois corporation; and so far as is legal and as such successor in trust it shall be and is authorized and empowered to receive from its said precedent corporations all trust funds and assets of every kind and character, real, personal or mixed, held by them or any one of them and it shall be and is authorized to administer such trusts and funds in accordance with the conditions under which they have been previously received and administered by said precedent corporations. Nothing herein contained, however, shall be construed to require the dissolution of any of the precedent corporations above listed, and they shall continue to administer such funds as may not be legally transferred to the new corporation (4210-4220).

### E. Indemnification of Officers

**4235.** The Wesleyan Church shall indemnify any director or officer or former director or officer of the Corporation against expenses actually or reasonably incurred by him in connection with the defense of any civil action, suit or proceeding in which he is made or threatened to be made, a party by reason of being or having been a director or officer, except in relation to matters as to which he is adjudged in the action, suit or proceeding to be liable for negligence or misconduct in the performance of duty to the corporation; however, this indemnification is not exclusive and does not impair any other rights those indemnified, or any person who may have served at its request as a director or officer of another corporation, may have under any provision of the Articles of Incorporation, Bylaws, resolution or other authorization adopted, after notice, by a majority of the members voting at an annual meeting; expenses incurred in defending any action, suit or proceeding, civil or criminal, may be paid by the corporation in advance of the final disposition of such action, suit or proceeding, notwithstanding any provisions of this article to the contrary upon receipt of an undertaking by or on behalf of the director, officer, employee or agent to repay the amount paid by the corporation if it shall ultimately be determined that the director, officer, employee or agent is not entitled to indemnification as provided in this section.

### F. Donations, Bequests, Devises

**4240.** The Wesleyan Church Corporation shall receive and hold in trust by donation, gift, grant, bequest, devise or otherwise, any property, real, personal or mixed, in any state in the United States of America or any other country, in behalf of The Wesleyan Church or any of its subsidiary interests, for any benevolent, charitable, religious or educational purpose and to administer the same and the income therefrom in accordance with the directions of the donor, trustor or testator and in the interests of the general department, office, institution, agency, society or other body contemplated by such donors, trustors or testators, the whole to be under the direction of and amenable to the General Conference (1590:4-5). The board of directors shall have power, with the advice of competent investment counsel, to invest, reinvest, buy, sell, transfer and convey any and all funds and properties which it may hold in trust, subject always to the terms of the legacy, devise or donation and shall, whenever it is necessary to do so, determine the use or uses of each such fund or trust which shall correspond with the general intentions of the donor, trustor or testator.

### G. Power of Intervention

**4250.** The General Board as the board of directors shall be authorized and empowered to intervene and institute all necessary legal and equitable actions in the name of The Wesleyan Church Corporation to protect the interests and rights of The Wesleyan Church anywhere, including all matters relating to property and rights to property, whether arising by gift, devise or otherwise, or where held in trust for the benefit and use of the members and ministers of The Wesleyan Church (1655:20; 4120:3; 4590; 4770; 4870-4880).

**4260.** Whenever any group of ministers or members shall put themselves in an attitude of insubordination or disobedience to The Wesleyan Church as set forth in 5070, the General Board shall be empowered to institute and carry out disciplinary proceedings as set forth in the Judiciary (5185-5195; 5218-

5240) and other pertinent provisions of *The Discipline*, and, when deemed necessary, may authorize a General Superintendent or other general official(s) to request an affirmation of loyalty and reorganize the district or other unit involved as set forth in the Judiciary (5190-5195; 5235-5240). Whenever such insubordination occurs in a local church, the General Board shall intervene only when the district officials or district board of administration over the local church shall fail or refuse to act.

### H. Amendments

**4270.** The articles of incorporation for The Wesleyan Church Corporation may be amended by the General Conference by a two-thirds vote at any regular or special session (1590:5).

# Chapter IV

# SUBSIDIARY AND AFFILIATE CORPORATIONS AND ADJUNCT ENTITIES

## A. Authorization of Subsidiary Corporations

**4300.** The General Conference may authorize the incorporation of any agency, institution (for matters relative to a general educational institution, cf. 2362), board, organization or similar body as a subsidiary corporation of The Wesleyan Church, and shall approve the articles of incorporation and bylaws and any amendments thereto (1590:6). The General Board shall carry out the directions of the General Conference regarding such subsidiary corporations, assign each one to the supervision of a General Superintendent (1915:3); and, in the interim of General Conference sessions, may authorize such an incorporation by a two-thirds majority vote of all its members, and may approve the articles of incorporation and bylaws and any amendments thereto for any subsidiary corporation except as otherwise restricted by the General Conference (1655:17).

## B. Subsidiary Corporations

**4310. Definition.** Those corporate units of The Wesleyan Church which are intrinsic to the priority mission of the Church are known as subsidiary corporations. These include the following:

(1) Districts (cf. 4100-4150). Local churches, whether incorporated or unincorporated (cf. 4000-4070), are units of the related district and subject to the authority of said district as set forth in *The Discipline* of The Wesleyan Church (cf. 1233:28-40; 1310:12-21; 4650-4780).

(2) General Educational Institutions (cf. 2365).

(3) The Wesleyan Pension Fund, Inc. (cf. 4400-4425).

(4) Hephzibah Children's Home. The Hephzibah Children's Home in Macon, Georgia, is incorporated under the laws of the state of Georgia. It is administered by a board of directors elected by and amenable to the General Board (1655:17). The board of directors shall administer all matters pertaining to Hephzibah Children's Home in accord with *The Discipline* (4570), the articles of incorporation and bylaws of the corporation.

(5) Wesleyan Investment Foundation, Inc. The Wesleyan Investment Foundation, Inc. is a not-for-profit corporation under the laws of the State of Indiana. It is governed by a board of directors of eleven members, with the

General Secretary as recording secretary, the General Treasurer and nine other members elected by the General Board (1655:18). The board of directors shall administer all matters pertaining to the Wesleyan Investment Foundation, Inc. in accord with *The Discipline* (4570), its articles of incorporation and bylaws, and is amenable to the General Board.

(6) Other corporate units may be designated as subsidiary corporations by the General Conference or a two-thirds vote of all members of the General Board.

### C. Basic Provisions of Subsidiary Corporations

**4320.** The articles of incorporation or charter for the incorporation of any agency, institution (other than a district, cf. 1000-1496, or a general educational institution, (cf. 2362), board, organization or similar body as a subsidiary corporation (4300; 4310:6), now established or hereafter created, and its bylaws, shall be in accord with the following basic provisions, provided that whenever such basic provisions shall conflict with the local laws under which the incorporation is effected, such provisions shall be modified to the extent required by local laws (4510):

(1) The purposes of the subsidiary corporation shall be in keeping with the religious, charitable, benevolent and educational purposes of The Wesleyan Church and consistent with its doctrines and principles as stated in *The Discipline* (cf. 100-105; 200; 2100; 2200; 2300); and pecuniary profit shall not accrue to the members of the corporation.

(2) The bylaws of the corporation shall include *The Discipline* of The Wesleyan Church as amended from time to time (4570); and no bylaws may be adopted that are inconsistent with the provisions of *The Discipline* or contrary to local laws as stated in 4510. The bylaws, and any amendments thereto, shall be subject to the approval of the General Board, who shall also have the right to initiate any such bylaws or amendments, provided they do not contravene any action of the General Conference (1655:17).

(3) The General Board shall be and constitute the board of directors or shall elect the members of the board of directors as required by the Constitution except where prohibited by local laws (340:2; 1655:18; 4510), and shall have the authority to remove for cause any member thereof (1655:39b).

(4) All members of the board of directors and all principal officers shall be covenant members or ministers of The Wesleyan Church.

(5) A member of the board of directors may not be held personally liable for any debts, liabilities or obligations of the corporation.

(6) All fiscal operations shall be under board control, with budget, investment and cash control by a board of directors of no less than seven members.

(7) The General Board shall be authorized to direct an annual audit of all assets, records and other affairs of the corporation, and at any other time as it shall deem necessary (1655:19), and all records shall be open to the General Superintendent having supervision over the corporation (1935:5) and to any other representative the General Board shall appoint for such a purpose.

(8) The board of directors shall make a complete and faithful report of finances and other activities to the General Board at any time as shall be required by such General Board (1655:21).

(9) An official copy of the minutes of all meetings of the board of directors and of the financial reports shall be forwarded to the General Secretary of The Wesleyan Church for permanent filing as requested.

(10) The bylaws shall establish proper safeguards for the borrowing or loaning of funds, and it shall be required that there will be adequate security by full mortgage protection or the like whenever there is an investment in property.

(11) All property, whether real, personal or mixed shall be held in trust for the use and benefit of the members and ministers of The Wesleyan Church and shall contain the appropriate trust clause as set forth in 4610.

### D. Affiliate Corporations

**4340. Definition.** An affiliate corporation may be formed and exist when a subsidiary corporation (cf. 4310) of The Wesleyan Church seeks to develop responses to social, humanitarian or community needs which can best be achieved by a separate legal entity. This may be for the purpose of carrying on specific religious, benevolent, charitable or educational activities apart from the usual activities of the subsidiary corporation, such as, but not limited to, the operation of nursing homes, retirement centers, special educational or recreational activities and the like. When the organization and operation of such a ministry is desired, it shall be incorporated apart from the subsidiary corporation and termed an affiliate corporation.

### E. Basic Provisions of Affiliate Corporations

**4350.** The articles of incorporation or charter for the incorporation of any affiliate corporation hereafter created (other than by an educational institution, (cf. 2362; 4320), and its bylaws, shall be in accord with the following basic provisions, provided that, whenever such basic provisions shall conflict with the local laws under which the incorporation is effected, such provisions shall be modified to the extent required by local laws:

(1) The principal purpose of an affiliate corporation shall be to augment one or more of the religious, charitable, benevolent or educational purposes of the subsidiary corporation with which it is affiliated, and pecuniary profit shall not accrue to the members of the affiliate corporation.

(2) The bylaws of the affiliate corporation shall be in accord with the bylaws of the subsidiary corporation with which it is affiliated, as amended from time to time, and no bylaw may be adopted by the affiliate corporation that is inconsistent with the provisions of the charter or bylaws of such subsidiary corporation or contrary to local, state or federal laws governing the affiliate corporation. The bylaws, and any amendments thereto, shall be subject to the approval of the board of directors of the subject subsidiary corporation, and the concurrence in writing of the supervising General Superintendent of The Wesleyan Church after the receipt of competent legal counsel (1935:5).

(3) The board of directors of the subsidiary corporation shall be and constitute, or shall elect, the members of the board of directors of the affiliate corporation, and shall be and constitute the membership of such corporation, except where prohibited by local laws, and shall have the authority to remove for cause any member.

(4) All members of the board of directors and principal officers of the affiliate corporation shall be covenant members or ministers of The Wesleyan Church with the exception of elementary and secondary educational institutions which are affiliate corporations to Wesleyan churches or districts. In such instances the school's bylaws (4350:2) may provide for up to 20 percent of the board of directors to be believers from outside the sponsoring Wesleyan community.

(5) Except where liability is allowed by law, a member of the board of directors of the affiliate corporation may not be held personally liable for any debts, liabilities or obligations of the corporation.

(6) All fiscal operations, including budget, investment and cash control, shall be under the control of a board of directors of not less than seven members.

(7) The board of directors of the affiliate corporation, other governing board or the supervising General Superintendent, shall be authorized to direct an annual audit of all assets, records or other affairs of the corporation, and at any other time as it or the supervising General Superintendent shall deem necessary, and all records shall be open to the supervising General Superintendent and to any other representative the board of directors of the subsidiary corporation shall appoint for such a purpose (1935:5).

(8) The board of directors of the affiliate corporation shall make a complete and faithful report of finances and other activities annually, and at any other time as shall be required, to the board of directors of the subsidiary corporation with which it is affiliated.

(9) An official copy of the minutes of all meetings of the board of directors and of the financial reports shall be forwarded to the chair and the secretary of the board of directors of the subsidiary corporation for permanent filing and to the supervising General Superintendent (1935:5).

(10) The bylaws of the affiliate corporation shall establish proper safeguards for fiscal soundness, legal requirements, integrity of purpose and protection of the assets of the corporation.

(11) All property of the affiliate corporation, whether real, personal or mixed, shall, in the event of the liquidation or dissolution of such corporation, devolve upon and pass to The Wesleyan Church Corporation or one of its subsidiary corporations.

## F. Adjunct Entities

**4370. Definition.** An adjunct entity may exist when an entity heretofore has been developed in response to social, humanitarian or community needs for the purpose of carrying on activities which are apart from the usual activities of a subsidiary corporation, such as, but not limited to, the operation of nursing homes, retirement centers, special educational or recreational activities and the like. Where the operation of such an adjunct ministry presently exists, and where such entity fails, prior to January 1, 1990, to incorporate and hereafter exist and conduct its affairs as an affiliate corporation (4340; 4350), it shall exist apart from any subsidiary, any affiliate corporation and The Wesleyan Church Corporation, and shall be termed an adjunct entity. In all such latter cases, the governing body of the subject subsidiary corporation shall use its best efforts on a continuing basis to cause the adjunct entity to meet the following conditions:

(1) The relationship between the adjunct entity and any subsidiary corporation, affiliate corporation or The Wesleyan Church, shall only be described and shown as "related through common religious heritage" rather than by use of name or such words as "agent," "agency," "subsidiary," or "affiliate."

(2) All financial responsibility arising from conduct of any activities of the adjunct entity shall be that solely of the adjunct entity, and no such responsibility shall fall upon any subsidiary corporation, affiliate corporation, The Wesleyan Church Corporation or any member or former member of the governing body thereof.

(3) No subsidiary corporation shall directly or indirectly elect, approve nominations for or confirm elections or selections of, members of the board of directors or other governing body of any adjunct entity.

(4) The real, personal or mixed property of the adjunct entity shall not be held in trust for a subsidiary corporation, an affiliate corporation or The Wesleyan Church.

(5) The adjunct entity shall, to the satisfaction of the subject subsidiary corporation or affiliate corporation, and the supervising General Superintendent, take all necessary and other reasonable measures to avoid creating the impression to the public, or any part thereof, that its existence or operation is in any fashion sponsored, controlled or operated by the subsidiary corporation, an affiliate corporation or The Wesleyan Church Corporation (1935:5).

**4390. Restriction.** Except as expressly permitted by paragraphs 4310, 4320, 4340 or 4350, no two or more members of the Board of Directors of The Wesleyan Church Corporation or of the board of directors or other governing body of any subsidiary corporation or affiliate corporation of The Wesleyan Church Corporation, whether acting individually or severally, shall directly or indirectly form or become members of any corporation, association, partnership or other legal entity which promotes, sponsors, encourages or in any manner engages in any activity which directly or indirectly purports to be sponsored or operated in any manner by or in the name of The Wesleyan Church or any subsidiary or affiliate corporation, except as authorized by a two-thirds vote of the General Board. Provided, however, that nothing contained in this paragraph 4390 or elsewhere in this Chapter IV of Part VIII of *The Discipline* is intended to prohibit the formation or operation of one or more private foundations or supporting organizations as described in Internal Revenue Code Section 170(b)(1)(E)(ii) or Section 509(a)(3) (or any successor provisions thereto of such Code) which benefit The Wesleyan Church.

# Chapter V

# PENSION CORPORATION

## The Wesleyan Pension Fund

**4400. Purpose**. The Wesleyan Church shall maintain and conduct a pension plan to be known and incorporated as The Wesleyan Pension Fund, Inc., for the benefit of its ministers and other persons as defined in the bylaws.

**4405. Government.** All matters pertaining to The Wesleyan Pension Fund shall be administered by a Board of Pensions who shall govern The Wesleyan Pension Fund in accord with *The Discipline* (4570) and its articles of incorporation and bylaws. The Board of Pensions is amenable to the General Board.

**4410. Duties and Powers.** This corporation shall receive and administer new trusts and funds and shall be and is directed and authorized to honor and carry out all commitments made by The Pilgrim Pension Plan, Inc., to its members through its bylaws and the commitments made by The Wesleyan Methodist Church of America to its ministers through the Superannuated Ministers' Aid Society and the Wesleyan Retirement Plan, as stated herewith:

(1) The Board of Pensions of The Wesleyan Pension Fund, Inc. shall be and constitute the Board of Pensions of The Pilgrim Pension Plan, Inc., which corporation shall continue in full force and effect until such time as all of its liabilities shall have been satisfied and discharged, at which time any remaining assets thereof shall, insofar as may be legal, by appropriate action of the General Conference be paid over to and become a part of The Wesleyan Pension Fund, Inc.

(2) The Wesleyan Pension Fund, Inc., insofar as may be legal shall be the successor in trust of the Superannuated Ministers' Aid Society of The Wesleyan Methodist Church of America, a New York corporation and as such successor in trust it shall be and is authorized and empowered to receive from its precedent corporation all trust funds and assets of any kind and character; real, personal or mixed held by it; and it shall be and is authorized to administer such trusts and funds in accordance with the conditions under which they have been previously received and administered by said precedent corporation. But nothing herein contained shall be construed to require the dissolution of the said precedent corporation and it shall continue to administer such funds as may not be legally transferred to the new corporation.

(3) The Wesleyan Pension Fund, Inc. insofar as may be legal, shall be the successor in trust for the Wesleyan Retirement Plan of The Wesleyan

Methodist Church of America, Inc., and as such successor in trust it shall be and is authorized and empowered to receive all trust funds and assets of any kind or character pertaining to the Wesleyan Retirement Plan; real, personal or mixed, held by said corporation; and it shall be and is authorized to administer such trusts and funds in accordance with the conditions under which they have been previously received and administered by said precedent corporation.

**4425. Bylaws of The Wesleyan Pension Fund.** The bylaws of the Wesleyan Pension Fund are to be maintained in a current and accurate form. Copies of the official and complete bylaws shall be provided upon request to any member of the Wesleyan Pension Fund.

The bylaws of the Wesleyan Pension Fund may be amended by the Board of Pensions, subject to ratification by a two-thirds vote of all the members of the General Board (1655:17).

# PART VIII

# PROPERTY

## Chapter I

## GENERAL REGULATIONS

### A. Application

**4500.** The general regulations set forth in this chapter shall be binding on all trustees and their governing bodies of The Wesleyan Church, whether local, district or general church, including all institutions, subsidiary corporations and similar bodies, unless otherwise stated in *The Discipline* or in the articles of incorporation and bylaws governing such trustees.

### B. Local Laws

**4510.** All provisions of *The Discipline* relating to property, both real and personal and relating to the formation and operation of any corporation, are conditioned upon their being in conformity with the local laws (4580) of the country, state, territory or other like political unit within the geographical bounds of which the property is situate; and in the event of conflict therewith, said provisions of *The Discipline* shall be modified to the extent required to conform with any such local laws. This regulation, however, shall not be construed to give the consent of The Wesleyan Church to deprivation of its property without due process of law, or to the regulation of its affairs by statute where such regulation violates the constitutional right of freedom of religion, separation of church and state or the rights of the Church to maintain its polity.

### C. Requirements

**4520.** A trustee must be a covenant member of The Wesleyan Church. Whenever a trustee ceases to be a covenant member of The Wesleyan Church for any reason, the office as trustee shall be declared vacant and a successor shall be elected for the unexpired term in the manner provided in *The Discipline*.

**4530.** All trustees shall administer their duties in accord with *The Discipline* as from time to time amended, as directed by the governing body to which they are amenable, and subject to local laws as set forth in 4510. Whenever a trustee refuses to carry out properly given orders and instructions and submit to the authority to which amenable, the trustee may be removed from office and a successor shall be elected for the unexpired term as provided for in *The Discipline*.

**4540.** A board of trustees shall have and hold in trust for the use and benefit of the members and ministers of The Wesleyan Church any and all property committed to it; shall see that titles are good; that deeds and all written instrumentalities are in harmony with *The Discipline* and with local laws as set forth in 4510; that all property deeds and titles contain the required trust clause as set forth in 4610; that they are promptly recorded; that abstracts and all other legal papers are properly stored and secured; and shall perform such other duties as are required of them in *The Discipline* or by the governing body to which they are amenable, and in the case of incorporated bodies, as set forth in the articles of incorporation and bylaws or charter of the corporation.

### D. Restrictions

**4550.** A trustee or board of trustees and/or its governing body may not divert property from the ownership and use of The Wesleyan Church .

**4560.** A board of trustees shall not normally accept a deed which contains a clause by which the land conveyed may revert to the original grantor, the heirs or assigns of the original owners.

### E. Terms

**4570.** "*The Discipline*" shall always refer to *The Discipline* of The Wesleyan Church as from time to time legislated and declared (125-175; 185; 385; 1590:1-2; 1920:27).

**4580.** "Local laws," whenever used in *The Discipline*, shall be construed to mean laws, including regulations and case law, of the civil jurisdiction(s) applicable to the matter at hand. With respect to property matters, this would normally be the law of the jurisdiction within which the property is located, and with respect to any other legal matters, would normally be the law of the civil jurisdiction(s) within which the matters arise.

### F. Trust Clause and Release Therefrom

**4590.** All property, whether real, personal or mixed, acquired by any local church, circuit, district, institution, agency or other similar body of The Wesleyan Church, whether incorporated or unincorporated, shall be held in trust for The Wesleyan Church, incorporated as The Wesleyan Church Corporation under the laws of the state of Indiana, and shall contain the trust clause as set forth in 4610 (cf. 315:6; 323:8). The absence of the trust clause in the evidence of the title or other written instruments, regardless of whether such absence is due to mistake, inadvertence or willful omission, shall in no way exclude a local church, circuit, district, institution, agency or similar body, whether incorporated or unincorporated, from or relieve it of its responsibility to The Wesleyan Church and subjection to the authority of said Church, and such property can only be sold, transferred or otherwise disposed of in accord with the provisions of *The Discipline*, concerning the sale, transfer or encumbrance of property.

(1) For property in developing districts see 542; 4650; 4800; 4920; cf. 4200-4260; 4500-4630.

(2) For property in provisional districts see 1025:3; 1030:1, 3; 4650; 4810-4820; cf. 4200-4260; 4500-4630.

(3) For local property in established districts see 510:4; 518:4; 528:5; 655:13-14; 725:24-25; 782:27-31; 850-859; 1038:3; 1180:21-22; 1233:13-14; 1310:11; 1345; 1360-1365; 4000-4070; 4100-4150; 4500-4630; 4660-4780; cf. 4250-4260; 4830-4880.

(4) For district property in established districts see 1038:3; 1180:21-22; 1233:13-14; 1310:11; 1345; 1360-1365; 4100-4150; 4250-4260; 4500-4630; 4830-4880.

(5) For general church property see 4200-4270; 4500-4630; 4900-4940; cf. 475; 2070.

(6) For property of a general educational institution see 4500-4630; cf. 2362; 4250-4260.

(7) For property of a subsidiary corporation, board or institution, other than a general educational institution see 4300-4370; 4500-4630; cf. 4250-4260.

**4610.** All titles, deeds and other written instruments for the conveyance of property to or for The Wesleyan Church as set forth in 4590 shall contain the following trust clause:

> In trust for the use and benefit of the ministry and members of The Wesleyan Church, incorporated under the laws of the state of Indiana as The Wesleyan Church Corporation, subject to *The Discipline*, regulations and appointments of said Church as from time to time legislated and declared.

**4620.** Real property acquired by a conveyance containing the foregoing trust clause in 4610 may be sold in conformity with the provisions of *The Discipline*, and when such provisions have been complied with, the real property so sold or conveyed shall be released from the foregoing trust clause, and the trustees enabled to give a good and sufficient deed (cf. 4690:1).

**4630.** Real property acquired by a conveyance containing the foregoing trust clause in 4610 may be mortgaged or otherwise encumbered in conformity with the provisions of *The Discipline*, and when such provisions have been complied with, the foregoing trust clause shall be subordinated to the mortgage lien (cf. 4690:2).

# Chapter II

# LOCAL CHURCH PROPERTY

## A. Developing Church Property

**4650. Developing District and Provisional District.** Developing churches within the bounds of a developing district or provisional district shall be under the jurisdiction of the General Department of Evangelism and Church Growth as set forth in 4800 and 4810-4820.

**4660. District.** The regulations concerning property for a developing church within the bounds of an established district are:

(1) The district board of administration shall be vested with power and authority to purchase, manage, sell, encumber, transfer and dispose of any and all property of a developing church, whether real, personal or mixed (510:4; 1233:13-14), and shall direct the pastor and the local advisory council concerning the same in keeping with *The Discipline* (1233:1, 30).

(2) The pastor and local advisory council of a developing church shall be responsible to supervise, control and maintain the property under their care as directed by the district superintendent and the district board of administration (510:3-4; 1233:1, 30).

(3) All property of a developing church shall be held by the district in trust for the use and benefit of the members and ministers of The Wesleyan Church as required in 323:8 and shall contain the trust clause as given in 4610 (cf. 4140; 4590-4630; 4830).

(4) Whenever a developing church has been organized as an established church (518-520), the district board of trustees may transfer the property to the local board of trustees as set forth in 4680, provided that the property is free of debt.

**4670. Reclassification.** Whenever an established church is reclassified as a developing church as set forth in 518:5; 1180:24; and 1233:29, the office of the members of the local board of administration and the local board of trustees shall thereupon cease (859:5) and the district board of administration shall be responsible for the property as set forth in 4660:1-4 (cf. 510:4). Whenever the property of such a church has been held by the local trustees, it shall be conveyed or transferred to the district to be held as set forth in 4830 (cf. 859:5).

## B. Church Property

### 1. Ownership

**4680.** Local property within an established district may be held by the local church or by the district, as decided upon by the district conference (cf. 1180:21-22). In those districts where the local churches are to hold their own property, all grants, conveyances, devises, gifts, transfers and assignments now owned or hereafter acquired of any property, real, personal or mixed, to or for any unincorporated local church or any organization, board or similar body connected thereto, shall be held by and/or conveyed to its duly elected board of trustees, and to their successors in office and their assigns, as the board of trustees of such local church, in trust for the benefit and use of the members and ministers of The Wesleyan Church, subject to its *Discipline*, regulations and appointments as from time to time legislated and declared and shall contain the appropriate trust clause as set forth in 4610 (cf. 4590; 4620). An omission of the name of any or all of the trustees shall not render any instrument invalid. (The regulations for an incorporated local church are set forth in 4000-4070.) In those districts where the district is to hold local property (cf. 323:8), such local property shall be held as set forth in 4140 or 4830.

### 2. Trust Clause and Release Therefrom

**4690.** All written instruments of conveyance by which property is held or hereafter acquired by any local church, whether incorporated or unincorporated, shall contain the trust clause in 4610, and release therefrom shall be as follows:

(1) Whenever the real property of a local church acquired by a conveyance containing the trust clause as set forth in 4610 is sold in conformity with the provisions of *The Discipline* (4700-4720), the written approval of the district board of administration (4700:3) shall constitute a release and discharge of the real property so sold and conveyed from the trust clause (cf. 4620).

(2) Whenever the real property of a local church, acquired by a conveyance containing the trust clause in 4610, is mortgaged or encumbered as provided for in *The Discipline* (4700-4720), the written approval of the district board of administration for such mortgage or encumbrance (4700:3) shall constitute a formal recognition of the priority of such mortgage lien and the subordination of the trust clause thereto (cf. 4630).

## B. Acquisition, Sale, Mortgage and Transfer of Property

**4700.** An unincorporated local church within an established district may acquire, purchase, sell, mortgage, transfer or otherwise dispose of real property in accord with the following authorization and conditions:

(1) A resolution authorizing such action shall be recommended by the local board of administration (782:31), and passed by the local church conference (655:13) by a majority of those present and voting, at any regular or special session duly called for such purpose, provided that notice of the intended action shall be given to the local church members by announcement from the pulpit in two regular services, the first of which shall be not less than one week before the date of the session of the local church conference at which the proposal shall be considered, and that notice shall also be given at least one week in advance in the church bulletin, when such is available, and that such other notice shall be given as may be required by local laws (cf. 633:1).

(2) The proposal shall be studied by the district building committee whenever it involves the purchase of property, the construction or remodeling of buildings or other work as set forth in 1345, and the written recommendation of the district building committee shall be forwarded to the district board of administration and the local church.

(3) The district board of administration, after receiving the recommendation of the district building committee, shall approve the proposal of the local church in writing and such approval shall be affixed to the written instrument involved (1233:32).

(4) The resolution authorizing such action shall direct that any contract, deed, bill of sale, mortgage or other necessary written instrument be executed by and on behalf of the local church by the proper officers of the local board of trustees, who thereupon shall be duly authorized to carry out the directions of the local church conference and the local board of administration in keeping with the requirements of *The Discipline* (cf. 850-859; 4500-4630; 4720); and any written instrument so executed shall be binding and effective as the action of the local church.

(5) The chair of the local board of trustees, or other designated trustee, shall submit all written instruments of conveyance and title for the acquisition of property to the district superintendent for approval as to their conformity with *The Discipline* as stated in 1310:11 and shall see that permanent legal and property records are properly stored as set forth in 4760.

(6) When real property is donated to a Wesleyan church for ministries or in a capital or fund raising campaign, and the donor's intent is that the property be sold and the proceeds invested accordingly, the local board of

administration shall have full power to authorize the reception and disposal of the property, subject to the express written approval of each transaction by the district superintendent.

**4720.** The proceeds from the sale of any real property of a local church whether incorporated or unincorporated, other than as provided for in 4700:6, shall be used for the purchase or improvement of property for that local church, unless otherwise authorized by the district board of administration (1233:32). In the event of a situation where two or more local churches have merged, proceeds from the sale of such property shall be used by the merged church unless otherwise authorized by the district board of administration. Whenever a local church does not wish to invest the money received as stated herewith, the money shall be forwarded to the district treasurer, and provided that all debts against such property being sold shall first be paid, it shall be used as ordered by the district conference or the district board of administration for the construction of churches or parsonages within the bounds of the district, for district property, or for purchase of property or construction of buildings involved in the planting of new churches. Such moneys may be used for other expenses involved in the planting of new churches only with the approval of the area General Superintendent.

### 4. Abandoned Church Property

**4730.** When the property of a local church is no longer used, a local church may be declared by the district board of administration as discontinued or abandoned (1233:29) and the title shall thereupon vest in the district corporation (4100), or in the district board of trustees in the case of an unincorporated district (4855). The district board of administration shall have the authority to order the sale of said property and to appropriate the proceeds for the purchase of property for a local church, for the construction of churches or parsonages within the bounds of the district, for district property, or for the purchase of property or construction of buildings involved in the planting of new churches. Such moneys may be used for other expense involved in the planting of new churches only with the approval of the area General Superintendent. The actions of the district board of administration shall be reported to the next session of the district conference. Any bequests, devises, gift annuities or other benefits to a local church that accrue or become available after said church has been discontinued shall become the property of the district corporation (4100), or, in the case of an unincorporated district, shall become the property of the district board of trustees (4855).

### C. Circuit Property

**4740.** The organization and government for a circuit within an established district are set forth in 525-535. The regulations concerning the acquisition, purchase, sale, encumbrance, transfer or other disposition of circuit property within an established district shall be the same as for local church property within the district as set forth in 4680 and 4700:1-5. The proceeds from the sale of circuit property shall also be disposed of in the same manner as the proceeds from the sale of local church property as set forth in 4720-4730. The circuit board of trustees shall carry such duties concerning circuit property as are required of a local church board of trustees (cf. 850-859) and shall be subject to the general regulations as set forth in 4500-4630.

**4750.** Whenever the discontinuance of a circuit shall be ordered by the district conference, or whenever a local church is separated from a circuit and established as a separate pastoral charge (1180:25), the district conference shall also order the sale or disposition of circuit property, for which a recommendation shall be received from the district board of administration (cf. 1233:9c). Each local church shall be entitled to receive its just share of the property in which it has invested funds; and the amount of such value and just share shall be determined by the district board of administration or a special committee appointed for that purpose.

### D. Property Records

**4760.** All deeds, titles and other legal or property records of each developing church, church or circuit within the bounds of the district shall be placed in the custody of the district superintendent (1310:11) who shall be responsible for their preservation and permanent filing as directed by the district board of administration (1233:15). The district superintendent may authorize a local church to retain such records when deemed necessary, in which case a certified or true copy shall be kept in the district files which are in the district superintendent's custody.

### E. Rights to Property

**4770.** The district board of administration, in the name of the district corporation (4100; cf. 4855), shall have the right to intervene or to institute any legal or equitable actions as may be deemed necessary against a local church or circuit within the bounds of the district to preserve the rights and interests of the district and The Wesleyan Church, in all matters relating to property and the rights to property within the bounds of the district, as set forth in the Judiciary (5185-5190) and as otherwise provided for in *The Discipline*. The General Board, in the name of The Wesleyan Church Corporation, shall also have the right to intervene and protect the rights and interests of The Wesleyan Church as set forth in 4250-4260.

**4780.** No local church may vote to withdraw as a body from The Wesleyan Church, or in any way sever its relation thereto, and no local church conference and/or local board of administration and/or local board of trustees can divert property from The Wesleyan Church (859:4; 4550). If any local church violates or in any way attempts to circumvent these provisions, then all right, title and interest in and to all real property of such local church shall thereupon immediately vest in the district corporation (4100) or in the district board of trustees in the case of an unincorporated district (4855); and all such property shall be vacated immediately by the offending party or parties. The district conference or, in the interim, the district board of administration shall have authority to deny the use of any such property to the offending party or parties and to order the immediate eviction of any such party or parties who do not comply therewith.

# Chapter III

## DISTRICT PROPERTY

### A. Developing District Property

**4800.** The regulations concerning property within the bounds of a developing district shall be set forth in the *Policy of the General Board for Evangelism and Church Growth* in accord with the following:

(1) The authority for the purchase, sale, encumbrance, transfer or other disposal of real property within a developing district shall be vested in the General Board (cf. 1655:34; 4810).

(2) All property shall be held by and/or conveyed to The Wesleyan Church Corporation and shall be general church property (4920), except when otherwise required by local laws or otherwise directed by the General Board (cf. 1655:38), in which case it shall be held in trust for the benefit and use of the members and ministers of The Wesleyan Church and shall contain the appropriate trust clause as set forth in 4610 (cf. 4590-4630).

(3) The superintendent and any other workers of the developing district shall supervise, control and maintain the property under their care in accord with *The Discipline*, the *Policy of the General Board for Evangelism and Church Growth* and other directives, and as supervised by the General Director of Evangelism and Church Growth.

(4) All legal and property records shall be in the custody of the General Secretary unless otherwise directed by the General Board, in which case certified or true copies shall be filed in the General Secretary's custody.

### B. Provisional District Property

**4810.** The regulations concerning property within the bounds of a provisional district shall be the same as for an established district, with the exception that the official actions of a provisional district are subject to the approval of the General Board (cf. 1020-1030), and that no property within a provisional district may be received, transferred, bought, leased or sold without the written permission of the General Director of Evangelism and Church Growth, and with the further exception that the General Board may give special directions as deemed necessary (cf. 1655:34).

**4820.** A provisional district may be incorporated when so recommended by the General Director of Evangelism and Church Growth and authorized by the General Board (1655:34) as set forth in 4100-4150.

## C. District Property

### 1. Ownership

**4830. Unincorporated District.** Except when local laws shall otherwise require, all grants, conveyances, devises, gifts, transfers and assignments, now owned or hereafter made, of any property, real, personal or mixed, to or for any unincorporated district or any organization, board or similar body connected thereto and for any local property held by such a district (4660; 4680), shall be held by and/or conveyed to its duly elected board of trustees (cf. 1360-1365; 4855), and to their successors in office and to their assigns, as the board of trustees, of said district, in trust for the benefit and use of the members and ministers of The Wesleyan Church and subject to its *Discipline*, regulations and appointments, as from time to time legislated and declared and shall contain the trust clause as set forth in 4610 (cf. 4590-4630). (The regulations for an incorporated district are set forth in 4100-4150.)

### 2. Management and Control

**4840.** The district board of administration shall have the following duties and powers concerning the district property and such local property as may be held by the district (4660; 4680):

(1) To carry out the directions of the district conference (1180:22; 1233:14), and, in the interim of its sessions, to have power to act on its own resolution to acquire, purchase, sell, exchange, mortgage, deed in trust, pledge, rent, lease and convey any property, real, personal or mixed, as may be deemed necessary or convenient for the purpose of the district and so to order the district board of trustees (1360-1365; 4855), provided that in transactions concerning real property used for district purposes such as a district parsonage, headquarters or campground, the district board of administration shall consult with the General Superintendent over the district (1935:17), and further provided that said district board of administration shall be subject to the general regulations concerning property as set forth in 4500-4630.

(2) To carry out the directions of the district conference (1180:22; 1233:14), and in the interim of its sessions, to direct the district board of trustees (1360-1365; 4855) concerning any and all donations, bequests and devises of any kind or character, real or personal, that may be given, devised, bequeathed or conveyed to the district, or to the district board of trustees as such, for any benevolent, charitable or religious purpose, and to direct the board of trustees in the administration of such in accordance with the

directions of the donor, trustor or testator, and in the interest of the church, institution, organization or agency contemplated by such donor, trustor or testator.

(3) To supervise, control and maintain all district property.

(4) To receive a report from the district building committee as set forth in 1345 and to approve in writing the proposal of a local church to acquire, purchase, encumber, sell, transfer or otherwise dispose of real property as set forth in 4040-4070 and 4700-4720.

(5) To act in regard to the disposition of the proceeds from the sale of local church or circuit property as set forth in 4720, and the discontinuance or disposal of abandoned property as set forth in 4730.

(6) To intervene and institute all necessary legal and equitable actions to safeguard and protect the rights and interests of the district and of The Wesleyan Church, including all matters relating to the property and rights to property, including any property held by a local church, circuit or other organization within the district, whether arising by gift, devise or otherwise, or where held in trust for the benefit and use of the members and ministers of the district and The Wesleyan Church (4770-4780).

(7) To direct the district superintendent in the care and preservation of all legal and property records for the local churches and the district (4760).

### 3. District Board of Trustees

**4855.** The district conference of each established district shall be incorporated or shall cause a corporation to be formed and maintained to facilitate the management of its legal and corporate affairs as set forth in 4100-4150. In places where local laws prohibit such incorporation, or where the local laws require property to be held by trustees, the district conference shall elect from among the members of the district board of administration the members of the district board of trustees in such number as desired (1180:22; cf. 1360-1365). The district trustees shall hold office as trustees until their term of office expires as members of the district board of administration and until their successors are qualified and elected. The district board of trustees shall be amenable to the district board of administration and shall hold all district property, and such local property as may be held by the district (cf. 4660; 4680), in trust for The Wesleyan Church as set forth in 4590-4610, shall attend to all legal matters pertaining to the district property and other business as directed, and shall carry out such transactions for the purchase, acquisition, sale, encumbrance, transfer or other disposal of district property as ordered by the district board of administration (4840). Whenever a trustee shall refuse to carry out the directions of the district board of administration, the trustee may be removed from office by a two-thirds vote of all the members of the district board of administration, who shall also fill the vacancy for the unexpired term (cf. 1233:27a; 1360).

### D. Rights to Property

**4870.** A district, whether incorporated or unincorporated, that has been placed under discipline in accord with the procedures set forth in the Judiciary (5070; 5218-5230), and each local church within that district, shall be suspended from the right to acquire, purchase, sell, mortgage, transfer or otherwise dispose of any real property without the approval of the General Superintendent or general official appointed to have charge of the district (5225). Whenever a district is reorganized as set forth in 5235, the members and ministers affirming loyalty to The Wesleyan Church shall be and constitute the district and shall have the right to control and manage all district property as set forth in *The Discipline*.

**4880.** No district conference may vote to withdraw as a body from The Wesleyan Church, or in any way sever its relation thereto, and no district board and/or committee and/or board of trustees can divert property from The Wesleyan Church (4540-4550). Provided, however, that no sale, exchange, mortgage, deed in trust, pledge, lease, conveyance or other alienation of property, in whole or in part, whether such property is real, personal or mixed, as may be necessary or convenient for the purposes of the district, and when undertaken in accordance with the provisions and requirements of *The Discipline*, shall constitute a "diversion" of such property from The Wesleyan Church. If a district conference violates or in any way attempts to circumvent these provisions, then all right, title and interest in and to all district real property shall thereupon immediately vest in The Wesleyan Church Corporation (4200-4270). The General Conference or, in the interim, the General Board shall have the authority to deny the use of any such property to the offending party or parties and to order the immediate eviction of any such party or parties who do not comply therewith from such property.

### E. Loan Guarantees

**4890.** The district board of administration of an unincorporated district may authorize and direct the district trustees to guarantee in writing any note, mortgage, contract or any other evidence of indebtedness, of any local church of said district.

## Chapter IV

## GENERAL CHURCH PROPERTY

### A. Incorporation

**4900.** The General Conference shall cause a corporation to be formed and maintained under the name of The Wesleyan Church Corporation, through which it shall acquire, sell, manage, encumber, transfer and otherwise dispose of general church property (4200-4260; cf. 1590:5).

### B. Ownership

**4920.** All grants, conveyances, devises, gifts, transfers and assignments now owned or hereafter made of any property, real, personal or mixed, to or for The Wesleyan Church, or any general office, department, institution, agency or organization connected thereto, with the exception of those that are separately incorporated (cf. 1590:6; 4300), shall be held by and/or conveyed to The Wesleyan Church Corporation in its corporate name, for the use and benefit of the members and ministers of The Wesleyan Church, subject to its *Discipline*, regulations and appointments as from time to time legislated and declared (cf. 4570).

### C. Suggested Forms for Bequests and Devises

**4940.** The General Director of Estate and Gift Planning (2070) shall be available for special advice and instruction for those who desire to make wills, donations or bequests to The Wesleyan Church or any of its various ministries (cf. 475).

(1) **Form for Bequests of Money or Personal Property.** I give, devise and bequeath to The Wesleyan Church Corporation, a corporation created and existing under and by virtue of the laws of the state of Indiana, the sum of ____________ dollars, (or if personal property, notes, bonds, etc., describe the same); to be used and appropriated by that body to religious, benevolent, missionary or educational purposes (or, if desired, state the specific purpose); and the receipt of the treasurer of the said corporation shall be a full and sufficient discharge of my executor for the same.

(2) **Form for a Devise of Land.** I give, devise and bequeath to The Wesleyan Church Corporation, a corporation created and existing under and

by virtue of the laws of the state of Indiana, the following described lands and premises, viz: (full description of land); to have and to hold the same with the privilege or appurtenances unto said corporation (state a specific purpose if desired), its successors and assigns forever; and the receipt of the treasurer of said corporation shall be a full and sufficient discharge of my executor for the same.

(3) **Form for a Devise of Residuary Estate or Any Part Thereof.** I give, devise and bequeath to The Wesleyan Church Corporation, a corporation created and existing under and by virtue of the laws of the state of Indiana, all (or some specific part of) the rest, residue or remainder of my estate, real or personal to said corporation (state specific purpose if desired), its successors and assigns forever; and the receipt of the treasurer of said corporation shall be a full and sufficient discharge of my executor for the same.

(4) Suggested forms for other types of donations and delayed gift giving are available from the General Director of Estate and Gift Planning (2070).

# PART IX

# JUDICIARY

## Chapter I

## GENERAL PRINCIPLES

### A. Meaning and Purpose of Church Discipline

**5000. Definition.** Church discipline is the orderly exercise of that authority, and the application of those principles and laws, which the Church has derived from the Word of God and has appointed for the governing of its members, ministers, congregations and official bodies.

**5005. Classification.** Church discipline may be referred to in the general sense of administrative discipline and in the more restricted sense of judicial discipline:

(1) **Administrative Discipline.** Administrative discipline is the general and orderly exercise of ecclesiastical authority for the government and preservation of the Church. The purpose of administrative discipline is to provide for the purity, effectiveness and spiritual influence of the church organization and the protection of the rights of its members, ministers, congregations and official bodies.

(2) **Judicial Discipline.** Judicial discipline is the proper exercise of the authority which Christ has vested in His church for the prevention and correction of offenses and the removal of scandal (cf. Matt. 18:15-18; 1 Cor. 5:1-5). The purpose of judicial discipline is the vindication of the truth, the preservation of the integrity of the body, the restoration and salvation of the guilty and the warning of the careless.

**5010. Subjects of Discipline.** All members and ministers of The Wesleyan Church are subject to its administrative discipline, and, if charged with an offense, are subject to its judicial discipline.

### B. The Administration of Judicial Discipline

**5015.** In order that the purposes of church discipline may be realized, judicial discipline for The Wesleyan Church shall be administered in accord with the following principles:

(1) A prayerful and Christlike spirit shall be maintained at all times by all parties (Eph. 4:15; 2 Tim. 4:2; 1 Cor. 13:4-7).

(2) The restoration and salvation of erring members shall ever be kept in view. Every effort that love can suggest shall be made to bring back to the Lord one who, while under the Church's care, has wandered from Him (cf. 268).

(3) A sincere and reasonable effort shall be made to clear up an accusation or to deal with an offending person without the formality of a church trial, in keeping with scriptural admonitions (Matt. 18:15-18; Gal. 6:1-2; James 5:16).

(4) Each accusation and all judicial proceedings shall receive prompt and careful attention by the proper authorities.

(5) The doctrines and standards of The Wesleyan Church shall be maintained without respect of persons. Any offending person shall be dealt with kindly, yet faithfully, according to the seriousness of the offense and as provided for in this Judiciary and in *The Discipline*.

(6) Legal technicalities shall not be permitted to obstruct the sincere search for truth, while at the same time the fundamental principles and procedures of justice shall be upheld. There shall be no attempt to confuse or entangle anyone in the process of an investigation or a trial (cf. 276).

(7) The accused person shall be presumed innocent until proven guilty. However, the moral conviction of the truth of the charge is all that is necessary in church discipline (5274).

### C. Fundamental Rights and Duties for Judicial Discipline

**5025. Right of Trial and Appeal.** The right to a fair and impartial trial and the right to appeal shall not be denied to any member, minister, local church, district or official body of The Wesleyan Church. No one shall be arbitrarily set aside without due consideration for both spiritual welfare and rights as a member of The Wesleyan Church and shall always have the right to request a trial or to appeal, even when placed under discipline (302:4; 305:3; 313:7; 315:8; 323:10; 360:3f; 375:4, 6; 380).

**5030. Rights of the Accused.** Any member or minister who is accused shall have the following rights:

(1) **Counsel.** The accused shall always have the right to be represented at a church trial by counsel of choice, provided such counsel is a covenant member in good standing in The Wesleyan Church, or to present a personal defense. Any covenant member against whom there are no charges shall be considered to be in good standing.

(2) **Examination.** The accused, or the counsel chosen by the accused, shall have the right to meet any accuser(s) face to face and to cross-examine any witnesses for the prosecution.

(3) **Objection.** The accused shall have the right to challenge for cause the qualifications of any member of the judicatory, the validity of which shall be determined by the presiding officer (5318).

(4) **Limitation.** A minister or member shall not be required to answer charges for any act which occurred more than five years before the filing of such charges, except in cases involving immorality or crime.

**5040. Right of Investigation.** The Church has a right to investigate the character of its members and ministers in order to maintain the purity of its doctrines and practices, and can, therefore, through its own officers, official bodies and judicatories, require members or ministers under investigation to testify, under penalty of dismissal if they refuse.

**5045. Duty of Cooperation.** It shall be the duty of every member, minister and church body to cooperate and to witness when properly requested to do so for an official investigation or trial.

## Chapter II

## OFFENSES

### A. Individual

**5050.** Any member, minister, special worker or district or general official of The Wesleyan Church shall be liable to disciplinary proceedings and trial for any of the following offenses:

(1) Holding or teaching any doctrine contrary to the doctrine of The Wesleyan Church as stated in *The Discipline*.

(2) Disobedience to the provisions of *The Discipline* or tolerating such disobedience.

(3) Insubordination or willful refusal to recognize Church authority.

(4) Conduct unbecoming a member or minister of The Wesleyan Church.

(5) Immorality or crime.

(6) Serious or persistent neglect of duty.

### B. Local Church, District or Official Body

**5070.** Any local church, district, official body or other agency of The Wesleyan Church shall be liable to disciplinary proceedings and trial for any of the following offenses:

(1) Disseminating or tolerating the teaching of any doctrine contrary to the doctrines of The Wesleyan Church as stated in *The Discipline*.

(2) Disobedience to the provisions of *The Discipline* or tolerating such disobedience.

(3) Insubordination or willful refusal to recognize Church authority.

## Chapter III

## LOCAL CHURCH JURISDICTION

**5100. Jurisdiction.** Original jurisdiction over a lay member belongs to the local church of which the lay person is a member.

(1) Accusations against a lay member shall be submitted to the pastor (725:15; 5254). If there is no pastor, or if the pastor does not attend to the matter, the accusation shall be submitted to a member of the local board of administration who shall present it to the local board of administration. Inquiry shall be made (5258), and the local board of administration shall have charge of ordering an investigation (5278:2) or trial (782:11), if necessary, as set forth in this Judiciary (cf. 5250-5347). Any charge against a lay member must be sustained by two or more responsible members of The Wesleyan Church. Whenever a trial is ordered, the district superintendent shall be notified.

(2) The authority of a local board of administration for a developing church shall be exercised by the district superintendent (1310:15).

(3) The district superintendent, when requested to do so by the local board of administration, shall have authority to provide for any unusual circumstances not provided for in *The Discipline*, and to appoint, when necessary, any members from another Wesleyan church or from the district to a local judicial committee (5115:1-2; cf. 1310:16).

(4) When a lay member, who resides away from the church in which membership is held and attends another Wesleyan church, is accused of improper or immoral conduct, the pastor and the local board of administration where the lay member attends shall have authority to make an official investigation of such accusation (5250-5258; 5278). If, pursuant to such investigation, a bill of charges is drawn up against such a member, it shall be presented to the pastor of the local church where the accused holds membership.

**5115. Local Judicial Committee.** Charges against a lay member shall be heard and determined by a local judicial committee:

(1) A local judicial committee shall consist of not less than three covenant members (5318), which shall be selected by the local board of administration, as the occasion may arise, from its own membership or the membership of the local church (782:11; 970; cf. 5100:3). The committee shall serve from the time of its appointment until it shall hear and determine the case, including any reopening (5335).

(2) The local board of administration shall designate the chair or may request the district superintendent to do so. The chair of the local judicial committee shall be the presiding officer and shall conduct the proceedings in accord with this Judiciary (cf. 5250-5347), and shall notify the accused of their rights (5030).

(3) It shall be the duty of the local judicial committee to hear and determine the charges, to render a verdict concerning the guilt or innocence of the accused, and to recommend to the body having authority over the accused (655:1, 6, 7; 782:11, 25) the penalty, if any, to be imposed (5350). A two-thirds majority vote of all members of the committee shall be required to render a verdict of guilty. Discipline, if required, shall be administered by the body having authority over the accused, and may take the form of admonition, rebuke, suspension, deposition or dismissal, and said body may require repentance, apology or restitution as deemed necessary (5350).

(4) Whenever the accused lay member is serving the Church under the jurisdiction of the General Board (5203), a certified copy of the findings of the local judicial committee shall be forwarded to the chair of the General Board (cf. 1935:1); and whenever the accused is licensed or commissioned by the district, a certified copy of the findings shall be forwarded to the district superintendent (cf. 1310:27).

(5) An appeal may be taken by the accused concerning the verdict and/or penalty to the district board of review, within thirty days (5162:1; 5338-5347).

**5130. Restrictions Under Discipline.** Whenever a lay member has been found guilty by a judicatory, and has been placed under discipline by being suspended from the rights and privileges of membership, the lay member shall not vote, hold or exercise any office, and shall not be eligible for a local license or a district license or commission for the duration of such suspension. If the suspension has been for an indefinite period, the local board of administration shall be responsible to declare an end to the suspension (782:11). If the person suspended shows the desired repentance and the offense has ceased, the suspension shall be terminated. If the offense has not ceased, in due time, the local board of administration shall recommend the dismissal of the accused from the Church or vote for such dismissal itself if such power has been delegated (cf. 655:1; 782:10).

**5140. Reinstatement.** After being dismissed from the Church, a lay member may be reinstated by the local church when such a person evidences a genuine repentance and amendment of life, and meets the requirements for membership.

# Chapter IV

# DISTRICT JURISDICTION

## A. Jurisdiction

**5150.** The district conference shall have original jurisdiction as set forth in 5153 over the following members and local units of the district (5203):

(1) An ordained, commissioned or licensed minister.

(2) A ministerial student.

(3) A commissioned or licensed special worker.

(4) A supply pastor.

(5) A developing church, established church, circuit or mission, within the district.

**5153.** The jurisdiction of the district conference (1180:12), and, in the interim of its sessions, the district board of administration (1233:1), over those persons listed in 5150:1-4 shall be over their standing in the ministry or as a ministerial student or a special worker, as the case may be, and their district conference relations and appointments (1240) with the exception of those who are first amenable to the General Board for their official duties (5203-5208; cf. 323:1; 360:2). The judicial authority of the district conference and/or its district board of administration is limited to standing, district conference relations and appointments and does not extend to local church membership, but the district conference or district board of administration may also decide upon the submission of charges to the local church having jurisdiction over the membership of the accused.

**5156.** The district conference, when in session, shall receive any complaint or accusation (cf. 5170) against any person or local unit under its jurisdiction, appointing an investigative committee (5278:1), and, if necessary, referring charges against a person to a district judicial committee appointed by the district conference (5175), and referring charges against a local unit to the district board of review (5162). If the judicatory is able to complete its work while the district conference is still in session, it shall report its findings to the conference which shall fix the penalty, if any, to be imposed (5350-5370). (Cf. 1180:44.) If the investigative committee or the judicatory completes its work after the close of the district conference session, it shall report its findings to the district board of administration which shall exercise the authority of the district conference over those under its jurisdiction and shall take charge of all judicial proceedings necessary in the interim of district conference sessions (1233:35, 39).

## B. District Board of Review

**5159.** Each established district shall have a district board of review consisting of four ordained ministers and three lay covenant members, elected annually by the district board of administration (1233:25; 1370). They shall be covenant members of The Wesleyan Church and of the district and shall not, at the same time, be members of the district board of administration. The district board of administration shall also elect two ordained ministers and two lay members as reserves who shall serve in the order of their election whenever a member is disqualified for a particular case (5318) and shall also fill any vacancies in the order of their election. The district board of review shall organize itself and elect its own officers, and shall see that complete records of all proceedings and cases are kept (cf. 5322). The board shall meet annually at the time of the regular district conference session and at other times and places as deemed necessary. The chair shall see that proceedings are conducted in keeping with the rules of procedure (5250-5347) and other provisions of *The Discipline*. The board shall also be authorized to cite any member(s), minister(s) or local church(es) through their officials to appear and to testify concerning matters brought before the district board of review (5040-5045). The records of the district board of review shall be in the custody of the district secretary (1332:6).

**5162.** The duties and powers of the district board of review are:

(1) To hear and determine the appeal of a lay member or of a local board of administration concerning the results of a local church trial (5115:3, 5); to sustain, modify or revoke, in whole or in part, the verdict and/or the penalty as set forth in 5338-5347, by a majority vote of all members of the district board of review (302:4; 5115:3), provided that if the accused has been previously found innocent, it shall require a two-thirds majority of all members of the district board of review to find the accused guilty.

(2) To hear and determine the appeal of a member(s) concerning an action of a local church conference or a local board of administration when such member(s) is aggrieved or adversely affected by such action, to determine the legality of such an action in regard to *The Discipline* and district regulations, and to report their findings to the district board of administration for appropriate action. (Cf. 5185:1.)

(3) To hear any charges against a local church alleging an offense as set forth in 5070 presented by the district conference (1180:44) or the district board of administration (1233:35); to determine the guilt or innocence of the local church with reference to such charges, with a two-thirds vote of the district board of review required for a verdict of guilty; and to report its findings and recommendations to the district conference, or in the interim of

its sessions, to the district board of administration. (Cf. 1233:35; 5156; 5185:2.)

(4) To hear and decide any complaint by a local church against another local church within the district (315:8), provided that such a complaint shall be sustained by a two-thirds majority vote of the local church conference, and further provided that sincere efforts have been made for an amicable settlement through the district board of administration; to report its findings and recommendations to the district conference, or in the interim of its sessions, to the district board of administration. (Cf. 1233:35; 5156; 5185:1.)

(5) To hear and decide any other cases as shall be referred to it by the district conference (1180:44) or the district board of administration (1233:35). (Cf. 5156; 5185.)

**5167. Appeals.** Appeals concerning a decision of the district board of review shall be made to the General Board of Review (5185:4; 5440:7).

## C. Ministers, Ministerial Students, and Special Workers

### 1. Procedure

**5170.** Accusations or complaints against those under the jurisdiction of the district as set forth in 5150:1-4 shall be cared for as follows:

(1) Accusations shall be submitted to the district superintendent who shall make inquiry (1310:27; 5254-5258), and the district conference, or in the interim of its sessions, the district board of administration shall decide on any official investigation (5278:1) or trial, if necessary, as set forth in the rules of procedure (1180:44; 1233:39; 5156; 5250-5347). Any charges alleging an offense as set forth in 5050 shall be heard and determined by a district judicial committee (5175:1-5). If guilt has been confessed by the accused, a trial is unnecessary and the district conference or the district board of administration shall proceed to fix the penalty, if any, to be imposed, which may consist of admonition, rebuke, suspension or deposition (5180; 5350-5370).

(2) If the accused is the district superintendent, a general official or other person amenable to the General Board (5203), the accusation shall be given to the General Superintendent and handled as set forth in 5212.

(3) If an accusation alleges an offense committed by a person under the jurisdiction of the district (5150:1-4) in a district other than that in which the accused holds membership, the district superintendent and the district board of administration of the district in which the offense was allegedly committed shall have jurisdiction over the official investigation (5278). If a bill of charges is to be drawn up, it shall be submitted through the General Superintendent(s) to the district in which the accused holds membership.

## 2. District Judicial Committee

**5175.** A district judicial committee shall be constituted and shall carry out such duties as provided herewith:

(1) A district judicial committee shall consist of four ordained ministers and three lay covenant members, selected by the district conference, or in the interim of its sessions, by the district board of administration (1233:25, 39), as the occasion may arise, from among its own members or the members of the district, and the appointing body may request that one member shall be a general official. The General Superintendent over the district shall be notified of the trial. The committee shall serve from the time of its appointment until it shall hear and determine the case.

(2) The appointing body shall appoint the chair or may request the General Superintendent to do so. The chair of the district judicial committee shall preside over the trial and shall conduct it according to the rules of procedure (5250-5347) and *The Discipline*, shall notify the accused of their rights (5030), and shall decide on the admissibility of evidence (5266).

(3) It shall be the duty of the district judicial committee to hear and determine the charges, to render a verdict concerning the guilt or innocence of the accused, and to recommend the penalty, if any, to be imposed by the body having jurisdiction over the accused (5350). A two-thirds majority vote of all members of the district judicial committee shall be required for a verdict of guilty. The penalty may take the form of admonition, rebuke, suspension or deposition as set forth in 5350-5370, and the body having jurisdiction may also require repentance, apology or restitution as deemed necessary.

(4) The records of a district judicial committee shall be filed with the district secretary (1332:6). Whenever the accused is a district superintendent, a general official or one who is serving under the General Board (cf. 5203), a copy of the findings of the committee shall be forwarded to the chair of the General Board (1935:1).

(5) An appeal may be taken by the accused concerning the verdict and/or penalty to the General Board of Review within thirty days (5338-5347; 5440:7).

## 3. Special Regulations for Ministers, Ministerial Students and Special Workers

**5180.** The administration of judicial discipline and penalties to those persons under the jurisdiction of the district (5150:1-4) shall be in accord with the following regulations:

(1) **Indiscreet Conduct.** Whenever a minister, ministerial student, or special worker has been charged with an offense alleging immorality or crime

and is not found guilty of such actions but rather of "high imprudence or indiscreet conduct," the offender shall be subject to admonition, rebuke, suspension or deposition, according to the seriousness of the offense.

(2) **Suspension.** Whenever a minister shall be suspended from the ministry, or a ministerial student, or special worker shall be suspended from such office, all ministerial credentials shall be surrendered to the custody of the district superintendent (cf. 1310:27). Whenever such a person shall furnish the district superintendent a written apology acknowledging guilt and pledging to correct the matter, and gives evidence that the offense has ceased and that the person is repentant, the district board of administration may end the suspension, reinstate the person, and authorize the return of all ministerial credentials. If the written apology and assurance are not forthcoming, and the accused does not exercise the right of appeal, the district board of administration shall declare that the said person has withdrawn from the district, and said person's credentials shall be forwarded to the General Secretary (cf. 1233:39; 1310:28; 3100:4; 3127).

(3) **Immorality and Crime.** Whenever a minister, ministerial student or special worker shall have been convicted by a judicatory of such immoral acts as fornication, adultery or homosexual behavior, or has confessed to such acts to the official body having jurisdiction, the individual shall be deposed from the ministry or from the office of a ministerial student or special worker, as the case may be. This shall not prohibit membership in a Wesleyan church when the guilty person repents and demonstrates a Christian life according to the standards of The Wesleyan Church. Anyone who has been deposed for such an offense may be restored as provided for in 3127-3148.

(4) **Deposition** (5350:4). A minister that has been deposed from the ministry, or a ministerial student or special worker that has been deposed from such office, shall immediately surrender all ministerial credentials to the district superintendent (cf. 1310:27; 3085:4; 3127), shall cease to exercise any of the functions of the ministry or of a commission, or license, as the case may be, and shall not occupy any pulpit in The Wesleyan Church. Such a person's compensation and benefits, or a comparable family living allowance, shall cease after 30 days, and, if the deposed person is a pastor, the parsonage shall be vacated within 30 days; any further compensation and/or benefits, or family allowance, or rights to occupy the parsonage, may be granted upon approval by the local board of administration, the district superintendent, and the area General Superintendent. Whenever anyone who has been expelled from the ministry or a commission or license shall appeal, the penalty may be deferred with the exception that such a person shall be suspended from the exercise of any office or of any particular service while the appeal is pending (cf. 5344).

(5) **Restoration.** Provisions for the restoration of an ordained, commissioned or licensed minister, and ministerial student are set forth in 3127-3148 and shall be the same for a special worker (3480).

## D. Local Churches

### 1. Procedure

**5185.** The procedure for the discipline of a local church or circuit shall be:

(1) Any complaint against a local church by a lay member, minister or another local church shall be submitted in writing to the district superintendent (1310:27), who, together with the district board of administration (1233:35) shall endeavor to make an amicable settlement. If such a settlement cannot be realized, the complaint shall be referred to the district board of review who shall hear and decide the complaint (5162:2, 4).

(2) Whenever a local church shall be charged with an offense as set forth in 5070, the district superintendent (1310:27) and the district board of administration (1233:35) shall make every effort to bring about an amicable settlement. The district board of administration shall have the authority to cite the offending church, in the person of its pastor and local officials or local board of administration, to appear before it to settle the matter or to show cause why it shall not be placed under discipline. Such a citation shall contain a clear and definite statement of the charges and any supporting evidence so that the accused local church may be properly informed of the grounds of the accusation. The order shall be served upon the pastor and the local church secretary. Whenever a settlement cannot be effected, a bill of charges and specifications against the local church shall be submitted to the district board of review who shall hear and determine the case (5162:3).

(3) Whenever a local church has been declared guilty of an offense as set forth in 5070 by the district board of review (cf. 5162:3), it shall be suspended by the district conference (1180:44), or, in the interim of its sessions, by the district board of administration (1233:35), from all the rights and privileges of a local church as set forth in the Constitution (315) and *The Discipline*. The suspension shall end when the local church, through its officials, shall make a written apology acknowledging its guilt and pledging loyalty to the district and the denomination, and when, in the opinion of the district board of administration, the offense has ceased. Whenever a local church does not offer such a written apology and assurance, and if it continues to offend, it shall be reorganized (5190).

(4) An appeal may be taken by the accused church concerning the verdict and/or penalty to the General Board of Review (5440:7).

### 2. Reorganization

**5190.** Whenever a local church, through its pastor and/or local church officials or local board of administration, shall refuse to answer the citations of the district board of administration to appear for a settlement (5185:2) or the citation of the district board of review to appear for the hearing of the case (cf. 5294), or whenever a local church that has been placed under discipline refuses to offer a written apology and assurance as set forth in 5185:3 and does not exercise the right of appeal, the district board of administration shall authorize the district superintendent and any two of its other board members to reorganize the local church. The district superintendent and the appointed representatives shall ask the members of the local church for an affirmation of loyalty to The Wesleyan Church, its *Discipline* as currently revised and amended, and its duly elected officials. Those members who affirm such loyalty shall be the members of that local church, and those members who refuse to affirm such loyalty shall be declared as having withdrawn from The Wesleyan Church and from that local church and all offices held by such persons shall thereby be vacated. The loyal members shall be entitled to hold and use the property as provided for by *The Discipline* and to carry on the functions of the local church. Whenever such members are ten or fewer, the church shall be automatically classified as a developing church and shall be under the supervision of the district superintendent and the district board of administration (cf. 510; 518:5).

**5195.** Any person who has been declared as withdrawn from The Wesleyan Church during the reorganization of a local church may be reinstated when the person gives evidence of a change of attitude, and is deemed to meet the requirements for membership.

# Chapter V

# GENERAL CHURCH JURISDICTION

### A. General Conference

**5200.** The General Conference, as the chief governing body, exercises supreme judicial authority within The Wesleyan Church. The General Conference shall hear appeals from rulings of the General Board of Review (380; 1590:22; 5445), and may, at its own pleasure, hear and determine such appeals, or appoint special committees to do so as desired who shall report their findings to the General Conference for final action (1590:24); shall appoint investigative committees to consider accusations against the various units under its jurisdiction, hear the reports of such committees, file charges, if necessary, against such units before the General Board of Review (375:6; 5218-5230), and upon hearing the findings and recommendations of the General Board of Review fix the penalty, if any, to be imposed (5440:5c). In the interim of General Conference sessions, the General Board shall hear the findings and recommendations of the General Board of Review and fix the penalty, if any, to be imposed (5440:5c).

### B. Officials

#### 1. Jurisdiction

**5203.** The General Board shall have jurisdiction over the following persons in regard to their official duties:

(1) A general official (1800; cf. 360:2; 1655:36).

(2) An area representative of the General Board (cf. 1655: 36).

(3) A district superintendent (cf. 323:1; 360:2; 1655: 36).

(4) A member or minister of The Wesleyan Church who is serving under the jurisdiction of the General Board, including any who are elected or employed by the General Board for full time service for the general church (cf. 323:1; 1655:26), missionaries or workers under the General Department of World Missions or the General Department of Evangelism and Church Growth (cf. 323:1; 1655:42), members of boards elected by the General Board (cf. 1655.17), and any others amenable to the General Board.

**5208.** The General Board shall have the authority to remove from office, for cause, any persons under its jurisdiction as listed in 5203:1-4 (cf. 1655:39), but shall not have authority to depose anyone from the ministry (cf. 5153) or to dismiss anyone from the Church (cf. 5100-5140). The purpose of any disciplinary or judicial proceedings, such as an official investigation or the hearing of any complaints or charges by a judicial committee, shall be to clear up any accusations or charges, or to determine the official standing and relationship of an accused person to the general church, or to decide upon the submission of charges to the official body having jurisdiction over the ministerial standing or membership of the accused, as the case may be.

### 2. Procedure

**5212.** Administrative or judicial discipline against persons listed in 5203:1-4 shall be administered as follows:

(1) If the accused is a general official, an area representative of the General Board, or a district superintendent, any accusation alleging an offense set forth in 5050 shall be submitted in writing (5254) to the chair of the General Board (1630; 1935:1) and must be sustained by at least three responsible members of The Wesleyan Church. If the accused is a General Superintendent, the other General Superintendents shall have charge of the matter. The General Superintendents shall make inquiry as required in 5258-5262. The General Board shall dispose of any charges or accusations as set forth in 5208. Whenever it is deemed necessary, the General Board may remove a general official, an area representative of the General Board or a district superintendent from office by a two-thirds majority vote of all its members (1655:39a), and shall also decide whether charges shall be submitted to the official body having jurisdiction over the accused concerning ministerial standing or membership in the Church (cf. 315:1; 323:1).

(2) If the accused is a member or minister under the jurisdiction of the General Board (5203:4), an accusation or complaint shall be submitted to the general official to which the accused is amenable or to a General Superintendent. The General Board or its Executive Board shall decide on the disposition of such accusations or charges as set forth in 5208. If it is deemed necessary, the General Board may remove such a person from office by a majority vote of all members of the General Board (1655:39b).

### 3. Power of Removal

**5215.** The General Board, the Board of Pensions, the Board of Directors of the Wesleyan Investment Foundation, the board of trustees of an educational or benevolent institution, and other such governing boards shall have full power and authority to discharge at their discretion any officer or employee thereof (with the exception of those in 5203:1-4 which shall be limited to the General Board) who shall be guilty of any immoral conduct or breach of trust, or who for any reason is unable, or who fails to perform the duties of their office, or for other misconduct which any of said boards may deem sufficient to warrant discharge. The action of such board in removing such officer or employee in the circumstances above set forth shall be final. Any governing board of a subsidiary corporation, or of any educational or benevolent institution, shall have the right to recommend the removal of any of its members to the General Board, who shall have power to sustain or reject such a recommendation (cf. 1655:17, 39b).

## C. Districts

### 1. Procedure

**5218.** Any charge or complaint against an established district alleging an offense set forth in 5070 shall be heard and determined by the General Board of Review (5440:5c). The General Superintendent(s) over the involved district(s), together with the General Board or its Executive Board shall make every effort to clear up such accusations or charges or to effect an amicable settlement (1655:40; 1935:18) before any district, through its officials or district board of administration, shall be brought to trial before the General Board of Review, unless a hearing is requested by the accused district.

**5220.** The General Board, or, in the interim of its sessions, the Executive Board, shall have the authority to cite a district, through its officials or its district board of administration, to appear before it to show cause, why it should not be brought to trial or declared to be in a state of disobedience or insubordination for an offense as set forth in 5070. Such a citation shall set forth a clear and definite statement of the charges and any supporting facts or evidence and shall be signed by the chair and secretary of the General Board, so that the accused district may be properly informed of the grounds of the accusation. The order shall be served upon both the superintendent and the secretary of the accused district. Should the hearing before the General Board or the Executive Board result in a satisfactory adjustment of the charges, with the accused district pledging its loyalty to the denomination, no further steps shall be taken. When it is impossible to reach an amicable settlement, in the opinion of the General Board, or should the cited district officials fail or refuse to appear, a bill of charges and specifications for offenses as listed in 5070 shall be prepared and submitted to the General Board of Review.

**5225.** After receiving the report of the findings of the General Board of Review and pursuant thereto, the General Board, by a two-thirds majority vote of all its members, may place a district found guilty under discipline and suspend all its rights and privileges as a district under the Constitution, or other provisions of *The Discipline*, and may thereupon appoint a General Superintendent or general official to have charge of the district (360:3c, e; cf. 1655:41). Such suspension shall continue until the district under discipline shall, through its officials, offer a written apology acknowledging its guilt and giving assurance of its loyalty to the denomination and shall also give evidence that the offense has ceased, whereupon the General Board shall end the suspension and reinstate the district (cf. 1655:43). A district under discipline shall also be suspended from all rights to acquire, purchase, mortgage, sell, transfer or otherwise dispose of any real property, unless approved by the general official appointed to have charge of the district.

**5230.** An appeal may be taken by the accused district concerning the verdict and/or penalty to the General Conference (5445). All appeals must be filed in the office of the General Secretary within sixty days after the date of the official decision on the matter.

### 2. Reorganization

**5235.** Whenever a district under discipline refuses to offer a written apology and assurance of loyalty as set forth in 5225, or whenever the district officials refuse to answer a citation to appear (5220), the General Board or its Executive Board may authorize the General Superintendent over the district to reorganize the district (1655:43). The General Superintendent shall ask for an affirmation of loyalty. Those members and ministers of the district who affirm their loyalty to The Wesleyan Church and to its *Discipline* as currently revised and amended and to its duly elected officials shall be and constitute the district. Those members of the district who refuse to affirm such loyalty to The Wesleyan Church shall be declared by the General Superintendent as having withdrawn from the district and from The Wesleyan Church, and all offices held by such persons shall thereupon be vacated. Those who are thus declared to be the members of the district shall be entitled to hold and to use all the district property in the manner as set forth in *The Discipline* and shall be organized to carry on the work of the district. Should the number of loyal ministers and members be fewer than that required for an established district, the district shall be reclassified by the General Board as a provisional district or developing district as the case may be (cf. 1034; 1042-1045.)

**5240.** If a minister that has been declared withdrawn from the district shall desire to be reinstated, the minister may be reinstated as provided for in 3120-3124.

# Chapter VI

## RULES OF PROCEDURE

### A. Procedure

**5250.** The procedure for handling accusations or complaints, investigations and trials by the various official bodies and judicatories of The Wesleyan Church shall be as hereinafter provided, with the exception of the Board of Review which shall provide its own rules of procedure (5420:2). Additional rules of procedure for such matters as evidence, testimony and other technicalities shall be issued with the approval of the General Board (1655:44) and be available upon request from the General Secretary.

### B. Accusation

**5254.** Accusations must be in writing, dated, signed by the accuser(s) and handed to the official having jurisdiction over the accused before official action shall be taken. Whenever, in the opinion of the accuser(s), proper action has not been taken, appeal may be made to the next higher Church authority.

### C. Preliminary Settlement

**5258.** A sincere effort shall be made in each case to meet with the accused personally in order to clear up the accusation or to avoid the necessity of a trial. Whenever an alleged offense involves an error in doctrine, disobedience to the order and *Discipline* of the Church, the indulging in sinful tempers or words, the sowing of dissension or other similar matters, the official having jurisdiction, or other designated representative, shall privately inquire, and, if necessary, instruct and admonish an offending person. If there is an acknowledgment of the fault and correction is made, the case shall be dropped. If the offense continues, the official in charge shall take along two or three other discreet members or ministers of The Wesleyan Church and give further instruction and reproof. If the offense continues, the offending members shall be brought to trial.

**5262.** If an aggrieved person shall allege a personal offense, the aggrieved person shall be first required to follow the Lord's directions in Matthew 18:15-17 before filing accusations or charges against the offending party.

## D. Evidence

**5266. Rules of Evidence.** An investigation committee, judicatory or other official body shall not be bound by any technical rules of evidence but shall adopt such rules as shall, in its opinion, be best adapted to ascertain the truth and determine accurately the substantial rights of the parties involved (5015:6). The presiding officer of the judicatory shall decide on the admissibility of evidence.

**5270. Testimony.** No one may be barred as a witness on the grounds that they are not a member of The Wesleyan Church. Whenever circumstances make it impossible for a witness to appear, a proper certificate or affidavit from such a person may be presented, provided that the party against whom it is sought to be introduced has had a proper opportunity to see the certificate or affidavit and to question before witnesses the person signing the affidavit regarding the contents thereof. Witnesses shall be examined first, by the party producing them, then cross-examined by the opposite party, after which any member of the judicatory or either party may put additional questions.

**5274. Proof of Charges.** The accused shall be presumed innocent until the contrary is proved (5015:7). However, the moral conviction of the truth of the charge is all that is necessary to find the accused guilty of the charges.* In all cases the accused may be questioned relative to the charges made.

## E. Committee of Investigation

**5278.** A trial may not be ordered until a proper inquiry is made by a committee of investigation.

(1) Such a committee shall be appointed by the official body having jurisdiction, and shall consist of two or more covenant members or ministers of The Wesleyan Church in good standing who can be relied on for impartial judgment, who are not involved in the case, and who are not closely related to the accuser or the accused. A member of the committee of investigation may not thereafter be a member of the judicatory that will hear the case (see 5318).

*"In acting upon the case, it must be borne in mind that there is a vast distinction between the evidence necessary to convict in a civil court and that required to convict in an ordinary society or ecclesiastical body. A notorious pickpocket could not even be arrested, much less convicted by a civil court, simply on the ground of being commonly known as a pickpocket; while such evidence would convict and expel him from ordinary society.

"The moral conviction of the truth of the charge is all that is necessary in an ecclesiastical or other deliberative body to find the accused guilty of the charges." —*Robert's Rules of Order*. Revised, Seventy-Fifth Anniversary Edition.

(2) The committee shall make a careful and thorough inquiry into the matter, meet with the accuser and the accused, endeavor to bring the accuser and the accused together in the presence of the committee, appoint a secretary to keep an accurate record of all committee proceedings, testimonies and evidence, and shall make a written report to the appointing body of its findings and recommendation. If the committee believes no reasonable grounds for such accusations exist or that there is insufficient evidence, it shall so report; and if its findings are otherwise, the committee shall draw up charges and specifications accordingly.

(3) The appointing body shall receive and pass on the report and recommendations of the committee of investigation. If there is insufficient evidence or if guilt is confessed, a trial shall not be ordered, and in no case shall a trial be ordered unless a charge is sustained by two responsible members or ministers of The Wesleyan Church. When guilt is confessed, the official body may pass on the offense and decide on the penalty to be imposed, if any, without further trial unless such is requested by the accused. If the official body decides that a trial shall be conducted for the hearing and determination of charges, it shall so order, setting the date and place for such trial; appointing the members of the judicatory and the prosecutor (5290), unless otherwise provided for in this Judiciary. The date of the trial shall not be less than ten days from the date that notice shall be given to the accused or more than thirty days (cf. 5015:4).

### F. Charges

**5285.** It is not required that the charges be written in any particular legal form, but it is recommended that they be written in the standard form as provided in *Robert's Rules of Order, Newly Revised.* Every charge must be in writing, dated, signed by the accuser or by those members or ministers of The Wesleyan Church sustaining the charge, and must clearly define the alleged offense by its proper term as stated in 5050-5070, and shall be accompanied by the specifications of the facts relied on to sustain the charge:

(1) A charge shall not allege more than one offense. However, more than one charge against the same person, with the specifications for each charge, may be presented to the judicatory at the same time and heard at the same time, provided that the vote on each charge shall be taken separately.

(2) The specifications shall declare as far as possible, the time, place and circumstances of the alleged offense, and shall be accompanied with the names of the witnesses and the title of each record or document to be cited for its support.

(3) No charge shall be entertained for any alleged offense committed more than five years before the filing of such charge, except in cases involving immorality or crime (5030:4).

### G. Counsel

**5290.** The official body ordering a trial shall, at the same time, appoint a prosecutor, whose duty it shall be to prepare in final form the bill of charges and specifications, present them at the proper time and place to the judicatory and represent the Church during the hearing. The accused shall have the right to choose counsel (5030:1), or to present a personal defense; but where this right is not exercised, a defense counsel may be appointed by the chair of the judicatory. Both the prosecutor and the counsel for the accused shall be covenant members or ministers of The Wesleyan Church in good standing.

### H. Notices

**5294.** All notices and citations to appear shall be given as directed by the chair of the judicatory and shall be in writing, in the name of the Church, and signed by the chair. An official notice of the date, time and place of the trial, together with an official copy of the bill of charges and specifications, and a citation to appear shall be delivered to the accused not less than ten days prior to the date set for the trial. No subsequent changes in such charges and specifications shall be permitted. Notices to appear shall be given to such witnesses as either party may name, and shall also be served at least ten days before the trial. Members or ministers of The Wesleyan Church shall be cited to appear, but others may only be requested to appear.

### I. Participants

**5298.** Only those who are covenant members or ministers of The Wesleyan Church shall be allowed to participate in a trial, except as witnesses, and only those participating in the trial shall be permitted to attend the hearing of the trial. All deliberations of a judicatory shall be considered confidential, and members of a judicatory shall not discuss the case with anyone outside the judicatory during the hearing of the case.

### J. Request for Withdrawal

**5302.** Whenever in the course of an investigation or trial, the accused person shall request a letter of withdrawal from the Church, the same shall be granted and the case shall end. It shall be noted on the membership records of the local church, and, when the accused is a minister, on the membership record of the district, as "withdrawn under accusation" whenever such request is during the investigation, and "withdrawn under charges" when such request is during the trial. (cf. 592.)

### K. Postponements

**5306.** The prosecutor, or the accused, shall have the right to petition the chair of the judicatory for a postponement of the trial date, and the chair may grant such a petition if deemed essential for proper preparation or other necessary reasons, provided that the other party shall be notified before the postponement is granted. A postponement shall not be granted for more than thirty days.

### L. Failure or Refusal to Appear

**5310.** Whenever an accused member or minister refuses to obey a properly issued citation to appear for trial, or fails to appear except for unavoidable circumstances, the accused member or minister shall be considered guilty of contempt and shall be censured by the chair of the judicatory. If such an accused person refuses or fails to appear after a second citation, it shall be considered as sufficient reason for summary dismissal from the Church (5040). A member or minister of The Wesleyan Church who refuses a properly issued citation to appear as a witness shall likewise be deemed guilty of contempt and shall be liable to censure (5045).

### M. Status of the Accused

**5314.** After the official notice of the date, time and place of the trial, together with a copy of the bill of charges and specifications, is delivered to the accused and until after judgment is rendered by the judicatory, the accused may be temporarily suspended from the exercise of any office by the judicatory at its discretion.

### N. Grounds for Challenge

**5318.** A person is disqualified to serve as a member of any judicatory who is personally interested in the case, closely related to either the accused or the accuser, has been active for or against either party in the matter referred to in the charges, is at personal variance with either party, or who has prejudged the case (see 5278). Any member of a judicatory may, on such grounds, be challenged by either party, provided that such challenge shall be made not later than the opening of any trial hearing, and the allowance of such challenge shall be decided by the remaining members of the judicatory.

### O. Records

**5322.** The chair of the judicatory shall appoint a secretary, who need not be a member of the judicatory, and shall see that complete and accurate records are kept by the secretary of all proceedings, testimonies, evidence, documents admitted, together with copies of the charges, specifications, notices, citations and findings of the judicatory. The records shall be attested to by both the chair and the secretary. The chair shall be the custodian of such records until the case is finished and shall then deliver such records to the proper secretary for permanent filing. Whenever the decision of the judicatory is appealed, the person having custody of the official records shall forward such records promptly to the chair of the appellate body, or a transcript of the same, when requested to do so by the chair of the appellate body.

### P. The Order of a Church Trial

**5326.** The following order should be observed in conducting a church trial:

(1) Devotional exercises.

(2) Statement of purpose, the reading of the official action ordering the trial, and the announcement of the members of the judicatory, by the chair of the judicatory.

(3) Challenges by either party of the members of the judicatory (5318), if any.

(4) Reading of the charges and specifications by the secretary.

(5) Answer by the accused or counsel chosen by the accused with a plea of "guilty" or "not guilty." If guilt is confessed, the judicatory may thereupon consider the penalty to be imposed, if any, and terminate the hearing, or it may request to hear the evidence in order to make a more proper determination of the cause and the penalties to be imposed.

(6) Statement of the case and line of evidence by the prosecutor.

(7) Evidence for the prosecution and cross-examination by the defense.

(8) Statement of the case and line of defense by the defense.

(9) Evidence for the defense and cross-examination by the prosecution.

(10) Rebuttal by the prosecution.

(11) Rebuttal by the defense.

(12) Summary of the case by the prosecution.

(13) Summary of the case by the defense.

(14) Should it be deemed proper to allow the prosecutor to reply, the defense shall also be permitted to reply.

(15) Instructions by the chair to the judicatory concerning the duties assigned to it as set forth in this Judiciary and especially to render a verdict in not more than three days, and to vote separately on each charge and by secret ballot, with a two-thirds vote of all the members required to render a verdict of guilty. Members of the judicatory who have been absent from more than one sitting shall not be permitted to vote on the verdict.

(16) The verdict.

(17) Announcement by chair of the verdict, and the recommendations, if any, being made to the official body having jurisdiction over the accused.

### Q. Motion to Reopen the Case

**5335.** If within thirty days after a conviction under the foregoing provisions, the accused shall make application in writing to the chair of the official body having jurisdiction for a reopening of the case on the ground of newly discovered evidence, and shall submit a written statement of the same, and if it shall appear that such evidence is material to the issue involved, the case may be reopened. In no case, however, shall a reopening of the case be granted when the failure to submit such evidence at the original hearing was the result of neglect or carelessness on the part of the accused. The judicatory may thereupon reopen the case or may refuse to do so. Upon such refusal, if it appears that the failure to submit such evidence was not the result of neglect or carelessness on the part of the accused, such additional evidence may become a part of the record of the appeal. The judicatory shall be considered to continue for a period of thirty days in order to receive and consider a petition for a reopening of the case and until the matter shall be decided upon, or a new judicatory may be constituted.

### R. Appeals

**5338. Right of Appeal.** The accused, if found guilty, shall have the right to appeal the verdict and/or the penalty unless such right has been forfeited for misconduct. Misconduct shall consist of withdrawing from the Church, publicly discrediting or slandering the members of the judicatory, refusing to abide by the decision of the judicatory, or by refusing to appear in person or by counsel if cited to appear by the appellate body, or by resorting to a suit in a civil court concerning the matter involved in the charges. Misconduct shall be decided upon by the appellate body. If, on the other hand, the accused was found innocent, the official body which ordered the trial has the right to appeal the verdict.

**5341. Procedure of Appeal.** The appellant or the counsel of appellant, within thirty days after being notified of the verdict and/or penalty, shall submit a request in writing and shall set forth the grounds of the appeal. The chair of the appellate body shall ask for a transfer of all the official records of the case, or a transcript of the same, which shall be forwarded promptly by the person having custody of such records. The appellant shall be responsible to pay the cost of the appeal, including the cost of preparing a transcript of the records. Upon modification or reversal of the verdict and/or penalty, such cost of the appeal shall be paid by the church or district from which such appeal is taken by the appellant.

**5344. Status of the Accused During Appeal.** While the appeal is pending, the penalty shall be deferred. Whenever the accused is a church or a district, it may continue to function but shall have the status of being under discipline and shall not be entitled to any representatives in a conference body and, in the case of a district, shall not have authority to buy, sell or transfer any real property, except with the approval of the General Superintendent over the area.

**5347. Judgment of the Appellate Body.** The appellate body shall promptly consider the case and the grounds for appeal and shall render judgment within thirty days, with the exception of the General Board of Review. The appellate body, by a majority vote, may affirm, modify or reverse the findings of the lower judicatory in whole or in part, or may remand the case for a new trial, provided that if the accused has been previously found innocent, it shall require a two-thirds majority vote of the appellate body to find the accused guilty. In all cases the right to present evidence shall be exhausted when the case has been heard once on its merits in the proper court, with the exception as provided for in 5335. The appellate body shall also have the right to cite the accused or the counsel of the accused to appear. Whenever a case is remanded for a new trial, a new judicatory shall be constituted if necessary, to provide for a fair and proper hearing of the case. When any appellate court shall reverse, in whole or in part, the findings of a trial court, or change the penalty imposed by the official body having jurisdiction, it shall return to the official body having jurisdiction, or to the judicatory, a statement of the grounds of its action.

# Chapter VII

# PENALTIES

## A. Definition of Penalties

**5350.** There shall be five degrees of penalty for the administration of discipline which are:

(1) **Admonition.** Admonition is the mildest penalty and consists of a general reproof, a warning and an exhortation to greater watchfulness by the offender.

(2) **Rebuke.** Rebuke is a stronger penalty for a more serious offense and consists in setting forth the offense, an official rebuke and correction, and a warning to the offender.

(3) **Suspension.** Suspension is that penalty by which the accused is placed "under discipline" and is deprived of certain rights and privileges for a period of probation.

(a) Suspension may be applied to the rights and privileges of membership, the rights and privileges of the ministry or the exercise of an office. A local church or a district may be suspended from the rights and privileges of a church and a district, respectively, as set forth in the Constitution and *The Discipline*.

(b) Suspension may be definite or indefinite as to duration. Definite suspension is administered when the name of Christ, the integrity of the Church, and the good of the offender demand it, even though the offender may have given evidence of repentance. Indefinite suspension is required when the offender is to be placed on probation until demonstrating a genuine repentance and reformation of life to the proper authorities. The official body having jurisdiction over the party placed "under discipline" for an indefinite suspension shall have the authority to end such suspension or, if necessary, to impose a stronger penalty when the accused continues to offend.

(4) **Deposition.** Deposition is that penalty by which a person is removed from an official position or appointment, or expelled from the ministry, or removed from the office of a ministerial student or special worker, as the case may be.

(5) **Dismissal.** Dismissal is the strongest penalty and is the expulsion of the offender from membership in the Church (305:3; 315:1; 585:3), which automatically includes all lesser penalties. Dismissal should be imposed only for the most serious offenses, or for obstinate persistence in a serious offense

and can only be imposed by the local church (655:1). The purpose of dismissal is to awaken the offender, deliver the Church from scandal and to warn others.

### B. Assignment of Penalties.

**5370.** Official bodies shall be governed by the seriousness of the offense and by the following regulations in the assignment of penalties:

(1) Anyone declared guilty of holding or teaching any doctrine contrary to the doctrines of The Wesleyan Church as stated in *The Discipline* (5050:1) shall be punished with deposition and/or dismissal (5350:4-5), unless the official body is of the opinion that the offense has ceased, in which case the penalty shall be either that of admonition, rebuke or suspension.

(2) Disobedience to *The Discipline*, or tolerating such disobedience (5050:2), shall be punished with such penalty as deemed advisable.

(3) Insubordination or willful refusal to recognize properly constituted church authority (5050:3) shall be punished by such penalty as deemed advisable.

(4) Conduct unbecoming a member or minister (5050:4), such as dishonesty, or sowing dissension by inveighing against the officials or ministers of the Church, shall be punished with deposition and/or dismissal (5350:4-5), unless the official body believes the offender is truly penitent, in which case the offender shall be rebuked or indefinitely suspended (5350:2-3) until such time as the proper authorities are satisfied that the accused has reasonably demonstrated genuine Christian character in accord with the standards of The Wesleyan Church.

(5) Immorality, such as adultery, fornication, homosexual behavior or other acts involving moral turpitude or crime, may be punished by immediate dismissal from the Church (265:5; 5050:5; cf. 5180:3).

(6) Serious or persistent neglect of duties (5050:6) shall be punished by suspension or deposition, unless corrected, in which case a lesser penalty may be imposed.

# Chapter VIII

## GENERAL BOARD OF REVIEW

### A. Membership

**5400. Members.** The General Board of Review shall consist of nine members, five of whom shall be ordained ministers and four of whom shall be lay members who are covenant members of The Wesleyan Church:

(1) Their term of office shall be for four years. They shall serve from the close of the session of the General Conference at which they are elected until the close of the next session of the General Conference or until their successors are elected and qualified.

(2) A member of the General Board of Review may not at the same time be a member of the General Board.

(3) The General Conference shall elect by majority vote the members of the General Board of Review, from nominations presented by the Committee on Special Nominations. Additional nominations may be made from the floor of the General Conference (1580:2; 1590:19).

(4) A member of the General Board of Review shall be disqualified for a particular case, when the member is personally interested or involved in the case, closely related to any parties involved, or has been active for or against either party in the matter to be heard and determined by the General Board of Review. Any member of the General Board of Review may be challenged for such reasons or for other reasons, and the allowance of such challenge shall be decided by the remaining members of the General Board of Review. Whenever a member is disqualified, the chair shall appoint an alternate for the hearing of that particular case (5408), provided that such appointment shall maintain the membership of the Board as five ordained ministers and four lay members.

**5405. Alternates.** The General Conference shall elect, in the same manner described in 5400:3, four ordained ministers and three lay members to serve as alternate members of the General Board of Review, with the same qualifications (5400:2) and term of office (5400:1) as the members (cf. 1590:19).

**5408. Vacancies.** A vacancy in the membership of the General Board of Review shall be filled by an alternate, who shall be appointed by the chair of the General Board of Review in such manner as to maintain the representation of ordained ministers and lay members as set forth in 5400. Whenever a vacancy occurs in the interim of General Conference sessions, an alternate shall be appointed to serve until the close of the next General Conference. An alternate shall also be appointed to serve for a particular case whenever a member of the General Board of Review is disqualified (5400:4), or for a temporary vacancy created by the absence of a member of the session of the General Board of Review held during the General Conference.

### B. Sessions

**5412. Regular Sessions.** The General Board of Review shall meet at the time and place of the General Conference and shall continue in session until the adjournment of that body. In the interim of General Conferences, the Board shall meet in annual session at a time and place of its own choosing, unless the chair of the Board shall certify in writing to all members that there is no pending business for the Board.

**5415. Special Sessions.** The General Board of Review shall meet at other times and places of its own choosing as deemed necessary, or as requested by the General Board or its Executive Board.

### C. Organization and Procedure

**5420.** Organization and procedure for the General Board of Review shall be:

(1) **Organization.** The General Board of Review shall organize itself and shall elect, from among its own members, a chair, vice-chair, secretary and such other officers as deemed necessary.

(2) **Procedure.** The General Board of Review shall decide on its own methods and rules of procedure and shall adopt such bylaws as deemed necessary, provided such do not contravene any provisions of *The Discipline*. All parties shall file their briefs and arguments and shall present evidence under such rules as the General Board of Review shall adopt from time to time (cf. 5347).

(3) **Quorum.** Seven members shall constitute a quorum. A decision of the General Board of Review on the constitutionality of an act by the General Conference shall require a two-thirds majority vote of all members of the Board, and on all other matters a majority vote of all members of the Board shall be sufficient.

**5425. Records.** The General Board of Review shall see that complete and accurate minutes are kept of all proceedings, testimonies, evidence, documents and findings, certified copies of which shall be forwarded promptly after each session to the General Secretary.

**5430. Notification.** After each session of the General Board of Review, an official summary of the Board's decisions on points of Church law or interpretations of *The Discipline*, as prepared by the secretary and attested to by the chair, shall be published in the official church publication. A decision of the General Board of Review which is not overruled by the General Conference shall be incorporated in *The Discipline*.

**5435. Finances.** Expense allowances for members of the General Board of Review shall be the same as for members of the General Board, when the members of the General Board of Review are engaged in official business, and payment therefor shall be made by the General Treasurer. The party making appeal shall be responsible for the expenses involved in attending to the appeal.

### D. Duties and Powers

**5440.** The jurisdiction and duties of the General Board of Review are set forth in the Constitution (370-380) and as provided for herewith:

(1) To determine the constitutionality of any act of the General Conference, upon the appeal of the Board of General Superintendents or one-fifth of the members of the General Conference (375:1; 1920:26). An act of the General Conference that is declared as unconstitutional by the General Board of Review shall be null and void (cf. 1590:3).

(2) To render a judgment on the constitutionality of any memorial or proposed legislation to be acted upon by the General Conference, when the General Conference shall so request, by a majority vote, and to notify the General Conference immediately of such judgment (cf. 375:1).

(3) To hear and determine any appeal from a ruling of the Board of General Superintendents on a point of church law, an interpretation of *The Discipline* or the validity of an action by a district as set forth in 1920:24-25 (375:2).

(4) To hear and determine any appeal concerning the legality of any action by any general church board upon appeal of one-third of the members thereof or by request of the Board of General Superintendents (375:3; 1920:25).

(5) To have jurisdiction over the issues arising between a district and the General Conference, or, in the interim of General Conference sessions, between a district and the General Board, as follows (375:6):

(a) To hear and determine a complaint by a district against the General Conference, provided that such a complaint shall be sustained by a two-thirds vote of the district conference (375:6; 1180:42).

(b) To hear and determine a complaint by a district against the General Board in the interim of General Conference sessions, provided that such a complaint shall be sustained by a majority vote of the district conference (1180:42) or by a two-thirds vote of the district board of administration (1233:40), and further provided that the subject of the complaint concerns the district by which it is presented.

(c) To hear and determine any charges against a district, alleging an offense as set forth in 5070, provided that such charges are preferred by the General Conference or the General Board; to determine the guilt or innocence of the accused district; and, if necessary, to recommend to the General Conference, or in the interim of General Conference sessions, to the General Board, the placing of the district under discipline (cf. 1590:21, 24; 1655:40; 5218-5235).

(6) To have jurisdiction over any complaints between districts, to hear and determine such complaints or charges, provided that such are sustained by a two-thirds vote of the district conference presenting the complaint (375:4; 1180:42).

(7) To hear and determine any appeal from the judgment of a district judicial committee or district board of review (5167; 5175:5; 5185:4).

(8) To hear and determine the validity of complaints against books used in the correspondence courses of study and by the educational institutions of The Wesleyan Church (375:5; cf. 2388:2).

(9) To hear and determine such cases as shall be referred to it by the General Conference or the General Board.

## E. Appeals

**5445.** A decision of the General Board of Review shall be final until overruled by the General Conference by a two-thirds majority of those present and voting (380). An appeal may be presented to the General Conference by either party involved in the judgment. The General Conference may hear and determine such appeals or may create a special judicial committee to hear the appeals and present its recommendations to the General Conference for final determination. All appeals must be filed in the office of the General Secretary within sixty days after the date of the official decision on the matter.

# Chapter IX

## DEFINITION OF TERMS FOR THE JUDICIARY

**5450.** The terms used in this Judiciary are defined as follows:

(1) **Accusation.** A written representation alleging an offense by a member or minister of The Wesleyan Church (5254).

(2) **Charge.** A written statement alleging an offense as set forth in 5050-5070, accompanied by specifications, for which a trial may be conducted (5285).

(3) **Church.** The Wesleyan Church, a denomination with its headquarters in Indianapolis, Indiana.

(4) **Complaint.** A written representation of a grievance by a member(s) or minister(s) against the local church or higher authority; a written grievance by one unit against a unit of equal authority, or of a lower church body against a higher church body.

(5) **Discipline.** *The Discipline* of The Wesleyan Church as currently legislated and declared from time to time (185).

(6) **Judicatory.** An officially constituted board or committee for the hearing of charges or appeals. The Judicatories of The Wesleyan Church are local judicial committee, district judicial committee, district board of review, General Conference judicial committee and the General Board of Review.

(7) **Lay Minister.** A covenant member of The Wesleyan Church who has been licensed as a lay minister by a local Wesleyan church (3400-3440).

(8) **Member.** A covenant member of The Wesleyan Church, and unless otherwise specified includes all ordained ministers, commissioned ministers, licensed ministers, ministerial students, special workers, lay ministers and others commissioned or licensed by a district or a local church.

(9) **Minister.** An ordained (3067-3089), commissioned (3059) or licensed minister (3030-3055) of The Wesleyan Church.

(10) **Ministerial Student.** A covenant member of The Wesleyan Church who has been granted a license as a ministerial student by a district (3015:1).

(11) **Official Body.** A conference or board having jurisdiction over members or ministers of The Wesleyan Church in matters of administrative or judicial discipline. The official bodies having jurisdiction over disciplinary proceedings are the local church conference and the local board of administration, the district conference and the district board of administration and the General Conference and the General Board.

(12) **Special Worker.** A covenant member of The Wesleyan Church commissioned or licensed as a special worker by the district conference as set forth in 3460-3470.

# PART X

# THE RITUAL

## Chapter I

## BAPTISM

### A. Dedication of Infants

**5500.** ***(When the parents, guardians or other sponsors have presented themselves with their children before the minister, the minister shall say:)***

Dear *friends*, you have brought *these children** whom God has given you to be dedicated to God and to His service. By this act you testify to your faith in the Christian religion, and also your desire that your *child*ren shall receive the benefits of consecration to God, and of the prayers of the church, and may early learn to know and follow the will of God; and therefore may live a Christian life.

In order for this to happen, it will be your duty as *parents* to teach your *child*ren early the fear of the Lord; to watch over *their* education, that *they* may not be led astray by false teachings or doctrines, to direct *their minds* to the Holy Scriptures as expressing the will and authority of God for all people, and to direct *their* feet to the sanctuary, to restrain *them* from evil associates and habits; and, as much you are able, to bring *them* up in the Lord's discipline and instruction. Will you endeavor to do so, by the help of the Lord?

*(Then the parents or guardians shall answer:)*

*We* will.

(*Then the minister shall read the following Scripture lesson*:)

"People were bringing little children to Jesus to have him touch them, but the disciples rebuked them. When Jesus saw this, he was indignant. He said to them, 'Let the little children come to me, and do not hinder them, for the

*Throughout the ritual, whenever instructions are given to the officiating minister, or a word may change form due to the gender or number of persons involved in the ritual on a given occasion, that word(s) is printed in italics to alert the minister who reads. "These children" may become "this child," "he" may become "she" or "they," etc.

kingdom of God belongs to such as these. I tell you the truth, anyone who will not receive the kingdom of God like a little child will never enter it.' And he took the children in his arms, put his hands on them and blessed them" (Mark 10:13-16, NIV).

*(Then the minister shall ask the parents or guardians the name of each child to be dedicated, take each child in arms, lay a hand upon the child's head, and say:)*

____________ ____________, in behalf of your *parents* and of this congregation, I dedicate you unto the Father, and the Son, and the Holy Spirit. Amen.

*(Then the minister may pray.)*

## B. Baptism of Infants

**5510.** *(When the parents, guardians or other sponsors have presented themselves with their children before the minister, the minister shall say:)*

Dear *friends*, you have brought *these children* whom God has given you to be baptized, thereby testifying to your own commitment of faith in Christ and the assurance you hold that the grace of God is even now at work in *their lives*. Forasmuch as *these children are* now presented by you, it will be your duty as *parents* to teach *them* as soon as *they are* able to learn, the nature and meaning of this sacrament. In order to testify to your faith and to your desire to nurture your *children* within this faith, please respond to these questions.

Do you present your *children* for baptism as a sign of the grace of God which is extended even now to your *children* through the atoning work of Christ and declares *them* to be a part of the family of God? And,

Do you promise with the help of God to bring your *children* up in the instruction and discipline of the Lord, to pray with *them* and for *him/her*, and to make every effort to so order your own life that you will not cause *these* little *ones* to stumble? And,

Do you intend to encourage your *children* as soon as *they* are able to comprehend its significance to acknowledge personally *his/her* own faith in the Lord Jesus Christ, and to serve God faithfully in the fellowship of His Church?

*(Then the parents will respond:)*

*We* do, God being *our* helper.

*(Then the minister shall ask the parents or guardians the name of each child, take it in arms, and baptize each child saying:)*

____________ ____________, I baptize you in the name of the Father, and of the Son, and of the Holy Spirit. Amen.

*(Then the minister may pray.)*

## C. Baptism of Believers

**5515.** *(When the candidates for baptism have presented themselves before the minister, the minister shall say:)*

Dear *friends*, in keeping with the example of Jesus, you have presented *yourselves* this day that you might receive the sacrament of baptism. Baptism is not itself the door to salvation, but rather is an outward sign of the new birth which God has wrought in your heart. It proclaims to all the world that you have taken Christ Jesus as the Lord of your *lives*, and that it is your purpose always to obey Him. In order that we may hear your testimony of what God has done for you, and that we may know that you understand the significance of the step you are taking, we want to ask you these questions:

Do you believe in God the Father, the Son and the Holy Spirit? That Jesus Christ the Son suffered in your place on the cross, that He died but rose again, that He now sits at the Father's right hand until He returns to judge all people at the last day? And do you believe in the Holy Scriptures as the inspired Word of God? That by the grace of God every person has the ability and responsibility to choose between right and wrong, and that those who repent of their sin and believe in the Lord Jesus Christ are justified by faith?

**Answer:** All this I steadfastly believe.

Do you intend by this act to testify to all the world that you are a Christian and that you will be a loyal follower of Christ?

**Answer:** I do.

*(Then the minister shall ask the name of each candidate and shall immerse the candidate in water, or if desired, sprinkle or pour water, saying:)*

____________, I baptize you in the name of the Father, and of the Son, and of the Holy Spirit. Amen.

*(Then the minister shall pray.)*

## D. Affirmation of Parental Vows

**5530.** *(Persons who were baptized as infants, upon coming to maturity and being converted, and desiring to make personal the vows earlier taken in their behalf by their parents, may do so by publicly answering the questions in the ritual of baptism as given in 5515 and as directed by the pastor.)*

Dear *friends*, ______________ *were* presented by *their parents* for baptism as children. *They* now desire to make personal the vows made in *their* behalf by publicly declaring *their* commitment to the faith in which *they were* baptized.

*(Then the minister shall address the candidate:)*

Do you believe in God the Father, the Son and the Holy Spirit? That Jesus Christ the Son suffered in your place on the cross, that He died but rose again, that He now sits at the Father's right hand until He returns to judge all people at the last day? And do you believe in the Holy Scriptures as the inspired Word of God? That by the grace of God every person has the ability and responsibility to choose between right and wrong, and that those who repent of their sin and believe in the Lord Jesus Christ are justified by faith?

**Answer:** All this I steadfastly believe.

Do you affirm the act of your *parents* as they presented you for baptism and do you hereby testify to all the world that you are a Christian and that you will be a loyal follower of Christ?

**Answer:** I do.

*(Then the minister shall pray.)*

# Chapter II

## RECEPTION OF MEMBERS

**5550.** When candidates for covenant membership or community membership have been approved for reception as given in 553-563, the pastor shall appoint a time during a regular worship service for their public reception, and shall preside over the service of reception, or appoint a representative to preside. In those churches in which the local churches must vote on the reception of covenant members, such vote should be taken at a meeting prior to the service of reception. Paragraphs 5565-5567, "Reception of Covenant Members," "Covenant Questions," and "Declaration of Purpose" have the authority of statutory law. The paragraphs must be followed as prescribed, except that paragraph 5566 may be addressed during membership preparation classes and omitted during the service of reception if a shortened service is desired.

**5555.** *The service of reception may begin with a hymn and scripture reading such as one of those listed below, and with the administration of the sacrament of baptism to any who have not previously received it.*

**Hymn.** "*The Church's One Foundation,*" "*I Love Thy Kingdom, Lord,*" "*Glorious Things of Thee Are Spoken,*" "*A Mighty Fortress Is Our God.*"

**Scripture Lesson.** *Romans 12:1-8; 1 Corinthians 12:4-27; Ephesians 4:1-7, 11-16; 5:25b-27.*

**5560. Introductory Remarks.**

**Minister**: Dear *friends*, the privileges and blessings which we have within the fellowship of the church of Jesus Christ are very sacred and precious. Christ so loved the church that He gave Himself for it, sanctifying Himself that the church might be sanctified. He chose to speak of Himself as the Head of the church and of the church as His body; and again He spoke of Himself as the husband and of the church as His bride. Christ gave Himself unselfishly, and He asked the church to share its glorious relationship with all humankind, sending it into the world to preach the Scriptures, to save the lost, to administer the sacraments, to maintain Christian fellowship and discipline, and to build up the believer until He comes again. All of us, whatever our age or position, stand in need of Christ's church and of those means of grace which it alone makes available.

It is in keeping with Christ's commission to the church, that we meet together now. There are some among us who testify to having been received already into the spiritual fellowship of the universal church, and who desire to be received into the official and visible fellowship of this local unit of the body of Christ.

**5565. Reception of Covenant Members.**

*(The minister shall call before the congregation those who are being received as covenant members.)*

*These persons* standing before you come to enter into covenant *as members* in full relationship with The Wesleyan Church, with all of the accompanying rights, privileges and responsibilities. *They testify* to having been born again. *They have* received the sacrament of baptism, *have* been instructed in and *have* accepted the doctrines and polity of The Wesleyan Church, and *have* been approved by vote as manifesting in spirit and practice God's work of grace within *their hearts*.

*(If a shortened service is desired, and the candidates have been asked the membership covenant questions and have responded appropriately, the presiding minister may add the statement* [*They have each* responded appropriately to the membership covenant questions as required by *The Discipline*, cf. 5550.], *omit the questions, and move to paragraph 5567. If the covenant questions have not been addressed previously, or if a public response to the questions is desired, the questions in paragraph 5566 shall be asked as prescribed.)*

**5566. Covenant Questions.**

**Minister:** We now propose, in the fear of God, to question *these persons* as to *their* experience, faith and purpose, that you may know that *they* are proper *persons* to be admitted into this Church.

Dear *friends*, you are come seeking union with the church of Jesus Christ. We rejoice that you have chosen to undertake the privileges and the responsibilities of membership in The Wesleyan Church. Before you are fully admitted thereto, you should here publicly and individually make your vows, confess your faith and declare your purpose, by answering the following questions:

**Minister:** Do you believe in God the Father, the Son and the Holy Spirit? That Jesus Christ the Son suffered in your place on the cross, that He died but rose again, that He now sits at the Father's right hand until He returns to judge all people at the last day? And do you believe in the Holy Scriptures as the inspired and inerrant Word of God? That by the grace of God every person has the ability and responsibility to choose between right and wrong, and that those who repent of their sin and believe in the Lord Jesus Christ are justified by faith? And do you believe that God not only counts believers as righteous, but that He makes them righteous, perfecting them in love at entire sanctification, and providing for their growth in grace at every stage of their spiritual life, enabling them through the presence and power of the Holy Spirit to live a victorious life?

**Candidate:** This I believe.

**Minister:** Do you have the witness of the Spirit that you are a child of God?

**Candidate:** I do.

**Minister:** Have you the assurance that you have experienced the deeper grace of heart cleansing through the infilling of the Holy Spirit? If not, do you purpose to diligently seek this grace?

**Candidate:** I do.

**Minister:** Do you cordially accept our Covenant Membership Commitments and Elementary Principles as biblical guidelines for your conduct, and do you accept the authority of *The Discipline* of The Wesleyan Church in matters of church government?

**Candidate:** I do.

**Minister:** Do you recognize your obligation to God and the Church, and do you purpose to contribute your resources as the Lord has prospered you for the support of the gospel as the Church fulfills its mission in the world?

**Candidate:** I do.

**5567. Declaration of Purpose.**

**Minister:** By coming before us today you indicate your purpose to publicly confess the Lord Jehovah, Father, Son and Holy Spirit, to be your God and the object of your highest love. You accept the Lord Jesus to be your Redeemer, and the Holy Spirit to be your Sanctifier, Comforter and Guide. You joyfully dedicate *yourselves* to God that within the everlasting covenant of His grace you might be used in His service to glorify and honor Him. And you promise to hold to Him as the highest good of your life; that you will give diligent attention to the commandments and principles of His Word; that you will seek the honor and advancement of His kingdom; and that forsaking all ungodliness and worldly desires, you will live soberly, righteously and godly in this present world.

You do also purpose to join *yourselves* to this church, submitting *yourselves* to its principles of government; and by walking in love and fellowship with all its members, seek its peace, purity and growth in grace.

Do you freely and sincerely devote *yourselves* to be the Lord's within the fellowship of this church?

**Candidate:** I do.

**5570. Reception of Transfers from Other Denominations.**

**Minister:** There are *those* who *have* found Christ in some other branch of His church, but who now *desire* to transfer *their* membership to The Wesleyan Church, and who present *themselves* for reception as covenant *members* by transfer. To *them* we address this question:

**Minister:** Dear *friends*, in transferring your covenant relation to this branch of Christ's church, you again renew your vows of church fellowship. Relying upon the grace of God, you promise to walk in all His commandments and ordinances, and to seek His service as your highest joy. You promise to submit to the rules and *The Discipline* of The Wesleyan Church; to strive earnestly for its peace, purity and growth in grace, and to walk with all its members in love and Christian faithfulness. Do you sincerely devote *yourselves* to be the Lord's and do you hereby renew your covenant with the church of Jesus Christ by joining yourselves to this fellowship of believers?

**Transferee:** I do.

**5575. Reception of Community Members.**

*(Paragraph 5575 is provided for those churches implementing community membership. For other churches or if no community members are being received, the minister will skip 5575 and go directly to 5580.)*

**Minister:** The church of Jesus Christ is not only for those who are spiritually strong and mature, but it is intended by its Head and Master for all who know Him as Savior and who love and serve Him as Lord. There are those who are not yet ready for covenant membership in The Wesleyan Church. For these, the Church has provided the category of community membership, that they may enjoy its pastoral care and spiritual nurture, and that they may grow in grace and knowledge until they take their place in full relation to the Church. *These* come now that *they* may be questioned and received as *their* experience makes fitting.

To you who have so recently been converted to Christ, and to *all* of you who desire to study and grow toward spiritual maturity, and who have here presented *yourselves* for reception as community *members*, we address these questions:

**Minister:** Does the Lord now forgive your sins?

**Candidate:** Yes, He does.

**Minister:** Is it your purpose to grow spiritually, to study daily in private devotions and regularly at the church, to become acquainted with the Scriptures and *The Discipline* of our Church, and to prepare to be received at the proper time in covenant membership?

**Candidate:** Yes, it is.

**5580. Response of the Church.**

**Minister:** May the members of the church now join me in welcoming *these* new *ones* to our fellowship, assuring *them* of our love, of our prayers and of our care over *them* in days to come. Do you, the members of this church, receive *these* to our communion and fellowship as beloved *brothers* and *sisters*, and promise to walk with them in love, to instruct, counsel, admonish and cherish *them*, and to watch over *them* with all long-suffering, gentleness and love?

**Congregation:** We do.

**5585. Prayer.**

**Minister:** O God of the church, we thank You for the blessing of Christian fellowship, for joining together in one body all those who truly believe in Jesus Christ, Your Son. We thank You for *these* who this day are becoming a part of this local church, this branch of Christ's body. Grant to *them* the grace and strength *they* shall need to fulfill *their* vows, and bind our hearts together in Your holy love, that we may aid each other and that together we may share Your gospel with the world for which Christ died. In His name we pray. Amen.

**5590. Right Hand of Fellowship.**

**Minister:** And now, in behalf of The Wesleyan Church and of this local congregation, I extend to you the right hand of fellowship, welcoming you as *members* with us of the body of Christ.

**5595.** *The service of reception may close with a hymn and a benediction such as the following:*

**Hymn.** "*Blest Be the Tie That Binds,*" "*Onward, Christian Soldiers,*" "*Lead On, O King Eternal,*" "*Soldiers of Christ, Arise.*"

**Benediction.** Now unto Him who is able to do exceeding abundantly above all that we ask or think, according to the power that works in us, unto Him be glory in the church by Christ Jesus throughout all ages, world without end. Amen.

## Chapter III

## THE LORD'S SUPPER

### A. General Directions

**5600.** The Lord's Supper shall be observed in each local Wesleyan church at least once each three months (cf. 293; 725:6).

**5605.** It is expected that Wesleyan ministers shall carefully admonish the people that only those who are in right relations with God and with their neighbors should come to the Lord's table, and that others should come only if in so doing they are expressing repentance and seeking forgiveness.

**5610.** Only unfermented grape juice shall be used in observing the Lord's Supper.

**5611**. The officiating minister may enlist the assistance of other ministers, persons preparing for the ministry or laypersons for the distribution of the elements.

### B. Order of the Lord's Supper—as Part of a Service

**5615.** *(The elements of the Lord's Supper shall be placed upon a table and covered with a white linen cloth. The minister shall read a Scripture lesson, such as one of the following: Isa. 53; Matt. 26:26-29; Luke 22:14-20; Rom. 5:1-2, 6-12, 18-21; 1 Cor. 10:16-17; 11:23-29; Eph. 1:3-12; 2:1-10, 12-22; Heb. 9:11-17, 22-28; 1 Peter 1:18-23; 2:21-25.)*

*(Then the congregation shall sing a hymn, such as one of the following: "Alas! and Did My Saviour Bleed," "Man of Sorrows, What a Name," "When I Survey the Wondrous Cross," "Arise, My Soul, Arise," "My Faith Looks Up to Thee," "Rock of Ages," "There Is a Fountain Filled with Blood.")*

*(Then the minister may preach a sermon on some phase of the Lord's Supper. Afterwards the congregation may sing another hymn such as one of those listed above. Then the minister shall direct the people as to the plan for distribution of the elements of the Supper, either directing them to come and kneel at the altar or to be served while seated, in either instance using this invitation:)*

You who are walking in fellowship with God, and are in love and harmony with your neighbors; and you who do truly and earnestly repent of your sin and intend to lead a new life, following the commandments of God, and walking from this time in His holy ways, draw near with faith, and take this holy sacrament to your comfort; and meekly make your humble confession to Almighty God.

*(Then the minister shall remove the cloth, folding it neatly, and laying it to one side. Then the minister shall pray the prayer of consecration:)*

O God of grace and mercy, we thank You that You ever loved us and provided for our redemption. We thank You for Your Son who died to save us, and for Your Spirit who invites us to draw near. Guide us now as we commemorate the suffering of our Lord. Help us to remember the cost of our salvation. Help us to commune with You and with each other. And so consecrate the bread and wine which are here prepared, that as we partake of them we may receive the spiritual benefits of Christ's broken body and shed blood. In His name we pray. Amen.

*(Then the minister shall first partake of the bread, and then distribute it to the people, saying:)*

The body of our Lord Jesus Christ, which was given for you, preserve your soul and body unto everlasting life. Take and eat this remembering that Christ died for you, and feed on Him in your heart, by faith, with thanksgiving.

*(Then the minister shall partake of the wine, and then distribute it to the people, saying:)*

The blood of our Lord Jesus Christ, which was shed for you, preserve your soul and body unto everlasting life. Drink this remembering that Christ's blood was shed for you, and be thankful.

*(After all have partaken, let that which remains of the consecrated elements be returned to the table, and covered with the white linen cloth. Then let the minister pronounce the benediction:)*

May the peace of God, which passes all understanding, keep your hearts and minds in the knowledge and love of God, and of His Son, Jesus Christ, our Lord; and the blessings of God Almighty, the Father, the Son and the Holy Spirit be among you and remain with you always. Amen.

## C. Order of the Lord's Supper—as an Entire Service

**5635.** *(The elements of the Lord's Supper shall be placed upon a table and covered with a white linen cloth. The minister shall address the congregation saying:)*

### Call to Worship

The Lord Jesus himself instituted the holy sacrament we call the Lord's Supper, giving it to the disciples as a means of remembering Him until He comes again, and as a seal of the new covenant between God and man. This service is therefore a time of special sacredness and we can only be properly prepared by giving our hearts and minds to reverent worship, and by being freed of all things contrary to the divine nature and purpose. Therefore let us bow in a period of silent prayer, asking the Holy Spirit to search our hearts and to bring us into conformity with the holiness of the God we serve.

*(The minister shall allow sufficient time for each person to prepare for the service, and then shall pray:)*

### Invocation

Almighty God, to whom all hearts are opened, all desires known and from whom no secrets are hidden: cleanse the thoughts of our hearts, through the presence of the Holy Spirit, that we may perfectly love You, and worthily magnify Your holy name, through Christ our Lord. Amen.

### Hymns

*(Then the congregation shall sing a hymn, such as one of the following: "Alas! and Did My Saviour Bleed," "Man of Sorrows, What a Name," "When I Survey the Wondrous Cross," "Arise, My Soul, Arise," "My Faith Looks Up to Thee," "Rock of Ages," "There Is a Fountain Filled with Blood.")*

### Scripture Readings

*(Then the minister shall read a Scripture lesson, such as one of the following: Isa. 53; Matt. 26:26-29; Luke 22:14-20; Rom. 5:1-2, 6-12, 18-21; 1 Cor. 10:16-17; 11:23-29; Eph. 1:3-12; 2:1-10, 12-22; Heb. 9:11-17, 22-28; 1 Peter 1:18-23; 2:21-25.)*

### Prayer

*(Then the minister shall pray an extemporaneous prayer or use the following:)*

Almighty God, father of our Lord Jesus Christ, maker of all things, judge of all men, we acknowledge that in Your sight all our righteous acts are like filthy rags. Outside of Christ we are sinners, and it is only through His atonement that we are forgiven and cleansed. Whatever there is of purity and virtue in our hearts or in our lives is the product of Your grace. We come today to remember once again how Christ obtained our salvation. And as we do, we ask that the Holy Spirit shall search our hearts. If we have committed any act which is displeasing to You, or neglected any duty which would have honored

You, reveal it and forgive, we pray. Or if there is any tendency to disobedience, to the love of the world, or to the exaltation of self, reveal it and purge it from our hearts, we pray. You have told us that if any man sin, we have an advocate with the Father, Jesus Christ the righteous. Our hope, our trust, our righteousness are in Him alone. Have mercy upon us for His sake, and grant that we may serve and please You in newness of life and purity of heart, world without end, in the name of our Lord Jesus Christ. Amen.

### Sermon, Hymn, Instructions

*(Then the minister may preach a sermon on some phase of the Lord's Supper. Afterwards the congregation may sing another hymn such as one of those listed above. Then the minister shall direct the people as to the plan for distribution of the elements of the Supper, either directing them to come and kneel at the altar or to be served while seated, in either instance using this invitation:)*

### Invitation

You who are walking in fellowship with God, and are in love and harmony with your neighbors; and you who do truly and earnestly repent of your sin and intend to lead a new life, following the commandments of God, and walking from this time in His holy ways, draw near with faith, and take this holy sacrament to your comfort; and meekly (*kneeling*) make your humble confession to Almighty God.

*(When all are in place, the minister shall remove the cloth, folding it neatly, and laying it to one side. Then the minister shall pray the prayer of consecration:)*

### Consecration of Bread and Wine

Almighty God, our heavenly Father, who in mercy gave Your only Son, Jesus Christ, to suffer death upon the cross for our redemption: accept our praise, we beseech You. We thank You for Your love, for the gift of Your Son, for the sacrifice He made in our behalf, for the forgiveness of our sins and the cleansing of our hearts, for the present witness of Your Holy Spirit to our hearts that we are Your children. Grant that, as we receive this bread and wine, in memory of Christ's death and suffering, in communion with You and with Your children, we may be made partakers of His body and blood; who, on the night He was betrayed, took bread,

*(Here the minister may take the plate of bread in hand.)*

and when He had given thanks, He broke it and said, Take, eat; this is my body which is given for you: do this in memory of me. In the same way, after supper He took the cup,

*(Here the minister may take in hand the vessel from which the wine is to be poured, or the tray of individual cups.)*

and gave it to them, saying, Drink from it, all of you, for this is my blood of the new covenant, which is poured out for many, for the forgiveness of sins; do this, whenever you drink it, in memory of me. Amen.

### Distribution of Bread and Wine

*(Then the minister shall direct the distribution of the elements, either first kneeling at the table and partaking, then serving others who may be assisting, and then serving the people; or directing first the distribution of the bread with all holding their portion until the time for simultaneous participation, and then the distribution of the wine in the same manner.)*

*(In either instance, either before or during the distribution, or immediately before the simultaneous partaking of the bread, the following shall be read:)*

The body of our Lord Jesus Christ, which was given for you, preserve your soul and body unto everlasting life. Take and eat this remembering that Christ died for you, and feed on Him in your heart, by faith, with thanksgiving.

*(And in like manner, either before or during the distribution, or immediately before the simultaneous partaking of the wine, the following shall be read:)*

The blood of our Lord Jesus Christ, which was shed for you, preserve your soul and body unto everlasting life. Drink this remembering that Christ's blood was shed for you, and be thankful.

*(After all have partaken, let that which remains of the consecrated elements be returned to the table, and covered with the white linen cloth. Then let the minister and congregation join in praying:)*

### Lord's Prayer

Our Father which art in heaven, hallowed be Thy name. Thy kingdom come. Thy will be done in earth, as it is in heaven. Give us this day our daily bread. And forgive us our debts, as we forgive our debtors. And lead us not into temptation, but deliver us from evil: for Thine is the kingdom, and the power, and the glory, forever. Amen.

## Benediction

*(Then the minister shall conclude the service with the benediction:)*

May the peace of God, which passes all understanding, keep your hearts and minds in the knowledge and love of God, and of His Son, Jesus Christ, our Lord; and the blessings of God Almighty, the Father, the Son and the Holy Spirit, be among you and remain with you always. Amen.

# Chapter IV

# MARRIAGE

## A. Marriage Ceremony-Long Form

**5650.** *(At the day and time appointed for the solemnizing of matrimony, the persons to be married standing together, the man on the right hand of the woman, the minister shall say:)*

Dearly beloved, we are gathered together in the sight of God, and in the presence of these witnesses, to join together this man and this woman in holy matrimony, which is an honorable estate, instituted of God, and signifying unto us the mystical union which exists between Christ and His church. It is therefore not to be entered into unadvisedly, but reverently, discreetly and in the fear of God. Into this holy estate these two persons come now to be joined.

*(Speaking to the persons to be married, the minister shall say:)*

I charge you both, as you stand in the presence of God, before whom the secrets of all hearts are disclosed, that, having duly considered the holy covenant you are about to make, you do now declare before this company your pledge of faith, each to the other. Be well assured that if these solemn vows are faithfully kept, as God's Word demands, and if steadfastly you endeavor to do the will of your heavenly Father, God will bless your marriage, will grant you fulfillment in it, and will establish your home in peace.

*(Then shall the minister address the man by name, and ask:)*

Will you have this woman to be your wedded wife, to live together in the holy estate of matrimony? Will you love her, comfort her, honor and keep her, in sickness and in health; and forsaking all others keep yourself only unto her, so long as you both shall live?

*(The man shall answer:)*

I will.

*(Then shall the minister address the woman by name, and ask:)*

Will you have this man to be your wedded husband, to live together in the holy estate of matrimony? Will you love him, comfort him, honor and keep him, in sickness and in health; and forsaking all others, keep yourself only unto him, so long as you both shall live?

*(The woman shall answer:)*

I will.

*(Then shall the minister ask:)*

Who gives this woman to be married to this man?

*(The father of the woman, or whoever gives her in marriage, shall answer:)*

I do (*or* Her mother and I).

*(Then the minister shall cause the man and woman to join right hands and shall cause the man, using their given names, to say after him:)*

I, ___________, take you, ___________, to be my wedded wife, to have and to hold, from this day forward, for better, for worse, for richer, for poorer, in sickness and in health, to love and to cherish, till death do us part, according to God's holy law; and thereto I pledge you my faith.

*(Then shall the minister cause the woman, using their given names to say after him:)*

I, ___________, take you, ___________, to be my wedded husband, to have and to hold, from this day forward, for better, for worse, for richer, for poorer, in sickness and in health, to love and to cherish, till death do us part, according to God's holy law; and thereto I pledge you my faith.

*(If an exchange of rings is desired, the minister shall ask for the rings, deliver the ring to the man and say:)*

___________, place this ring on the finger of your bride and repeat after me: This ring I give you, in token and pledge of our constant faith and abiding love.

*(The minister shall then deliver the ring to the woman and say:)*

___________, place this ring on the finger of your groom and repeat after me: This ring I give you, in token and pledge of our constant faith and abiding love.

*(Here may be offered the following prayer, or an extemporaneous prayer closing with the Lord's Prayer.)*

O eternal God, creator and preserver of all mankind, giver of all spiritual grace, the author of life everlasting, let Your blessing descend and rest upon these Your children, whom we bless in Your name. Bless this marriage and make it to them the source of abundant and enduring good. Look graciously upon them that they may love, honor and cherish each other. May their mutual affection never know change, doubt, nor decay. Direct and strengthen them in the discharge of all their duties. Bless the home which they establish. Teach them to order their household wisely and well, and to regard all their possessions as Your gifts to be employed in Your service. May they so live together in faithfulness and patience, in wisdom and true godliness, that their home may be a haven of blessing and a place of peace, through Jesus Christ our Lord. Amen.

*(Then shall the minister cause the man and woman to join right hands and placing a hand on top of theirs shall say:)*

Forasmuch, as ___________ and ___________ have consented together in holy wedlock, and have witnessed the same before God and this company and thereto have pledged their faith each to the other, and have declared the same by joining hands [*and by giving and receiving rings*]; I pronounce that they are husband and wife together, in the name of the Father, and of the Son, and of the Holy Spirit. Those whom God has joined together let not man put asunder. Amen.

*(Then the minister shall give this blessing,)*

God the Father, God the Son, God the Holy Spirit, bless, preserve and keep you; the Lord mercifully with His favor look upon you, and so fill you with all spiritual benediction and grace, that you may so live together in this life, that in the world to come you may have life everlasting. Amen.

### B. Marriage Ceremony—Shorter Form

**5680.** *(At the day and time appointed for the solemnizing of matrimony, the persons to be married standing together, the man on the right hand of the woman, the minister shall say:)*

My friends, the ordinance of marriage was instituted by God himself in the garden of Eden, and is one of the most solemn and binding of obligations, because it involves the sacred relations of the home and the family. Your happiness for the future will largely depend upon the faithfulness with which the marriage vows are cherished and kept. There must be mutual affection the one for the other, and the marriage covenant must be kept in purity of spirit, as well as in actual word and deed, if you would reap the full fruition of happiness in your marriage.

If, with full and free consent, and thoughtful determination to keep the marriage covenant, you desire to enter the holy estate of marriage, you will acknowledge the same by taking the other by the right hand.

*(With their hands joined, the minister shall address the man by name, and ask:)*

Will you have this woman to be your wedded wife, to live together after God's ordinance in the holy estate of matrimony? Will you love her, comfort her, honor and keep her, in sickness and in health; and forsaking all others, keep yourself only unto her, so long as you both shall live?

*(The man shall answer:)*

I will.

*(Then the minister shall address the woman by name, and ask:)*

Will you have this man to be your wedded husband, to live together after God's ordinance in the holy estate of matrimony? Will you love him, comfort him, honor and keep him, in sickness and in health; and forsaking all others, keep yourself only unto him, so long as you both shall live?

*(The woman shall answer:)*

I will.

*(Then the minister shall place a right hand upon their joined hands and say:)*

Since they have taken the marriage covenant before God, and in the presence of these witnesses, by the authority committed unto me as a minister of the church of Jesus Christ, I declare that ____________ and ____________ are now husband and wife, according to the ordinance of God and the law of the state, in the name of the Father, and of the Son, and of the Holy Spirit. Those whom God has joined together let not man put asunder. Amen.

*(Then the minister shall offer an appropriate prayer.)*

# Chapter V

## BURIAL OF THE DEAD

### 5700. At the House, Church or Funeral Chapel.

#### Opening Sentences

*(The minister shall open the service with an opening sentence, such as one of the following:)*

"I know that my Redeemer lives,
and that in the end he will stand upon the earth.
And after my skin has been destroyed,
yet in my flesh I will see God;
I myself will see him
with my own eyes—I, and not another" (Job 19:25-27a, NIV).

"God is our refuge and strength,
an ever present help in trouble.
Therefore we will not fear, though the earth give way
and the mountains fall into the heart of the sea,
though its waters roar and foam
and the mountains quake with their surging" (Ps. 46:1-3, NIV).

"I tell you the truth, a time is coming and has now come when the dead will hear the voice of the Son of God and those who hear will live" (John 5:25, NIV).

"Jesus said to her, 'I am the resurrection and the life. He who believes in me will live, even though he dies; and whoever lives and believes in me will never die'" (John 11:25-26a, NIV).

"Praise be to the God and Father of our Lord Jesus Christ, the Father of compassion and the God of all comfort, who comforts us in all our troubles, so that we can comfort those in any trouble with the comfort we ourselves have received from God" (2 Cor. 1:3-4, NIV).

"For our light affliction, which is but for a moment, is working for us a far more exceeding and eternal weight of glory, while we do not look at the things which are seen, but at the things which are not seen. For the things which are seen are temporary, but the things which are not seen are eternal" (2 Cor. 4:17-18, NKJV).

"For I am already being poured out like a drink offering, and the time has come for my departure. I have fought the good fight, I have finished the race, I have kept the faith. Now there is in store for me the crown of righteousness, which the Lord, the righteous Judge, will award to me on that day—and not only to me, but also to all who have longed for his appearing" (2 Tim. 4:6-8, NIV).

**Hymn**

*(Then a hymn shall be sung, or played. Then the minister shall read a scripture lesson, such as one of the following:)*

**Scripture Readings**

"Show me, O Lord, my life's end
  and the number of my days;
  let me know how fleeting is my life.
You have made my days a mere handbreadth;
  the span of my years is as nothing before you.
  Each man's life is but a breath.
Man is a mere phantom as he goes to and fro:
  He bustles about, but only in vain;
  he heaps up wealth, not knowing who will get it.
But now, Lord, what do I look for?
  My hope is in you" (Ps. 39:4-7, NIV).
"Lord, You have been our dwelling place
  in all generations.
Before the mountains were brought
  forth,
Or ever You had formed the earth
  and the world,
Even from everlasting to everlasting,
  You are God.
For a thousand years in Your sight
Are like yesterday when it is past,
And like a watch in the night.
We finish our years like a sigh.
The days of our lives are seventy years;
And if by reason of strength they are
  eighty years,
Yet their boast is only labor
  and sorrow;
For it is soon cut off, and we fly away.
So teach us to number our days,
That we may gain a heart of wisdom" (Ps. 90:1-2, 4, 9b-10, 12, NKJV).

"But Christ has indeed been raised from the dead, the firstfruits of those who have fallen asleep. For since death came through a man, the resurrection of the dead comes also through a man. For as in Adam all die, so in Christ all will be made alive. But each in his own turn: Christ, the firstfruits; then, when he comes, those who belong to him. Then the end will come, when he hands over the kingdom to God the Father after he has destroyed all dominion, authority and power. For he must reign until he has put all his enemies under his feet. The last enemy to be destroyed is death. Listen, I tell you a mystery: We will not all sleep, but we will all be changed—in a flash, in the twinkling of an eye, at the last trumpet. For the trumpet will sound, the dead will be raised imperishable, and we will be changed. When the perishable has been clothed with the imperishable, and the mortal with immortality, then the saying that is written will come true: 'Death has been swallowed up in victory.'

'Where, O death, is your victory?
Where, O death, is your sting?'

The sting of death is sin, and the power of sin is the law. But thanks be to God! He gives us the victory through our Lord Jesus Christ. Therefore, my dear brothers, stand firm. Let nothing move you. Always give yourselves fully to the work of the Lord, because you know that your labor in the Lord is not in vain" (1 Cor. 15:20-26, 51-52, 54-58, NIV).

"After this I looked and there before me was a great multitude that no one could count, from every nation, tribe, people and language, standing before the throne and in front of the Lamb. They were wearing white robes and were holding palm branches in their hands. And they cried out in a loud voice:

'Salvation belongs to our God,
who sits on the throne,
and to the Lamb.'

All the angels were standing around the throne and around the elders and the four living creatures. They fell down on their faces before the throne and worshipped God, saying:

'Amen!
Praise and glory
and wisdom and thanks and honor
and power and strength
be to our God for ever and ever.
Amen!'

Then one of the elders asked me, 'These in white robes—who are they, and where did they come from?' I answered, 'Sir, you know.' And he said, 'These are they who have come out of the great tribulation; they have washed their robes and made them white in the blood of the Lamb. Therefore,

'they are before the throne of God
and serve him day and night in his temple;

and he who sits on the throne will spread his tent
over them.
Never again will they hunger;
never again will they thirst.
The sun will not beat upon them,
nor any scorching heat.
For the Lamb at the center of the throne will be
their shepherd;
he will lead them to springs of living water.
And God will wipe away every tear from their eyes.'" (Rev. 7:9-17, NIV).

### Prayer

*(Then the minister shall pray an extemporaneous prayer or use the following prayer:)*

O God of life, as we have learned to do in all our experiences, we come to You in the hour of death. We know that You love us, and that You can turn even the shadow of death into the light of morning. Help us now to wait before You with reverent and submissive hearts. Make this a time of opening our eyes and our understanding, and a time of admonition to our hearts and souls. Bless those who feel this sorrow most keenly, and cause the bonds of Christian love to bind us closer together, so that we may share with them that spiritual strength and that faith in God which is ours through the love of Christ, in whose name we pray. Amen.

### Message and Prayer

*(Then the minister shall preach a funeral message. The service may be closed with an extemporaneous prayer, and the following benediction:)*

### Benediction

May the grace of the Lord Jesus Christ, the love of God the Father, and the communion of the Holy Spirit abide with us now and evermore. Amen.

### 5725. At the Graveside

#### Scripture Readings

*(The minister shall read a brief scripture lesson, such as one of the following:)*

"I lift up my eyes to the hills—
where does my help come from?
My help comes from the Lord,
the Maker of heaven and earth.
He will not let your foot slip—
he who watches over you will not slumber;
indeed, he who watches over Israel
will neither slumber nor sleep.
The Lord watches over you—
the Lord is your shade at your right hand;
the sun will not harm you by day,
nor the moon by night.
The Lord will keep you from all harm—
he will watch over your life;
the Lord will watch over your coming and going
both now and forevermore" (Ps. 121, NIV).

"'Do not let your hearts be troubled. Trust in God, trust also in me. In my Father's house are many rooms; if it were not so, I would have told you. I am going there to prepare a place for you. And if I go and prepare a place for you, I will come back and take you to be with me that you also may be where I am. You know the way to the place where I am going.' Thomas said to him, 'Lord, we don't know where you are going, so how can we know the way?' Jesus answered, 'I am the way and the truth and the life. No one comes to the Father except through me'" (John 14:1-6, NIV).

#### Committals

*(Then the minister shall read one of the following committals:)*

"And now, we commit this body to its resting place; and we commit the spirit, O our Father, together with every sacred interest of our hearts, into Your keeping; praying that You will deal graciously and mercifully with each of us, until we too shall come to You in glory, through the riches of grace in Jesus our Lord."

"Then I saw a new heaven and a new earth, for the first heaven and the first earth had passed away, and there was no longer any sea. I saw the Holy City, the new Jerusalem, coming down out of heaven from God, prepared as a bride beautifully dressed for her husband. And I heard a loud voice from the throne saying, 'Now the dwelling of God is with men, and he will live with them. They will be his people, and God himself will be with them and be their God. He will wipe every tear from their eyes. There will be no more death or mourning or crying or pain, for the old order of things has passed away.' He who was seated on the throne said, 'I am making everything new!' Then he said, 'Write this down, for these words are trustworthy and true.' He said to me: 'It is done. I am the Alpha and the Omega, the Beginning and the End. To him who is thirsty I will give to drink without cost from the spring of the water of life. He who overcomes will inherit all this, and I will be his God and he will be my son'" (Rev. 21:1-7, NIV).

"Then the angel showed me the river of the water of life, as clear as crystal, flowing from the throne of God and of the Lamb down the middle of the great street of the city. On each side of the river stood the tree of life, bearing twelve crops of fruit, yielding its fruit every month. And the leaves of the trees are for the healing of the nations. No longer will there be any curse. The throne of God and of the Lamb will be in the city, and his servants will serve him. They will see his face, and his name will be on their foreheads. There will be no more night. They will not need the light of a lamp or the light of the sun, for the Lord God will give them light. And they will reign for ever and ever" (Rev. 22:1-5, NIV).

### Prayer and Benediction

*(Then the minister may offer a brief extemporaneous prayer, and conclude with the following benediction:)*

Now the God of peace, that brought again from the dead our Lord Jesus, that Great Shepherd of the sheep, through the blood of the everlasting covenant, make you perfect in every good work to do His will, working in you that which is well-pleasing in His sight, through Jesus Christ; to whom be glory for ever and ever. Amen.

# Chapter VI

## ORDINATION OF MINISTERS

### A. Regulations

**5750.** That portion of the ritual of ordination entitled, "Examination of Candidates" (5772) has the authority of statutory law, and must be followed as prescribed.

**5752.** The ordination service shall be planned by the Council of Ordination (1405; 3070:6) and shall be presided over by the General Superintendent (1935:15), or by a representative appointed by the General Superintendent (3091), or if neither of the above is present, by the district superintendent (1310:23). They shall be assisted in the various parts of the service and in the act of ordination by the Council of Ordination (1405; 3070:6).

### B. The Order of the Ordination of Ministers

#### Call to Worship

**5755.** *(The appointed minister shall commence the service with a Call to Worship, such as Isa. 52:7; 1 Cor. 1:21-24; 2 Cor. 4:5-6).*

#### Hymn

*(Then the congregation shall join in singing a hymn, such as: "Lord, Speak to Me, That I May Speak," "A Charge to Keep I Have," "Lead on, O King Eternal," "Soldiers of Christ, Arise," "Conquering Now and Still to Conquer.")*

#### Invocation

*(Then the minister appointed shall give the invocation:)*

Almighty God, giver of all good things, who by the Holy Spirit has appointed ordained ministers in the church, grant us Your assistance in this service given to the ordination of such ministers, and mercifully behold *these* Your *servants*, now called to this office, and replenish *them* so with the truth of Your doctrine, and adorn *them* with innocence of life, that both by word and good example *they* may faithfully serve You in this office to the glory of Your name and the edification of Your church, through the merits of our

Savior, Jesus Christ, who lives and reigns with You and the Holy Spirit, world without end. Amen.

### Sermon

*(Then the General Superintendent or the minister appointed (3091) shall preach the ordination sermon, cf. (1935:15.)*

### Presentation of Candidates

**5758.** *(Then the district superintendent or the appointed representative shall have those to be ordained to stand and shall present them to the General Superintendent, saying:)*

I present *(read names aloud)* to be ordained as *(a) minister(s)* in The Wesleyan Church and in the church universal.

### Acceptance of Candidates

*(Then the presiding minister (5752) shall say to the people:)*

Dear friends, *these are they* whom we purpose, God willing, this day to ordain *ministers*. For, after due examination, we find that *they are* truly called to this function and ministry, and that *they are* qualified for the same.

*(The ordinands shall be seated, after which the appointed ministers shall read the Epistle and the Gospel, respectively:)*

### The Epistle

**5762.** "I became a servant of this gospel by the gift of God's grace given me through the working of his power. Although I am less than the least of all God's people, this grace was given me: to preach to the Gentiles the unsearchable riches of Christ, and to make plain to everyone the administration of this mystery, which for ages past was kept hidden in God, who created all things" (Eph. 3:7-9, NIV).

"It was he who gave some to be apostles, some to be prophets, some to be evangelists, and some to be pastors and teachers, to prepare God's people for works of service, so that the body of Christ may be built up until we all reach unity in the faith and in the knowledge of the Son of God and become mature, attaining to the whole measure of the fullness of Christ" (Eph.4:11-13, NIV).

### The Gospel

**5765.** "Therefore Jesus said again, 'I tell you the truth, I am the gate for the sheep . . . I am the gate; whoever enters through me will be saved. He will come in and go out, and find pasture. The thief comes only to steal and kill and destroy; I have come that they may have life, and have it to the full. I am the good shepherd. The good shepherd lays down his life for the sheep. The hired hand is not the shepherd who owns the sheep. So when he sees the wolf coming, he abandons the sheep and runs away. Then the wolf attacks the flock and scatters it. The man runs away because he is a hired hand and cares nothing for the sheep. I am the good shepherd; I know my sheep and my sheep know me—just as the Father knows me and I know the Father—and I lay down my life for the sheep. I have other sheep that are not of this sheep pen. I must bring them also. They too will listen to my voice, and there shall be one flock and one shepherd'" (John 10:7, 9-16, NIV).

### The Charge

**5768.** *(Then the presiding minister [3091;5752] shall ask the candidates to stand for the Charge and the Examination and shall address the candidates, giving the Charge:)*

Dear *Servant(s)* of God:

You have heard, both in your private examination by the district board of ministerial development and in the message which has just been delivered, something of the importance of the ministry to which you are called. You are *undershepherd(s)* of the Good Shepherd, the Lord Jesus, called to teach and admonish, to feed and provide for the Lord's family, to bring the lost into the fold, to bring each person unto the fullness of the stature of Christ.

Remember always the greatness of this responsibility and give yourselves without reservation unto the ministry to which God has called you. We charge you to pray daily for divine guidance and strengthening so that by your study of the Scriptures and your own personal growth and development you may both model the ideal of Christ and lead your people to live in keeping with His example and instructions.

### Examination of Candidates

**5772.** *(Then while the candidates remain standing, the presiding minister [3091; 5752] shall administer the Examination to the candidates:)*

This assembled congregation represents the church of Jesus Christ everywhere as they witness your responses to the inquiries we shall make of you. In this way we shall understand your mind and will in these things, and you may also be moved to greater faithfulness in doing your duties.

**Question:** Is it your sincere conviction that you have been called of God to the office and work of a minister, and are you persuaded that you ought to fulfill that call by serving as an ordained minister in The Wesleyan Church and among God's people everywhere?

**Answer:** That is my sincere conviction.

**Question:** Do you believe the Holy Scriptures are the fully inspired and inerrant written Word of God, containing sufficiently all doctrine necessary for eternal salvation through faith in Christ Jesus? Are you determined to instruct people from the Scriptures in order that they may be born again in Christ, become committed to holy living, and be prepared to serve for the upbuilding of the Christian community in this present age?

**Answer:** All of this I believe, and accept as my duty.

**Question:** Do you cordially accept our Articles of Religion and Membership Commitments, and agree to declare and defend them? And do you recognize your responsibility and cheerfully accept your obligation to promote and support The Wesleyan Church and all institutions and ministries approved by The Wesleyan Church?

**Answer:** Yes, I do.

**Question:** Will you with diligence minister the doctrines, sacraments and disciplines of Christ, being always ready to challenge strange doctrine which is contrary to God's Word wherever it may arise?

**Answer:** I will, as God enables me.

**Question:** Do you intend to make reading of the Word and effectual prayer your earnest pursuit, and will you seek to make your lifestyle and family government exemplary so far as is possible for you?

**Answer:** Yes, the Lord being my helper.

**Question:** Believing that accountability and acceptance of authority is God's design for His church, will you cheerfully accept the direction of those whom the Church may place over you in the doing of your work?

**Answer:** I will cheerfully do so.

### Covenant with Candidates' Spouses

**5775.** *(Then, if it is so desired, the presiding minister (3091; 5752) may call the spouses of the candidates to come and stand beside them, and shall address them saying:)*

It is the teaching of Scripture that a spouse shall be a loving companion in the ministry of a mate. You have witnessed the examination of your marriage partner in which commitment to the work and responsibilities of ministry has been stated. Your participation in God's purposes for ministry through your marriage partner is important also. You will be needed to share in prayer, to extend love and compassion to all, to carry forward the example of marriage harmony and family wholesomeness. As the companion of your loved one who is now entering the ranks of ordained ministers in the Church, will you dedicate yourself to complement and embrace that ministry as God enables you?

**Answer:** I will, by God's grace.

### Act of Ordination

**5782.** *(Then the candidates for ordination shall kneel, and, if so desired, their spouses may kneel at their sides, and the presiding minister [3091; 5752] and the Council of Ordination shall lay their hands severally upon the head of each one, and the presiding minister [3091; 5752] shall say:)*

__(name)__, as we lay our hands upon you we ask the Lord to give the unusual outpouring of the Holy Spirit needed for your service as an ordained minister in the Church. May God's anointing enable you to be a faithful exponent of His Word, and an instrument for His holy sacraments, in the name of the Father, the Son and the Holy Spirit. Amen!

__(name)__, take authority to preach the Word of God, to administer the holy sacraments, and to perform the duties of an ordained minister in the Church.

### Prayer for Enduement

**5785.** *(Then the presiding minister [3091; 5752] or other appointed minister shall pray an extemporaneous prayer of enduement or use the following:)*

Our Father, we beseech You to send upon *these* Your *servants* Your heavenly blessings: that *they* may be clothed with righteousness and with the power of the Holy Spirit, that Your Word spoken in *their mouths* may have success and that it may never be spoken in vain. Grant also that we may have grace to hear and to receive what *they* shall deliver out of Your holy Word, as the means of our salvation; and that in all our words and deeds we may seek Your glory, and the increase of Your kingdom, through Jesus Christ our Lord. Assist us, O Lord, in all our doings, with Your most gracious favor, and further us with Your continual help, that in all our works begun, continued and ended in You, we may glorify Your holy name, and finally by Your mercy obtain everlasting life through Jesus Christ our Lord. Amen.

### Right Hand of Fellowship

**5788.** *(The newly ordained ministers shall then arise, and the presiding minister (3091; 5752) and the members of the Council of Ordination shall extend to each the right hand of fellowship, welcoming the newly ordained ministers to the work and labors of the ministry. Then the presiding minister may direct the congregation to file by and greet the newly ordained ministers, or the service may be closed with the following benediction:)*

### Benediction

**5792.** May the God of peace, who through the everlasting covenant brought back from the dead our Lord Jesus, that great Shepherd of the sheep, equip you with everything good for doing his will, and may he work in us what is pleasing to him, through Jesus Christ, to whom be glory for ever and ever. Amen! (Heb. 13:20-21, NIV).

# Chapter VII

## COMMISSIONING OF MINISTERS

### A. Regulations

**5800.** That portion of the ritual of commissioning ministers entitled "Examination of Candidates" (5825), has the authority of statutory law, and must be followed as prescribed.

**5805.** The commissioning service shall be planned by the Council of Ordination (1405) and shall be presided over by the General Superintendent (1935:15), or a representative appointed by the General Superintendent (3091), or if absent by the district superintendent (1310:23). They shall be assisted in the various parts of the service and in the act of commissioning by the Council of Ordination (1405; 3059:1c).

### B. The Order of the Commissioning of Ministers

#### Invocation

**5810.** *(The minister appointed shall give an extemporaneous invocation.)*

#### Hymn

*(Then the congregation shall join in singing a hymn, such as "Lord, Speak to Me, That I May Speak," "A Charge to Keep I Have," "Take My Life and Let It Be.")*

#### Scripture Reading

*(Then the minister appointed shall read a Scripture lesson, such as 1 Tim. 6:3-16; 2 Tim. 1:6-14; 2:1-16, 22-26; 4:1-8; Titus 2:11-15; 3:3-9.)*

#### Sermon

*(Then a sermon or address may be given.* cf. 1935:15; 3091.*)*

## Presentation of Candidates

**5815.** *(Then the appointed minister shall bring the candidates and present them to the General Superintendent, saying:)*

I present *(read names)* to be commissioned as *ministers* in The Wesleyan Church.

*(Then the presiding minister (3091; 5805) shall say unto the people:)*

Dear friends, *these are they* whom we purpose, God willing, this day to commission as *ministers*. For, after due examination, we find that *they are* truly called to this function and ministry, and that *they are* qualified for the same.

## The Charge

**5820.** *(Then the presiding minister (3091; 5805) shall address the candidates, giving the charge:)*

Dear *Servant(s)* of God:

You have heard, both in your private examination by the district board of ministerial development and in the message which has just been delivered, something of the importance of the ministry to which you are called. You are *undershepherd(s)* of the Good Shepherd, the Lord Jesus, called to teach and admonish, to feed and provide for the Lord's family, to bring the lost into the fold, to bring each person unto the fullness of the stature of Christ.

Remember always the greatness of this responsibility and give yourselves without reservation unto the ministry to which God has called you. We charge you to pray daily for divine guidance and strengthening so that by your study of the Scriptures and your own personal growth and development you may both model the ideal of Christ and lead your people to live in keeping with His example and instructions.

## Examination of Candidates

**5825.** *(Then the presiding minister (3091; 5805) shall administer the examination to the candidates:)*

Is it your sincere conviction that you have been called of God to serve as a commissioned minister in The Wesleyan Church?

**Answer:** That is my sincere conviction.

**Question:** Do you believe the Holy Scriptures are the fully inspired and inerrant written Word of God, containing sufficiently all doctrine necessary for eternal salvation through faith in Christ Jesus? Are you determined to instruct people from the Scriptures in order that they may be born again in Christ, become committed to holy living and be prepared to serve for the upbuilding of the Christian community in this present age?

**Answer:** All of this I believe, and accept as my duty.

**Question:** Do you cordially accept our Articles of Religion and Membership Commitments, and agree to declare and defend them? And do you recognize your responsibility and cheerfully accept your obligation to promote and support The Wesleyan Church and all institutions and ministries approved by The Wesleyan Church?

**Answer:** Yes, I do.

**Question:** Will you with diligence minister the doctrines, sacraments and disciplines of Christ, being always ready to challenge strange doctrine which is contrary to God's Word wherever it may arise?

**Answer:** I will, as God enables me.

**Question:** Do you intend to make reading of the Word and effectual prayer your earnest pursuit, and will you seek to make your lifestyle and family government exemplary so far as is possible for you?

**Answer:** Yes, the Lord being my helper.

**Question:** Believing that accountability and acceptance of authority is God's design for His Church, will you cheerfully accept the direction of those whom the church may place over you in the doing of your work?

**Answer:** I will cheerfully do so.

### Covenant with Candidates' Spouses

**5835.** *(Then if it is so desired, the presiding minister (3091; 5805) may call the spouses of the candidates to come and stand beside them, and shall address them saying:)*

It is the teaching of Scripture that a spouse shall be a loving companion in the ministry of a mate. You have witnessed the examination of your marriage partner in which commitment to the work and responsibilities of ministry has been stated. Your participation in God's purposes for ministry through your marriage partner is important also. You will be needed to share in prayer, to extend love and compassion to all, to carry forward the example of marriage harmony and family wholesomeness. As the companion of your loved one who is now entering the ranks of commissioned ministers in the Church, will you dedicate yourself to complement and embrace that ministry as God enables you?

**Answer:** I will, by God's grace.

### Act of Commissioning

**5840.** *(Then the candidates for commissioning shall kneel, and if so desired, their spouses may kneel at their sides, and the presiding minister (3091; 5805) and the Council of Ordination shall lay their hands severally upon the head of each one, and the presiding minister shall say:)*

__(name)__, as we lay our hands upon you we ask the Lord to give the unusual outpouring of the Holy Spirit needed for your service as a commissioned minister in the Church. May God's anointing enable you to be a faithful exponent of His Word, and an instrument for His holy sacraments, in the name of the Father, the Son and the Holy Spirit. Amen!

__(name)__, take authority to preach the Word of God, to administer the sacraments, and to perform the duties of a commissioned minister in the Church.

### Prayer of Enduement

**5845.** *(Then the appointed minister shall pray an extemporaneous prayer for the anointing of the Holy Spirit upon each candidate.)*

### Right Hand of Fellowship

*(The newly commissioned ministers shall then arise, and the presiding minister (3091; 5805) and the members of the Council of Ordination shall extend to each the right hand of fellowship, welcoming them to the work and labors of the ministry. Then the presiding minister may direct the congregation to file by and greet the newly commissioned ministers, or the service shall be closed with the following benediction:)*

### Benediction

May the God of peace, who through the blood of the everlasting covenant brought back from the dead our Lord Jesus, that great Shepherd of the sheep, equip you with everything good for doing his will, and may he work in us what is pleasing to him, through Jesus Christ, to whom be glory for ever and ever. Amen! (Hebrews 13:20-21, NIV).

# Chapter VIII

## COMMISSIONING OF LAY WORKERS

**5850.** The commissioning service shall be planned by the Council of Ordination (1405) and shall be presided over by the General Superintendent when present (1935:15), or if absent by a representative appointed by the General Superintendent (3091), or, if not, by the district superintendent (1310:23).

**5855. Order of Commissioning of Lay Workers.**

*(This ritual is adaptable for use in commissioning any type of lay worker, including special workers, such as director of music, director of Christian education, youth director, song evangelist, chalk artist, children's worker, spouse in ministry; including lay missionaries, such as doctors, nurses, teachers, spouses of ordained missionaries, office workers; and including any other lay worker commissioned by a district conference. In each case, the presiding minister (3091; 5850) and others helping in the commissioning service [cf. 1405; 1935:15; 3470; 3490] shall insert the title of the commission being granted in the blanks, and make such other adaptations or modifications as are needed.)*

### Invocation

**5860.** *(The presiding minister or other appointed minister shall give an extemporaneous invocation.)*

### Hymn

*(Then the congregation shall join in singing a hymn, such as one of the following: "Take My Life, and Let It Be," "Hear Ye the Master's Call," "Give of Your Best to the Master," "Hark! The Voice of Jesus Calling.")*

### Scripture Reading

*(Then the presiding minister or other appointed minister shall read a scripture lesson, such as one of the following: Acts 2:41-44 and 6:1-8; Rom. 12:4-15; 1 Cor. 12:4-12.)*

### Sermon

*(Then the presiding minister or other appointed minister may give a sermon or address declaring the need and function of lay workers.)*

### Presentation of Candidates

**5865.** *(Then the district superintendent shall present the candidates individually to the General Superintendent, saying:)*

I present ___________ ___________ unto you to be commissioned as ___________.

*(Then the the presiding minister (3091; 5850) shall address the congregation, saying:)*

Dear Friends, *these are they* whom we purpose this day to commission as ___________ in The Wesleyan Church. After inquiry and examination, we discover that *they have* met the stated requirements of the Church, and we believe *them* to be worthy and proper persons for this service.

### Address to Candidates

**5870.** *(Then the the presiding minister (3091; 5850) shall address the candidates, saying:)*

Dear *Friends*, we rejoice that in the providence of God a door of usefulness has been opened to you in the service of the Church. It is with infinite wisdom that God has provided diversities of gifts for His workers, distributing and administering them according to His good pleasure through the Holy Spirit. It is with joy that we have watched God's will revealed in your *lives*, and your own resolve grow firm to use your *gifts* for His glory. Turning aside from worldly interests and pursuits, you are devoting *yourselves* to the Lord's work, and to being *helpers* of the ministry. You will be pouring out of your talent, your time, your possessions, your strength, your very *selves* in a living sacrifice to Christ. You have not entered upon this solemn responsibility lightly, and doubtless already in the sacred stillness of the sanctuary of your heart you have consecrated *yourselves* to this service. What you have done alone with God, you do now formally and publicly in the presence of the Church.

### Questioning of Candidates

**5875.** *(Then the the presiding minister (3091; 5850) shall question the candidates:)*

Do you believe that you have been led by the Spirit and the providences of God to engage in this work and to assume the duties of this service?

**Answer:** I do.

Do you, in the presence of God and of this congregation, promise faithfully to perform the duties of ___________ in The Wesleyan Church?

**Answer:** I do.

Do you accept the Bible as God's Word, and will you make it a lamp to your feet, and a light unto your path?

**Answer:** I accept it, and will walk in its light.

Will you be diligent in prayer, in the study of the Holy Scriptures, and in such other devotions as will help you to grow in the knowledge and love of God?

**Answer:** I will.

Will you cheerfully accept the direction of those whom the Church may place over you in the doing of your work?

**Answer:** I will cheerfully do so.

### Consecration of Candidates

**5880.** *(Then the candidates shall kneel for a brief season of silent prayer, after which the presiding minister or other appointed minister shall pray extemporaneously or use the following:)*

Our Father, who called Stephen, Philip and other lay members into the service of Your church, look upon *these* Your *servants* who *are* to be set apart to service as ___________. Give, we pray, such understanding of Your holy gospel, such firmness of Christian purpose, such diligence in service, and such beauty of life in Christ, that *they* may be to all whom *they teach* or *serve* a worthy revelation of the meaning and power of the Christian life. May *they* so order *their* time and nourish *their minds* and *hearts* that *they* may constantly grow in grace and in the knowledge of our Lord Jesus Christ, and steadily increase in the ability to lead others unto Him. Grant that *they* may have strength of body, mind and soul for the fulfillment of Your will in the holy task to which You have called *them*; and grant *them* Your Holy Spirit, that *they* may worthily discharge the work committed to *them*, to the blessing of mankind and to the praise of Christ our Savior. Amen.

*(Then the presiding minister shall address the candidates, saying:)*

May the Spirit of the living God descend upon you and abide with you always. May His holy anointing impart to you the grace for every trial, and gifts for every duty. May His presence be to you a pillar of cloud by day, and pillar of fire by night, all along the journey of life. And may the blessing of God, Father, Son and Holy Spirit, be with you now and evermore. Amen.

## Act of Commissioning

**5885.** *(Then the candidates shall rise, and the presiding minister shall take each by the hand and say:)*

I commission you to service as ____________ in The Wesleyan Church, in the name of the Father, and of the Son, and of the Holy Spirit. Amen.

## Hymn

*(Then the congregation shall join in singing a hymn, such as one of the following: "O Master, Let Me Walk with Thee," "O Jesus, I Have Promised," "Work, for the Night Is Coming," "I'll Go Where You Want Me to Go.")*

## Benediction

*(Then the presiding minister or other appointed minister shall pronounce the benediction:)*

The peace of God, which passes all understanding, keep your hearts and minds in the knowledge and love of God, and of His Son, Jesus Christ our Lord; and the blessing of God Almighty, the Father, the Son and the Holy Spirit, be among you and remain with you always. Amen.

# Chapter IX

## INSTALLATION CEREMONIES

### A. General Regulations

**5900.** The installation ceremonies provided herewith shall normally be used as a part of some general service of worship, and in most instances the other parts of the service, such as hymns, scripture readings and prayers, will need to be supplied, being chosen in such a manner as to give the entire service unity and dignity.

### B. Installation of a Pastor

**5905. Order of Installation of a Pastor.**
*(The district superintendent or representative shall preside over the installation of a pastor [1310:23]. The presiding minister or other appointed minister shall give the invocation:)*

O Lord, You have made known your will to us that we should pray for You to send forth laborers into Your harvest. We earnestly ask you to send forth into the world true teachers and ministers of Your Word, and to enlighten their minds with the knowledge of Your truth, that they may faithfully make known the whole counsel of God unto salvation, to the glory of Your name and the saving of souls; through Jesus Christ, our Lord and Savior. Amen.

*(The presiding minister or other appointed minister may read a scripture lesson such as John 15:1-8 and may deliver an appropriate message. At the proper time, the presiding minister shall address the congregation, saying:)*

Dear friends, we are assembled before God to install the Reverend ____________________, who has answered your call to become the pastor of this church, and whose installation has been duly authorized by the ____________________ District of The Wesleyan Church.

*(The pastor shall come and stand before the presiding minister, who shall address the pastor, saying:)*

Dear fellow minister, the duties of your holy office are clearly set forth in the Word of God. As an ambassador of our Lord Jesus Christ, you are first of all to preach both Law and Gospel, as they are comprehended in the Holy Scriptures and defined in *The Discipline* of The Wesleyan Church. This you are to do without the addition of private opinion, as the apostle admonishes, "If anyone speaks, he should do it as one speaking the very words of God" (1 Peter 4:11, NIV).

Whatever is contrary to sound doctrine shall be refuted with all restraint as the Scripture warns, "The Lord's servant must not quarrel; instead, he must be kind to everyone, able to teach, not resentful. Those who oppose him he must gently instruct" (2 Tim. 2:24-25a, NIV).

Those who are committed to your pastoral care are to be diligently admonished to walk in the commandments of the Lord blamelessly. The erring are to be warned with the fidelity which the Word of the Lord demands of faithful pastors, as the Prophet Ezekiel was instructed, "Son of man, I have made you a watchman for the house of Israel" (Ezek. 3:17, NIV).

You are also to be the steward of the holy sacraments which you are to administer to the comfort of troubled souls.

In view of the Savior's gracious words, "Let the little children come to me" (Mark 10:14, NIV), the children and youth of the church must in a special sense be the object of your pastoral instruction and care.

The measure of faithfulness with which you are to seek the erring is set forth in the Holy Scriptures in the words of the Apostle Paul who said, "I never stopped warning each of you night and day with tears" (Acts 20:31, NIV).

The example of holy men and women of God will impel you to pray diligently for your people and to be a pattern unto them in faith and good works.

Do you therefore earnestly purpose to diligently fulfill these duties, and thus be able in this life to answer before The Wesleyan Church and the church universal, and in the life to come to give an account before the judgment seat of Christ?

**Answer:** Yes, I do so purpose, by the help of God.

"In the presence of God and of Christ Jesus, who will judge the living and the dead, and in view of his appearing and his kingdom, I give you this charge: Preach the Word, be prepared in season and out of season; correct, rebuke and encourage—with great patience and careful instruction . . . keep your head in all situations, endure hardship, do the work of an evangelist, discharge all the duties of your ministry" (2 Tim. 4:1-2, 5, NIV).

*(The congregation shall rise, and the presiding minister shall address them, saying:)*

And now, dear friends, I admonish you to receive as your pastor, the Reverend _____________, whom God has given you. Accept the Word of God as preached by His messenger to you, whether it be for your comfort, your admonition or your instruction, even as Christ has said, "Consider carefully how you listen" (Luke 8:18, NIV).

Use all diligence that your children receive instruction in the Christian faith and are present with you in the services at God's house, in accordance with the counsel of the Apostle Paul to Christian parents to bring children "up in the training and instruction of the Lord" (Eph. 6:4, NIV).

Pray for your pastor that the ministry offered in this place may tend to the salvation of many souls, and that through sacrificial labors, you, together with your pastor, may be saved.

Honor and esteem the one who is to minister to your souls. As the Apostle Paul exhorts, "Respect those who work hard among you, who are over you in the Lord and who admonish you. Hold them in the highest regard in love because of their work. Live in peace with each other" (1 Thess. 5:12-13, NIV).

Do you now, as becomes a Christian church, accept these obligations?

**Answer:** Yes, by the help of God.

*(Then the presiding minister shall address the pastor, saying:)*

Upon these, your solemn mutual promises, I now install you, the Reverend ____________, as pastor of the ____________ Wesleyan Church, in the name of the Father, and of the Son, and of the Holy Spirit. Amen.

*(Then the presiding minister shall lead in prayer, concluding by leading the congregation in the Lord's Prayer. Then the presiding minister shall address the congregation and the pastor, saying:)*

The Lord bless you that you may bring forth much fruit and that your fruit may remain.

*(Then the congregation shall join in singing a hymn such as, "A Charge to Keep I Have." Then the congregation may come forward to greet the pastor and family at the altar. The pastor shall pronounce the benediction.)*

## C. Installation of Local Church Officers

### 5915. Order of Installation of Local Church Officers.

*(This installation may be held during a Sunday morning service or other appropriate service just prior to the time when the newly elected officers shall assume their duties. The congregation may join in singing a hymn, such as: "A Charge to Keep I Have," or "I'll Live for Him Who Died for Me." The pastor may read a scripture lesson such as Acts 2:41-44 and 6:1-8. Depending upon the number of officers involved, the pastor may wish to read something concerning their duties from* The Discipline. *At the proper time, the pastor shall call the newly elected officers before the congregation, and shall address them, saying:)*

Dear friends, it is recorded in the Acts of the Apostles that when the early church was growing and the number of disciples was multiplying, and the duties of the church so increased, and so became diversified, that the church called its members together and chose those of good report, full of the Holy Spirit and wisdom, to assist in administering the affairs of the church; and that the officers thus chosen by the church were set before the apostles, who laid hands on them and prayed, thus setting them apart in the presence of the church to the duties of their honorable office.

In like manner this church, having first sought the guidance of the divine Spirit, has chosen you to similar offices to be associated with those already in office and with the pastor before whom you have now come for public consecration.

Therefore, we, the pastor and the people of this church, call upon you to hear and join in this pledge of trust to Christ and His church.

### The Officers' Pledge

**5920.** Trusting in Jesus Christ, the great Head of the church, I humbly promise Him and His church that I will be faithful to the extent of my ability to all known duties and responsibilities assigned to me as an officer of this church. I will endeavor to be regular in my attendance, cheerful in my service, wholehearted in my giving, open-minded in my planning, patient in the face of trials, persistent in the face of difficulty, and Christlike in my faithfulness to His service. I will seek by example and precept the promotion of Christian fellowship among all our members and the spreading of the message of full salvation at home and abroad. Do you cheerfully and yet solemnly accept the obligations of this pledge?

**Answer:** I do.

*(Then the pastor shall address the congregation, asking them to stand, and saying:)*

We, the pastor and officers of this church, call upon the members and friends of this church to hear and join in this pledge of loyalty to those called of God and elected by the church as its leaders.

### The Church's Pledge

**5925.** Having chosen these officers to guide us in the administration of the church, we, its members and friends, do now pledge our loyalty to its work and promise our consideration of the plans and our friendly cooperation in the service suggested to us. We acknowledge our duty and declare our determination to pray for all our leaders and to share with them in the glorious responsibility of spreading the good news, thus hastening the coming of Christ. Do you cheerfully and yet solemnly accept the obligations of this pledge?

**Answer:** We do.

*(The officers shall then kneel at the altar while the pastor and people offer prayer in their behalf.)*

## D. Installation of District Superintendent

**5930. Order of Installation of a District Superintendent.**

*(The General Superintendent or representative shall be in charge of installing the district superintendent before the adjournment of the district conference in which election to the office has occurred (1935:10). The newly elected district superintendent, and such other district officers as are desired, shall be called before the General Superintendent, who shall first address the district superintendent, saying:)*

District superintendent ________________, today you stand before us along with the other duly elected officers of the district. You have been prayerfully selected by this district conference to serve as leader of the ____________________ District of The Wesleyan Church. It is in you that the ministers and members of the various churches within the bounds of this district are investing their confidence and trust. Yours is indeed a position of significant honor and responsibility, and it is only as God is with you that you will be enabled to fill it.

In counseling, may He grant needed grace; in decisions, may He impart of His wisdom; in labors, may your secret be His all-sufficient strength; in administration's numerous phases, may He be your "very present help." The support and cooperation of this body are assured you in the days that lie ahead. Together may you build a district that knows its best days spiritually, numerically and materially as well.

And now, that we may hear publicly your intentions to accept this charge with proper regard for all that is therewith involved, we ask you in the presence of God and of these witnesses, do you accept the office of superintendent of the ______________ District, and do you hereby solemnly covenant to discharge your duties to God, to The Wesleyan Church and to all the members of the __________________ District, according to *The Discipline* and in the fear of God?

**Answer:** I do, God being my helper.

*(The General Superintendent shall address the other district officers, saying:)*

Do you, as officers representing the ______________ District, covenant to support the district superintendent and to discharge your several duties to God, to The Wesleyan Church and to all the members of this district, according to *The Discipline* and in the fear of God?

**Answer:** We do, God being our helper.

*(Then the General Superintendent shall address the district superintendent, saying:)*

As representative of The Wesleyan Church, I charge you with this responsibility and declare you to be formally installed as superintendent of the ________________ District, entitled to the rights and privileges thereunto pertaining.

*(Then the General Superintendent shall lead in prayer.)*

### E. Installation of General Officials

**5935. Order of Installation of General Officials.**

*(In the parts of the service prior to the actual installation, a scripture lesson such as 1 Corinthians 12:14-28 shall be read. The person appointed to preside over the service shall be responsible for giving the various charges, and shall address the congregation, saying:)*

According to Acts, chapter 6, the Holy Spirit led the first-century church to select persons for positions of service according to gifts bestowed upon them. So the Holy Spirit has led The Wesleyan Church to choose persons believed to be blameless in heart as well as in life, possessing in measure the qualifications for the offices to which they are called. These persons we now come to set apart as General Officials.

*(Then the chair shall address those elected as General Superintendents, saying:)*

Will the *General Superintendents-elect* please stand. __________, __*Names of elected*__, ______________, the Church has called you to its most honored and responsible place of leadership, to the office of General Superintendent. This high office is one of great importance and dignity, imposing weighty responsibilities and demanding earnest, arduous and self-sacrificing labor. In assuming your duties, you become stewards over the spiritual and temporal affairs of the Church worldwide.

You have been chosen for the office of General Superintendent because the Church recognizes in you the leadership abilities to carry spiritual and administrative authority in humility that is born of love. Further, you exemplify the high standard for Christian leadership set forth in the Word of God by Paul in the first chapter of his epistle to Titus, when he said, "Since an overseer is entrusted with God's work, he must be blameless—not overbearing, not quick-tempered, not given to drunkenness, not violent, not pursuing dishonest gain. Rather he must be hospitable, one who loves what is good, who is self-controlled, upright, holy and disciplined. He must hold firmly to the trustworthy message as it has been taught, so that he can encourage others by sound doctrine and refute those who oppose it" (Titus 1:7-9, NIV).

Do you accept the office of General Superintendent, and promise that you will faithfully endeavor to discharge your duties as set forth in *The Discipline* of The Wesleyan Church?

**Answer:** I do.

Inasmuch as the Church has elected you to this high office, and you have declared your willingness to accept it and your sincere purpose to discharge faithfully your duties as a General Superintendent, you are hereby set apart to this service in the Church.

May faith, courage, knowledge, temperance, patience, godliness, brotherly kindness and charity be in you and abound, so that you shall neither be barren nor unfruitful in your leadership of the Church. Amen.

*(Then the General Superintendents shall be seated, and the chair shall address those others elected as General Officials, saying:)*

The Church is served by General Officials, some elected by this General Conference, and some elected by the General Board.

Will _______________, elected as General Secretary; ____________ elected as General Director of Communications; _______________, elected as General Director of Sunday School and Discipleship Ministries ;_________________, elected as General Director of Evangelism and Church Growth; ___________________, elected as General Director of Education and the Ministry; ___________________, elected as General Director of World Missions; ______________________, elected as General Director of Youth; _______________________________, elected as General Treasurer; ___________________, elected ___________________, as General Publisher; and ___________________, elected as General Director of Estate and Gift Planning please stand.

The Wesleyan Church has honored you by electing you to stand with the General Superintendents as the general officials of the Church. These are highly esteemed places of leadership. In assuming these offices, you become the recipients of respect and deference from faithful Wesleyans around the world.

In connection with your respective offices, *The Discipline* charges you under the direction of the General Board with the responsibility of the secretarial and corporate affairs of the Church, the editorship of the official Church publication, the development and promotion of the work of the Sunday schools, the promotion and administration of the outreach of the Church into new areas of the homeland, the promotion and correlation of the Church's educational institutions, the administration of a program of worldwide missions, the development and promotion of the work of the youth of the Church, the administration of the financial affairs of the Church, the publication and distribution of materials as resources for the growth of the Church, the communication of the gospel through the written and spoken word, and the promotion of the current and ongoing stewardship of those who make up our fellowship. Your service in these offices will impose duties which cannot be faithfully performed without self-denial and self-sacrifice. You must spend and be spent for the Church in the spirit of joyful service. Your election to these offices is evidence of the confidence the Church has in you as Christian leaders. May your leadership always inspire such confidence, to the glory of God.

Do you accept the office to which the Church has elected you, and do you promise to discharge your duties as God may help you?

**Answer:** I do.

Inasmuch as the Church has elected you to these high offices, and you have declared your willingness to accept them and your sincere purpose to discharge faithfully your several duties, you are now set apart to this service in the Church.

May you be strong to do God's will and have great joy in your labors. Amen.

*(Then the other general officials shall be seated, and the chair shall address the area representatives of the General Board, saying:)*

Will the area representatives of the General Board please stand.

Having carefully considered the responsibilities and obligations of service as members of the General Board as set forth in *The Discipline* of The Wesleyan Church, will you, with just appreciation of these responsibilities and obligations, accept this service to which you are called?

**Answer:** I will.

Will you promise that, always seeking divine help, you will faithfully serve as a member of the General Board of The Wesleyan Church, assisting to govern and direct its affairs in a manner which will make for peace, purity and spiritual growth throughout the denomination?

**Answer:** I will.

*(The General Superintendents and other general officials shall stand once again, and the chair shall address them and the area representatives of the General Board collectively, saying:)*

Forasmuch as you have been chosen and have declared your willingness to accept the service to which you have been elected, you are hereby formally recognized as the general officials and General Board of The Wesleyan Church. May you always be worthy of the honor conferred upon you and the trust reposed in you by the Church. And may God, by whose providence you have been set apart to this service, grant that "the whole body, joined and held together by every supporting ligament, grows and builds itself up in love, as each part does its work." Amen.

*(Then the chair shall address the congregation, saying:)*

Have you, members and representatives of The Wesleyan Church, worldwide, seeking the guidance of divine wisdom, chosen the persons who now stand before you to take charge of your denominational activities and interests as general officials and members of the General Board?

**Answer:** We have.

Will you pledge to honor, encourage and cooperate with them in all things consistent with the will of God, and will you zealously aid them in the discharge of their official duties?

**Answer:** We will.

*(Then the chair shall address the General Superintendents, other general officials and area representatives of the General Board, saying:)*

Take to yourselves the office to which you have been called, in the name of the Father, and of the Son, and of the Holy Spirit. Amen.

*(Then the chair shall pray:)*

O Lord, we ask that you set apart these Your servants unto the work to which You have called them by the voice of the Church.

Endue them with heavenly vision. Grant to them Your grace that they may serve You well, being full of the Holy Spirit and of faith, administering the work of their office in the fear of the Lord.

Give these Your servants favor and influence throughout Your Church. May Your work increase and advance because of Your blessings and their diligence.

Equip these officers for their respective duties and enable them to be faithful in all things, so that when the Great Shepherd shall appear, each may receive a crown of glory that does not fade away.

Through Christ we bring this petition. Amen.

## F. Installation of a College/University President

**5945. Order of Installation of a College/University President.**

*(The General Superintendent, chair of the board of trustees or other appointed official shall formally and officially install a college/university president at the proper time during the convocation of inauguration. The chair shall address the president, saying:)*

President ___________, you have been chosen as the leader of ___________ College/University. The Wesleyan Church is placing under your guidance and leadership not only the physical plant which is about us, the loyal faculty which serves here, but also the sons and daughters from our homes who are to be nurtured in the Christian tradition. They are the foundation both for tomorrow's Church and for your future constituency.

As president of ___________ College/University, yours is both a priceless heritage and a grave responsibility. You are to be the one to whom all institutional personnel are responsible. It will be your task to interpret the college/university program to the faculty, the student body, the board of trustees, the constituency and the general public. Yours is one of many educational institutions which through an unending stream of trained youth constantly condition the thought life of our age. The heritage, the doctrines and the ideals of The Wesleyan Church will be projected to succeeding generations only as you dedicate yourself to their preservation in the present. And if free institutions are to endure in the society of which we are a part, you must carry a flaming torch of democratic idealism.

You have been called to this important task because we have confidence in your leadership, in your ability, in your Christian integrity and in your consecration to the sacred task before you. We pledge to you our cooperation, our financial support and our prayers for the days which are ahead.

By the authority vested in me as chair of the board of trustees of ____________ College/University, I hereby place in your hands the official seal of the institution as the insignia of your authority and declare you formally installed as president of ____________ College/University.

# Chapter X

# DEDICATION SERVICES

## A. Dedication of a Church Building

### 5950. Order of Dedication of a Church Building.

#### Call to Worship

*(The pastor or other appointed minister shall give the call to worship:)*

"Worship the Lord with gladness; come before him with joyful songs. Know that the Lord is God. It is he who made us, and we are his; we are his people, the sheep of his pasture. Enter his gates with thanksgiving, and his courts with praise; give thanks to him and praise his name" (Ps. 100:2-4, NIV).

#### Invocation

*(Then the pastor or other appointed minister may pray an extemporaneous invocation or use the following:)*

O God, eternal and ever blessed, who delights in the assembling of your people in the sanctuary; receive us graciously as we come into your house, and grant that peace and prosperity may be found within its walls, that the glory of God may be the light thereof, and that we may be satisfied with the goodness of your house; through Jesus Christ our Lord. Amen.

#### Hymns

*(Then the congregation shall join in singing a hymn, such as one of the following: "All Hail the Power of Jesus' Name," "O Worship the King," "The Church's One Foundation," "I Love Thy Kingdom, Lord.")*

#### Scripture Readings

*(Then the pastor or other appointed minister shall read a scripture lesson, such as one of the following: 2 Chron. 6:1-2, 18-21, 40-42; 7:1-4; Ps. 24; Ps. 84; Heb. 10:19-25.)*

### Sermon

*(The General Superintendent, the district superintendent or other appointed minister may be asked to deliver a message on the nature and task of the church.)*

### Offering

*(It is much to be desired that all money required for the erection and completion of a house in which to worship God shall be fully provided before the day of dedication; but where this is not done, appeals may be made either just before or following the sermon. No building shall be dedicated to God until approved as financially secure and properly deeded as specified in* The Discipline.*)*

### Presentation of Building for Dedication

*(Then the district superintendent or representative shall stand at the pulpit facing the trustees of the church. The chair of the trustees shall address the district superintendent, saying:)*

On behalf of the trustees, the members and this congregation, I present you this building to be dedicated to God as a place of worship and of service in His kingdom.

### Acceptance of Building for Dedication

*(Then the district superintendent shall respond, saying:)*

Dear friends, for countless centuries people have erected buildings for the public worship of God, and have separated these buildings from all unhallowed uses in order to increase their reverence for God and for those places in which they commune with Him. We rejoice that God has put it into the hearts of His people to build this house in this place to the glory of His name. I now accept this building, to be known as the ____________ Wesleyan Church, to dedicate it and to set it apart for the worship of Almighty God and the service of all people. Let us therefore, as we are assembled, solemnly dedicate this place to its proper and sacred uses.

### Litany of Dedication

*(Then the district superintendent shall cause the congregation to stand and to join in the responsive litany of dedication:)*

**Leader:** To the glory of God the Father, who has called us by His grace; to the honor of His Son, who loved us and gave Himself for us; to the praise of the Holy Spirit, who illumines and sanctifies us;
**Congregation:** We dedicate this house.
**Leader:** For the worship of God in prayer and praise;
**Congregation:** For the preaching of the everlasting gospel;
**Leader:** For the celebration of the holy sacraments;
**All:** We dedicate this house.
**Leader:** For the comfort of all who mourn;
**Congregation:** For strength to those who are tempted;
**Leader:** For light to those who seek the way;
**All:** We dedicate this house.
**Leader:** For the hallowing of family life;
**Congregation:** For teaching and guiding the young;
**Leader:** For the perfecting of the saints;
**All:** We dedicate this house.
**Leader:** For the conversion of sinners;
**Congregation:** For the sanctification of believers;
**Leader:** For the promotion of righteousness; for the extension of the kingdom of God;
**All:** We dedicate this house.
**Leader:** In the unity of the faith; in the bond of Christian brotherhood; in charity and goodwill to all;
**Congregation:** We dedicate this house.
**Leader:** In gratitude for the labors of all who love and serve this church; in loving remembrance of those who have finished their course; in the hope of a blessed immortality through Jesus Christ our Lord;
**Congregation:** We dedicate this house.
**All in Unison:** We now, the people of this church and congregation, surrounded by a great cloud of witnesses, grateful for our heritage, sensible of the sacrifice of our fathers in the faith, confessing that apart from us their work cannot be made perfect, do dedicate ourselves anew to the worship and service of Almighty God; through Jesus Christ our Lord. Amen.

### Prayer of Dedication

*(Then the district superintendent shall give an extemporaneous prayer of dedication, or use the following:)*

Almighty God, we are not worthy to offer unto You anything belonging unto us. We humbly acknowledge that "except the Lord build the house, they labor in vain that build it." Yet we ask that in Your great goodness you would accept the dedication of this place to Your service. Prosper this our undertaking. Receive the prayers and intercessions of all your servants who shall call upon You in this house. Give them grace to prepare their hearts to serve You with reverence and godly fear. Affect them with a solemn apprehension of Your divine majesty, and a deep sense of their own unworthiness. May they always approach Your sanctuary with lowliness and devotion. May they always come before You with clean thoughts and pure hearts, with bodies undefiled and minds sanctified. May they always perform a service acceptable to You, through Jesus Christ our Lord. Amen.

**Hymn**

*(Then the congregation shall join in singing a hymn, such as: "Lead On, O King Eternal.")*

**Benediction**

*(Then the pastor or other appointed minister shall pronounce the benediction:)*

May You, O Lord our God, make this house Your abiding place from this day forth, and let Your ministers be clothed with salvation, let Your saints rejoice in goodness all their days, as the blessings of God the Father, the Son and the Holy Spirit rest and abide upon them. Amen.

## B. Dedication of Parsonage

**5975. Order of Dedication of a Parsonage.**

*(At the time appointed for the dedication service, an appropriate hymn may be sung by the congregation or by a soloist or choir. Suitable numbers include: "Happy the Home When God Is There," and "Bless This House." Then the pastor or other appointed minister shall give an extemporaneous prayer. Then the pastor or other appointed minister shall give a scripture reading, such as 1 Cor. 9:7-10, 13-14. Then the district superintendent [cf. 1310:11] or representative shall address the congregation, saying:)*

The Scriptures clearly teach that as Aaron was divinely appointed to the priesthood, even so today persons are called to the ministry for the purpose of preaching the Word and otherwise giving aid and comfort to the spiritually needy. In the same divine program it is also "commanded that those who preach the gospel should receive their living from the gospel" (1 Cor. 9:14, NIV). Providing a house for the pastor is a recognition of the minister's high office and great value to the church. It is a wise provision contributing to proper temporal support. This house about to be dedicated as a pastor's home has been made possible by the generous gifts of those who are interested in the ministry and the church such ministry represents.

*(Then the trustees of the church shall come and stand before the district superintendent, and the chair of the trustees shall address the district superintendent, saying:)*

On behalf of the trustees, the members and this congregation, I present this house to be dedicated to God as the home for the person whom He has appointed to pastor this people.

*(Then the district superintendent may give an appropriate discourse, gratefully commending the people for providing this house and charging the pastor to live here in the fear of God and as a faithful servant of the people. Then the district superintendent shall offer a prayer of dedication, such as the following:)*

O most gracious Lord, we acknowledge that we are not worthy to offer unto You anything belonging to us. Yet we ask that You accept the dedication of this home to Your service, and that You will prosper this our undertaking.

Grant that whoever shall dwell in this house shall be so yielded and dedicated to Your service as "vessels sanctified and meet for the Master's use, prepared unto every good work," that their ministry shall be a heavenly benediction to all they meet.

Grant, O Lord, that whoever shall enter this the home of Your ministering servants shall be made to sense Your presence, and as they depart shall be strengthened to walk in Your holy commandments, and that all who minister to the material comforts of Your servants in this home shall be richly rewarded by You.

Grant, O Lord, that all who come to this home for spiritual counsel and comfort, shall be made both to perceive and know what things they ought to do, and may have power and strength to fulfill the same.

Grant, O Lord, that whoever shall be joined together in the holy estate of matrimony in this home may faithfully perform and keep the vow and covenant made between them, and may remain in perfect love together all of their lives.

Grant, O Lord, that at the family altar of this home, when prayer with thanksgiving and supplication shall be offered, that they may receive from Your hand such things as are necessary. Also, that as Your servants study and search Your Word, that divine illumination for life and duty may be given as in Your infinite wisdom You shall see to be most expedient for them.

All of this we ask in the name of Jesus Christ, our most blessed Lord and Savior. Amen.

*(Then the district superintendent shall address the congregation, saying:)*

I now declare this house duly set apart as the residence of the pastor of the ____________ Wesleyan Church.

*(Then the district superintendent or other appointed minister shall pronounce the benediction:)*

The Lord bless you, and keep you: the Lord make His face to shine upon you, and be gracious unto you: the Lord lift up His countenance upon you, and give you peace. Amen.

# PART XI

# FORMS

## Chapter I

## CHURCH LETTERS

### A. Letter of Transfer – Covenant Member

**6000. Letter Sent by Church Granting Transfer to Another Wesleyan Church** (cf. 575-580).

To the pastor and secretary of the ____________ Wesleyan Church.

This certifies that ______________ is a covenant member in good standing in the ____________ Wesleyan Church, and being desirous of transferring membership to your church, is hereby transferred and commended to your care and fellowship.

By authority and in behalf of the ______________ Wesleyan Church, this ______ day of ________, A.D. ________.

________________________
Pastor

________________________
Secretary

The member's relationship at the church granting the letter continues until the member is duly received by the church to which the member is being transferred.

**6010. Acknowledgment Sent by Receiving Church** (cf. 575).

To the pastor and secretary of the _____________ Wesleyan Church.

This certifies that _______________, for whom you issued a letter of transfer dated the ______ day of _________, A.D. ________, has been duly received by the ________________ Wesleyan Church on the ______ day of

________, A.D. ________, and we send you this acknowledgment in order that you may complete your record of this transfer.

________________________
Pastor

________________________
Secretary

**6020. Notice Sent to Member Being Transferred.**

We have on this date, the ______ day of __________, A.D. ________, issued a letter of transfer of your membership to the ________________ Wesleyan Church, commending you to its care and fellowship. May the Lord bless you in your new relationship.

________________________
Pastor

________________________
Secretary

**B. Letter of Recommendation – Covenant Member**

**6030. Letter Given to Person Desiring to Transfer to Another Denomination** (cf. 590).

This certifies that ____________, the bearer, has been up to this date an acceptable covenant member of the ______________ Wesleyan Church, and being desirous of removing from said church, is hereby released and cordially recommended to the Christian confidence of those to whom this certificate may be presented.

By authority and in behalf of the ______________ Wesleyan Church, this ______ day of __________, A.D. ________.

________________________
Pastor

________________________
Secretary

It is understood that this letter of recommendation terminates the bearer's membership in The Wesleyan Church immediately.

### C. Letter of Withdrawal – Covenant or Community Member

**6040. Letter Given to Person Desiring to Withdraw from the Church** (cf. 592; 5302).

This certifies that ___________, the bearer, has been up to this date a _____________* member of the _____________ Wesleyan Church, and being desirous of withdrawing from said Church, is hereby declared to be withdrawn.

By authority and in behalf of the _____________ Wesleyan Church, this ______ day of __________, A.D. ________.

_________________________
Pastor

_________________________
Secretary

It is understood that this letter of withdrawal terminates the bearer's membership in The Wesleyan Church immediately.

(*Insert the proper term, namely covenant or community.)

# Chapter II

# SERVICE CREDENTIALS

## A. Ministerial Credentials

**6200. Lay Minister's License** (cf. 3410).

This certifies that ________________, having been duly examined concerning ___________ gifts, graces and usefulness, and being deemed qualified for such service, is hereby licensed according to the usages of The Wesleyan Church as a lay minister, for one year, provided that ________________ spirit, practice and teachings are in keeping with the Scriptures and *The Discipline* of The Wesleyan Church.

By order and in behalf of the local church conference of _____________ Wesleyan Church, this _____ day of __________, A.D. ________.

_______________________
Pastor

_______________________
Secretary

(This license may be renewed annually, and when so renewed, notation shall be made on the reverse side of this form of the date on which such renewal was ordered, and the same shall be attested by the signature of the pastor and the local church secretary.)

**6220. Lay Minister's Letter of Standing** (cf. 3440:3).

This certifies that ________________ has been up to this date a lay minister in good standing in the ________________ Wesleyan Church, and being desirous of transferring ___________ membership from this church, is granted this letter of standing to recommend __________________ to whomsoever it may concern as a person worthy of consideration for license as a lay minister.

By the authority and in behalf of the ________________ Wesleyan Church, this _____ day of _________, A.D. ________.

_______________________
Pastor

_______________________
Secretary

**6240. Certificate of Authorization as a Supply Pastor** (cf. 3260).

This certifies that ___________ has been appointed on a temporary basis as a supply pastor of the _______________ Wesleyan Church, and is hereby authorized to fill its pulpit, to provide spiritual leadership to the congregation and to perform such other duties as shall be authorized by the district superintendent.

By the authority and in behalf of the ____________ District of The Wesleyan Church, this _____ day of _________, A.D. ________.

_________________________
District Superintendent

_________________________
District Secretary

**6260. District License** (cf. 3015:1, 5b; 3033:9).

This certifies that _________________, having been duly examined concerning ____________ gifts, graces and usefulness, and being deemed qualified for such service, is hereby made ____________* according to the usages of The Wesleyan Church, for one year, provided that ___________ spirit, practice and ministry are in keeping with the Scriptures and *The Discipline* of The Wesleyan Church.

By order and on behalf of the district conference of the _________________ District of The Wesleyan Church, this _____ day of _________, A.D. _______.

_________________________
District Superintendent

_________________________
District Secretary

(*Insert the proper term, namely licensed minister or ministerial student. This license may be renewed annually; and when so renewed notation shall be made on the reverse side of this form on which such renewal was ordered, and the same shall be attested by the signature of the district superintendent and the district secretary.)

**6280. Commission Certificate for a Minister** (cf. 3059:1).

This certifies that ______________, having been judged worthy and well qualified for such a ministry, and having been duly elected by the ____________ District Conference of The Wesleyan Church, has been set apart this day, by the laying on of hands and prayer, to service as a commissioned minister in The Wesleyan Church so long as ___________ spirit, practice and ministry are in keeping with the Scriptures and *The Discipline* of The Wesleyan Church, and __________________ is hereby empowered and fully authorized to administer the sacraments of baptism and the Lord's Supper, to solemnize matrimony and to feed the flock of Christ, taking oversight thereof, not as lord over God's heritage, but as being an example to the same.

By the order and in behalf of the district conference of the ________________ District of The Wesleyan Church, this _____ day of _________, A.D. ________.

________________________
General Superintendent

________________________
District Superintendent

________________________
District Secretary

**6300. Certificate of Ordination** (cf. 3070).

This certifies that ____________, having been judged worthy and well qualified for such a ministry, and having been duly elected by the ___________ District Conference of The Wesleyan Church, has been set apart this day, by the laying on of hands and prayer, to the office and work of an *ordained minister* in The Wesleyan Church so long as ________________ spirit, practice and ministry are in keeping with the Scriptures and *The Discipline* of The Wesleyan Church, and __________ is hereby empowered and fully authorized to administer the sacraments of baptism and the Lord's Supper, to solemnize matrimony and to feed the flock of Christ, taking oversight thereof, not as lord over God's heritage, but as being an example to the same.

By order and in behalf of the district conference of the ________________ District of The Wesleyan Church, this _____ day of _________, A.D. ________.

________________________
General Superintendent

________________________
District Superintendent

________________________
District Secretary

**6320. Certificate of Validation for Minister Transferring from Another Denomination** (cf. 3104).

This certifies that the ______________ District Conference of The Wesleyan Church, having examined the credentials of ___________, a(n) ___________* of the __________ Church, and having received other testimonials of ___________ graces, gifts and usefulness, and being satisfied that ___________ is a person worthy and well qualified for such a ministry, has this day accepted and recognized ___________ in due form as a(n) ___________* in The Wesleyan Church, entitled to exercise under its authority all the functions pertaining to a(n) ______________* so long as __________________ spirit, practice and ministry are in keeping with the Scriptures and *The Discipline* of The Wesleyan Church.

By order and in behalf of the district conference of the __________ District of The Wesleyan Church, this _____ day of __________, A.D. _______.

______________________
General Superintendent

______________________
District Superintendent

______________________
District Secretary

(*Insert the proper term, namely ordained minister, commissioned minister or licensed minister.)

**6340. General Evangelist's Certificate** (cf. 3285).

This certifies that ______________, a(n) ______________* of the ___________ District of The Wesleyan Church, having been appointed by the district to the work of evangelism and being recommended by that district as a person qualified for such service to the Church at large, is hereby authorized to exercise the ministry of a *general evangelist* for one year from the date hereto affixed and is recommended to all whom it may concern for employment as an evangelist.

By order and in behalf of the district conference of the __________ District of The Wesleyan Church, this _____ day of _________, A.D. _______.

______________________
General Director of
Evangelism and Church Growth

______________________
District Superintendent

______________________
District Secretary

(*Insert the proper term, namely ordained minister or commissioned minister.)

(This certificate may be renewed annually; and when so renewed, notation shall be made on the reverse side of this form of the date on which such renewal was ordered, and the same shall be attested by the signature of the district superintendent and the district secretary.)

## B. Special Worker's Credentials

**6360. Special Worker's License** (cf. 3460).

This certifies that ___________, having been duly examined concerning _______ gifts, graces and usefulness, and being deemed qualified for such service, is hereby made a *licensed special worker* according to the usages of The Wesleyan Church, and is authorized to serve as a _________* for one year, provided that ________ spirit, practice and service are in keeping with the Scriptures and *The Discipline* of The Wesleyan Church.

By order and in behalf of the district conference of the _________ District of The Wesleyan Church, this _____ day of __________, A.D. _________.

_________________________
District Superintendent

_________________________
District Secretary

(*Insert the proper term, such as director of music, director of Christian education, youth director, song evangelist, chalk artist, children's worker, spouse in ministry, lay evangelist or social worker.)

(This license may be renewed annually; and when so renewed, notation shall be made on the reverse side of this form of the date on which such renewal was ordered, and the same shall be attested by the signature of the district superintendent and the district secretary.)

**6380. Special Worker's Commission** (cf. 3470).

This certifies that ________________ has this day been consecrated according to the usages of The Wesleyan Church to service as a *commissioned special worker*, having been judged worthy and well qualified for such service, and this commission shall recommend ______________ to all whom it may concern as a proper person to do the work of a ____________* so long as ___________ spirit, practice and service are in keeping with the Scriptures and *The Discipline* of The Wesleyan Church, and _____________ continues to be actively engaged in such work.

By order and in behalf of the district conference of the ________ District of The Wesleyan Church, this _____ day of _________, A.D. ________.

_________________________
General Superintendent

_________________________
District Superintendent

_________________________
District Secretary

(*Insert the proper term, such as director of music, director of Christian education, youth director, song evangelist, chalk artist, children's worker, spouse in ministry, lay evangelist or social worker.)

**6400. Lay Missionary's Commission** (cf. 3490).

This certifies that ___________ has been appointed by the General Board of The Wesleyan Church to service as a *lay missionary* under the direction of the General Department of ___________*, that ___________ has been consecrated to such service by the ___________________ District of The Wesleyan Church, and that this commission shall remain in effect throughout ______________ period of service under such appointment and direction as listed on the reverse side of this commission.

By order and in behalf of the district conference of the __________ District of The Wesleyan Church, this _____ day of ________, A.D. ________.

_________________________
General Superintendent

_________________________
District Superintendent

_________________________
District Secretary

(*World Missions or Evangelism and Church Growth.)

(This certificate may be renewed annually; and when so renewed, notation shall be made on the reverse side of this form of the date on which such renewal was ordered, and the same shall be attested by the signature of the district superintendent and the district secretary.)

On reverse side:

Renewal ordered on: ______(date)______

_______________________
District Superintendent

_______________________
District Secretary

### C. General Credentials

**6410. Course of Study Certificate** (cf. 3033:3; 3040:2; 3070:3; 3170; 3200; 3470).

This certifies that ___________, has completed the Course of Study for ____________* authorized in *The Discipline* of The Wesleyan Church and provided by the General Board, *or the equivalent* of said Course, having satisfactorily passed examination in each subject.

By order and in behalf of the district conference of the __________ District of The Wesleyan Church, this _____ day of _________, A.D. ________.

_______________________
Director of Ministerial Study Course Agency

(*Insert the name of the particular Course of Study, namely that of Lay Minister, Pre-Ordination, Ministers of Music, Ministers of Christian Education, Special Workers, Directors of Music, Directors of Christian Education, Evangelistic Singers, Chalk Artists, Children's Workers, Spouses in Ministry, Lay Evangelists or Social Workers.)

**6420. Recommendation for District License** (cf. 3015:1; 3033:4; 3410; 3460).

This certifies that ____________, a covenant member in good standing of the ____________________ Wesleyan Church, is hereby recommended by ___________ local church conference to the ____________ District Conference of The Wesleyan Church as having the graces, gifts, usefulness and other qualifications necessary for district authorization to serve as a _________*.

By order and in behalf of the local church conference of the ____________ Wesleyan Church, this _____ day of _______, A.D. _____.

____________________
Pastor

____________________
Secretary

(*Insert the proper term, namely ministerial student, licensed minister or licensed special worker. If licensed special worker, add the particular type of service, such as licensed special worker - director of music, director of Christian education, youth director, song evangelist, chalk artist, children's worker, spouse in ministry, lay evangelist or social worker.)

**6430. Pocket Certificate of Standing** (cf. 3015:5b; 3055:2; 3059:4b; 3089:2).

This certifies that ________________ was, on this _____ day of __________, A.D. ________, a(n) __________* in good standing of the ______________ District of The Wesleyan Church.

____________________
District Secretary

Valid only for one year, and only when signed by the secretary.

(*Insert the proper term such as ordained minister, commissioned minister, licensed minister, ministerial student, commissioned special worker or licensed special worker.)

**6440. District Letter of Transfer** (cf. 3100:1; 3480).

To the superintendent of the ________________ District of The Wesleyan Church.

This certifies that ____________ is a(n) ___________* in good standing in the ______________ District of The Wesleyan Church, and, having requested a transfer, is hereby transferred and recommended to your district, subject to the action of said district.

By the authority and in behalf of the ______________ District of The Wesleyan Church, this _____ day of _________, A.D. _______.

____________________
District Superintendent

The person for whom the letter is granted shall continue as a member of the district granting the letter until the district receiving the letter replies on form 6450.

(*Insert the proper term, namely appointed ordained minister, ordained minister on reserve, ordained minister on educational leave, retired ordained minister, ordained minister without appointment, commissioned minister, licensed minister, ministerial student, commissioned special worker or licensed special worker. If licensed special worker, add the particular type of service, such as licensed special worker - director of music, director of Christian education, youth director, song evangelist, chalk artist, children's worker, spouse in ministry, lay evangelist or social worker. If the person being transferred is a licensed minister or licensed special worker, the transfer is not valid unless accompanied by a properly attested statement of standing in the course of study and of the person's service record in the district.)

**6450. Acknowledgment of District Letter of Transfer** (cf. 3100:1; 3480).

To the superintendent of the ________________ District of The Wesleyan Church.

This certifies that _____________, for whom you issued a letter of transfer as a(n) ______________* dated the _____ day of ___________, A.D. _______, has been duly enrolled by the District as a(n) ______________*, the transfer having been completed on the _____ day of _________, A.D. _______, and we send you this acknowledgment in order that you may complete your record of the transfer.

By the authority and in behalf of the ____________ District of The Wesleyan Church, this _____ day of _________, A.D. _______.

________________________
District Superintendent

(*Insert the proper term, namely appointed ordained minister, ordained minister on reserve, ordained minister on educational leave, retired ordained minister, ordained minister without appointment, commissioned minister, licensed minister, ministerial student, commissioned special worker or licensed special worker. If licensed special worker, add the particular type of service, such as licensed special worker - director of music, director of Christian education, youth director, song evangelist, chalk artist, children's worker, spouse in ministry, lay evangelist or social worker.)

**6460. District Letter of Standing** (cf. 3100:3; 3480).

This certifies that ___________ has been up to this date a(n) ______________* in good standing in the _____________ District of The Wesleyan Church, and being desirous of removing from The Wesleyan Church, is hereby released and cordially recommended to the Christian confidence of those to whom this letter may be presented.

By the authority and in behalf of ________________ District of The Wesleyan Church, this ______ day of __________, A.D. ________.

____________________________
District Superintendent

It is understood that this letter terminates immediately any relationship the bearer may have had to The Wesleyan Church as a minister or special worker.

(*Insert the proper term, namely ordained minister, commissioned minister, licensed minister, ministerial student, commissioned special worker or licensed special worker. If licensed special worker, add the particular type of service, such as licensed special worker - director of music, director of Christian education, youth director, song evangelist, chalk artist, children's worker, spouse in ministry, lay evangelist or social worker.)

# APPENDICES

## APPENDIX A

## CHARTER OF THE WESLEYAN WORLD FELLOWSHIP

**6500. Article 1. Name.** The name of the organization shall be the Wesleyan World Fellowship.

**6505. Article 2. Purpose.** The purpose shall be to provide an inclusive fellowship and mutual understanding among the various Wesleyan-Arminian churches which have originated from within or have otherwise affiliated with The Wesleyan Church; to preserve unity in faith and doctrine while recognizing national, language and cultural distinctives; to promote holiness evangelization worldwide; to foster interrelation/interaction toward joint planning and cooperative functions.

**6510. Article 3. Membership.**

### A. Membership Categories

(1) The Wesleyan World Fellowship shall make provision for full members and associate members.

(2) **Full Members.** Full members shall be as follows:

(a) They shall consist of those bodies which have originated in or which have affiliated with The Wesleyan Church which adhere to the Essentials of The Wesleyan Church and subscribe to the provisions of this Charter.

(b) A church body which has not originated in but wishes to affiliate with The Wesleyan Church, if it is deemed by the General Council of the Wesleyan World Fellowship to qualify for full standing as a general conference in keeping with Article 3:B:2, and if it agrees to adhere to the Essentials of The Wesleyan Church and to subscribe to the other provisions of this Charter, may be received by vote of the General Council and the approval of the general administrative boards of the several fully established general conferences.

(c) A church body which has not originated in but wishes to affiliate with The Wesleyan Church, if it is deemed by the General Council of the WWF not to qualify for general conference status, may be directed by the General Council or its Executive Committee to a member general conference for affiliation.

(3) **Associate Members.** Associate members shall consist of church bodies of comparable general conference status which have not originated in or affiliated with The Wesleyan Church. An associate member shall be in harmony with the Essentials of The Wesleyan Church, shall subscribe to other provisions of The Wesleyan World Fellowship Charter and shall be received by vote of the General Council and approval of the general administrative boards of the several fully established general conferences. Their members shall have all rights of the General Council except being officers or members-at-large of the Executive Committee.

(4) Full and associate members shall meet the financial obligations of membership as determined by the General Council.

### B. Membership Status

(1) There shall be three ranks of members: general conferences, provisional general conferences and mission units.

(2) A general conference is a body that has full power over the Church in its assigned territory, in keeping with the Charter of the Wesleyan World Fellowship and other regulations for the World Organization of The Wesleyan Church as shall be legislated and declared from time to time (cf. 1015-1017).

(3) A provisional general conference is a body which has originated in or affiliated with one of the general conferences of The Wesleyan Church and which has been authorized by its general conference on the grounds that the following requirements have been satisfied:

(a) An effective church organization on the local, district, and/or general levels.

(b) Effective programs for the nurture and training of members, new converts, children, young people, and lay workers.

(c) An effective program for ministerial training.

(d) Evidence of responsible stewardship of life and possessions, including the proper management of funds and the provision for the support of its own pastors, workers, and officers.

(e) A definite program of evangelism, church extension, and missionary outreach on an indigenous basis.

(f) The existence of a property-holding body, or more than one such body if required by local laws.

(g) Agreement to adhere to the Essentials of The Wesleyan Church.

(h) A discipline as approved by the general administrative board of the originating/initiating general conference. If the use of the name, "The Wesleyan Church," is impossible or impractical, the general administrative board of the originating/initiating general conference, after consultation with the equivalent boards of the other fully established general conferences, may approve an adaptation for use by the new provisional general conference.

A provisional general conference may be advanced to the status of a general conference by its originating/initiating general conference following a satisfactory record as a provisional general conference for at least four years, and upon recommendation from the General Board of Administration of its originating/initiating general conference.

(4) Mission units shall be bodies such as national or regional multi-district conferences, established districts, provisional districts, or pioneer districts functioning under a missions department of a general or a provisional general conference.

## THE ESSENTIALS

**6520. Article 4. The Essentials of The Wesleyan Church.**

(1) **Statement of Definition and Purpose.** The Essentials of The Wesleyan Church consist of an historic statement of faith and practice. Each general conference of The Wesleyan Church must subscribe to the Essentials. While each general conference is free to express its beliefs and practices in the terms most meaningful to its immediate mission and culture, it shall not in its constitution, articles of religion, or discipline contravene or contradict any provision of the Essentials.

(2) **Statement of Faith.**

### Articles of Religion

#### *1. Faith in the Holy Trinity*

**6530.** We believe in the one living and true God, both holy and loving, eternal, unlimited in power, wisdom and goodness, the Creator and Preserver of all things. Within this unity there are three persons of one essential nature, power and eternity—the Father, the Son and the Holy Spirit.

**Gen. 1:1; 17:1; Ex. 3:13-15; 33:20; Deut. 6:4; Ps. 90:2; Isa. 40:28-29; Matt. 3:16-17; 28:19; John 1:1-2; 4:24; 16:13; 17:3; Acts 5:3-4; 17:24-25; 1 Cor. 8:4, 6; Eph. 2:18; Phil. 2:6; Col. 1:16-17; 1 Tim. 1:17; Heb. 1:8; 1 John 5:20.**

#### *2. The Father*

**6540.** We believe the Father is the Source of all that exists, whether of matter or spirit. With the Son and the Holy Spirit, He made man in His image.

By intention, He relates to man as Father, thereby forever declaring His goodwill toward man. In love, He both seeks and receives penitent sinners.

**Ps. 68:5; Isa. 64:8; Matt. 7:11; John 3:17; Rom. 8:15; 1 Peter 1:17.**

### *3. The Son of God*

**6550.** We believe in Jesus Christ, the only begotten Son of God. He was conceived by the Holy Spirit and born of the Virgin Mary, truly God and truly man. He died on the cross and was buried, to be a sacrifice both for original sin and for all the transgressions of men, and to reconcile us to God. Christ rose bodily from the dead, and ascended into heaven, and there intercedes for us at the Father's right hand until He returns to judge all men at the last day.

**Ps. 16:8-10; Matt. 1:21, 23; 11:27; 16:28; 27:62-66; 28:5-9, 16-17; Mark 10:45; 15; 16:6-7; Luke 1:27, 31, 35; 24:4-8, 23; John 1:1, 14, 18; 3:16-17; 20:26-29; 21; Acts 1:2-3; 2:24-31; 4:12; 10:40; Rom. 5:10, 18; 8:34; 14:9; 1 Cor. 15:3-8, 14; 2 Cor. 5:18-19; Gal. 1:4; 2:20; 4:4-5; Eph. 5:2; 1 Tim. 1:15; Heb 2:17; 7:27; 9:14, 28; 10:12; 13:20; 1 Peter 2:24; 1 John 2:2; 4:14.**

### *4. The Holy Spirit*

**6560.** We believe in the Holy Spirit who proceeds from the Father and the Son, and is of the same essential nature, majesty and glory, as the Father and the Son, truly and eternally God. He is the Administrator of grace to all mankind, and is particularly the effective Agent in conviction for sin, in regeneration, in sanctification and in glorification. He is ever present, assuring, preserving, guiding and enabling the believer.

**Job 33:4; Matt. 28:19; John 4:24; 14:16-17; 15:26; 16:13-15; Acts 5:3-4; Rom. 8:9; 2 Cor. 3:17; Gal. 4:6.**

### *5. The Sufficiency and Full Authority of the Holy Scriptures for Salvation*

**6570.** We believe that the books of the Old and New Testaments constitute the Holy Scriptures. They are the inspired and infallibly written Word of God, fully inerrant in their original manuscripts and superior to all human authority, and have been transmitted to the present without corruption of any essential doctrine. We believe that they contain all things necessary to salvation; so that whatever is not read therein, nor may be proved thereby, is not to be required of any man that it should be believed as an article of faith, or be thought requisite or necessary to salvation. Both in the

Old and New Testaments life is offered to mankind ultimately through Christ, who is the only Mediator between God and man. The New Testament teaches Christians how to fulfill the moral principles of the Old Testament, calling for loving obedience to God made possible by the indwelling presence of His Holy Spirit.

The canonical books of the Old Testament are:

Genesis, Exodus, Leviticus, Numbers, Deuteronomy, Joshua, Judges, Ruth, 1 Samuel, 2 Samuel, 1 Kings, 2 Kings, 1 Chronicles, 2 Chronicles, Ezra, Nehemiah, Esther, Job, Psalms, Proverbs, Ecclesiastes, The Song of Solomon, Isaiah, Jeremiah, Lamentations, Ezekiel, Daniel, Hosea, Joel, Amos, Obadiah, Jonah, Micah, Nahum, Habakkuk, Zephaniah, Haggai, Zechariah and Malachi.

The canonical books of the New Testament are:

Matthew, Mark, Luke, John, Acts, Romans, 1 Corinthians, 2 Corinthians, Galatians, Ephesians, Philippians, Colossians, 1 Thessalonians, 2 Thessalonians, 1 Timothy, 2 Timothy, Titus, Philemon, Hebrews, James, 1 Peter, 2 Peter, 1 John, 2 John, 3 John, Jude and Revelation.

**Ps. 19:7; Matt. 5:17-19; 22:37-40; Luke 24:27, 44; John 1:45; 5:46; 17:17; Acts 17:2, 11; Rom. 1:2; 15:4, 8; 16:26; 2 Cor. 1:20; Gal. 1:8; Eph. 2:15-16; 1 Tim. 2:5; 2 Tim. 3:15-17; Heb. 4:12; 10:1; 11:39; James 1:21; 1 Peter 1:23; 2 Peter 1:19-21; 1 John 2:3-7; Rev. 22:18-19.**

### *6. God's Purpose for Man*

**6580.** We believe that the two great commandments which require us to love the Lord our God with all the heart, and our neighbors as ourselves, summarize the divine law as it is revealed in the Scriptures. They are the perfect measure and norm of human duty, both for the ordering and directing of families and nations, and all other social bodies, and for individual acts, by which we are required to acknowledge God as our only Supreme Ruler, and all men as created by Him, equal in all natural rights. Therefore all men should so order all their individual, social and political acts as to give to God entire and absolute obedience, and to assure to all men the enjoyment of every natural right, as well as to promote the fulfillment of each in the possession and exercise of such rights.

**Lev. 19:18, 34; Deut. 1:16-17; Job 31:13-14; Jer. 21:12; 22:3; Micah 6:8; Matt. 5:44-48; 7:12; Mark 12:28-31; Luke 6:27-29, 35; John 13:34-35; Acts 10:34-35; 17:26; Rom. 12:9; 13:1, 7-8, 10; Gal. 5:14; 6:10; Titus 3:1; James 2:8; 1 Peter 2:17; 1 John 2:5; 4:12-13; 2 John 6.**

### *7. Marriage and the Family*

**6590.** We believe that man is created in the image of God, that human sexuality reflects that image in terms of intimate love, communication, fellowship, subordination of the self to the larger whole, and fulfillment. God's Word makes use of the marriage relationship as the supreme metaphor for His relationship with His covenant people and for revealing the truth that that relationship is of one God with one people. Therefore God's plan for human sexuality is that it is to be expressed only in a monogamous lifelong relationship between one man and one woman within the framework of marriage. This is the only relationship which is divinely designed for the birth and rearing of children and is a covenant union made in the sight of God, taking priority over every other human relationship.

**Gen. 1:27-28; 2:18, 20, 23, 24; Isa. 54:4-8; 62:5b; Jer. 3:14; Ezek. 16:3ff.; Hosea 2; Mal. 2:14; Matt. 19:4-6; Mark 10:9; John 2:1-2, 11; 1 Tim. 5:14; 1 Cor. 9:5; Eph. 5:23-32; Heb. 13:4; Rev. 19:7-8.**

### *8. Man's Choice*

**6600.** We believe that man's creation in the image of God included ability to choose between right and wrong. Thus man was made morally responsible for his choices. But since the fall of Adam, man is unable in his own strength to do the right. This is due to original sin, which is not simply the following of Adam's example, but rather the corruption of the nature of every man, and is reproduced naturally in Adam's descendants. Because of it, man is very far gone from original righteousness, and of his own nature is continually inclined to evil. He cannot of himself even call upon God or exercise faith for salvation. But through Jesus Christ the prevenient grace of God makes possible what man in himself cannot do. It is bestowed freely upon all men, enabling all who will to turn and be saved.

**Gen. 6:5; 8:21; Deut. 30:19; Josh. 24:15; 1 Kings 20:40; Ps. 51:5; Isa. 64:6; Jer. 17:9; Mark 7:21-23; Luke 16:15; John 7:17; Rom. 3:10-12; 5:12-21; 1 Cor. 15:22; Eph. 2:1-3; 1 Tim. 2:5; Titus 3:5; Heb. 11:6; Rev. 22:17.**

### *9. The Atonement*

**6610.** We believe that Christ's offering of himself, once and for all, through His sufferings and meritorious death on the cross, provides the perfect redemption and atonement for the sins of the whole world, both original and actual. There is no other ground of salvation from sin but that alone. This atonement is sufficient for every individual of Adam's race. It is unconditionally effective in the salvation of those mentally incompetent from birth, of those converted persons who have become mentally incompetent, and of children under the age of accountability. But it is effective for the salvation of those who reach the age of accountability only when they repent and exercise faith in Christ.

**Isa. 52:13-53:12; Luke 24:46-47; John 3:16; Acts 3:18; 4:12; Rom. 3:20, 24-26; 5:8-11, 13, 18-20; 7:7; 8:34; 1 Cor. 6:11; 15:22; Gal. 2:16; 3:2-3; Eph. 1:7; 2:13, 16; 1 Tim. 2:5-6; Heb. 7:23-27; 9:11-15, 24-28; 10:14; 1 John 2:2; 4:10.**

### *10. Repentance and Faith*

**6620.** We believe that for man to appropriate what God's prevenient grace has made possible, he must voluntarily respond in repentance and faith. The ability comes from God, but the act is man's.

Repentance is prompted by the convicting ministry of the Holy Spirit. It involves a willful change of mind that renounces sin and longs for righteousness, a godly sorrow for and a confession of past sins, proper restitution for wrongdoings, and a resolution to reform the life. Repentance is the precondition for saving faith, and without it saving faith is impossible. Faith, in turn, is the only condition of salvation. It begins in the agreement of the mind and the consent of the will to the truth of the gospel, but issues in a complete reliance by the whole person in the saving ability of Jesus Christ and a complete trusting of oneself to Him as Savior and Lord. Saving faith is expressed in a public acknowledgment of His Lordship and an identification with His church.

**Mark 1:15; Luke 5:32; 13:3; 24:47; John 3:16; 17:20; 20:31; Acts 5:31; 10:43; 11:18; 16:31; 20:21; 26:20; Rom. 1:16; 2:4; 10:8-10, 17; Gal. 3:26; Eph. 2:8; 4:4-6; Phil. 3:9; 2 Thess. 2:13; 2 Tim. 2:25; Heb. 11:6; 12:2; 1 Peter 1:9; 2 Peter 3:9.**

### *11. Justification and Regeneration*

**6630.** We believe that when man repents of his sin and believes on the Lord Jesus Christ, he in the same moment is justified, regenerated, adopted into the family of God, and assured of his salvation through the witness of the Spirit.

We believe that we are accounted righteous before God only on the basis of the merit of our Lord and Saviour Jesus Christ, being justified by faith alone, and not on the basis of our own works.

We believe that regeneration is that work of the Holy Spirit by which the pardoned sinner becomes a child of God. This new life is received through faith in Jesus Christ, and by it the regenerate are delivered from the power of sin which reigns over all the unregenerate, so that they love God and through grace serve Him with the will and affections of the heart, receiving the Spirit of Adoption.

**Justification:** **Hab. 2:4; Acts 13:38-39; 15:11; 16:31; Rom. 1:17; 3:28; 4:2-5; 5:1-2; Gal. 3:6-14; Eph. 2:8-9; Phil 3:9; Heb. 10:38.**
**Regeneration:** **John 1:12-13; 3:3, 5-8; 2 Cor. 5:17; Gal. 3:26; Eph. 2:5, 10, 19; 4:24; Col. 3:10; Titus 3:5; James 1:18; 1 Peter 1:3-4; 2 Peter 1:4; 1 John 3:1.**
**Adoption:** **Rom. 8:15; Gal. 4:5, 7; Eph. 1:5.**
**Witness of the Spirit: Rom. 8:16-17; Gal. 4:6; 1 John 2:3; 3:14, 18-19.**

### *12. Good Works*

**6640.** We believe that although good works cannot save us from our sins or from God's judgment, they are the fruit of faith and follow after regeneration. Therefore they are pleasing and acceptable to God in Christ, and by them a living faith may be as evidently known as a tree is discerned by its fruit.

**Matt. 5:16: 7:16-20; John 15:8; Rom 3:20; 4:2, 4, 6; Gal. 2:16; 5:6; Eph. 2:10; Phil. 1:11; Col. 1:10; 1 Thess. 1:3; Titus 2:14; 3:5; James 2:18, 22; 1 Peter 2:9, 12.**

### *13. Sin After Regeneration*

**6650.** We believe that after we have experienced regeneration, it is possible to fall into sin, for in this life there is no such height or strength of holiness from which it is impossible to fall. But by the grace of God one who has fallen into sin may by true repentance and faith find forgiveness and restoration.

**Mal. 3:7; Matt. 18:21-22; John 15:4-6; 1 Tim. 4:1, 16; Heb. 10:35-39; 1 John 1:9; 2:1, 24-25.**

### *14. Sanctification: Initial, Progressive, Entire*

**6655.** We believe that sanctification is that work of the Holy Spirit by which the child of God is separated from sin unto God and is enabled to love God with all his heart and to walk in all His holy commandments blameless. Sanctification is initiated at the moment of justification and regeneration. From that moment there is a gradual or progressive sanctification as the believer walks with God and daily grows in grace and in a more perfect obedience to God. This prepares for the crisis of entire sanctification which is wrought instantaneously when the believer presents himself a living sacrifice, holy and acceptable to God, through faith in Jesus Christ, being effected by the baptism with the Holy Spirit who cleanses the heart from all inbred sin. The crisis of entire sanctification perfects the believer in love and empowers him for effective service. It is followed by lifelong growth in grace and the knowledge of our Lord and Saviour, Jesus Christ. The life of holiness continues through faith in the sanctifying blood of Christ and evidences itself by loving obedience to God's revealed will.

**Gen. 17:1; Deut. 30:6; Ps. 130:8; Isa. 6:1-6, 35; Ezek. 36:25-29; Matt. 5:8, 48; Luke 1:74-75; 3:16-17; 24:49; John 17:1-26; Acts 1:4-5, 8; 2:1-4; 15:8-9; 26:18; Rom. 8:3-4; 1 Cor. 1:2; 6:11; 2 Cor. 7:1; Eph. 4:13, 24; 5:25-27; 1 Thess. 3:10, 12-13; 4:3, 7-8; 5:23-24; 2 Thess. 2:13; Titus 2:11-14; Heb. 10:14; 12:14; 13:12; James 3:17-18; 4:8; 1 Peter 1:2; 2 Peter 1:4; 1 John 1:7, 9; 3:8-9; 4:17-18; Jude 24.**

### *15. The Gifts of the Spirit*

**6670.** We believe that the Gift of the Spirit is the Holy Spirit himself, and He is to be desired more than the gifts of the Spirit which He in His wise counsel bestows upon individual members of the Church to enable them properly to fulfill their function as members of the body of Christ. The gifts of the Spirit, although not always identifiable with natural abilities, function through them for the edification of the whole church. These gifts are to be exercised in love under the administration of the Lord of the church, not through human volition. The relative value of the gifts of the Spirit is to be tested by their usefulness in the church and not by the ecstasy produced in the ones receiving them.

**Luke 11:13; 24:49; Acts 1:4; 2:38-39; 8:19-20; 10:45; 11:17; Rom. 12:4-8; 1 Cor. 12:1-14:40; Eph. 4:7-8, 11-16; Heb. 2:4; 13:20-21; 1 Peter 4:8-11.**

### *16. The Church*

**6680.** We believe that the Christian church is the entire body of believers in Jesus Christ, who is the founder and only Head of the church. The church includes both those believers who have gone to be with the Lord and those who remain on the earth, having renounced the world, the flesh and the devil, and having dedicated themselves to the work which Christ committed unto His church until He comes. The church on earth is to preach the pure Word of God, properly administer the sacraments according to Christ's instructions, and live in obedience to all that Christ commands. A local church is a body of believers formally organized on gospel principles, meeting regularly for the purposes of evangelism, nurture, fellowship and worship. The Wesleyan Church is a denomination consisting of those members within district conferences and local churches who as members of the body of Christ, hold the faith set forth in these Articles of Religion and acknowledge the ecclesiastical authority of its governing bodies.

**Matt. 16:18; 18:17; Acts 2:41-47; 9:31; 11:22; 12:5; 14:23; 15:22; 20:28; 1 Cor. 1:2; 12:28; 16:1; 2 Cor. 1:1; Gal. 1:2; Eph. 1:22-23; 2:19-22; 3:9-10, 21; 5:22-33; Col. 1:18, 24; 1 Thess. 1:1; 2 Thess. 1:1; 1 Tim. 3:15; Heb. 12:23; James 5:14.**

### *17. The Sacraments: Baptism and the Lord's Supper*

**6690.** We believe that water baptism and the Lord's Supper are the sacraments of the church commanded by Christ and ordained as a means of grace when received through faith. They are tokens of our profession of Christian faith and signs of God's gracious ministry toward us. By them, He works within us to quicken, strengthen and confirm our faith.

We believe that water baptism is a sacrament of the church, commanded by our Lord and administered to believers. It is a symbol of the new covenant of grace and signifies acceptance of the benefits of the atonement of Jesus Christ. By means of this sacrament, believers declare their faith in Jesus Christ as Savior.

**Matt. 3:13-17; 28:19; Mark 1:9-11; John 3:5, 22, 26; 4:1-2; Acts 2:38-39, 41; 8:12-17, 36-38; 9:18; 16:15, 33; 18:8; 19:5; 22:16; Rom 2:28-29; 4:11; 6:3-4; 1 Cor. 12:13; Gal. 3:27-29; Col. 2:11-12; Titus 3:5.**

**6700.** We believe that the Lord's Supper is a sacrament of our redemption by Christ's death and of our hope in His victorious return, as well as a sign of the love that Christians have for each other. To such as receive it humbly, with a proper spirit and by faith, the Lord's Supper is made a means through which God communicates grace to the heart.

**Matt. 26:26-28; Mark 14:22-24; Luke 22:19-20; John 6:48-58; 1 Cor. 5:7-8; 10:3-4, 16-17; 11:23-29.**

### *18. The Second Coming of Christ*

**6705.** We believe that the certainty of the personal and imminent return of Christ inspires holy living and zeal for the evangelization of the world. At His return He will fulfill all prophecies made concerning His final and complete triumph over evil.

**Job 19:25-27; Isa. 11:1-12; Zech. 14:1-11; Matt. 24:1-51; 25; 26:64; Mark 13:1-37; Luke 17:22-37; 21:5-36; John 14:1-3; Acts 1:6-11; 1 Cor. 1:7-8; 1 Thess. 1:10; 2:19; 3:13; 4:13-18; 5:1-11, 23; I2 Thess. 1:6-10; 2:1-12; Titus 2:11-14; Heb. 9:27-28; James 5:7-8; 2 Peter 3:1-14; 1 John 3:2-3; Rev. 1:7; 19:11-16; 22:6-7, 12, 20.**

### *19. The Resurrection of the Dead*

**6710.** We believe in the bodily resurrection from the dead of all mankind--of the just unto the resurrection of life, and of the unjust unto the resurrection of damnation. The resurrection of the righteous dead will occur at Christ's Second Coming, and the resurrection of the wicked will occur at a later time. The resurrection of Christ is the guarantee of the resurrection of those who are in Christ. The raised body will be a spiritual body, but the person will be whole and identifiable.

**Job 19:25-27; Dan. 12:2; Matt. 22:30-32; 28:1-20; Mark 16:1-8; Luke 14:14; 24:1-53; John 5:28-29; 11:21-27; 20:1--21:25; Acts 1:3; Rom. 8:11; 1 Cor. 6:14; 15:1-58; 2 Cor. 4:14; 5:1-11; 1 Thess. 4:13-17; Rev. 20:4-6, 11-13.**

### *20. The Judgment of Mankind*

**6715.** We believe that the Scriptures reveal God as the Judge of all mankind and the acts of His judgment are based on His omniscience and eternal justice. His administration of judgment will culminate in the final meeting of mankind before His throne of great majesty and power, where records will be examined and final rewards and punishments will be administered.

**Eccl. 12:14; Matt. 10:15; 25:31-46; Luke 11:31-32; Acts 10:42; 17:31; Rom. 2:16; 14:10-12; 2 Cor. 5:10; 2 Tim. 4:1; Heb. 9:27; 2 Peter 3:7; Rev. 20:11-13.**

### *21. Destiny*

**6720.** We believe that the Scriptures clearly teach that there is a conscious personal existence after death. The final destiny of man is determined by God's grace and man's response, evidenced inevitably by his moral character which results from his personal and volitional choices and not from any arbitrary decree of God. Heaven with its eternal glory and the blessedness of Christ's presence is the final abode of those who choose the salvation which God provides through Jesus Christ, but hell with its everlasting misery and separation from God is the final abode of those who neglect this great salvation.

**Dan. 12:2; Matt. 25:34-46; Mark 9:43-48; Luke 13:3; John 8:21-23; 14:2-3; 2 Cor. 5:6, 8, 10; Heb. 2:1-3; 9:27-28; 10:26-31; Rev. 20:14-15; 21:1-22:5, 14-15.**

**6725.** (3) **Statement of Practice.**

(a) **Identification with the church.** To be identified with an organized church is the blessed privilege and sacred duty of all who are saved from their sins, and are seeking completeness in Christ Jesus. From the church's beginnings in the New Testament age, it has been understood that such identification involves the putting off of the old patterns of conduct and the putting on of the mind of Christ, and a unity of witness and worship.

(b) **Biblical principles.** In maintaining the Christian concept of a transformed life, The Wesleyan Church intends to relate timeless biblical principles to the conditions of contemporary society in such a way as to respect the integrity of the individual believer, yet maintain the purity of the church and the effectiveness of its witness. This is done in the conviction that there is validity in the concept of the collective Christian conscience as illuminated and guided by the Holy Spirit. While variations in culture may require variations in which the transformed life is evident or demonstrated, each general conference of The Wesleyan Church will be expected to adopt guidelines for its members providing for such evidence and demonstration in conformity with biblical principles.

(c) **Worship and language.** The Wesleyan Church believes in the miraculous use of languages and the interpretation of languages in its biblical and historical setting. But it is contrary to the Word of God to teach that speaking in an unknown tongue or the gift of tongues is the evidence of the baptism of the Holy Spirit or of that entire sanctification which the baptism accomplishes; therefore, only a language readily understood by the congregation is to be used in public worship. The Wesleyan Church believes that the use of an ecstatic prayer language has no clear scriptural sanction, or any pattern of established historical usage in the Church; therefore, the use of such a prayer language shall not be promoted among us.

**6730.** (4) **Statement of Relationship.** The unity of The Wesleyan Church worldwide shall be recognized and maintained in the following:

(a) The right of a member or minister to transfer from one unit (general conference, provisional general conference, regional/national church) to any other such unit of The Wesleyan Church worldwide, with the understanding that consideration must be given to differences in requirements for licensing and ordination of ministers as provided for in the various disciplines of units worldwide.

(b) The right of a member or minister to election to office in any unit (as defined in Article 4:4a) of The Wesleyan Church worldwide provided that the qualifications of said office are met, with the understanding that the right to hold such office shall be subject to the transfer of church membership to the unit within which the election occurs and subject to *The Discipline* governing that unit.

(c) The right of any member body which has not reached the status of a fully established general conference to participate with full or partial powers through its duly elected representatives in the respective general conference to which it relates.

*(This concludes The Essentials of The Wesleyan Church)*

**6735. Article 5. General Council.**

(1) The Wesleyan World Fellowship shall function through its General Council composed of the Executive Committee and delegates elected by the following member groups:

(a) **General Conferences.** Each full member general conference shall be entitled to one ministerial and one lay delegate. After said conference has a total membership of 7,000, it shall be entitled to one additional ministerial and one additional lay delegate for each additional 7,000 members or major fraction thereof, with a maximum of 10 delegates from any one such conference. Each associate member general conference shall be entitled to one delegate.

(b) **Provisional General Conferences.** Each provisional general conference shall be entitled to one lay and one ministerial delegate.

(c) **Mission Units.** Mission units, as identified on Article 3:B:4, shall be entitled to one delegate.

(2) The General Council may provide for nonvoting delegates at its own discretion.

(3) In each case the highest interim administrative body of the general conference, provisional general conference, or other unit shall be responsible for designating delegates, and for all interrelations with the official bodies of the Wesleyan World Fellowship.

**6740. Article 6. Officers.**

(1) The officers of the General Council shall be the chairman, vice-chairman, secretary and treasurer. The offices of secretary and treasurer may be combined. The officers shall be elected by the General Council. They are *ex officio* members of the General Council.

(2) The officers shall take office at the adjournment of the General Council session electing them and shall continue in office until the adjournment of the next regular session or until their successors are elected.

(3) The person elected to the office of chairman shall not succeed himself in office.

(4) A vacancy in any office shall be filled by the Executive Committee.

(5) An executive secretary may be authorized by the General Council which shall outline his duties. His selection and conditions of service shall be under the control of the Executive Committee.

(6) The General Council may create and fill other offices as needed.

**6743. Article 7. Meetings.** The General Council shall meet at the call of its Executive Committee. If practicable it shall be held in conjunction with a meeting of one of the general conferences. It shall be the responsibility of the Executive Committee of the General Council to arrange for its meeting, considering the cost of travel, entertainment and the general interests of the entire Wesleyan World Fellowship.

**6745. Article 8. Powers and Duties.** With full respect for the authority of the several full general conferences and in harmony with the fellowship purpose of the Wesleyan World Fellowship, the powers and duties of the General Council shall be:

(1) To promote evangelism.

(2) To stimulate the deeper spiritual life of Wesleyans worldwide.

(3) To promote Wesleyan doctrines as set forth in the Essentials of The Wesleyan Church.

(4) To encourage development of each member body in support, government and propagation.

(5) To conduct a continuing study of world trends and opportunities with a view to securing united Wesleyan action.

(6) To further mutual understanding of cultural, economic, political and linguistic factors affecting the progress of the gospel.

(7) To conduct public meetings in connection with its sessions.

(8) To receive reports from member conferences and other bodies, to evaluate the same and to make recommendations to the appropriate bodies

(9) To consider the special needs common to member bodies and to make recommendations to the appropriate bodies through their respective general conference officers.

(10) To have the Executive Committee indicate, at least one year prior to the General Council, the requested assessment of each member body and to adopt a budget based on the financial obligation to be met by each member body.

(11) To receive and to process new applications for membership.

(12) To organize area fellowships where geographic situation, mutual interest and need for spiritual counsel and encouragement make it advisable.

**6750. Article 9. Executive Committee.**

(1) The Executive Committee shall consist of the Wesleyan World Fellowship officers (Article 6), one representative from each member general conference without representation by election (who shall be the highest ranking officer of that General Conference), and four ministerial and four lay members-at-large elected by the General Council with a view toward broad representation. The General Council shall set the terms of office for members at-large.

(2) Any vacancy for a member-at-large shall be filled in the same manner as a vacancy for an officer (6:4).

(3) The Executive Committee shall meet at least one year prior to the regular meeting of the General Council at a time and place consistent with the plans of its members. Special meetings may be called as deemed necessary by a majority vote of its members.

(4) The quorum shall consist of four members, two of whom shall be officers.

(5) The Executive Committee shall carry out the will of the General Council serving as necessary in the interim of General Council sessions.

(6) In the interim of General Council sessions the Executive Committee shall exercise such powers and have such duties as are assigned to it by the WWF Charter or by the General Council, and to develop plans and arrangements for the quadrennial meeting of the General Council. It may initiate, and shall review, and recommend all resolutions for the WWF General Council.

**6755. Article 10. Commissions.**

(1) The Wesleyan World Fellowship may establish commissions as it deems necessary to assist in the fulfillment of the purposes and objectives of the Fellowship.

(2) The General Council shall authorize the establishment of each commission and approve its organizational and operational guidelines which shall become its bylaws.

(3) Each commission shall be amenable to the General Council.

(4) Each commission shall report through its chair to the General Council at every regular session and to the executive committee as requested.

(5) Each commission shall submit a proposed budget for the ensuing period to the General Council for its approval along with a financial report for the concluding period.

**6760. Article 11. International Board of Review.**

(1) The International Board of Review shall be established by the several general conferences to maintain fidelity to the Essentials of The Wesleyan

Church, to adjudicate matters of comity and to supervise referendums involving more than one general conference.

(2) The International Board of Review shall be composed of the general superintendents or equivalent officers representing the fully established general conferences on the General Council of the Wesleyan World Fellowship.

(3) The International Board of Review shall elect from among its members a chair and such other officers as it shall deem necessary. It shall determine the term of their service.

(4) The provisions of the Charter of the Wesleyan World Fellowship do not give to the International Board of Review any powers which are not listed below in relation to the fully established general conferences. Its duties shall be:

(a) To hear and determine any appeals from actions of any fully established general conference as to its adherence to the Essentials of The Wesleyan Church. If the International Board of Review shall find a general conference in violation of the Essentials, that general conference shall be expected to rescind the violating action. If it does not, the International Board of Review shall report its findings and the response to the General Council, which shall have authority to expel the erring general conference. At the discretion of the General Council, it may provide for the reorganization of the loyal elements of The Wesleyan Church within the area of that general conference and for the declaration that the other ministers and members are withdrawn from The Wesleyan Church.

(b) To review the adherence of associate members to the conditions of associate membership and to recommend to the General Council the termination of their membership if violation of these conditions persist.

(c) To adjudicate any problem that may arise between general conferences involving boundaries or other matters of comity.

(d) To supervise the voting by the several fully established general conferences and/or their respective general administrative bodies on the reception of affiliating bodies and on proposed amendments to the Charter.

(5) The International Board of Review shall meet on a regular basis in conjunction with meetings of the General Council. A special meeting may be called by the chair.

**6765. Article 12. Amendments.**

(1) Amendments to the Essentials of The Wesleyan Church in Article 4 must be approved by a two-thirds aggregate vote of all general conferences who are members of the Wesleyan World Fellowship.

(2) Provisions of this Charter, other than the Essentials in Article 4, may be amended by a two-thirds vote of those present and voting at any meeting of

the General Council and are subject to the approval of the general conferences or their interim administrative bodies if so authorized.

(3) All amendments are subject to review by the International Board of Review.

(4) The International Board of Review shall supervise the referendum voting on amendments.

# APPENDIX B

# INTERPRETATIONS OF CHURCH LAW

**6800.** This section contains the official interpretations of *The Discipline* by the Board of General Superintendents which have been sustained by the General Conference and are therefore in full force and effect as church law (1920:26). Each interpretation is identified by the paragraph number of *The Discipline* to which it refers.

Whenever a revision of *The Discipline* makes an interpretation unnecessary or renders it obsolete, the interpretation is to be deleted from *The Discipline* by order of the General Conference (Minutes of the 1976 General Conference, proceeding 276).

### Trafficking

**6805. 265:4.** *The General Superintendents on November 7, 1983, officially interpreted subparagraph 265:4 and the General Conference on June 20, 1984, sustained the interpretation (GC-1984-175), thereby authorizing this provision to mean:*

"Trafficking," as used with reference to alcoholic beverages in 265:4, means "production, sale or purchase." "Production" means "activity which is a part of the manufacturing or primary distribution process." "Sale" means "giving up property to another for money or other valuable consideration."

# APPENDIX C

# WESLEYAN MEDICAL FELLOWSHIP

## Constitution of Wesleyan Medical Fellowship

**7000. Article 1. Name.** The name of this organization shall be Wesleyan Medical Fellowship.

**7010. Article 2. Purposes.** The purposes of Wesleyan Medical Fellowship are to enlist the interests of physicians, dentists and members of other medical professions in Christian projects around the world sponsored by The Wesleyan Church; to establish effective communications on a regular basis with the people in The Wesleyan Church who are in medical and related professions; to collect and to disburse funds for the operation of medical, educational, charitable and religious activities; to provide professional counsel when desired to any agency of The Wesleyan Church, especially the General Department of World Missions; to offer guidance, assistance and fraternal interest to students preparing for medical professions; to provide a means of bringing together Christian medical personnel and others for social, religious and educational benefits; and to promote by seminars and other types of learning forums the professional ethics of its members.

**7020. Article 3. Function.** The Wesleyan Medical Fellowship shall function as an auxiliary of The Wesleyan Church.

**7030. Article 4. General Wesleyan Medical Fellowship Officers.**

(1) **Identification.** The general officers of Wesleyan Medical Fellowship shall include the General Director of Wesleyan Medical Fellowship and four persons elected by the General Board to serve with the General Director of Wesleyan Medical Fellowship as the general WMF executive committee (7040:3).

(2) **Election procedure.** The general WMF executive committee shall appoint a nominating committee of not less than three members to present nominations for the General Director of WMF and the general WMF executive committee to the General Board for election, prior to each General Conference. The General Board shall elect the officers to allow proper distribution throughout the geographic expanse of The Wesleyan Church.

(3) **Term of service.** The General Director of WMF and other members of the general WMF executive committee shall serve for four years, beginning at the close of General Conference, or until their successors are elected and qualified.

(4) **Qualifications.** The general WMF officers shall be covenant members of The Wesleyan Church at the time of election and throughout their tenure.

(5) **Amenability and vacancies.** The General Director of WMF and other members of the general WMF executive committee shall be amenable to the General Board. They may be removed from office by a majority vote of all members of the General Board, which shall have power to fill any vacancy (1655:39b).

**7040. Article 5. Duties.**

**(1) Criteria.** The General Director of WMF and the general WMF executive committee shall perform their duties in keeping with the Constitution of Wesleyan Medical Fellowship, the *Policy of the General Board for Wesleyan Medical Fellowship* and *The Discipline* of The Wesleyan Church.

(2) **General Director of WMF.** The General Director of WMF shall exercise general leadership over the Wesleyan Medical Fellowship; preside over area conventions of Wesleyan Medical Fellowship whenever present; publicize and promote the interests of Wesleyan Medical Fellowship; and shall report to the General Board annually and to the General Conference quadrennially. The General Director of Wesleyan Medical Fellowship shall be a nonvoting member of the General Conference unless qualified as a voting member by some other right (1503:2).

(3) **General WMF Executive Committee.** The general WMF executive committee shall advise the General Director of WMF in all phases of this work, make recommendations to the General Board concerning Wesleyan Medical Fellowship membership dues (1655:26), and cooperate with the General Secretary of The Wesleyan Church in developing procedures for the compiling of statistics so that a record of the work may be readily maintained.

**7050. Article 6. Special Committees.** The general WMF executive committee may appoint such other committees as deemed necessary.

**7060. Article 7. General Treasurer.** The General Treasurer of The Wesleyan Church shall be the treasurer for Wesleyan Medical Fellowship (1976), receiving, holding and disbursing all funds in keeping with the financial policies adopted by the General Board for the support of auxiliaries and the recommendations of the general WMF executive committee (1655:26).

**7070. Article 8. Membership and Dues.** Membership in the Wesleyan Medical Fellowship is open to all persons of good character. Members of the medical and allied professions may be full members. Other persons of good character who support the goals and purposes of Wesleyan Medical Fellowship may be associate members. Dues shall be recommended by the general WMF executive committee and set by the General Board (7040:3).

**7080. Article 9. Meetings.** The Wesleyan Medical Fellowship shall have a quadrennial meeting at the time and place of General Conference and other meetings at the call of the general WMF executive committee with adequate notices to all members.

**7090. Article 10. Amendments.** The Constitution of Wesleyan Medical Fellowship may be amended by the General Board at any regular or special session by a majority vote (cf. 1557).

# APPENDIX D

# WESLEYAN MEN

## A. Constitution of Local Wesleyan Men

**7100. Article 1. Name.** The name of this organization shall be Wesleyan Men of ______ Wesleyan Church. (If the chapter serves more than one local church, the name of the city or region may be used.)

**7105. Article 2. Purpose.** Wesleyan Men shall seek to extend the kingdom of God through the ministries of The Wesleyan Church through soul-winning, service, stewardship and fellowship.

**7110. Article 3. Relationship.** The local chapter of Wesleyan Men shall function as a part of the local Wesleyan church, shall be subject to the supervision of the pastor (725:16) and shall be amenable to the local board of administration (782:3, 23). If the chapter serves more than one local church, it shall be amenable to the district superintendent and the district board of administration (1233:23; cf. 1310:8).

**7115. Article 4. Membership.** Membership in Wesleyan Men shall be open to all men of good character.

**7120. Article 5. Meetings.**

(1) The chapter should meet monthly for inspiration, instruction, business and fellowship.

(2) The annual meeting for the election of officers shall be held during the month preceding the close of the district fiscal year (1180:18).

**7125. Article 6. Local Wesleyan Men Officers.**

(1) **Executive Officers.** The executive officers of the local Wesleyan Men shall be the president, vice-president, secretary and treasurer, who, together with the pastor (725:18), shall constitute the local WM executive committee.

(2) **Other Officers.** Each local WM may also have such other officers and committees as it shall deem necessary, subject to the approval of the local board of administration (782:23).

(3) **Delegates.** In addition to the president of each WM chapter, who is a member of the district WM convention by virtue of his office (7130:2; 7155:2), each WM chapter shall be entitled to at least one delegate to the district WM convention. The district WM convention may establish a system of multiple representation from larger chapters.

(4) Qualifications. The executive officers and delegates of the local WM shall be laymen and members of The Wesleyan Church, except that the

membership requirement may be waived in the case of a developing church. All officers and committee members must be members of the local WM and in harmony with the doctrines and standards of The Wesleyan Church.

(5) **Election Procedure.** Executive officers, delegates and such other officers and committee members as the bylaws shall require, shall be elected by the local WM at its annual business meeting (7120:2). Preceding the annual WM election, the local WM shall elect or the local WM executive committee shall appoint, a nominating committee consisting of three to five members, over which the pastor or his representative shall preside (725:18). The nominating committee shall select two or more nominations for the local WM president, to be approved by the local board of administration and elected at the annual WM business meeting, provided that the local board of administration may make such other nominations as desired. The nominating committee shall present nominations to the local WM for all other officers, committee members and delegates. Executive officers shall be elected by ballot, and other officers, delegates and committee members may be elected in any manner desired. In all cases, election shall be by majority vote of the members of the local WM present and voting. The election must be ratified by the local board of administration before becoming final (782:23).

(6) **Term of Service.** Local WM officers shall take office at the beginning of the district fiscal year (1180:18), and shall serve until the end of the district fiscal year or until their successors are elected and qualified.

(7) **Amenability and Vacancies.** All officers and committee members of the local WM shall be amenable for their official duties to the local board of administration, and may be removed for cause or whenever the best interests of the church or the local WM so require by a majority vote of the local board of administration (782:25). The local board of administration shall have authority to see that all vacancies are filled in the manner it deems best (782:26).

**7130. Article 7. Duties of Local WM Officers.**

(1) **Criteria.** All officers shall carry out their duties in keeping with *The Discipline*, the constitution of Wesleyan Men, and the official WM handbook authorized by the General Board and issued by the general WM executive committee (cf. 1655:26; 7195:3).

(2) **Local WM President.** The president shall cooperate with the district WM president, exercise general leadership of the local Wesleyan Men under the general oversight of the pastor (725:16), preside over business meetings and meetings of the local WM executive committee (7130:6), serve as an *ex officio* member of all local WM committees, report to each regular session of the local church conference (650:2; 655:5) and to the local board of administration as it shall order (782:4), and shall serve as an *ex officio* member of the district WM convention (7155:2).

(3) **Local WM Vice-President.** The vice-president shall assist the president as the president shall request, and shall assume the duties of the president in case the president is unable to serve.

(4) **Local WM Secretary.** The secretary shall keep a record of members, and shall record the minutes of all meetings, including those of the local WM executive committee (7130:6).

(5) **Local WM Treasurer.**

(a) **Fiscal Procedures.** The treasurer shall receive, record, hold and disburse all funds of the chapter in keeping with the financial plans of the general and district organizations of Wesleyan Men, and as ordered by the chapter or its executive committee subject to the approval of the local board of administration (782:23), remitting monthly all funds intended for the district or general church to the district WM treasurer (7165:5).

(b) **Reports.** The treasurer shall make a financial report to all regular meetings of the chapter, to the local WM executive committee and to the monthly session of the local board of administration as requested (782:4), and to all regular sessions of the local church conference (650:3; 655:5). He shall submit an annual statistical report of the local WM to the district WM convention and shall assist the pastor and the local WM president as they shall request in the preparation of their reports. His books shall be submitted to the local church auditing committee annually (863), and as ordered by the local board of administration (782:4).

(6) **Local WM Executive Committee** (7125:1). The local WM president shall be chairman *ex officio* of the local WM executive committee (7130:2), and the local WM secretary shall be secretary *ex officio* (7130:4). The local WM executive committee shall direct the affairs of the local WM between business meetings of the chapter, shall make recommendations to the chapter and shall appoint all committee members not elected by the chapter. All plans and actions of the local WM executive committee may be reviewed by the local board of administration, which may veto any of the committee's plans or actions (782:23).

**7135. Article 8. Local Bylaws**. The local WM chapter may adopt such bylaws as it deems necessary, provided that they do not conflict with *The Discipline* or other directives of the general church and district, and provided they are approved by the local board of administration (782:23), or in the case of a city or regional chapter, by the district board of administration (1233:22).

## B. Constitution of District Wesleyan Men

**7140. Article 1. Name.** All local Wesleyan Men chapters within the bounds of a district shall be known collectively as Wesleyan Men of the ________ District of The Wesleyan Church.

**7145. Article 2. Purpose.** The district Wesleyan Men shall carry out the basic purpose of Wesleyan Men (7105) within the bounds of the district, organizing chapters and securing their cooperation as an effective district unit of Wesleyan Men.

**7150. Article 3. Relationship.** The district WM shall function as a part of the district of The Wesleyan Church to which it belongs, shall be subject to the supervision of the district superintendent (1310:8) and shall be amenable to the district board of administration (1233:23, 27b).

**7155. Article 4. District Wesleyan Men Convention.**

(1) **Purpose and Organization.** There shall be an annual district Wesleyan Men convention in each district at such a time and place as the district board of administration shall approve (1233:23), to receive reports (7165:2, 5), to elect district WM officers (7160:4), to make recommendations to the district board of administration and/or the general WM executive committee, to carry on all other business pertaining to the district WM, and to provide the members of the convention with a time of inspiration, fellowship and Christian challenge. The General Director of Wesleyan Men shall preside over the district WM convention when present (7195:2), and when he is absent, the district WM president shall preside (7165:2).

(2) **Membership.** The district WM convention shall be composed of the district superintendent (1303:6), the district WM officers (7165), the presidents of all local chapters (7130:2), and delegates from the local chapters (7125:3). Delegates shall be members of The Wesleyan Church, and shall be elected by the chapters at the annual meeting for the election of officers (7120:2).

(3) **Committees.** There shall be a nominating committee as set forth in 7160:4. The district WM convention may elect such other committees as it may deem necessary, and shall define the duties of the same.

(4) **Approval.** All plans and actions of the district WM convention shall be subject to the approval of the district board of administration (1233:23).

**7160. Article 5. District WM Officers.**

(1) **Executive Officers.** The executive officers shall be the president, vice-president, secretary and treasurer, who together with the district superintendent (1310:10) shall constitute the district WM executive committee.

(2) **Other Officers.** Each district WM may also have such other officers and standing committees as the district WM convention shall deem necessary.

(3) **Qualifications.** All officers and committee members must be covenant members of The Wesleyan Church, and wherever practicable, members of a local chapter of Wesleyan Men within the district. Executive officers shall be laymen.

(4) **Election Procedure.** The executive officers of the district WM and such other officers and committee members as the bylaws shall require shall be elected by the district WM convention (7155:1). The district WM convention shall elect or the district WM executive committee shall appoint a nominating committee, over which the district superintendent or his representative shall preside. Preceding the district WM convention, the nominating committee shall select two or more nominees for district WM president, for approval by the district board of administration and election by the district WM convention, provided that the district board of administration may make such other nominations as desired. The nominating committee shall present nominations to the district WM convention for all other officers and positions as requested (7155:1-3). Executive officers shall be elected by ballot and other officers may be elected in any manner desired. All offices and positions shall be filled by majority vote of the district WM convention present and voting. The election must be ratified by the district board of administration before becoming final (1233:23).

(5) **Term of Service.** District WM officers shall assume office at the close of the district convention at which they are elected and shall serve for one year or until their successors are elected and qualified.

(6) **Amenability and Vacancies.** All officers and committee members of the district WM shall be amenable to the district board of administration, and may be removed for cause or when the best interests of the WM or the district so require by a majority vote of the district board of administration. The district board of administration shall fill all vacancies. (Cf. 1233:27b.)

**7165 Article 6. Duties of District WM Officers.**

(1) **Criteria.** All officers shall carry out their duties in keeping with *The Discipline*, the constitution of Wesleyan Men and the official handbook authorized by the General Board and issued by the general WM executive committee (cf. 7195:3).

(2) **District WM President.** The president shall be responsible to cooperate with the General Director of Wesleyan Men and the general WM executive committee; to exercise general leadership of the district WM under the general oversight of the district superintendent (1310:8); to preside over meetings of the district WM executive committee (7165:6); to preside over sessions of the district WM convention except when the General Director of Wesleyan Men is present and presiding (7155:1; 7195:2); to seek to organize chapters of Wesleyan Men so as to serve each local church, whether through local church chapters, city, metropolitan, county, regional or zone chapters; to visit the local chapters as time and funds shall permit; and to report annually to the district conference (1180:13) and to the district WM convention, and at other times as ordered by the district board of

administration (1233:11). He shall be a nonvoting member of the district conference (1090:8) unless he is elected as a lay delegate by his local church.

(3) **District WM Vice-President.** The vice-president shall assist the president as the president shall request and shall assume the duties of the president in case the president is unable to serve.

(4) **District WM Secretary.** The secretary shall record the minutes of the district WM convention (7155:1) and of the meetings of the district WM executive committee (7165:6) and shall perform such other duties as the district WM convention shall determine.

(5) **District WM Treasurer**. The district WM treasurer shall receive, record and hold all funds remitted by local WM treasurers or raised by the district WM itself, forwarding specified funds and disbursing other funds in keeping with the financial plans of the general WM executive committee and the district WM convention, and as directed by the district WM executive committee. All funds intended for the general church shall be transferred monthly to the General Treasurer. The district WM treasurer shall report to the district WM executive committee as required, to the district board of administration quarterly (1233:11) and to the district conference (1180:13) and the district WM convention (7155:1) annually. His books shall be submitted to the district auditing committee annually (1340), and as ordered by the district board of administration (1233:18).

(6) **District WM Executive Committee** (7160:1). The district WM president shall be chairman *ex officio* of the district WM executive committee (7165:2), and the district WM secretary shall be secretary *ex officio* (7165:4). The district WM executive committee shall direct the affairs of the district WM between the annual district WM conventions, subject to the approval of the district board of administration (1233:23).

**7170. Article 7. District Bylaws.** The district convention of Wesleyan Men may adopt such bylaws as it deems necessary, providing that they are in accord with *The Discipline*, the constitution and purpose of WM, and other directives of the general church and district, and subject to the approval of the district board of administration (1233:23).

### C. Constitution of General Wesleyan Men

**7175. Article 1. Name.** All local and district WM organizations shall be known collectively as Wesleyan Men, an auxiliary of The Wesleyan Church.

**7180. Article 2. Purpose.** General Wesleyan Men shall carry out the basic purpose of Wesleyan Men (7105) throughout the Church, securing the cooperation of the local and district WM organizations and coordinating them as an effective arm of the Church.

**7185. Article 3. Relationship.** Wesleyan Men shall function as a part of The Wesleyan Church, and shall be amenable to the General Board.

**7190. Article 4. General WM Officers.**

(1) **Identification.** The general officers of Wesleyan Men shall include the General Director of Wesleyan Men and four persons elected by the General Board (7190:3) to serve with him as the general WM executive committee.

(2) **Qualifications.** The general WM officers shall be covenant members of The Wesleyan Church and members of a local chapter of Wesleyan Men at the time of their election and during their term of service.

(3) **Election Procedures.** The General Director of Wesleyan Men and the members of the general WM executive committee shall be elected by the General Board following a regular session of the General Conference (1655:18), selecting one executive committee member from each representative area insofar as is practicable.

(4) **Term of Service.** The general officers of Wesleyan Men shall take office at such time as the General Board shall determine (1655:26), and shall serve for four years or until their successors are elected and qualified.

(5) **Amenability and Vacancies.** The General Director of Wesleyan Men, and the other members of the general WM executive committee shall be amenable to the General Board and may be removed by a majority vote of all its members. The General Board shall fill all vacancies (1655:39b).

**7195. Article 5. Duties of General WM Officers.**

(1) **Criteria.** The General Director of Wesleyan Men and the general WM executive committee shall perform their duties in keeping with *The Discipline*, the constitution of Wesleyan Men and the *Policy of the General Board*.

(2) **General Director of Wesleyan Men.** The General Director of Wesleyan Men shall exercise general leadership of Wesleyan Men; preside over district conventions of Wesleyan Men whenever present (7155:1); publicize and promote the interests of the organization; promote the organization of Wesleyan Men on the district and local levels, devoting as much time as possible to the work; and shall report annually to the General Board (1655:21), and quadrennially to the General Conference (1590:7). He shall be a nonvoting member of the General Conference unless he is a voting member by some other right (1503:2).

(3) **General WM Executive Committee.** The general WM executive committee shall advise the General Director of Wesleyan Men in all phases of his work, and shall prepare and issue the official WM handbook (1655:26). It shall cooperate with the General Secretary in developing procedures for the compiling of statistics on the local, district and general levels, so that a record of the work may be readily maintained.

**7200. Article 6.** General Treasurer of Wesleyan Men. The General Treasurer shall be the general treasurer of Wesleyan Men (1976), receiving, holding and disbursing all funds in keeping with the financial policies adopted by the General Board for the support of auxiliaries, and the recommendations of the general WM executive committee.

### D. Amendments to Wesleyan Men Constitutions

**7210.** The local, district or general constitutions of Wesleyan Men may be amended by majority vote of the General Board at any regular or special session.

# APPENDIX E

# WESLEYAN WOMEN

**7300. Purpose:** The purpose of Wesleyan Women is to develop mature, godly women who recognize and respond to the spiritual and physical needs of persons worldwide. Core values of the auxiliary include providing fellowship and support for women, motivating a benevolent spirit of generosity, and encouraging a desire for excellence in Christian women's leadership.

**7302. Vision Statement:** Wesleyan Women doing what we can, when we can (Mark 14:8, The Message).

### A. Constitution of Local Wesleyan Women

**7306. Article 1. Name**. The name of a local organization may be Wesleyan Women of _______ Wesleyan Church or (church name) Wesleyan Women. A registered local organization is called a chapter.

**7308. Article 2. Purpose.** The local executive committee shall carry out the purposes of the auxiliary by developing an effective women's ministry in their church and providing information, instruction, and guidance. Motivation for benevolence shall be provided by promotion of local, district, and area projects and missions support.

**7310. Article 3. Relationship.** The chapter shall function as a part of the local Wesleyan Church, be subject to the supervision of the pastor, and be amenable to the local board of administration.

**7315. Article 4. Ministries.** The executive committee shall plan ministries consistent with the stated purposes of Wesleyan Women.

**(1)** Chapters are encouraged to develop a variety of ministry cells based on common interests and/or convenient meeting times.

**(2)** The women of the local church are encouraged to meet annually to evaluate the effectiveness of their ministry.

**(3)** Women who take part in any women's ministry activities in the local church shall be identified as participants.

**7320. Article 5. Finances.** Benevolence is a core value of the auxiliary. The local chapter shall cooperate with the district, area, and general organization in promoting and raising funds for administration, approved ministries, projects, and missions support. All funds raised for district and general projects and missions support are to be sent to the district Wesleyan Women treasurer.

**7325. Article 6. Local Wesleyan Women Officers.**

**(1) Executive Committee.** It is recommended that the director, assistant director, outreach director, secretary, treasurer and coordinator of Wesleyan Kids for Missions (WKFM) constitute the local executive committee. The pastor is a voting member by virtue of his office.

**(a)** Registered chapters may choose a leadership team, rather than the traditional officers listed above. This team should be established in cooperation with the pastor and the local board of administration.

**(b)** The executive committee shall direct the affairs of the chapter and the WKFM, subject to the approval of the local board of administration.

**(2) Other Officers.** Other officers and committees may be elected by the chapter or appointed by the executive committee, subject to approval of the local board of administration.

**(3) Delegates to District Wesleyan Women Convention.** Registered chapters shall be entitled to the following representation at the district convention: director, WKFM coordinator, women pastors, pastor's wife (when a church has multiple staff, she may designate another ministry wife to serve in her place), and at least one elected delegate.

**(a)** Registered chapters with team leadership may send two leaders (same as local director and local WKFM coordinator) plus the pastor's wife and elected delegate(s) according to the representation system of their district.

**(b)** The district convention may establish a system of multiple representation from larger registered chapters.

**(c)** Women's ministry groups (not registered as Wesleyan Women chapters) may send two delegates who shall be voting members of the convention.

**(4) Qualifications.** Executive officers and delegates shall be members of The Wesleyan Church and be active in that chapter's ministry.

**(5) Nominating Committee.** The nominating committee shall consist of three to five members who were elected during the previous year's annual business meeting. The pastor or his representative is a voting member by virtue of his office and shall preside over committee meetings. The nominating committee shall endeavor to present two or more nominations for director. The local board of administration must approve the nominations for local director and may make other nominations. The nominating committee should endeavor to present two or more nominations for all other elected positions.

**(6) Election Procedures.** Executive officers, delegates, nominating committee members, and other officers shall be elected at an annual business meeting. Executive officers shall be elected by ballot and by majority vote.

Other officers and committee members may be voted on or appointed in the manner desired. The election of the executive committee must be ratified by the local board of administration.

**(7) Term of Service**. The initial election of a local director is for one year and reelection thereafter may be for terms of two years. All other officers may serve for one year. However, the local executive committee, in cooperation with the pastor and the local board of administration, may recommend that the chapter vote on whether or not they wish to offer longer terms for their officers. Officers shall serve from the beginning of the district fiscal year through the agreed term or until their successors are elected.

**(8) Amenability and Vacancies**. All chapter officers, committee members, and delegates shall be amenable to the local board of administration, and may be removed for cause or whenever the best interests of the church or the chapter so require by a majority vote of the local board of administration. The local board of administration shall fill a vacancy for director from nominations by the executive committee or by the board. Other vacancies may be filled by the executive committee.

**7330. Article 7. Duties of Local Officers.**

**(1) Criteria.** Officers shall carry out their duties in keeping with *The Discipline,* the Constitution, and the *Handbook* of Wesleyan Women.

**(2) Local Director.** The local director shall cooperate with the district director, provide leadership to the chapter under the oversight of the pastor, serve as a member of all local Wesleyan Women committees except the nominating committee, report to the local church conference and to the local board of administration as requested, and shall serve as a member of the district Wesleyan Women convention.

**(3) Local Assistant Director.** The assistant director shall cooperate with the director as requested and shall be ready to assume the duties of the director when necessary.

**(4) Local Outreach Director.** The outreach director shall promote local, district, and world outreach ministries and projects.

**(5) Local Secretary.** The secretary shall keep a record of all participants at all Wesleyan Women events and shall record the minutes of all executive and chapter meetings.

**(6) Local Treasurer.**

**(a) Fiscal Procedures.** The treasurer shall receive, record, and disburse funds raised by the chapter, remitting monthly all funds intended for the district or general church to the district Wesleyan Women treasurer in keeping with the financial plans of the district and general Wesleyan Women. Funds not sent through Wesleyan Women should be handled by the church treasurer.

**(b) Reports.** The treasurer shall report to the executive committee, the local board of administration, and the local church conference as requested. She shall submit an annual report to the district Wesleyan Women treasurer. The treasurer's books shall be submitted to the local church auditing committee annually or as requested by the local board of administration.

**(7) Local Wesleyan Kids for Missions (WKFM) Coordinator.** The coordinator shall strive to lead boys and girls to Christ, to prepare them for Christian service by the study of the Bible and missions, and to raise funds for worldwide projects. She shall cooperate with the local Wesleyan Women director and executive committee. She shall receive, record, and disburse funds raised by the local WKFM, remitting monthly all funds intended for district or general projects to the district coordinator and submitting financial records to the local church auditing committee. She shall report to the district coordinator, the local church conference, and the local board of administration as requested. The coordinator is a member of the district Wesleyan Women convention.

**(8) Assistant Coordinator of Wesleyan Kids For Missions.** An assistant coordinator may be nominated by the local WKFM coordinator to be approved by the local Wesleyan Women executive committee. The assistant shall cooperate with the coordinator as requested and shall be ready to assume the duties of the coordinator when necessary.

**7335. Article 8. Local Wesleyan Kids for Missions. (WKFM).**

**(1) Purpose and Relationship**. The Wesleyan Kids for Missions is an auxiliary of Wesleyan Women that seeks to lead boys and girls to Christ, to train them for Christian service by the study of the Bible and missions, to promote among them a true interest in Christian missions, and to raise funds for worldwide evangelism. If there is no local Wesleyan Women, the local board of administration may elect a local WKFM coordinator to provide the WKFM program.

**(2) Membership and Dues**. Active membership shall include all children through grade six who pay the membership dues. Honorary membership shall be open to all persons who have completed the sixth grade or are over twelve years of age who pay the membership dues. Membership dues shall be approved by the General Board of The Wesleyan Church. For a local WKFM to be organized, there must be members paying the annual membership dues.

**(3) Meetings.** Meetings of the local WKFM shall use program materials produced by the general WKFM coordinator. Offerings will go for projects approved by the general Wesleyan Women executive committee and promoted by the general WKFM coordinator.

## B. Constitution of District Wesleyan Women

**7340. Article 1. Name**. All local chapters within the bounds of a district may be known collectively as Wesleyan Women of the ________ District of The Wesleyan Church.

**7345. Article 2. Purpose.** The district executive committee shall carry out the purposes of the auxiliary by promoting and helping develop effective women's ministries in all local churches and providing information, instruction, and guidance to chapters. Motivation for benevolence shall be provided by promotion of district, area, and general projects, and missions support.

**7350. Article 3. Relationship.** The district Wesleyan Women shall be subject to the supervision of the district superintendent and be amenable to the district board of administration.

**7355. Article 4. Ministries.** The ministries of district Wesleyan Women shall be:

**(1)** To help develop effective women's ministries in every local church. This ministry will be registered as a chapter, and leadership may be structured as the church chooses. They shall carry out the purposes of Wesleyan Women.

**(2)** To help develop WKFM units that promote ministry to children and carry out the purposes of Wesleyan Kids For Missions.

**7360. Article 5. Finances.** Benevolence is a core value of the auxiliary. The district shall cooperate with the local, area, and general organizations in promoting and raising funds for administration, approved ministries, projects, and missions support. All funds received from local chapters or raised by the district for general projects and missions support are to be sent to the general Wesleyan Women office.

**7365. Article 6. District Officers.**

**(1) Executive Committee.** It is recommended that the director, assistant director, outreach director, secretary, treasurer, and WKFM coordinator constitute the district executive committee. The district superintendent is a voting member by virtue of office.

**(a)** Some districts may choose to elect a leadership team, rather than the traditional officers listed above. This team should be established in cooperation with the district convention body, the district superintendent, and the district board of administration.

**(b)** The executive committee shall direct the affairs of the district and the WKFM, subject to the approval of the district board of administration.

**(2) Qualifications.** District officers, committee members, and general convention delegates shall be covenant members of The Wesleyan Church and active in a local chapter.

**(3) Other Officers.** Other officers and committees may be elected as desired.

**(4) Nominating Committee.** The district nominating committee shall consist of three or more members who were elected during the previous year's district convention or appointed by the executive committee. The district superintendent or a representative is a voting member by virtue of his office and shall preside over committee meetings. The nominating committee shall endeavor to present nomination(s) for director. The district board of administration must approve the nomination(s) for district director and may make other nominations. The nominating committee should endeavor to present two or more nominations for all other elected positions. It is recommended that the nominating committee represent the entire district and serve staggered terms. Members shall not serve more than three consecutive years.

**(5) Delegates to General Wesleyan Women Convention.** District delegate(s) and alternate delegates to the general convention shall be elected by ballot at the district convention preceding the general convention. If the last annual session is within sixty days of the opening date of the general convention, the district convention may elect its delegate(s) at the previous session. The (newly elected) district director, district WKFM coordinator, and elected delegate(s) shall be voting members of the general Wesleyan Women convention. If either the director or the WKFM coordinator is unable to attend, her elected assistant shall attend in her place. Alternate delegates shall fill vacancies in the order of their election. The number of delegates for which each district is eligible will be determined by the general executive committee.

**(6) Election procedure**. Executive officers, delegate(s), and other officers shall be elected at the annual district convention. Executive officers shall be elected by ballot and by majority vote. Other officers, nominating committee members, and other committee members may be elected or appointed as desired. The election of the executive committee must be ratified by the district board of administration.

**(7) Term of Service.** The initial election of a district director is for one year and reelection thereafter may be for terms of two years. All other officers may serve for one year. However, the district executive committee, in cooperation with the district superintendent and the district board of administration, may recommend that delegates to the district convention be given the opportunity to vote on longer terms for their officers. Officers shall serve from the close of the convention through the agreed term or until successors are elected.

**(8) Amenability and Vacancies.** All officers and committee members shall be amenable to the district board of administration and may be removed for cause or when the best interests of Wesleyan Women or the district so require by a majority vote of the district board of administration. The district board of administration shall fill vacancies for director from nomination(s) presented by the district Wesleyan Women executive committee; however, the district board of administration may make other nominations, if desired. Other vacancies may be filled by the executive committee.

**7370. Article 7. Duties of District Officers.**

**(1) Criteria**. All officers shall carry out their duties in keeping with *The Discipline,* the Constitution, and the *Handbook of Wesleyan Women.*

**(2) District Director.** The director shall cooperate with the General Director and the general executive committee, give leadership to the district Wesleyan Women under the oversight of the district superintendent, preside over executive committee meetings, preside over the district convention unless the General Director or her representative is present and presiding, help organize chapters in every church by working with the pastors and local boards of administration, give leadership to chapter directors, and report to the district conference, the district convention, and the district board of administration as requested. She shall be a voting member of the general Wesleyan Women convention.

**(3) Assistant District Director.** The assistant director shall cooperate with the director as requested and shall be ready to assume the duties of the director when necessary.

**(4) District Outreach Director.** The outreach director shall be responsible for coordinating local, district and general Wesleyan Women outreach ministries and projects.

**(5) District Secretary.** The secretary shall record the minutes of the district Wesleyan Women convention and of the executive committee meetings. She shall provide materials for the annual district conference journal.

**(6) District Treasurer.** The treasurer shall receive, record, and disburse funds remitted by local treasurers or raised by the district in keeping with the financial plans of the district and general Wesleyan Women. All funds intended for the general church shall be transferred monthly to the general Wesleyan Women office. The district treasurer shall report to the district executive committee, district convention, district board of administration, and district conference as requested. The treasurer's financial records shall be submitted to the district auditing committee, as directed by the district board of administration.

**(7) District Wesleyan Kids for Missions (WKFM) Coordinator.** The coordinator is encouraged to conduct an annual meeting with local WKFM coordinators for inspiration, fellowship, and instruction. The coordinator shall serve under the oversight of the district director, the district executive committee, and the district superintendent. She shall endeavor to organize units in every church by working with the pastors and the local boards of administration and provide instruction and resources to the local coordinators. The district coordinator shall receive, record, and disburse all funds remitted by local units or raised by the district WKFM in keeping with the financial plans of the district and general WKFM. The coordinator shall report to the district executive committee, the district convention, the district board of administration, and district conference as requested. The WKFM financial records shall be submitted to the district auditing committee, as directed by the district board of administration. An annual report shall be sent to the general coordinator. The district coordinator shall be a voting member of the district and general Wesleyan Women conventions.

**(8) Assistant District Coordinator of Wesleyan Kids For Missions.** An assistant coordinator may be elected by the Wesleyan Women convention body or appointed by the district coordinator subject to the approval of the executive committee. The assistant coordinator shall assist the coordinator as requested and shall be ready to assume the duties of the coordinator when necessary.

**7375. Article 8 District Convention.**

**(1) Purpose and Organization.** An annual convention shall be held to provide a time of inspiration, motivation, fellowship, and Christian challenge; to receive reports, elect district officers, make recommendations to the district board of administration and/or to the general executive committee; and to care for all district business. The General Director of Wesleyan Women or her representative shall preside over the district convention when present; otherwise, the district director shall preside. The district convention may establish and appoint convention committees as desired. A time and place for the annual convention shall be recommended by the district executive committee and approved by the district board of administration.

**(2) Voting Members of District Wesleyan Women Convention**. District officers, local directors, local WKFM coordinators, elected delegates or alternates, women pastors, the district superintendent's wife, pastors' wives, and zone chairs shall be voting members of the district convention.

**(a)** Registered chapters with team leadership may send two leaders (same as local director and local WKFM coordinator) plus the pastor's wife and elected delegate(s) according to the representation system of the district.

**(b)** With recommendation of the executive committee, the convention body may elect to establish a system of multiple representation from larger registered chapters.

**(c)** Women's ministry groups (not registered as Wesleyan Women chapters) may send two delegates who shall be voting members of the convention.

**(3) Approval.** All plans and actions adopted by the Wesleyan Women district convention shall be subject to the approval of the district board of administration.

## C. Constitution of General Wesleyan Women

**7380. Article 1. Name**. All local and district Wesleyan Women organizations shall be known collectively as Wesleyan Women, an auxiliary of The Wesleyan Church.

**7385. Article 2. Purpose**. The general executive committee shall carry out the purposes of the auxiliary by promoting and helping develop effective women's ministries for local and district levels and providing information, instruction, and guidance. Motivation for benevolence shall be provided by promotion of area and general projects and missions support.

**7390. Article 3. Relationship**. Wesleyan Women shall function as an auxiliary of The Wesleyan Church.

**7395. Article 4. Ministries**. The ministries of Wesleyan Women shall be:

**(1)** To help develop and equip district leaders to establish effective women's ministries in every local church.

**(2)** To promote a spirit of benevolence throughout the organization.

**(3)** To help develop and equip district WKFM coordinators to establish WKFM units in every local church.

**7400. Article 5. Finances**. Wesleyan Women shall promote systematic giving for general funds and approved projects, with all promotion and projects subject to the direction of the general church.

**7405. Article 6. General Wesleyan Women Convention.**

**(1) Purpose and Organization.** A general convention shall be held to provide a time of inspiration, motivation, fellowship, and Christian challenge; to receive reports, elect general Wesleyan Women officers, make recommendations to the General Board of The Wesleyan Church and/or to the general executive committee; and care for all business pertaining to the auxiliary. The general convention shall be held the year preceding General Conference at a time and place recommended by the general executive committee and approved by the General Board of The Wesleyan Church.

**(2) Voting Members.** General Wesleyan Women officers, district directors, district WKFM coordinators, and elected delegates or alternates shall be voting members of the general convention. Districts with team leadership may send two leaders (same as district director and district WKFM coordinator) and elected delegate(s) according to the representation system. Nonvoting participants shall be encouraged to attend.

**(3) Planning.** The general executive committee shall plan the general convention program, appoint necessary committees, make assignments for workshops and seminars, and receive reports for evaluation and action.

**(4) Finances.** The general executive committee shall develop a plan for the collection of funds to subsidize the expenses of the general convention.

**7410. Article 7. General Wesleyan Women Officers.**

**(1) Identification.**

**(a) Executive Officers.** The executive officers are the General Director of Wesleyan Women and the assistant general director. The General Director shall recommend an assistant general director to be approved by the executive committee and ratified by the General Board of The Wesleyan Church.

**(b) General Executive Committee**. The executive committee members are the general director, assistant general director, area representatives, and the general WKFM coordinator.

**(2) Qualifications**. Members of the executive committee shall be covenant members of The Wesleyan Church and active in a local women's ministry at the time of election and during the term of service. Each area representative must reside within the represented area.

**(3) Nominating Committee.** The nominating committee shall consist of two members from each representative area who were elected during the previous general convention. One of these shall be from the executive committee and the other from a different district in the area. No members shall succeed themselves. The supervising General Superintendent or a representative is a voting member by virtue of office and shall preside over the meetings. The nominating committee shall present the nomination(s) for General Director and area representatives. The General Board of The Wesleyan Church must approve the nomination(s) for General Director and may make other nominations. The nominating committee shall serve from the close of the general convention through the close of the following general convention.

**(4) Election Procedure.** The general convention body shall elect the General Director from the approved nominee(s).

**(5) Area Caucus.** The General Director shall appoint persons to convene caucuses of the area delegates for the purpose of electing two area representatives who will serve on the general executive committee. Consideration should be given to the names that are presented by the nominating committee; however, other nominations may be made from the floor. In addition to electing area representatives, the caucus will elect two members to the nominating committee who will serve for the following general convention. Election may be by acclamation or ballot as determined by the caucus members. Election must be ratified by the general convention.

The newly elected executive committee shall meet at the close of the general convention to establish the time and place of their first meeting.

**(6) Term of Service.** The members of the general executive committee shall be elected for a term of four years or until the next general convention. They shall serve from the close of the convention in which they are elected until the close of the next convention, or until their successors are elected

**(7) Amenability and Vacancies.** The general officers shall be amenable to the General Board of The Wesleyan Church and may be removed by a majority vote of all its members. The General Board of The Wesleyan Church shall fill the vacancy of General Director from nominations presented by the general executive committee or the General Board of The Wesleyan Church. The salary of a retiring General Director of Wesleyan Women shall continue for one month beyond the date of her termination of service. Other vacancies may be filled by the executive committee.

**7415. Article 8. Duties of General Wesleyan Women Officers.**

**(1) Criteria.** The officers shall perform their duties in keeping with *The Discipline,* the Constitution of Wesleyan Women, and the *Policy of the General Board for Wesleyan Women.*

**(2) General Director**. The General Director of Wesleyan Women shall give leadership to Wesleyan Women and WKFM under the general oversight of the supervising General Superintendent and the Wesleyan Women executive committee; be responsible for the general office; submit a nomination for an assistant director to be approved by the executive committee and ratified by the General Board of The Wesleyan Church; employ the general WKFM coordinator; preside over the general convention; preside over the general executive committee; preside over district conventions when present; endeavor to visit each district at least once during the quadrennium for inspiration and promotion of general programs and interests; authorize the assistant general director, the general WKFM coordinator or the area representatives to preside over district conventions; publicize and promote the interests of Wesleyan Women; help district directors organize local chapters; and report to the general executive committee and the General Board of The Wesleyan Church annually or as requested. She is a voting member of the General Conference.

**(3) Assistant General Director.** The assistant general director shall work under the oversight of the General Director and in cooperation with the executive committee. Her duties shall be assigned in keeping with her gifts and strengths as well as the needs of the ministry. She is nominated by the General Director, approved by the executive committee, and ratified by the General Board of The Wesleyan Church.

**(4) General Wesleyan Kids for Missions (WKFM) Coordinator.** The general WKFM coordinator shall work under the oversight of the General Director of Wesleyan Women and in cooperation with the general executive committee. She shall be chosen and employed by the General Director with ratification by the executive committee. The coordinator shall seek to carry out the purposes of WKFM by working with district and local coordinators. She shall plan, promote, and conduct a meeting of the district coordinators in conjunction with the general Wesleyan Women convention; prepare program and promotional materials for use by local and district coordinators; promote projects approved by the general executive committee; and report to the general convention and the executive committee as requested.

**(5) General Executive Committee.** The newly elected general executive committee shall meet at the close of the general convention to establish the time and place of their first meeting. The general executive committee shall hear the reports and approve the plans of the General Director and the general WKFM coordinator, assist the General Director in preparing recommendations to the General Board of The Wesleyan Church, prepare the official *Handbook of Wesleyan Women*, establish Wesleyan Women and WKFM financial plans, promote service projects, hear progress reports from area representatives, initiate plans for the advancement of the ministry, and provide for such Wesleyan Women and WKFM publications as authorized by the *Policy of the General Board for Wesleyan Women*. It shall recommend to the General Board of The Wesleyan Church the time and place for the general convention, be responsible for planning the program, and recommend to the General Board of The Wesleyan Church a plan for subsidizing the expenses of delegates attending the general convention. It shall cooperate with the General Secretary in developing procedures for compiling statistics on the local, district, and general levels.

**(6) Advisory Committee.** During the first regular meeting of the executive committee, a vice-chair and a member-at-large will be elected to serve on the advisory committee. The advisory committee members are the General Director, assistant general director, general WKFM coordinator, the vice-chair, and the member-at-large. This committee shall meet at the call of the General Director. Minutes of these meetings shall be sent to the general executive committee and the supervising General Superintendent.

**7420. Article 9. General Treasurer of Wesleyan Women.** The General Treasurer of The Wesleyan Church shall be the general treasurer of Wesleyan Women.

## D. Amendments to Wesleyan Women Constitutions

**7425.** The local, district, or general constitutions of Wesleyan Women and those parts relating to its auxiliary, WKFM, may be amended by majority vote of the General Board of The Wesleyan Church at any regular or special session.

# APPENDIX F

# WESLEYAN YOUTH

## A. Constitution of Local Wesleyan Youth

**7500. Article 1. Name.** The name of this organization shall be Wesleyan Youth of ___________ Wesleyan Church, or a local WY may select its own name and logo for local identification purposes.

**7505. Article 2. Mission.** The mission of Wesleyan Youth is to glorify God through evangelizing, nurturing and equipping youth to be spiritual leaders committed to lifelong service to Christ and His church. Wesleyan Youth ministry shall be characterized by an effective organization of youth committed to active sharing of their faith, personal and collective study of God's Word, edifying the body of Christ through the use of spiritual gifts, positive Christian fellowship, and service to their family, church, community and the world.

**7510. Article 3. Organization.** A local WY shall be considered an organized WY if it has an adult youth leader, a WY president, a secretary-treasurer, meets regularly and has registered with the General Department of Youth. In case there are no youth qualified to serve as officers, the local board of administration may grant an exemption on youth officer elections and register them as an official WY with the General Department of Youth.

**7515. Article 4. Relationship.** The local WY shall be a ministry of the local Wesleyan church, shall be subject to the supervision of the pastor (725:16), in all actions shall be amenable to the local board of administration (782:3, 23), and shall be under the direction of the local board of Christian education (880:2).

**7520. Article 5. Membership.** Any youth completing grade six (or age thirteen) through age nineteen (or high school graduation), who is in any way touched by the local church ministries and who desires to participate in the meetings and activities of WY shall be listed by the local WY secretary-treasurer as a member of the local WY.

**7525. Article 6. Meetings.**

(1) **Regular Meetings.** The local WY shall hold meetings and activities which will help it to fulfill the mission of WY (7505).

(2) **Annual Business Meetings.** The local WY shall hold an annual business meeting at a time set by the local executive youth council for the election of officers and delegates and other necessary business (cf. 7530:2).

(3) **Special Business Meetings.** The local executive youth council may call a special business meeting, subject to the approval of the pastor (725:16).

**7530. Article 7. Officers.**

(1) **Qualifications.**

(a) **Adult Youth Leader.** The adult leader shall be a covenant member of The Wesleyan Church and live a life which will inspire youth to holy living. The position may be filled by either a minister or a lay member (7530:3).

(b) **Local WY President.** The local WY president shall be a covenant member of The Wesleyan Church or a Christian youth who is in harmony with the doctrines and standards of The Wesleyan Church, and a member of the local WY.

(c) **Other WY Officers.** The local WY secretary-treasurer and any other WY officers the local WY chooses to elect shall be Christian youth who are members of the local WY and in harmony with the doctrines and standards of The Wesleyan Church.

(d) **Adult Youth Staff.** If the adult youth leader chooses to recruit additional adult staff, they shall be persons who live a life which will inspire youth to holy living and are in harmony with the doctrines and standards of The Wesleyan Church.

(2) **Elections.**

(a) **Adult Youth Leader.** The adult youth leader shall be elected by the local board of administration (782:22), considering input from local youth.

(b) **WY Officers.** The local WY president, WY secretary-treasurer, other officers and delegates to the district WY convention shall be elected by the local WY under the direction of the adult youth leader. These elections are subject to ratification by the local board of administration.

(3) **Duties of Officers.**

(a) **Adult Youth Leader.** The adult youth leader is the primary spiritual and administrative head of the local WY and shall seek to lead the youth in fulfilling the mission of WY (7505), overseeing the activities and programs of the local WY and leading by spiritual example. The adult youth leader shall serve as the chair of the annual business meeting and any special business meetings. The adult leader shall work in cooperation with and be amenable to the pastor and local board of administration.

(b) **Local WY President.** The local WY president shall cooperate with the adult youth leader in implementing the mission of WY (7505), as the local WY president seeks to lead peers by spiritual example.

(c) **Local WY Secretary-Treasurer.** The local WY secretary-treasurer, in cooperation with the adult youth leader, shall be responsible for written correspondence, membership records, minutes, statistical and financial records, and annual reports. The office of secretary-treasurer may be divided into two positions by the executive youth council.

(d) **Other Officers.** Each local WY may elect other officers, such as directors of evangelism, fellowship, service projects and others as needed to fulfill the mission of WY (7505).

(e) **Adult Youth Staff.** The adult youth leader, in consultation with the pastor, may recruit other adult staff to help carry out the ministry of WY.

(f) **Executive Youth Council.** The executive youth council shall be composed of the adult youth leader as chair, local WY president, local WY secretary-treasurer and the pastor as an *ex officio* member. All actions of the executive youth council shall be subject to the review of the local board of administration (782:23). The executive youth council may also include other adult staff or other local WY officers (7530:3e).

(g) **Delegates.** In addition to the local adult youth leader and local WY president who are members of the district WY convention by virtue of their offices, each organized local WY shall be entitled to two youth delegates to the district WY convention (7585:3). In addition, each organized local WY whose average attendance is 20 or more shall be entitled to an additional adult and youth delegate for each additional 20 youth in average attendance.

(4) **Term of Service.** Local WY officers shall take office at the beginning of the local WY year and shall serve for one year or until their successors are elected and qualified. A shorter term of service may be adopted by action of the executive youth council.

(5) **Vacancies.** All officers of the local WY shall be amenable for their official duties to the local board of administration and may be removed whenever the best interests of the church or the local WY so require by a majority vote of the local board of administration (782:25). The local board of administration shall have authority to see that all vacancies are filled in the manner it deems best (782:26).

**7540. Article 8. Age-Level Divisions.** The executive youth council may approve the organization of the local WY into two or more separate age-level divisions.

**7545. Article 9. Bylaws.** The local Wesleyan Youth may adopt such bylaws as it deems necessary, provided that they do not conflict with *The Discipline* or other directives of the general church and district, and provided they are approved by the local board of Christian education (880:2) and the local board of administration (782.23).

## B. Constitution of District Wesleyan Youth

**7550. Article 1. Name.** All local WY organizations within the bounds of a district shall be known collectively as Wesleyan Youth of the __________ District of The Wesleyan Church.

**7555. Article 2. Purpose.** The purpose of the district Wesleyan Youth is to carry out the mission of WY (7505) on the district level and to train local WY leaders for effective ministry to youth.

**7560. Article 3. Relationship.** The district WY shall be a ministry of the district of The Wesleyan Church to which it belongs, operating for the benefit of local WY organizations, subject to the supervision of the district superintendent, coordinating its programs with the district board of Christian education, being amenable to the district board of administration.

**7565. Article 4. District WY Leadership.**

(1) **District WY Cabinet.** The district WY cabinet shall be composed of the district WY president as chair, the district WY treasurer, two teen members, two or more members appointed by the district WY president, and the district superintendent.

(a) **District WY President.** The district WY president is elected by the district WY convention (7585:4a). The initial election shall be for a term of one year, and reelection thereafter shall be for a term of two years. Total years of service as district WY president shall not exceed seven years.

(b) **District WY Treasurer.** The district WY treasurer shall be elected by the district WY convention for a term of one year.

(c) **Teen Members.** There shall be two teen members elected by the district WY convention for a term of one year.

(d) **Appointed Members.** The district WY president, in consultation with the district superintendent, shall appoint two or more additional members for one-year terms within thirty days after the district WY convention, subject to ratification by the district board of administration.

(e) **District Superintendent.** The district superintendent shall be an *ex officio* member of the cabinet (1310:10).

(2) **Qualifications.** All cabinet members must be covenant members of The Wesleyan Church within the district and have a burden and vision for youth ministry.

(3) **Amenability and Vacancies.** The district WY cabinet members shall be amenable to the district board of administration and may be removed when the best interests of the WY or district so require by a majority vote of the district board of administration. Vacancies of elected positions shall be filled by the district board of administration, and vacancies in appointed

positions shall be filled by the district WY president subject to the approval of the district board of administration.

**7575. Article 5. Duties of District WY Leaders.**

(1) **Criteria.** Cabinet members shall carry out their duties in keeping with *The Discipline,* the WY Constitution and the official WY handbook authorized by the General Board and issued by the General Department of Youth.

(2) **Duties of the District WY President.**

(a) To exercise leadership by coordinating and directing the ministry of district WY.

(b) To appoint two or more members to the district WY cabinet within 30 days after the district WY convention (cf. 7565:1).

(c) To appoint a chair pro tem of the WY cabinet to serve in case the district WY president is absent.

(d) To assign such responsibility to cabinet members as are needed to carry out the purpose of district WY (cf. 7555).

(e) To preside over meetings of the district WY cabinet.

(f) To serve as an *ex officio* member of all district WY committees.

(g) To preside over sessions of the district WY convention, except when the General Director of Youth or a representative designated by the General Director of Youth, is present and presiding.

(h) To supervise the recruiting and equipping of local youth leaders in cooperation with pastors and local boards of administration, seeking to organize local WYs in every church.

(i) To report annually to the district conference (1180:13) and the district WY convention regarding the state of the youth movement, including realization of goals and the vision for the future.

(j) To cooperate with the general WY director and the general WY executive committee (7620; 7625).

(k) To be a nonvoting member of the district conference by virtue of this office (1090:8) unless the district WY president is a voting member by some other right.

(l) To appoint one member of the district WY cabinet to serve as secretary of the cabinet and the district WY convention.

(3) **Duties of the District WY Treasurer.**

(a) To receive, record and hold all moneys remitted by local WY secretary-treasurers or raised by the district WY.

(b) To disburse funds in accordance with the financial plans of the district WY cabinet, the district WY convention and the General Department of Youth.

(c) To report annually to the district conference (1180:13) and district WY convention (7585:6), and to the district WY president and cabinet as requested.

(d) To submit the district WY treasurer's books annually to the district auditing committee (1340-1343), and when ordered by the district board of administration.

(4) **Duties of the District WY Cabinet.**

(a) The district WY cabinet shall direct the ministries of the district WY between the annual district WY conventions, including local leadership development, spiritual development and service opportunities, finances, communications, fellowship and other ministries.

(b) The district WY cabinet may also appoint others to direct specific youth ministries as necessary.

(5) **Other Committees.** Each district WY may also have such other committees as the district WY cabinet shall deem necessary.

**7585. Article 6. District WY Convention.**

(1) **Purpose.** The district WY convention shall rally the district youth movement to the mission of WY through inspiration, a call to commitment and the transaction of business (cf. 7505).

(2) **Organization.**

(a) There shall be an annual district WY convention at a time and place as recommended by the district WY cabinet and approved by the district board of administration (1233:24).

(b) The district WY president shall preside over the district WY convention unless the General Director of Youth, or a representative designated by the General Director of Youth, is present and presides .

(3) **Membership.**

(a) Voting members of the district WY convention shall include the district superintendent, the district WY cabinet, each local adult youth leader or pastor/youth pastor and WY president plus delegates from each organized local WY (7585).

(b) The district WY convention may have such honorary members as it desires.

(4) **Committees.**

(a) **Nominating Committee.** The district WY convention shall elect three members to serve with the district WY president and the district superintendent as the nominating committee. The district superintendent shall serve as chair. Elected members of the nominating committee shall not succeed themselves. The nominating committee shall present nomination(s) for district WY president to the district board of administration for their approval, or additional nominations, prior to the district WY convention (1233:24). The nominating committee shall then present to the convention the nomination(s) for district WY president, district WY treasurer, teen cabinet members (7565:1c) and nominating committee members.

(b) **Other Committees.** The district WY convention may appoint other committees as it deems essential.

(5) **Election Procedure.** The district WY president shall be elected by majority ballot from the nominees submitted by the nominating committee and approved by the district board of administration. The district WY treasurer and two teen cabinet members shall be elected by a majority ballot of the district WY convention from the nominations submitted by the nominating committee or other nominations from the floor. The nominating committee may be elected in any manner desired by the district WY convention. All elections other than district WY president must be ratified by the district board of administration before becoming final (1233:24).

(6) **Amenability.** All plans and actions of the district WY convention shall be subject to the approval of the district board of administration (1233:24).

**7595. Article 7. Zones.** A district WY cabinet may organize activities within one or more zones which meet for inspiration and fellowship (cf. 1233:12).

**7600. Article 8. Bylaws.** The district WY convention may adopt such bylaws as it deems essential, provided they are in accord with *The Discipline*, the constitutions and mission of WY, and other directives of the general church and district in coordination with the district board of Christian education and subject to the approval of the district board of administration.

### C. Constitution of General Wesleyan Youth

**7605. Article 1. Name.** All local and district WY organizations shall be known collectively as Wesleyan Youth, an auxiliary of The Wesleyan Church.

**7610. Article 2. Purpose.** General Wesleyan Youth shall carry out the mission of Wesleyan Youth, securing the cooperation of local and district WY organizations, providing resources and motivating them to accomplish the mission of Wesleyan Youth (cf. 7505).

**7615. Article 3. Relationship.** General Wesleyan Youth shall be a ministry of The Wesleyan Church and shall be subject to the direction of the General Department of Youth.

**7620. Article 4. General Director of Youth.** The General Director of Youth shall be the general WY director, serving as the executive officer of the general WY organization.

**7625. Article 5. General WY Executive Committee.**

(1) **Membership.** The general WY executive committee shall be composed of the general WY director as chair and the area WY directors.

(2) **Duties.** The WY executive committee shall hear the reports of the general WY director and the area WY directors; approve the official WY handbook; adopt recommendations to the General Director of Youth which the General Director of Youth may present to the General Board; serve as an advisory body to provide counsel and assistance to the general WY director (2335); submit memorials to the General Conference including proposed changes in *The Discipline* (1557); supervise area finances; approve area budgets; approve dates of area functions. All plans of the general WY executive committee shall be subject to the approval of the General Board.

**7630. Article 6. Area Wesleyan Youth Director.**

(1) **Qualifications.** Each area WY director shall be a covenant member of The Wesleyan Church and shall reside and hold church membership within the area represented and served.

(2) **Election Procedure.** The general WY director, after polling the district WY presidents, shall present nominations for an area WY director for each area to the General Board for election. The area WY director shall take office at a time determined by the General Board, shall serve for four years or until a successor is elected and qualified, and shall be amenable to the general WY executive committee. The area WY director may be removed by the General Board by a majority vote of all the members when it is in the best interests of Wesleyan Youth or the Church. The General Board shall have power to fill any vacancies.

(3) **Duties.** The area WY director shall be responsible to cooperate with the general WY director and the general WY executive committee, exercise leadership of the area WY, report when requested to the general WY executive committee, nominate an assistant area WY director and other officers as deemed necessary to the general WY executive committee for election, and assume other duties assigned by the general WY executive committee in keeping with *The Discipline* and the *Policy of the General Board for Youth.*

**7635. Article 7. General WY Treasurer.** The General Treasurer of The Wesleyan Church shall be the general treasurer of WY (1976), receiving, holding and disbursing all general WY funds in keeping with the actions of the general WY executive committee as approved or authorized by the General Board.

**7640. Article 8. General WY Convention.** There may be WY conventions, primarily for inspiration, instruction, and fellowship. They shall be held at a time and place recommended by the General Wesleyan Youth Executive Committee (7625:2) and approved by the General Board.

## D. Amendments to WY Constitutions

**7650.** The local, district or general constitutions of Wesleyan Youth may be amended by majority vote of the General Board at any regular or special session.

# APPENDIX G

# YOUNG ADULTS INTERNATIONAL

## A. Constitution of Local Young Adults International

**7700. Article 1. Name.** The name of this organization shall be Young Adults International of The Wesleyan Church or such name as the local YAI chapter may select.

**7705. Article 2. Mission.** The purpose of Young Adults International is to encourage members to adopt an obedient Christian life-style, to mobilize members for active involvement in Christian mission both locally and worldwide, and to provide opportunities for fellowship in the body of Christ.

**7710. Article 3. Organization.** A local YAI shall be considered an organized chapter if it has a chair, a secretary-treasurer, meets regularly and is registered with the General Department of Youth.

**7715. Article 4. Relationship.** The local YAI shall be a ministry of the local Wesleyan church, shall be subject to the supervision of the pastor (725:16), in all actions shall be amenable to the local board of administration (782:3, 25, 26, 28), and shall be under the direction of the local board of Christian education (880:2).

**7720. Article 5. Membership.** Any young adult of post high school status up to and including age thirty and who desires to participate in the meetings and activities of YAI, shall be listed as a member of this organization. An adult over age thirty who has been elected to lead a local chapter or is a district or general director of YAI shall also be listed as a member.

**7725. Article 6. Meetings.**

(1) **Strategy Meetings.** Strategy meetings of the local YAI shall be held monthly to develop plans for personal and group ministry projects, to encourage and support one another prayerfully in accomplishment of ministry projects, to review ministry projects and to establish accountability for accomplishment of purpose.

(2) **Annual Business Meeting.** The local YAI shall hold an annual business meeting at a time set by the YAI executive committee for the election of officers and a delegate, and other necessary business.

(3) **Additional meetings** may be held as necessary for the accomplishment of its purpose.

**7730. Article 7. Officers.**

(1) **Executive Officers.** The executive officers of the local YAI shall be the chair of the local chapter and a secretary-treasurer, who together with the

pastor as an *ex officio* member (725:18) shall constitute the local YAI executive committee (7740:4).

(2) **Other Officers.** Each local YAI shall select other officers and committees as it deems necessary, such as a singles coordinator, college age coordinator, young marrieds coordinator or a prison ministries coordinator.

(3) **Delegates.** In addition to the local YAI chair who is a member of the district YAI convention by virtue of office, each organized local YAI chapter shall be entitled to one delegate to the district YAI convention (7710; 7765:2).

(4) **Qualifications.** The local YAI chair shall be a covenant member of The Wesleyan Church and if necessary, may be over thirty years of age.

(5) **Election Procedure.** The local YAI chair, local YAI secretary-treasurer and the delegate to the district YAI convention shall be elected by the local YAI at its annual business meeting (7725:2). Preceding the annual YAI election, the local YAI shall elect or the local YAI executive committee shall appoint, a nominating committee consisting of three members. The pastor, or a representative appointed by the pastor, shall preside over the nominating committee (725:18). The nominating committee shall present nomination(s) for local YAI chair to the local board of administration for its approval prior to the election. The nominating committee shall then present to the annual business meeting the nomination(s) for local YAI chair, local YAI secretary-treasurer, delegate to district YAI convention and all other officers of the local YAI. All officers and the delegate shall be elected by a majority vote of the members of the local YAI present and voting. All elections other than that of the local YAI chair must be ratified by the local board of administration before becoming final.

(6) **Term of Service.** Local YAI officers shall take office at the beginning of the district fiscal year and shall serve until the end of the district fiscal year or until their successors are elected and qualified (1180:18).

(7) **Amenability and Vacancies.** All officers of the local YAI shall be amenable for their official duties to the local board of administration and may be removed whenever the best interests of the church or the local YAI so require by a majority vote of the local board of administration (782:25). The local board of administration shall have authority to fill all vacancies in the manner it deems best (782:26).

**7740. Article 8. Duties of Officers.**

(1) **Criteria.** All officers shall carry out their duties in keeping with *The Discipline* and the constitution of Young Adults International.

(2) **Local YAI Chair.** The local YAI chair shall exemplify an obedient Christian life-style including involvement in Christian mission, exercise general leadership of the local YAI under the general oversight of the pastor (725:16) and the local board of administration (782:4), preside over all business meetings of the local YAI and all meetings of the local YAI executive

committee. The local YAI chair shall serve as *ex officio* member of the district YAI convention if the local YAI chair represents an organized local YAI chapter (7710; 7765:2).

(3) **Local YAI Secretary-Treasurer.** The local YAI secretary-treasurer shall be responsible for membership records, minutes, statistical and financial records and annual reports, including those of the local YAI executive committee.

(4) **Local YAI Executive Committee.** The local YAI executive committee shall be composed of the local YAI chair who shall be chair *ex officio*, the local YAI secretary-treasurer and the pastor as an *ex officio* member (7730:1). All actions of the local YAI executive committee shall be subject to the review of the local board of administration. The local YAI executive committee may also include other local YAI officers.

**7745. Article 9. Bylaws.** The local YAI may adopt such bylaws as it deems necessary provided that they do not conflict with ***The Discipline*** or other directives of the general church and district and provided they are approved by the local board of Christian education (880:2) and the local board of administration (782:23).

## B. Constitution of District Young Adults International

**7750. Article 1. Name.** All local YAI organizations within the bounds of a district shall be known collectively as Young Adults International of the ___________ District of The Wesleyan Church.

**7755. Article 2. Purpose.** The district Young Adults International shall carry out the mission of YAI (7705), seeking to establish and motivate local chapters, to train local YAI directors and to mobilize young adults for ministry projects.

**7760. Article 3. Relationship.** The district YAI shall be a ministry of the district of The Wesleyan Church to which it belongs, shall be subject to the supervision of the district superintendent (1310:8), shall be amenable in all actions to the district board of administration (1233:24, 25), and shall be under the direction of the district board of Christian education (1455:1).

**7765. Article 4. District Convention.**

(1) **Purpose and Organization.** There shall be an annual district YAI convention, held at such time as the district board of administration shall approve (1233:24) to elect district YAI officers, to receive reports, to train local officers, to commission young adults involved in ministry projects and to recognize participants who have completed service in ministry projects. The district YAI director shall preside over the district YAI convention unless the general director of YAI, or a representative appointed by the General Director of YAI, is present and presides (cf. 7815).

(2) **Membership.** The annual YAI district convention shall be composed of the district superintendent (1303:6), the district YAI officers, local YAI chairs from each organized chapter and one delegate named by each local chapter.

(3) **Committees.** There shall be a nominating committee as set forth in 7770:4. The district YAI convention may elect other committees as it deems necessary and shall define their duties.

(4) **Approval.** All plans and actions of the district YAI convention shall be subject to the review and coordination of the district board of Christian education (1455:1) and the approval of the district board of administration (1233:24).

**7770. Article 5. District YAI Officers.**

(1) **Executive Officers.** The executive officers of the district YAI shall be the district YAI director, district YAI finance chair and the district YAI projects chair. These officers together with the district superintendent (1310:10) shall constitute the district YAI executive committee (7775:5).

(2) **Other Officers.** Each district YAI may have such other officers and committees as the district YAI convention shall deem necessary.

(3) **Qualifications.** All district YAI officers and committee members must be covenant members of The Wesleyan Church within the district in which they serve. If necessary, executive officers of the district YAI may be over thirty years of age.

(4) **Election Procedure.** The district YAI director, and any other officers and committee members as the bylaws shall require, shall be elected by the annual district YAI convention. The district YAI convention shall select, and the district YAI executive committee shall appoint, a nominating committee over which the district superintendent, or a representative appointed by the district superintendent, shall preside (1310:10). The nominating committee shall present nomination(s) for the office of district YAI director to the district board of administration for their approval, or additional nominations, prior to the district YAI convention (1233:24). The nominating committee shall then present the nomination(s) for district YAI director and other officers to the annual district YAI convention. Executive officers shall be elected by ballot and other officers elected in any manner desired. All elections other than that of the district YAI director must be ratified by the district board of administration before becoming final.

(5) **Terms of Service**. District YAI officers shall take office at the beginning of the district fiscal year and shall serve until the end of the district fiscal year or until their successors are elected and qualified (1180:18).

(6) **Amenability and Vacancies.** All district YAI officers and committee members shall be amenable to the district board of administration, and may be removed by majority vote of the district board of administration when the

best interest of YAI or the district so requires. The district board of administration shall fill all vacancies.

**7775. Articles 6. Duties of Officers.**

(1) **Criteria.** All officers of district YAI shall carry out their duties in keeping with *The Discipline*, the constitution of YAI and the official handbook authorized by the General Board and issued by the General Department of Youth.

(2) **District YAI Director.** The district YAI director shall be responsible to cooperate with the general YAI director; to exercise general leadership of the district YAI under the general oversight of the district superintendent (1310:8); to preside over the district YAI executive committee meetings; to preside over the district YAI convention, except when the general YAI director, or a representative appointed by the General YAI Director, is presiding; to appoint one member of the YAI executive committee to serve as secretary of the committee and the district YAI convention; to report annually to the district conference (1180:13), the district YAI convention and at other times as ordered by the district board of administration (1233:11); to organize local YAI chapters; and to equip local YAI chairs in cooperation with pastors and local boards of administration. The district YAI director shall be a nonvoting member of the district conference (1090:8), unless the district YAI director is a voting member by some other right.

(3) **District YAI Projects Chair.** The district YAI projects chair shall be responsible to organize ministry projects on the district level, to recruit young adults to participate and to assist local YAI chapters in organizing ministry projects in cooperation with pastors and local boards of administration.

(4) **District YAI Finance Chair.** The district YAI finance chair shall receive, record, hold and disburse all moneys remitted by the local YAI chapters or raised by the district YAI.

(5) **District YAI Executive Committee.** The district YAI director shall be the chair *ex officio* of the district YAI executive committee (7770:1). The district YAI executive committee shall direct the ministry of district YAI between the annual district YAI conventions and shall appoint others to direct specific ministries of district YAI as necessary.

**7785. Article 7. Bylaws.** The district YAI may adopt such bylaws as it deems necessary, provided that they are in accord with *The Discipline*, the constitution and purpose of YAI and other directives of the general church and district. Such bylaws are subject to the review and coordination of the district board of Christian education (1455:1) and the approval of the district board of administration (1233:24).

## C. Constitution of General Young Adults International

**7800. Article 1. Name.** All local and district YAI organizations shall be known collectively as Young Adults International, an auxiliary of The Wesleyan Church.

**7805. Article 2. Purpose.** General Young Adults International shall carry out the mission of YAI (7705), seeking to provide resources, materials and service opportunities to the district and local levels.

**7810. Article 3. Relationship.** Young Adults International shall be a ministry of The Wesleyan Church, and shall be subject on the general level to the direction of the General Department of Youth (2318:3).

**7815. Article 4. General Director.** The General Director of Youth, or a person designated by the General Director of Youth, shall be the general director of YAI and shall serve as the executive officer of YAI. The general director of YAI shall be responsible to seek to accomplish the mission of YAI with particular emphasis given to the spiritual vitality of the leaders; to train district YAI leaders; to provide resources for district and local YAI organizations; to provide information on YAI programs to district and local YAI leaders; to oversee the quadrennial general YAI convention; and to study prayerfully general church and worldwide needs in order to develop viable YAI ministry projects. The general YAI director, or a representative appointed by the General YAI Director, may preside over the district YAI convention when present (7775:2).

**7820. Article 5. General Treasurer of Young Adults International.** The General Treasurer of The Wesleyan Church shall be the general treasurer of YAI (1976), receiving, holding and disbursing all general YAI funds in keeping with the financial policies adopted by the General Board for the support of auxiliaries.

**7825. Article 6. Quadrennial General YAI Convention.** There shall be a quadrennial general YAI convention, primarily for inspiration, instruction and fellowship. It shall be held at a time and place recommended by the General Director of Youth and approved by the General Board .

## D. Amendments to Young Adults International Constitutions

**7840.** The constitution of Young Adults International of The Wesleyan Church may be amended by majority vote of the General Board at any regular or special session.

## APPENDIX H

## AFFILIATE CHURCHES

**7900.** An independent congregation of the Wesleyan tradition which seeks a less than full relationship with The Wesleyan Church may commit to Articles of Agreement and be recognized and listed as an affiliate church. The district board of administration shall be authorized on behalf of the district conference to develop and agree to the terms of the Articles of Agreement. Such relationships shall exist to encourage fellowship and to include the affiliated body in adult, youth and children ministries of The Wesleyan Church and to benefit the affiliated unit through acquaintance with and involvement in Wesleyan institutions of higher education, global outreach ministries and helpful publications of the denomination. The relationship may be terminated at any time, either by vote of the district board of administration or the ruling body of the affiliate church.

**7905. Membership.** All persons who have met the membership requirements of the independent congregation shall be listed by the district as affiliate members. Any affiliate member who seeks to transfer membership to The Wesleyan Church shall be examined by the pastor and the local board of administration. If it is discovered that the person involved had indeed been previously converted and is fully committed to the doctrines and standards of The Wesleyan Church, said affiliate member may be received by letter into the covenant membership of The Wesleyan Church (cf. 570; 578). If the affiliated church elects to become a Wesleyan congregation, the Procedures of Organization as set forth in The Wesleyan Church *Discipline*, paragraph 520 shall be followed.

**7910. Pastors**. The calling of pastors to an affiliated church shall be determined by said church's by-laws and shall not require approval of the Wesleyan district conference. A change of pastor or senior pastor of an affiliate church shall automatically give rise to a review of the affiliate status and shall require a renewal vote by the district board of administration to extend the relationship. In the event the affiliate church seeks to secure the leadership of a Wesleyan minister, that arrangement shall require the consent of the district superintendent and the ratifying vote of a majority of the district board of administration. An ordained minister serving on staff of an affiliate church may be appointed by the district conference as affiliate church pastor (cf.3346).

**7915. Government**. The Wesleyan Church shall not regulate the governance of an affiliate church. However, the district board of administration shall review the governmental structure of the church seeking affiliate status and shall be satisfied it is founded upon biblical principles prior to authorizing affiliate status. Conversely, any affiliate church desiring to adopt The Wesleyan Church *Discipline* as a governance model for the local church may do so.

**7920. Property and Support Obligations**. As long as the independent unit retains the status of an affiliate church it is not subject to the trust clause and other provisions for holding property as set forth in *The Discipline of The Wesleyan Church.*

It is anticipated that the affiliate church will financially support The Wesleyan Church and its various ministries. The details of such support shall be agreed upon between the affiliate church and the district board of administration.

It is expected that the various agencies of The Wesleyan Church shall have access to the affiliate church for the presentation of their programs and for the solicitation of support in the same manner as with all Wesleyan churches.

**7925. District/General Conference Representation.** Each affiliate church may send the pastor and one lay representative as honorary delegates, having voice but not vote, to the annual district conference. The listed affiliate members shall not be included in the membership count which determines the number of persons a district conference is authorized to elect as General Conference delegates.

**7930. Continuance of Status**. The district board of administration shall be empowered to renew the status of an affiliate church for up to five years from inception of the relationship. If the affiliate church has not begun the process leading to acceptance as an established church by the fifth year, renewal of the affiliate status shall require the annual recommendation of the district board of administration and annual approving vote of the district conference.

**7935. Use of Name**. The affiliate church may not adopt the name The Wesleyan Church nor utilize such benefits as coming under the denominational umbrella for IRS recognition as a 501 (C) (3) not-for-profit entity until said unit is received as a developing or established Wesleyan church and conforms to *The Wesleyan Church Discipline* in all matters of governance. It may choose to advertise with such language as "A congregation of the Wesleyan tradition" or "affiliated with The Wesleyan Church ."

*No two church "joinings" will be characterized by identical circumstances. The district board of administration may modify the following sample agreement to reflect levels of monetary support from the affiliate church or other mutual agreements which detail commitments to a developing unified ministry.*

**THE WESLEYAN CHURCH**
**AFFILIATE CHURCH**
**ARTICLES OF AGREEMENT**

**______________________________ CHURCH**

**AND**

**THE __________________________ DISTRICT OF THE**

**WESLEYAN CHURCH**

## PREAMBLE

The _______________________ Church, an independent congregation of the Wesleyan tradition (hereafter referred to as church) and the _______________ District of The Wesleyan Church (hereafter referred to as district), upon the signing of these Articles of Agreement do establish and commit to an affiliate relationship between church and district.

## OBJECTIVE

It is the objective of church and district, as co-laborers, to advance the Kingdom of Christ through the encouragement of fellowship, cooperation in varied ministries of evangelism, discipleship and education and a sharing of denominational benefits by making available literature, publications and personnel.

## ARTICLE I
## STATEMENT OF FAITH

Both the church and the district affirm the foundation for such affiliate relationship lies in the mutual embrace of and commitment to the following Statement of Faith:

> We believe in God the Father, the Son and the Holy Spirit.
>
> We believe that Jesus Christ the Son suffered in our place on the cross, that He died but rose again, that He now sits at the Father's right hand until He returns to judge every person at the last day.
>
> We believe in the Holy Scriptures as the inspired and inerrant Word of God.

We believe that by the grace of God every person has the ability and responsibility to choose between right and wrong, and that those who repent of their sin and believe in the Lord Jesus Christ are justified by faith.

We believe that God not only counts the believer as righteous, but that He makes such persons righteous, freeing them from sin's dominion at conversion, purifying their hearts by faith and perfecting them in love at entire sanctification, and providing for their growth in grace at every stage of spiritual life, enabling them through the presence and power of the Holy Spirit to live victorious lives.

**ARTICLE II**
**GOVERNANCE**

During the time period the church and district retain the affiliate church relationships, the district superintendent shall be expected to make periodic visits and provide such counsel as the church's pastor and board may welcome. The district board of administration shall annually review the ongoing relationship. The church shall establish its own organizational by-laws and shall be exempt from the property trust clause established for congregations holding full relationships to the denomination. During the period of affiliate relationship, the church may choose to advertise with such language as "a congregation of the Wesleyan tradition" or "affiliated with The Wesleyan Church," but may not assume/use the name The Wesleyan Church.

The affiliate church may send the (senior) pastor and one lay delegate to the annual district conference to enjoy voice but not vote.

**ARTICLE III**
**ADVANCEMENT**

Advancement to full relationship is possible. While no commitment to such is implied by the church or the district in affixing signatures to these Articles of Agreement, mutual approval by both entities can result in the church coming into full relationship with the district and The Wesleyan Church with all rights and privileges pertaining thereto.

## ARTICLE IV
## CONTINUANCE

Subject to annual review by the district board of administration, the affiliate relationship may be renewed up to five years by said district board of administration. If the affiliate church has not begun a process leading to acceptance as an established church by the end of the fifth year, renewal of the affiliate status shall that year and each successive year require the recommendation of the district board of administration and an approving vote of the district conference. A change in pastoral leadership in the church shall automatically give rise to a review of the relationship and, to renew affiliate status, shall require the consent of the district superintendent and the ratifying vote of a majority of the district board of administration. The relationship may be terminated at any time by either the vote of the district board of administration or the ruling body of the church.

## AGREEMENT

Sustained by the mutual belief that God in His providences has led together the people of the ________________________ Church and the ____________________ District of The Wesleyan Church, and upon the voted authority of the church's ruling body and the district board of administration, the authorized officials herewith affix their signatures to duplicate copies of these Articles of Agreement, thereby evidencing establishment of an affiliate relationship between church and district.

The________________ District of The Wesleyan Church:

___________________________
District Superintendent

___________________________
Assistant District Superintendent

___________________________
District Secretary

The__________________ Church:

___________________________
Pastor

___________________________
Board Chairman/Vice-Chairman

___________________________
Secretary

The numbers refer to *The Discipline* paragraphs. A subparagraph is separated from the related paragraph by a colon. Main references or definitions are in boldface type.

**B**

E

G

## J

## Q

T

## Z